SEVEN HELLS

Holocaust Library

Statement of Purpose

The Holocaust spread across the face of Europe almost fifty years ago. The brutality then unleashed is still nearly beyond comprehension. Millions of innocents—men, women and children—were consumed by its flames.

The goal of Holocaust Library, a non-profit organization founded by survivors, is to publish and disseminate works on the Holocaust. These will include survivors' accounts, testimonies and memoirs, historical and regional analyses, anthologies, archival and source documents and other relevant materials that will help shed light on this cataclysmic era.

These books and studies will be made available to the general public, scholars, researchers, historians, teachers and students. They will be used in Holocaust Resource Centers, libraries and schools, synagogues and churches. They will help foster an increased awareness of the Holocaust and its implications. They will help *to preserve the memory* for posterity and to enable this awesome time to be better understood and comprehended.

THADDEUS STABHOLZ

SEVEN HELLS

Translated from the Polish
by
Dr. Jacques Grunblatt
and
Hilda R. Grunblatt

Holocaust Library
New York

Printed in the United States of America

Cover Design by The Appelbaum Company

Library of Congress Cataloging-in-Publication Data

Stabholz, Thaddeus, 1916-
Seven hells / by Thaddeus Stabholz: translated from the Polish by Jacques Grunblatt and Hilda R. Grunblatt.
p. cm.
ISBN 0-89604-146-8 : $21.95.—ISBN 0-89604-147-6 (pbk.) : $12.95
1. Holocaust, Jewish (1939-1945)—Personal narratives. 2. Stabholz, Thaddeus, 1916- . I. Title.
D804.3.S7 1990
940.53'18-dc20 90-19307
CIP

Special edition of the magazine "Ojf der Fray"
Licence HQ Economic Affairs Division
AG 387.7 GEC–AGO 15 of May 1947

To my daughters Peggy and Betty
with the hope that
they may always live in freedom.

Contents

Introduction / Acknowledgement

When the American Army liberated me on that day in April of 1945, my life was saved, but I was too sick, too numb, too indifferent to comprehend its importance.

I cannot remember the days that followed. Much later I was told that, for weeks, I was lying in a bed unaware of my surroundings. Eventually, the dense fog clouding my brain lifted. At first I responded to simple stimuli. Then, when I tried to get out of bed without help, I remember falling flat on my face. It was difficult to accept the fact that I had to learn to walk all over again, but I tried and did my best.

By mid-September of 1945, I almost doubled my April weight. I felt reasonably well and began planning each day and the future. It was then that disaster struck.

Suddenly, one night, a terrible, invisible power paralyzed me, then seized me and effortlessly brought me back to Birkenau. For a while I stood on the ramp between Crematoria II and III. How could I forget the sight of those gray buildings with their few small, barred windows and their two huge chimneys belching fire to the sky? Before I knew it, I was placed in the middle of a cavernous gas chamber. The ceiling lights were blinding. I heard the heavy steel doors slam and the iron bolts screeching as they were turned and tightened, sealing the doors. The light was switched off; it was pitch black. A desperate voice screamed, "Gas! They're going to kill us!" My heart pounded wildly. Thousands of red-hot needles pierced my chest. I gasped for breath. I knew that I was about to die.

With my heart still beating violently, I awoke. I lay in a pool of sweat.

This same nightmare haunted me night after night. Always real, always frightening, it robbed me of sleep and slowly drove me mad. I began to fear darkness. I refused to close my eyes. In an attempt to allay this horrific dream, I read omnivorously: novels, poetry, medical books, anything and everything on which I could lay my hands. Alas, without relief. I knew that I needed professional help, but it was unavailable at that time.

One night when the nightmare was particularly intimidating, I arose, switched on the light, found an old notebook and pen, and started to write. Night and day I wrote, like a man possessed. In two weeks, half of my story was completed. Like a viper, the nightmare tried to sneak by, but, with pen in hand, I stabbed it repeatedly, pushing it back. Gradually, the nightmare receded until it disappeared completely. I had begun my journey back to sanity.

The book, SEVEN HELLS, was originally printed in a Displaced Persons Camp in Stuttgart, West Germany shortly after Liberation. People carried copies with them to many places in the world.

One summer day many years later, in 1981, I found a letter from Dr. Jacques Grunblatt in my mail. It was strange; I had never heard of him. In his letter, he wrote that he and his wife Hilda started translating my book into English after finding it in a friend's library. He asked my permission to continue. Needless to say, it was readily granted.

In the Fall of 1981, I met Jacques and Hilda in North Creek, NY. He had retired from his medical practice because of his heart condition. What a wonderful couple it was my good fortune to meet! Always busy, always active in the affairs of their community, Jacques and Hilda translated books from French and Polish. He was also fluent in German and Spanish. As a young doctor, Jacques had served with the International Brigades, helping the Spanish Republicans in their fight against Franco. He was the author of five chapters in OUR FIGHT in which he told of his experiences during the tragic Spanish Civil War.

Hilda and he worked long hours translating; they even worked while they were on vacation. Were it not for Jacques and Hilda, this book would never have been rendered into English. Dr. Jacques died in January, 1989. Hilda kept polishing the translation. In March of 1990, the completed book was accepted for publication by Holocaust Library, Sol Lewis, Editor.

Thank you, Jacques, for all of your efforts. I am very sorry that you did not live to see SEVEN HELLS published. Thank you, Hilda, for your tireless efforts. Dr. William Fagan and his wife Joy of Stowe, Vermont helped to convince me that the book should be published.

1 The Uprising in the Warsaw Ghetto

It is the end of April 1943. We are sitting in the depths of the cellar—about one hundred persons: men, women, children; young and old; the major part of the Jewish Hospital staff. Above us are the ruins of a house destroyed in 1939 during the fight over Warsaw.

Several days before the uprising, or rather, the hopeless attempt at resistance, *Untersturmführer* Brandt cordially invited us to take a "transport" to somewhere near Lublin and added, "It'll be good for you there, very good. In the Lublin area we'll set up model camps for over one hundred thousand workers. Naturally they'll need doctors and nurses."

Long ago we lost all trust in German promises. In the summer of 1942, the commander of the Warsaw Ghetto still solemnly assured us that Jews went East to work. They were going East, but not too far, and not to work. In the thick forest a hundred kilometers northeast of Warsaw, almost half a million Warsaw Jews found a "friendly reception" in Treblinka's spacious gas chambers. By a miracle, several persons from among those who were selected to sort the belongings of the gassed, were saved. They returned in the same railroad cars in which they had loaded the loot and told what they had seen in Treblinka. Nobody believed them; no one would accept that. It was too horrible for the human mind to conceive. "Gas chambers? Gas? Even the young and strong as well as those unable to work? Those are horror stories invented by sick minds. It's impossible! What will the world say to that!!" Then, when no help comes, the mind gets used to the tragic reality, and we begin to believe. In the face of death we are condemned to rely on our own strength.

Hell rages over our heads as frequent explosions rend the air, houses collapse, acrid smoke from the fires seeps through our small observation opening, and street fighting continues. One isolated hand grenade explosion followed by several revolver shots—those are ours; a few rounds of machine gun fire and a powerful explosion—those are the Germans'.

From day to day we get weaker and some die. Less often do we hear "our" isolated shots and explosions. More soot gets into our cellar as German mines destroy more and more houses. We hear the desperate cries of people pulled from cellars and chased along the street not far from us, mingled with the whistle of whips and the shrill shrieks of the victims, and from time to time, the word *Gnadenschuss* (*coup de grâce*).

Where are they chasing our brothers? What is going on up there? We must get out and look around.

Today is the 30th of April. The liquidation of the Ghetto and its last defenses had begun on the 18th. For twelve days we have been sitting in this hole. We are not sleeping; we are not moving; we are not talking. Instead, we lie silently on the bunks and think—of what?—of death, and why we must die, and of the hopelessness of our situation.

A mine explodes nearby, breaking our eardrums. Dirt falls on our heads, and our hearts beat wildly as we snuff out candles and lamps. Was it our hospital? A few of us run to our observation point. Yes, it was the hospital. The extra-thick walls of the four-story building were blown asunder and the pieces landed with a crash. Huge chunks fell on our hideout.

One hour later we hear German voices laughing and cursing in the hospital yard. Then we hear the sound of women's weak voices and sobs, a girl's cry, "Mother!", one shot . . . and silence. The Germans leave.

As night falls, Dr. Stein, our hospital director, makes a short speech. "Some of our men must go out and look around. Is contact with the Polish Aryan underground possible? Can we escape through the sewer lines? Where do they take the people whom they've driven out of the cellars? Our fate depends on what you learn."

Everyone wants to go, so we draw lots. Five are chosen, I am one of them. My fiancée grabs my hand and pleads, "Tadzek, don't go! I'm afraid you'll die. Oh God!" Almost by force, I tear myself away.

Dr. Stein gives us revolvers, ammunition, and a few hand grenades and says, "If you meet Germans, fight as much as you can, but remember boys, you must come back!"

We crawl through the underground tunnel that leads to the morgue on the hospital grounds, open the cover, and creep out. All that remains of the hospital is a heap of ruins: bare walls, twisted iron, chimneys, and smoldering wood. From time to time, a piece of wall falls.

"Fellows," I say through clenched teeth, "in case we fall into those hoodlums' hands, not a word of where our bunker is, even if they torture us."

We shake hands in silence. We may die, but we will not betray our loved ones.

The street looks horrible. The entire Jewish sector is destroyed. Smoke from the raging fires chokes us and makes our eyes tear. Quite often we trip over piles of ruins or fall into holes. Many charred, deformed bodies lie about. After walking for several minutes, we still do not know exactly where we are. Then Zenek Gurwicz says, "Dr. Brantwein's hiding place ought to be nearby. I know the entrance. From his place, we can go down to the sewers. Let's go there."

In the darkness, it takes Zenek a good hour before he finds the entrance among the ruins. We knock; nobody answers. We bang on the door and shout, "Friends, open!" Silence. After hesitating a few minutes, we break the sealed cover. When we finally free the entrance, we find two corpses clutching shovels. The cellar is terribly hot; we must retreat.

Returning one hour later, we crawl in, light our lamps, and look for people. In the first room we find potatoes and other supplies. The potatoes are soft; they are cooked. In the next room we find people—red, monstrously swollen, naked bodies—cooked. We count thirty of them; six are children. With some difficulty, I recognize Dr. Brantwein. We bow our heads for a minute in silence thinking of the horrible, tragic moments these people must have endured. They are not burned, just cooked. COOKED!! Cooked alive! The house burned on top of them. They wanted to save themselves by trying to break the sealed cover but they did not succeed. The terrible heat killed them. We are shaken to our very depths. Yes, today you—tomorrow, us!

Someone says in a broken voice, "Fellows, let's not forget why we're here. We can't help the dead, and others wait for us to return." Yes, that is true. Our object is to find the entrance to the street sewers, but unfortunately, they are buried.

We see two human silhouettes nearby. For six days these fellow sufferers dragged themselves through the rubble. The Germans had found and blown off the door of their hideout, and ordered everyone out. No one obeyed; they decided to die together. The Germans, afraid to go in, waited a while and then, threw in smoke bombs, and finally, hand grenades. Of the twenty persons inside, only these two survived. They tell us that thousands of Germans from different units using special listening devices and armed with the most modern weapons for street fighting, pursue the remaining Jews. Sections of *Waffen-SS* and police are used to finish off the Ghetto. The Germans also have at their command, companies of engineers and armed cars, and in the sky during the day, planes fly over the Ghetto.

"What's happening to the people?" we ask.

"It's bad, very bad. The Germans, enraged by the resistance and the losses they've suffered, chase the people to the Jewish Community Center where, over an open grave, they shoot all those they've caught. The behavior of their accomplices, the wild Vlasov gang, is even worse. This gang has been made part of the SS and given a free hand which the group exploits to the fullest. They chase people into fires. They torture women in the most horrible way to the accompaniment of insults and curses. They kill children in their usual manner: two brutes, each grabbing a leg, tear the child apart.

The milder ones smash the little heads on the pavement. This goes on in front of the dumbfounded, horrified mothers. God help you if you fall into the hands of the Vlasov gang!"

"Is there no escape?"

They laugh sadly, "Where to? How? The Ghetto walls are guarded; the sewers are patrolled. There's little help for us. We're doomed!" As they pull two Mausers from holsters, they say softly, "We've a few bullets left to avenge the death of our dear ones. We'll aim and shoot straight. The last two bullets are for us. Good-by, friends."

Cold sweat covers our foreheads. Yes, this is the end. What "good news" we will bring to those in the bunker! We are angry, yet those two gave us some good ideas. To die?—but before our throats utter our last cry, let us have some revenge by killing at least a few Germans with our own bullets, then we will die easier. We cock our guns, check our hand grenades, and go out into the street.

When we reach Powazkowska Street, we hear a motor and see some lights moving slowly toward us. We cling to a wall. As Zenek Gurwicz readies a hand grenade, he hisses, "I throw; you shoot!" The lights come closer. A German patrol in a big open police car is moving slowly over the ruins in the street. We quiver with emotion. "Oh, you beasts! What a reception we have planned for you!" The car is near enough to see the helmeted SS men with their "Schmeissers" ready to shoot. The explosion rips the air; the echo repeats a thousand times through the burned Ghetto. Clouds of smoke are emitted from the car. We shoot blindly and hear the Germans' wild shouts. As Zenek reaches for another hand grenade, a burst of machine gun fire smashes his head. He falls. We fire a few more shots, and Pinek Lewin throws a hand grenade. Henio Grin shouts hoarsely, "Fellows! Remember we must go back!" We can still hear the armed car; we must retreat. One minute more and it will be too late. We crawl backwards as the SS men open heavy machine gun fire. In a few minutes we are out of reach of their bullets. Zenek is missing. Dear boy, maybe you are better off, but what will we tell your little sisters?

We are back in the bunker; they surround us. Their faces

exhibit fear and tension, but no one dares to ask questions. The silence is broken by Dr. Stein asking, "Where's Zenek?" At the mention of their brother's name, his sisters awaken and run to us demanding, "Where's our brother?" We stand silently for a minute. Finally Natek Remba loses control of himself and cries, "Zenek is dead! And there's little life left for us."

Incoherently we tell them what we have seen during our wandering. Not a word is said. The bunker resounds with the sobbing of Zenek's sisters. Dr. Stein takes us aside. Truly, we have little to relate. There is nothing left but to await our fate, and we return to our holes.

We are given a reception: soup. It is the first warm meal in nearly two weeks, and we swallow our food with difficulty.

Dead tired, I stretch out. Fredzia sobs silently as she sits and strokes my hair. I am shaken by a spasm and feel as though I am losing my mind. This is the last human being left for me in this world, and she has to die. Despair, helplessness, humiliation alternate with rage to tear my very being. I reach for a medicine bag. Luminal, morphine, strychnine . . . quite a choice.

Fredzia watches every move I make and pleads, "Tadzek, I beg you! Don't do it! Maybe, in spite of all, we'll survive. Maybe they'll send us to work."

A fraction of a second later I think, "To what kind of work will they send me? To do the work of the Vlasov gang?" I control myself and repeat in a low voice, "Maybe they'll give us work." Then, from the depths of my soul comes a cry, "To die, my God, to die!"

Several days pass. Judging from the sounds, we could easily be on the front line. Explosion after explosion rattle the walls of our cellar. Meanwhile, the women shake off their apathy and check our supplies. Several kerosene burners are lighted. "If we must die," says Natek Remba with a wan smile, "let's do so on a full stomach."

Bela and Sabinka, nurses and my fiancée's close friends, enter our cellar. Both are beautiful girls with the perfect "Aryan" look. They have Polish I.D. cards and were out of the Ghetto for two weeks. Thinking that the safest place was in the wolf's jaws, they had registered to go to work in Germany and had come to the hospital two days ago to pick up a few things and to get some money for the road. Both of them were caught in the midst of the Ghetto Uprising. Now they sit with us in the bunker and cannot believe that the situation is so tragic. They will discover how tragic it really is in just a few more hours.

It happened, unexpectedly. After taking a strong dose of luminal, I slept in a corner with Fredzia. Suddenly I hear low voices whispering nearby, "The Germans are mining our cellar. In a while we'll be blasted into the air. It's the end!"

Jumping from my resting place, I run to the observation hole. The activity overhead is intense. "Sullivans" rumble and German voices call, "Here, one mine; there, the other. We'll soon smoke those God-damned *Schweinehunde* out of their rat holes."

My knees buckle under me. With great effort, I try to control myself. I return to the others and say, "Get ready for the road! We must run!" No one says a word. I run through the corridor and yell into the different rooms, "Everyone out through the tunnel! Keep quiet!"

We crawl to the exit. As I open the cover, a chunk of wall falls from above, and I retreat. Excited voices behind me whisper, "Hurry! What the hell is going on?" I emerge into the blinding daylight and blink. Through holes in the wall, I see many SS men among the ruins, some with dogs on leashes. Where can we hide? I crawl through the destroyed rooms deep inside the house to get as far away as possible from those hellish creatures. At last I find a sort of small cellar and jump into it. Fredzia, Henio, Bela and Sabinka follow. A wooden door hanging above us protects us somewhat. The place is small, and we must crouch. Water seeps from a wall—probably a burst water pipe. We are up to our knees in mud. If only we can hold out until nightfall, then, under cover of darkness, we may be able to do something. Meanwhile, others are coming out of the tunnel. Blinded by the light, disoriented, they fall into the hands of the SS men. These thugs line them up and march them off in groups.

Minutes later, a great explosion rends the air. Our hideout goes heavenward, our protective door flies off, and some bricks fall. The water, which had only seeped through, now becomes a shower, and in seconds we are drenched. Soon the water reaches our knees. It is evident that we must abandon our hiding place; we hold a short conference. The girls think it is better to give ourselves up to the mercy of the Germans than to drown like rats. "Tadzek," Fredzia says, "at the worst, Treblinka. I'll see how my parents perished."

Resignedly, I look for an exit, and we crawl out. No hiding place is in sight; we are in the open. Our appearance is greeted with loud laughter by the SS men who exclaim, "This is splendid! What a sight! Where have they been hiding?" Our teeth are chattering from the cold; the SS men think it is from fear. An *Untersturmführer* approaches and shouts, "Hands up!" We are searched; we have no weapons. "Wait!" he orders.

For two hours we stand silently while our group gets larger as more people are discovered. I recognize some of them, young people with old faces. Oh God, how people can change in such a short time! Now we are thirty. Several SS men surround us, their rifles cocked ready to shoot. "March!" one orders.

Our stiff legs refuse to obey, but we march. Sabinka trips on a rock and falls. An SS man jumps toward her, hits her over the head with his rifle, and yells, "Get up, you!" Fredzia and I help her. We, too, get a taste of whiplashes and German rifle butts.

We march to Nalewki Street where several hundred people are gathered on one side of the street. I recognize Director Stein and Natek Remba with their wives, and many others. Sabinka faints. The handkerchief she held to her nose is full of blood. A while ago, she spat out three teeth. Fredzia has a red mark on her forehead from the whip. We are completely apathetic, feeling neither exhaustion, nor thirst, nor hunger, nor pain. In a while, it will be the end. May God help us so that our suffering will not last long.

Several white-gloved officers with smiles on their faces approach our group. Invitingly, they announce, "don't be afraid. You're going to be taken to work. Nothing will happen to you. The only thing you have to do is to give up your valuables and money. You won't need them now."

The bully's "friendly talk" is interrupted by cries from the upper floor of the house at 11 Nalewki. One wall of this four-story house is left standing. The staircase is visible from the street, and we see soldiers climbing upstairs. Some human shapes are huddled in front of a window on the fourth floor—they probably know that the SS men are after them. At a certain moment, the door to the balcony opens, and a woman appears with a child in her arms. She takes a step forward, looks down . . . and retreats. Meanwhile, the thugs are almost upstairs. The woman with the child turns around and backs up to the edge of the balcony. One more step . . . she utters a horrible, blood-curdling cry as she falls. An interesting scene . . . the German officers' Leicas click. Two men follow the woman and jump. We hear a few loud words and then a girl's voice shouting, "Leave me alone!", then glass breaking. A young girl stands on the balcony and, without hesitation, jumps. The officers' smiles disappear as they say, "What's happening here? We don't harm anyone. We send you to work. You'll work, each one at his own trade."

Suddenly they remember. "Oh yes, money and valuables!" Cameras are taken away. Body searches are made. With insults and sneering smiles, the brutes pull off the women's dresses and panties in front of everyone. Those who hide the smallest item of value are killed mercilessly. After minutes that seem an eternity, the search finally ends, and we are chased across the street to join a group that has already been checked.

We are about 500 persons. SS men with guns ready to shoot stand nearby. Fredzia says, "Tadzek, maybe they're taking us to work." Although I can sense a faint hope in her voice, I fear the worst.

Dr. Szymek Stockhammer comes through the crowd. Compared to the rest of us, he looks good—he had managed to shave a few hours before the catastrophe. For months, he has not parted with a file to cut through bars. He keeps it hidden in the leg of one of his high boots. In a low voice he says, "Tadzek, we'll stick together. If we go to Treblinka, we'll jump." Pinek Lewin, standing nearby, overhears, smiles, and says, "Yes, we'll jump. It isn't hard."

Pinek has jumped twice before en route to Treblinka: in August 1942 and January 1943. In January three bullets were shot into him. He lay in the snow and cold for several days, but somehow he recovered.

Suddenly a big black limousine arrives, and *Untersturmführer* Brandt emerges. He looks at us for a minute. His small, pig-like eyes express satisfaction. In a derisive tone he says, "So we did get you!" He shouts a few orders. The SS men surround us. "March! Get going!"

We march. After several minutes on the road, we come to an assembly point known as Umschlagplatz. In the language of the Warsaw Ghetto, the two big schoolhouses adjacent to the railroad station are known as pre-funeral homes. From there, in July and August to the middle of September 1942, four hundred fifty thousand Jews were sent to their deaths in Treblinka. The Umschlagplatz is witnessing a scene unheard-of in the history of humanity—an immense tragedy. Now we, too, will be part of it.

A triple row of SS guards with machine guns aimed at the doors and windows stand in front of the two schoolhouses. We are not the first group to arrive; almost all the rooms are occupied. SS men divide us into three groups. My group of about two hundred people is chased into a small room on the first floor. About fifty people are already there. They have been sitting without food and water for five days; their agony is apparent on their faces. The floor is full of clotted blood covered over with rags and newspapers. In one corner, a few women are agonizing, dying of thirst. Little space is left for us, but somehow we find a spot on the floor and pull up our legs. When we ask what is happening here, no one replies. A young woman with prematurely gray hair and an insane expression on her face shouts, "Don't ask! You'll see! We're in hell!" Several hours pass in silence. No one arrives. We are thirsty and must satisfy our needs of nature. Szymek Stockhammer goes to the door. Someone yells, "Stop! Don't open it! Ten people went into the corridor and were murdered. Sit if you value your life!" Szymek retreats clumsily.

Director Stein says in a mild voice, "Listen! We'll designate one corner of the room for a toilet. We can't relieve ourselves like pigs. Let's remain human until the end." Someone sitting near the window stands up to go to the corner. At that very moment, a shot is fired, and the bullet whistles by his head, goes through the upper part of the door, and makes a hole in the ceiling of the corridor. Two SS men run into the room shouting, "You pigs!! Who was shooting?! Who has a gun?" They walk over the people lying on the floor and stop before Dr. Munwes, our chief of internal medicine. "Did you shoot?" one of them yells. Munwes is as pale as a white sheet. His teeth chatter from fear. He cannot utter a sound. "Admit!" they scream and drag him into the corridor by his collar. "Now talk!"

They leave the door open so that everyone can see how they search him. Of course they find no gun. "Where'd you hide the gun? Talk!!" One thug hits him over the head with an iron pipe. Munwes, covered with blood, falls to the floor. His brother watching the scene cannot contain himself and runs into the corridor shouting, "That shot came from below. We've no guns here." "Who's asking you, pig?" yells the other SS man and kicks him in the stomach. Both SS men beat the luckless brother with clubs. Using their heels, the SS men pound the prostrate, bleeding bodies as their victims moan weakly.

While this is going on, there is movement on the stairs. Another group is being brought up. The thugs leave their victims and go downstairs. Szymek jumps into the corridor and pulls the half-conscious brothers into the room. Fredzia clings to me. Her whole body shakes as she says, "I'm afraid, Tadzek." I remain silent. What can I tell her? How can I console her? My heart is breaking. I know what those beasts are capable of.

It is getting dark. From the rooms downstairs, we hear horrible screams from women. In the yard, SS men organize orgies with prisoners. We hear whips cracking, sometimes a cry of pain or despair. The scene usually ends with a shot.

We are so thirsty that our tongues stick to our palates and our lips swell, but we have no time to think about it. The doors to our room open and three hooligans enter. With the stance of heroes, they plant themselves in the middle of the room. Holding whips in their hands, they look around carefully, eyeing the women especially. Fredzia grabs me convulsively by the hand. My heart is dying. "You! You!" they exclaim, pointing to Bela and Marysia. "Quick! Stand up!" Bela and Marysia look at us, horrified. Suddenly Bela falls on her knees in front of the SS man and begs, "We know these are our final moments. Let us die in peace! Have mercy on us!" You must have a heart of steel not to heed her pleading. The sadists stick to their demand. Seeing that the girls do not move from their places, one grabs Marysia's hair and pulls her while the other beats Bela's back with his whip. One of the hooligans waiting in the corridor looks in and roars, "What in hell takes you so long?" When he notices the selected women, he smiles lasciviously.

An hour later the door opens. Bela enters with unsteady steps. She sits down beside Fredzia and cries uncontrollably. In a few minutes, Marysia enters. She is naked and blood runs down her legs. Without a word, she goes to the window and leans out—she wants to jump. Szymek grabs her by her legs and sits her down on the floor. The women give Marysia a few clothes. Rage tears at the heart. The bastards! If only we could revenge ourselves on them!

In the meantime, the SS men have devised another game. We hear them moving a heavy object in the corridor. Something high blocks the door. A voice calls through a window, "Ready!" At the same time we hear a low whistle. Through the broken window, two objects thrown from below fall into our room. They are smoke bombs which emit a horrible odor. We begin sneezing, coughing and choking. Our eyes tear. A searchlight is focused on our window. Several people want to jump; they fall, shot through the neck and head. Ricocheting bullets injure many in the room including Dr. Stein who puts a handkerchief around his hand and says to his wife, "It's a pity they didn't shoot me in the head." Thick smoke blankets the room, a foretaste of the gas chamber. Do you suffer much there? Does it take so long there? The bombs burn out in a few minutes. The smoke drifts out through the window. We do not recover before morning. Our throats are scratchy; our eyes burn; breathing is painful. We choke and cough, but this suffering has one benefit: nobody comes into our room. We continue to hear screams from the other rooms. The "game" lasts all night.

It is morning. The life-sustaining air of May permeates our room and dissipates the remaining smoke. The light bothers us terribly as we look around with red, swollen eyes. Our area is a horror scene: pools of clotted blood near the window, seven corpses of young boys and an eighth of a young girl with a bullet through her head. Oh, she is still alive! Another fifteen people are dying from thirst. How long will they keep us here? Our nerves are at the breaking point. In spite of it all, we do not fully realize how much a man can endure.

The guards change—new torturers. Someone pushes the heavy closet away. An SS man and his three Latvian assistants enter. "You have money! Give up everything, otherwise . . ." he exclaims and, looking at his wrist-watch, adds, "You've got ten minutes!" He walks out. With an insane expression on her face, Bela looks at us and pleads, "I beg you! Give them everything. I've seen what those bastards can do!" From secret pockets people pull out whatever they hid during the search in Nalewki Street. In all, it is very little.

In exactly ten minutes, the gangsters return. Pinek Lewin hands the SS man the collected money in a hat. Smiling derisively, the SS man insists, "You have more! Give it! Five minutes more!" A few rings fall into the hat, and that is all. They enter the five minutes later. Dr. Stein stands up and reports to the SS man, "This is everything we have. The rest was taken from us during the first search." The SS man turns red with anger, hits Dr. Stein in the face, and yells, "We'll see!"

The thugs pull three men and an old woman into the corridor and leave the door open. They force their victims to undress completely. The old woman has a little silver locket around her neck. "And what's this?!" one brute yells and yanks it off. "Mister, it's a picture of my husband. Please give it to me!" The fiend kicks her and she falls. The four stomp on her face with their boots. Lucky Marysia, she does not see that. For several hours now, she has been unconscious. We cannot rouse her.

The SS man looks through the men's clothes inch by inch. He cannot find a thing, but he wants to vent his anger on someone. He has an idea. He hands one of the three men a whip and orders the other two to bend over. "You must beat very hard. If you spare them, we'll kill you!" After ten minutes, the one with the whip is tired. The fiends take the whip from him and hit the naked bodies, legs, backs, and heads causing blood to spurt. Finally they, too, are exhausted. "For doing such a good job, we'll give you some water." One of the brutes brings some water. The fellow drinks greedily. A minute later he doubles up with cramps. The water was loaded with pepper. Some joke! The three bodies are left in the corridor. The dead old woman's open eyes seem to be imploring heaven for revenge.

It is noon; the sun beats down mercilessly. The bodies of the slain and tortured are decomposing. When a young *Untersturmführer* enters the room, Dr. Stein rises and begs him to have the bodies removed. The SS man smiles sneeringly as he says, "It won't be necessary. It'll show you how you'll look very soon!"

He notices Fredzia hiding behind me; she does not want to see the bully's face. He says, "You're pleased to sit close to your fellow, eh? You really have everything here, you Jews. I think we're too good to you!" I agree; that is why they must invent more tortures. He calls in two SS men from the corridor. My heart beats wildly. Maybe it is Fredzia's turn. I cannot utter a single word of consolation.

The SS men come in. The three consult quietly for a minute. Nodding understandingly they approach Fredzia and grab her hair. The *Untersturmführer* orders me to kneel facing the wall opposite the door. It is the spot designated as a latrine. He takes a sawed-off shotgun from one SS man and yells to me, "Don't turn around!" He says to Fredzia, "Now I'll shoot your lover. I'm aiming at his head. His brains will mix with shit. Jewish brains and shit are all the same." He shoots. The bullet whistles by my ear and lodges in the wall. The smoke gets into my eyes. I hear Fredzia's terrified scream. "Don't holler!" scolds the *Untersturmführer*. Fredzia is having a convulsion. They beat her with a whip. I feel like revolting. "Kill me, you dogs! Torture me! Why do you torture women?"

A second shot rings out. The same thing happens: he misses. The *Untersturmführer* has a longer explanation now. He "explains": His hand shakes; he cannot aim; he has shot Jews from longer distances; he has killed those vermin by the thousands. "Don't be afraid," he says to Fredzia, "the next shot will be more on target." He shoots and talks again.

How long will this beast torture Fredzia? A few more missed shots, but Fredzia no longer looks. She faints and falls. The "game" is over, and the brutes leave. We hear their beastly laughter in the corridor. I get up. My pants stink. Szymek removes his and gives them to me. Sabinka tries to revive Fredzia. Poor Sabinka almost passes out. Fredzia finally revives and exclaims joyfully, "Tadzek, you're alive!" My heart is sinking. Oh God!

The odor is unbearable in our room. Thirst is killing us. Some women begin shouting, "Water! Give us water!" One ruffian enters the room and says, "You want water? Come! We'll give it to you." The women rise. One holds a beautiful girl of about six in her arms. "Mother, we'll get water! Oh, good! I want a drink so much."

The hours slip by. It is five o'clock and the women have not returned. Nobody dares to call for water. The room is silent.

In the Ghetto, the action still goes on. The last of the houses are demolished with explosives and by fire. No one survives. Locomotives maneuver under our windows. We will go soon. My God, as quickly as possible! It does not matter where, just so we get out of here.

It is night. In the yard the soldiers are singing in hoarse, drunken voices. Only God knows what the night will bring.

Fredzia says, "Tadzek, if they'd only give us a little water, even a few drops." This is her first complaint in a long time. How brave the poor thing is! Since we left the bunker, one and a half days have passed. It seems more like one and a half years.

Szymek pulls a pencil from his pocket, crawls to the wall, and draws a black frame. In the dim light's illumination from outside, he writes:

JEWISH HOSPITAL 75 PERSONS died after long and terrible suffering

Similar obituaries appear on the walls by the thousands, some since 1942, others from January 1943. "After long and terrible suffering"—those words can be written in blood.

Exhaustion is stronger than thirst. Sleep! I hug Fredzia and fall into blessed unconsciousness. I am awakened by a commotion. What is it? Where am I? SS men are running through the corridors. I hear, "Get up! Quick!!!" being shouted and feet clattering on the stairs. Fredzia and Henio still sleep soundly. Unfortunately, I must wake them. "Fredzia, we're going!" Just then several thugs brandishing clubs burst into the room. They hit out blindly as they scream, "Out! Out!"

We run. At the door I am hit on the head. My sight dims and I instinctively raise my arm defensively only to receive a blow on my forearm. This was meant for Fredzia. We run down the stairs. Every few meters, SS men beat us with clubs. People fall like dead flies. I trip on the stairs, fall on my back and pull Fredzia with me. In this way we avoid more blows. We finally reach the yard. As they chase us to the ramp, we run by a deep hole full of dead and half-dead people. I glance down and recognize the women who called for water yesterday. The child is still alive.

Freight cars are at the ramp.

"Get going! Get in!"

The car is small with two tiny sealed windows and two open ones. The floor is covered with lime for "proper" hygiene. I pull Fredzia to an open window. Near us are Henio, Bela, Sabinka, Marysia, Dr. Stein and his wife, Szymek, Pinek, Natek Remba, his wife, and others. It continues to get more crowded. SS men at the door count, "One hundred twenty! Stop!" They close the door. In the room in the Umschlagplatz it was packed. Here in the car?! . . .

The lime chokes us. A thin stream of air wafts slowly through the window. In the middle of the car, it is difficult to breathe even now. It is early; the sun is not high enough to warm much. What will happen later?

We hear a voice outside announcing to someone that in every car there are one hundred and twenty Jews.

"What?! One hundred twenty!? God damn it!!! Are they going on a picnic, those Jews?! 150!"

"*Jawohl!*"

With a screech resembling a banshee's wail, the doors open. In spite of our groans and shouts and the squeezing, they cannot add more than twenty-eight people.

"*Jawohl!* Only 148!!"

The lime chokes even more as the heat rises. Oh, for a drink! We stand on our toes, seemingly glued to one another. Chests burst under the terrible pressure. Blood rises to our heads and runs from our noses and mouths. People are dying in awkward positions. One of the first victims is Renia Kopelowicz, a nurse in our hospital. She is nineteen years old. Until the last minute and in spite of the hopeless situation, she was optimistic and buoyed the morale of her husband, a medical student. Now her face is turning gray. She desperately gasps for breath and looks at her husband imploringly. One minute later her head falls and she dies. Renia is better off. She suffers no more.

Szymek is measuring the window with his eyes, calculating how one can jump out of it. But how do you broach it in this crowd? Maybe if we took off, riding would be better. Sabinka begins hemorrhaging; blood gushes from her nose. Marysia has a terrible stomach ache and cries from the pain. Fredzia keeps her head close to the window and tries, from time to time, to breathe deeply.

Not far from the car is a shower where "soldiers", naked to

the waist, are washing themselves. Oh God, if we only had a drop of water! . . .

With difficulty, Renia's husband feels in his pocket and pulls out a vial of pills. He chews and swallows. In a little while he will double over with pain. He begs to be thrown out of the window. He took strychnine and will suffer in agony for another two hours.

Meanwhile, the rest of the cars are being loaded. Ukrainians and SS men are stationed on the steps. It will be difficult to jump. On one side are two "soldiers" and on the other, another two—four guards for each car. Only four? What kind of criminals are we? We hear footsteps on the roof. A fifth Ukrainian pounds on the roof with his rifle butt to let us know that he is there.

It is noontime. The long blast of the locomotive's whistle pierces the air. The train moves slowly after those horrible minutes of waiting. We will know the verdict as soon as we cross the bridge over the Vistula. Will it be Maidanek or Treblinka? Which is better? Treblinka—death. Maidanek—more suffering. But in Maidanek there is water. WATER!

The last cars have crossed the bridge. The tracks are separating. Clack, clack, clack! The wheels switch tracks. Now!! There is a deadly silence in the car. The road to Maidanek is receding. We are on our way to Treblinka! Good-by Warsaw! Farewell life!

2 Treblinka

"Tadzek, where are we going? Tadzek, why don't you talk to me?" Fredzia asks as she pulls my hand. She is disoriented and bewildered. Luckily, I do not have to reply. The person watching from the other window calls out for all to hear, "Brothers! We're going to Treblinka!" The women begin sobbing loudly.

The train moves more rapidly. People are jumping from the other cars. We hear frequent shots as the SS men fire their machine guns at those who leap while the Ukrainians throw hand grenades. From my window I observe that, unfortunately, all who jumped are dead. In spite of the tragic situation, I try to keep calm.

The sun is shining; the sky is blue; the world is beautiful. We pass lovely resorts near the outskirts of the city. Lilacs are blooming; children play merrily in the fields, but we are riding toward death, toward a terrible death. Our ghastly train speeds toward our destination, the gas chambers. I look at Fredzia, and my heart sinks. I know that in a minute I will lose my self-control. I bite my lips until they bleed.

Szymek is trying to tell me something, but I do not hear; I do not understand. He smacks me and shouts, "You! Wake up! Get hold of yourself! We're jumping!" For that we need some space. We push. I pull myself up and stick out one arm; my head touches the roof. I turn and place my left leg out of the window. Szymek and Pinek help me, as much as possible, to climb out of the car. At the critical moment when seconds separate me from the jump, Fredzia grabs me. She sobs heartbreakingly, "Tadzek, I beg you! Don't do it! It's hopeless." Then she exclaims all in one breath, "You're not sure if they'll kill you immediately. Maybe they'll just wound you, and you'll lie in this heat. You'll suffer so much!!" I retreat. She adds, "Yes, Tadzek, it's right this way. You're not going to jump. It's better to die together."

From the center of the car I hear Dr. Stein's voice as calm and as friendly as always, "Tadzek, Fredzia's right. Even if you're lucky, the outlook isn't good. They'll recognize you, and you'll die! Bela and Sabinka have the best chances of any of us. They should jump." Dr. Dtein's words are effective. We are resigned. Instead, Bela starts pushing herself slowly toward the window. She hugs and kisses Fredzia, says farewell to us, and adds, "Help me." Our hands tremble as we lift her. The train races madly. Maybe their shots will not hit her, and she will succeed. "Much luck, Bela!" She is outside, and, following Pinek Lewin's instructions, she pushes herself away from the car with her knees. She flies! We watch and hold our breath. We hear many shots and see the bullets pass through her body. Oh no! She fell between the rails on the opposite track!

In the car, people become insane from thirst. A small ten year old boy takes a canteen from his belt. For several days now, there has not been a drop of water in it, but he lifts it to his mouth anyway. A group of men around him make some inarticulate noises, more animal than human. Several pairs of hands reach out to snatch the canteen, tearing it from the boy's hands. Now they are fighting over it among themselves. It is so crowded that they cannot even hit one another with their fists so they bite each other on the cheeks, on the nose, and on the ears. May God forgive them. They do not know what they are doing.

With every turn of the wheels, I no longer think about death. Instead, I keep wondering if these crimes will ever be avenged, and who will pay for the innocent blood spilled, or for these calculated crimes executed so meticulously. Someone at the other end of the car screams, "There is no God! God is no more! The devil rules our world!" With a smile Fredzia says, "Tadzek, this is our last trip. We'll meet in Heaven. Maybe it'll be better there." The train's wheels click: Death, death, death! Gas, gas, gas!

We pass the Tluszcz railroad station. It is fifty kilometers from there to Treblinka. We look anxiously through the window. We want to remember everything about this, our last trip: every lilac bush, every blooming tree, everything, everything!

Henio whispers softly, "Tadzek, is it true that, once upon a time, life was normal, that people could exist without the constant fear that, when they wake up, it will be the last day of their lives? Was human dignity always debased? Could any hoodlum be the master of life and death for thousands of people? Will no one stand up against the wronging and torturing?"

Henio is sixteen years old. He does not remember any other times. He looks at his sister, Fredzia, and thinks of his parents who perished in Treblinka during the German action in 1942. Now his sister and he must die. Of his entire family, none will be left to accuse the murderers.

The train starts to brake. We hear many rifle shots and hand grenades exploding loudly. The Jews in one car break the door and several of them jump, get up quickly, and run into the nearby forest. Shots are heard more frequently. In a little while, all the fugitives are laid out peacefully on the grass among the flowers.

The train moves again. If we were only there already! Waiting for death is worse than dying. In this macabre situation Szymek is jocular as usual. He wishes he had cologne so that, when we are converted into soap, we will smell nice. I would gladly hit him in the face. He keeps saying, "Remember, breathe deeply in the gas chamber. You'll die faster.", also, "Tickle me under the arms. I'll croak with a smile on my face." "Shut up, you fool!" I hiss through clenched teeth. I do not care to smile.

More people are dying in the car. They will spare themselves the "pleasure" of looking at the gas chambers. Pinek whispers, "From every transport the sadists select people for orgies." Now Symek has another opportunity for his brand of levity. "I would choose . . ." he says as he furtively looks around the car. He leaves the sentence unfinished and has no more witticisms.

Malkinia . . . five to six kilometers more to go. We stop for fifteen minutes while they add a new locomotive so that we may ride in the opposite direction. Some people take advantage of the short stop to commit suicide. It is very simple: They stick their heads out of the window, are immediately shot through the head . . . and that is the end of them. In the station, an overcrowded passenger train headed for Warsaw stands on a nearby track. The passengers look with horror at the scene being enacted before them.

A jerk, and we start moving along on a single-track line. The newly added locomotive huffs and puffs carrying its heavy load over a bridge, over a creek, past a small red house to the station, Treblinka. We stop, but we are not there yet. Half the cars are left on this track while we ride farther. On the horizon is a forest; eyewitnesses have told us about this place and the secrets it holds.

"Get ready, friends. We're going to take a bath. We're going to be deloused," Szymek jokes again. He must be completely crazy. I hold Fredzia in a strong embrace and say, "Fredzia, we'll not part! We'll go together!" "Yes we'll go together," she replies.

We move into the woods. The outskirts of the camp are encircled by three rows of ditches and three rows of heavy wire. Small towers with searchlights are placed ten meters apart. In every one, an SS man with a machine gun watches. The factory of death is extremely well guarded. As we ride, the woods become so dense that it is dark inside the car. After a short while, light enters, and the train brakes sharply. We have reached our destination.

The ramp is full of SS men. Some civilians run to every car, remove the hooks, open the doors, and shout, "Get out! Run! Run!" They are the *Sonderkommando*.

We jump out—I, Fredzia and Henio. We hold Fredzia tightly by the hands; we do not want to be separated. Suddenly we hear, "Women and children to the right! Move!"

I do not understand. I do not want to understand. An SS man is upon us at once. He kicks Fredzia, hits me over the head with the butt of his gun, and shouts something. My knees buckle and I fall. I am fighting with myself: Oh God, I must see Fredzia one more time, and I shout, "Henio, help!" Henio helps me. Dimly, I see Fredzia among a group of women near the gate in the fence. She notices me, waves her hand, and shouts something. An SS man beats her with his whip, and she disappears!

Natek, Szymek, and Pinek come over to us. Natek has just said goodby to his wife. He sobs uncontrollably. Director Stein, his head drooping sadly, stands nearby. He is probably thinking of his beautiful five year old daughter who is hiding somewhere in the Aryan sector. He does not know if she will ever see her father and mother again.

The last of the women pass through the gate. Marysia has an insane expression on her face. Sabinka calls to us, "The end of our tortures at last! Good-by! Hold out!"

Where did the women disappear? We hear no sounds from the forest, but we will know soon enough. Now everything seems indifferent to me, and I am very tired of life. Although I am only twenty-seven years old, I feel as if I were eighty and perhaps more.

I look around. On one side is the train where the *Sonderkommando* are pulling the corpses from the cars. They are quite busy. On the other side is a log fence about four meters high with two small doors. One, about fifty meters from us, is the gate through which Fredzia disappeared with all the women and children. In front of the other gate, an SS man is stationed with some of the *Sonderkommando*.

Now it is our turn. SS men surround us and show us which direction to take. "Run! Move!" they shout from all sides. To expedite their orders, they start beating. Whips crack; dogs bark as the SS men turn them loose on the people. Powerful beasts, they tear parts of our bodies while we maneuver in an effort to prolong our lives even for one minute longer. Nobody has the courage to cross the gate. I make my decision and shout, "Henio, let's go!" Szymek yells, "What's the hurry? Are you crazy?"

I have had enough. We run. A few people are in front of us. We are still a few meters from the gate. Suddenly, I trip and fall. Henio passes me, runs to the gate, and crosses over. I rise quickly and run. At the gate, a white-gloved hand stops me. Dumbfounded, I stand there for a while. I do not understand. One of the *Sonderkommando* grabs me by the collar, kicks me, and pushes me to one side. "You idiot," he hisses.

I run a few steps. An SS man hits me on the arm and sits me down near the fence. For a moment I think what this may mean as I recall Pinek's words. Cold sweat covers my forehead while I think, almost with envy, about the lucky ones who are now running through the gate toward the gas chamber.

From time to time, the SS man bars the way for someone. Several people are being stopped. The same scene is repeated: The fellow in the *Sonderkommando* shows them where I am sitting, and, with a kick, starts them off in my direction. Szymek and Dr. Stein are running. As they near the gate, they look at me, but the SS man boots them, and the *Sonderkommando* pushes them in. Natek, Pinek, and the brothers Tempelhof are hurrying. The hand comes down, and they go to the side. There are still two hundred people on the ramp. Half of them pass through the gate; the other half joins us. Among the latter are two elderly, gray-bearded Jews wearing long black coats. Now I have no doubt that we have been selected for torture.

The *Sonderkommando* is finishing its work. Hundreds of corpses lie near the cars. Some members of this unit use handcarts in which they throw the corpses and, on top, some garbage and manure. All will go into the oven anyway.

The locomotive pulls up again. The empty cars are closely inspected and then shunted to the side track. Now the other part of the train will follow.

In the meantime, an SS man arranges us in groups of ten. He counts, "One hundred." Surprise is evident in his voice. Our small group is bewildered. Pinek yells, "The hoodlums! They don't even let one die in peace!" while my whole being cries, "Fredzia! Fredzia!"

When the other cars arrive, the scene is the same. The women cry out piteously, "We know we're going to die! We beg you, give us some water!" The SS men and *Sonderkommando* brutally separate families: women to the right, men to the left. They chase the women through the gate now. Whips crack. Women go insane from fear and despair; children cling; the thugs scream, "Faster! Move!" Women are whipped; dogs tear their bodies. They get no water. They will be gassed.

The organization is perfect. Everything moves quickly and efficiently. One dare not even think of revolt. What can a half-corpse do who is dying from thirst and exhaustion, who has spent several days in the Umschlagplatz, and who has ridden for several hours jammed into a freight car with one hundred fifty other poor souls?

Now it is the men's turn. Some of them fall and slowly, very slowly crawl toward the cars. Will they succeed? Treblinka's ramp is high. The men inch their way between two cars trying to reach the other side. As they disappear from my sight, I hear machine guns firing, followed by two brief cries of despair and . . . finished. Meanwhile the rest of the men are chased to the gate. Half of them have already disappeared into this monstrous abyss.

It is hot. The SS man looks indifferently at the runners, takes off his cap, and wipes his forehead with his handkerchief. One of the *Sonderkommando* brings him some beer in a cup. He drinks with gusto as people dash past him to their death. When he finishes drinking and is obviously satisfied, he makes a number of movements with his hands, and a few people come toward us. I see my friend, Lolek Kamengiser, running. He sees us and starts in our direction, even though the SS man did not give the sign and yells, "Stop! Where are you going, *Schweinehund!*" Three SS men catch up with Lolek and beat him with a whip. They bludgeon his head and push him inside.

The bedlam at the station is almost at an end. The transport is over. In a while, Act II will start: the gas chambers. Then probably Act III will feature us.

Natek whispers, "Why have they selected only men?" We will soon know. Several of the *Sonderkommando,* husky, suntanned fellows, approach us. They ask where we come from and if we know their families in Warsaw. We learn that they have been working in this *Sonderkommando* for almost a year. A number of them work on the cars, some in the gas chamber, and others service the crematoria. They lack for nothing. The Jewish transports, especially those from Western Europe, bring plenty of food. These men are aware that their hours of life are few; they have seen too much. When Treblinka is liquidated, they will suffer the same fate. Many of them have witnessed close family members on their way to the gas chambers. Others who work in the crematoria have personally burned their dear ones. Their hearts have turned to stone. Just as no one pities them, they in turn do no longer pity anyone.

They are asked if they know what will happen to us. One *Sonderkommando* replies, his face twisting into an ugly smile, "Why are you so afraid for your life? It isn't such a *tzimmes.* One million Jews have died in Treblinka before you came, and so may you. It won't make a hole in the sky. Don't be afraid."

It is not death we fear, but the way we will die. Another *Sonderkommando* rushes to explain, "Lately, there's been much activity in Treblinka. The crematoria can't accomodate the demand, so we must burn the victims in trenches. You'll carry corpses from the gas chamber and throw them into the ditch. For this, you won't be gassed but shot by machine guns. It's happened before."

Shot. Shot! It is heavenly music. Fate does not abandon me. I am lucky. This is the first good news I have had in a long time. Natek and Pinek are also happy . . . anything but the gas chamber. We will have an easy death. Our hearts are lighter. Even our thirst does not bother us too much.

At the aproach of SS men, the *Sonderkommando* jump aside.

The SS count us. Altogether we total one hundred seventy-five. A few orders are given, then, "Give them water!"

Five minutes later, a large barrel of water is brought on a cart. It is dirty and foul smelling, but it is water. They place it on the ground.

TO DRINK!! People go insane. With their last ounce of strength, they throw themselves on the barrel. They fight; they scream; they fall. Everyone wants to be first. The barrel tips over, and the contents sink into the sand. The SS men laugh and enjoy taking several pictures of the whole scene.

An *Untersturmführer* arrives with a piece of paper in his hand. He says a few words to the SS guards and ends by exclaiming, "Heil! Heil!", and to us he shouts, "Get up!"

Act III begins. The railroad cars are nearby. After the guards divide us among the cars so that there are nearly sixty of us in each one, they close the doors. What is happening? We do not understand what is going on. The floor of the car has been nicely cleaned of lime. We hear a group of guards approaching and then the commander announcing loud enough for us to hear and remember, "At every stop, check the prisoners in each car. If one has escaped, all the others are to be shot."

I am in the same car with Natek, Pinek, and the brothers Tempelhof. The older Tempelhof, an engineer and office manager in the hospital, suffers terribly. He has cancer of the rectum and has had a colostomy. He is supposed to irrigate the bag once a day. Now he is rotting alive.

We wait an hour. Suddenly the locomotive's whistle blows. The guard takes up his post on the steps of the car. We ride through the woods, going back the way we came. Now we are in an open field. Above the forest, a large cloud of dense, black smoke rises. Fredzia! Fredzia!

3 Maidanek

The train is moving. We do not talk. Almost everyone of us has left a dear one in Treblinka. From time to time, somebody moans; someone sobs. A young boy jumps up with a blood-curdling yell, "They killed my mother and two sisters. I'll avenge them!" I am stretched out on the floor. Natek is near me and whispers in my ear, "My wife was four months pregnant. We wanted to have a child so much."

I have my own thoughts. Sometime in 1938, before the war, my mother was dying of cancer and was in severe pain. In 1941, the SS killed my father. After his death, I was left alone like a homeless dog. The only living member of my family was my old grandmother whom I cared for and protected in the Ghetto until she was beaten to death on the street in front of the hospital in January of 1943. From that time on, we were left alone, Fredzia and I. We lived only for ourselves buoying one another's spirits in the most difficult moments in the hope that maybe better times will come.

My thoughts dwell on my parents. After their death, I felt very unhappy. I thought that God had punished me harshly by taking away my loved ones. Today, I am almost content that they are not alive to see and live through this hell.

It is night when we reach the Malkinia station. Most of my fellow sufferers are sleeping. The older Tempelhof tinkers with his colostomy bag. It stinks terribly. Someone yells; my head whirls; I feel hopelessly lost and very sad.

When I wake from a fitful sleep, the train is moving. Everyone in the car is asleep, and I go to the window. It is another beautiful, bright, sunny day in May. We are approaching Warsaw! I recognize the neighborhood of the East Station. The city is alive: cars, trolleys, many people in the streets! My beloved city! Is it possible that I am seeing you again!?

We stop on a side track while the locomotive is detached. The sun is scorching. Ukrainian guards are moving around our car. A worker sitting on a rock nearby has put down his shovel and begins to eat his breakfast. We watch him avidly as he takes a bottle of tea from his pail. Pinek places his hands together as though to pray and then points to his mouth. To drink! To drink! He raises his five fingers to indicate that, for five days, we have been without water. The worker moves his head and looks at the Ukrainians. Taking advantage of a minute's distraction, he runs to our car. At that very moment we hear a shout, "Stop, you son-of-a-bitch!" Two guards run toward him, tear the bottle from his hands, and throw it on the ground. They beat him and scream, "You help the Jews! Maybe you're a Jew, too!"

Meanwile, I am wondering how many days a human being can survive without water in this heat, in cramped quarters, in a stuffy car.

Natek, who speaks Russian, observes that we have nothing to lose. He calls the Ukrainian and begs, "Give us a pail of water. We got out of Treblinka alive, but we'll surely be dead by the time we reach our next destination. Have a little mercy!"

The Ukrainian thinks a minute and asks, "Do you have dollars!? Give them to me and you'll have water, otherwise you'll die! It's none of my business!"

An elderly man hearing the Ukrainian's words, says, "I'll get you water."

He pulls down his trousers in a corner of the car and sits and strains as if he were having a bowel movement. Suddenly a package wrapped in thin rubber emerges from his rectum. The man tears off the cover, takes out five one hundred dollar bills, straightens them out, and hands them to Natek.

"I was keeping them for a dark hour. I thought we'd get to some concentration camp where I'd be able to use them to help my wife and three daughters, but they've been left in Treblinka. Drink water, children!"

Natek calls the Ukrainian and shows him one bill. He refuses to consider it. "What? A pail of water for one hundred dollars?!" He has made better deals with Jews. With his fingers he shows Natek three hundred. Natek hesitates and asks the donor who says, "Give him the five hundred."

Natek hands three hundred dollars to the Ukrainian. Now we are afraid that he will take the money and not bring the water. It seems that we are dealing with a "gentleman". He turns around and looks for a pail. Laborers are working nearby and have one which is used to carry plaster. That is good enough for the Jews. He takes the pail, rinses it under a faucet, wipes it a bit with a piece of paper, and then fills it. He opens the car door and growls, "Here's water, you Jews!"

He is an unusually "honest" fellow; he gives us the top of a thermos bottle without charge since we have nothing with which to drink the water. Oh, God! How delightful is water with plaster! The nectar of millionaires! We have ten liters of water for fifty-eight people. Every one of us could gladly drink the whole pailful. We dole out a little more than half a glass of water per person. I instruct each, in his turn, to drink slowly and to keep the water in his mouth for as long as possible. My turn comes. Thoughts strike me like a whip: "Oh, Fredzia! You suffered so much from thirst and went to the gas chamber without a drop a water!" I cry like a little child.

The Ukrainian comes to the car and asks, "Did it taste good? If you have dollars, you'll get more."

The old man whispers, "Give him the rest of the money so we'll have some water for later on. God knows how long we'll ride."

When Natek gives him the two hundred dollars, the Ukrainian says with a cynical smile, "I can't give you a full pail for two hundred dollars."

It costs him a lot, the hoodlum! Natek begs, "This truly is the last of our money."

The Ukrainian moves his head understandingly and brings somewhat more than half a pail of water. The next words the guard utters have great importance for us, "It isn't far to Lublin, only two hundred kilometers. We'll be there soon."

So it is to Lublin . . . to Maidanek for more suffering. The older Tempelhof says that it would have been better to die in the gas chamber in Treblinka. There, all is over in a few minutes. Who knows what is in store for us now?

"It isn't far to Lublin, some two hundred kilometers." We remain on a side track until late at night. When the activities in the city finally stop and the last trolleys have gone to the depot, they couple us to a freight transport. Near us is a cattle train. All night long we hear a cows' concert. The animals are destined for the slaughterhouse and will be killed humanely. And we, people? And our families? One thought, lucky cows!

We take turns guarding the pail of water, in teams of two in the event that someone succumbs to temptation. In the morning we reach Deblin. A whole night was spent in traveling one hundred kilometers. After a relatively short stop, we start to move again, this time more quickly. In less than two hours we arrive in Lublin. They separate us from the freight train and push us onto a side track, the "air-strip". Flying from a high tower is a black flag on which are embroidered two silver lightning bolts, the insignia of the SS.

Several Ukrainians enter the car to count us. They take advantage of this occasion to help themselves to several pairs of boots. It is about time to apportion the water.

The doors are opened and we jump out. A few SS men watch us while the *Kommandant* of the guard reports, "One hundred and seventy-five Jews. Five of them are dead."

One officer laughs, "They must have died from fear."

Another says, "Were I in their place, I'd also die."

"What's the difference? They won't live long anyway."

We line up five abreast while the officers whisper a few words to the *Kommandant* of the guards and then go to the other end of the square. An officer signals with his hand. The *Kommandant,* with a whip, shouts to the first five, "On the run, go!" They run some fifty meters toward the officers.

The second five run. One of them, in spite of his best efforts, can barely move his legs and fails the test. Two guards hasten to him and put him to one side. It is our turn to run, Pinek, Natek, the Tempelhofs, and I. Our lives depend on our succeeding.

We stand in line at the other end of the square as others run. Every few minutes someone is removed. At the end, ten unfortunate persons are on one side; the Ukrainians surround them and march them away; their fate is sealed. One hundred sixty of us are going to Maidanek.

About one hundred SS men with rifles cocked to shoot and with fixed bayonets, escort us as if we were dangerous criminals.

"Get going! Move!"

We walk along a wide, dusty road in the searing sun. Whoever lags behind is prodded with a bayonet. After some fifteen minutes of this, we notice, on the right side of the road, guard towers, some barracks, and large white signposts on which are painted a black skull with the inscription in five languages: Stop! Limits of camp! Trespassers will be shot without warning!

When we turn to the right, we observe the first signs of camp life. Inmates wearing striped prison garb and wooden shoes that clatter on the cobblestones, strain on ropes to pull a cart filled with stones. Sweat streams down their blackened, emaciated faces. A menacing man in civilian clothes with an armband reading: *Oberkapokommando-Strassenbau* stands on the cart with a whip in his hands. He is obviously dissatisfied because they probably do not pull fast enough, so he helps by beating the poor souls with his whip and shouting menacingly. It is too bad that Szymek does not see this. He would probably have material for his sarcastic remarks.

They chase us to a barbed wire enclosure. While we wait, several SS men stand at the wire, laugh, and throw stones at us. Beasts, why don't they shoot!?

A small group of *Häftlinge* dressed in striped prison uniforms but with leather shoes approaches us. These are the barbers who will shave our heads. Among them are several Jewish survivors of the first days of the Warsaw Uprising.

We ask, "How is it here?"

Not wanting to worry us, they shake their heads. Reluctantly they say, "Life's hard in Maidanek. There are four camps or fields, one next to the other. Fields 1 and 2 are bearable. The *Kommandant* is 'so-so'. Fields 3 and 4 are punitive. May God help you if you fall into those fields! They're slaughterhouses!"

Our heads are shaved. The SS men order us to take off our clothes and shoes and then rush us to the bath. Oh, God! Water! A minute later, we are under a hot shower. Finally we have water to our hearts' content. Never mind if it is hot, if it burns our palates and throats. DRINK! Drink! Drink! Drink! Now they chase us away, and we go to the clean side. SS men and two *Häftlinge* search us even though we are naked! "Open your mouth! Lift your arms! Go!"

Camp uniforms are issued a few meters away. Everything is done very quickly. They push some rags into our hands and order us to dress. The underwear is too small. We get patched shirts, faded striped pants, and civilian jackets with a red band on the back on which are big black letters: K.L. "You'll get shoes in the barrack," they add, to console us.

An *Untersturmführer* and two civilians with armbands reading *Lagerschreiber* come over to us. The SS man divides us into two lines and orders, "These go to Field 4; the others, to Field 3!"

I am in the same line with Pinek. The Tempelhofs and Natek are in the other. We are going to Field 4. Pinek, who considered our outfits a good masquerade, makes no more jokes.

Maidanek is actually composed of five fields. In the first and second, the barracks have good windows. These are for the lucky ones. In the third and fourth, the barracks are horse stables. The fifth field is for women. A small wooden structure, the *Blockführerstube,* stands at the gate to each field.

We stop in front of the *Blockführerstube* for Field 4 while the *Lagerschreiber* guiding us reports, "Enter eighty Jews."

We enter the camp and stop on a wide street with twelve barracks on each side. The *Lagerschreiber* calls a certain *Blockältester* who is *Reichsdeutsche* and wears a black triangle, the insignia of a professional criminal—he is a bandit. He tells him, "Here are eighty Jews. Do whatever you want with them."

This thug is now the master of life and death. He looks at us suspiciously and says angrily, "They always send me half-dead Jews! March!"

When we reach Barrack 12, the *Blockältester* shouts to the *Stubendiensts,* "Hey there! Come out! You have newcomers!" A few shadowy, miserable figures with ghastly-looking faces come from the barrack. The *Blockältester* says, "Tell them how they must behave and what the punishment is for disobeying."

The *Blockschreiber* steps forward. He seems to be a Jew for, on the left side of his jacket below his camp number, he wears the Star of David. We have some hope, but when he speaks, these vanish very quickly.

"Above all," he says in German, "you must realize where you are. Forget all your illusions. Forget whatever you have been before the war. The *Blockältester* is the highest authority, and he may decide to kill you. If any of you think that you came here to rest in a sanatorium, you are definitely mistaken. This is not a health facility; it is a crematorium. Here, no one pities anyone. A brother has no pity for a brother, a son for a father. If you want to prolong your life, you must keep your mouth shut. Don't be surprised at anything. Be obedient and work hard. For stealing, we hang you from the beams. In a minute, you will enter the barrack and be given shoes and a cap. Tomorrow morning, you will get tin tags with numbers to be worn around your neck, and a star and number for your jacket and pants. Now be quiet and go in, one at a time."

We enter the barrack. It is a large stable with triple bunks arranged in four rows. On one side, blankets screen off a few beds for the *Blockältester* and *Stubendiensts.* It is two hours before the evening roll call, and the barrack is empty. The inmates have not returned from work. We are tired, but there is no place for us to sit so we squat on the floor to think about the *Blockschreiber*'s words. Suddenly we hear voices shouting outside, *"Kaffeeholen! Kaffeeholen!"* Two *Stubendiensts,* one Ukrainian and one Polish, burst into the barrack.

"Our guests are sitting?! A few hours in the camp and you're tired already, you sons-of-bitches!? Go and run! Carry the coffee! What! You're still sitting!?" We get our first greetings, kicks. "Get going! Quickly!"

We run out of the barrack. The *Stubendiensts* select Pinek, myself and two others. We run to the kitchen for the heavy cauldrons of coffee. An SS man, the kitchen *Kapo,* comes out and shouts, "Stand still! Caps off!"

The *Stubendiensts* report that the team has come to get the coffee. An SS man moves his hand condescendingly. The reporting ceremony is over, and the *Kapo* calls the barrack numbers. We must grab the cauldron and run. "Always tempo, man!"

When our turn comes, we grab the handles and run with the full, one hundred liter cauldron. It has no cover; the hot liquid splashes and burns our hands. Since we are barefoot, the cobblestones and glass fragments hurt our feet. "Hurry!" the *Stubendienst* prods.

The load is too much for us. We are utterly exhausted and must stop for a minute at least. In the blinking of an eye, there is a disturbance. The *Kapo* runs over wanting to beat us, but he notices our miserable faces. The lashes that were meant for us he gives to the *Stubendiensts.* Meanwhile, we grab the cauldron and run out of the kitchen. The *Stubendiensts* hold their injured noses and threaten us, "You just wait! You'll pay for it later!"

They do not let us catch our breath for a moment. We still have one hundred meters to go before we reach the barrack. When we are just a few meters away, Pinek falls, pulling the cauldron so that it tips over spilling the liquid. Now the *Stubendiensts* have a case against us. They call the *Blockältester.* The old bandit stands in front of us, looks at Pinek, then at me, the empty cauldron, and shakes his head in silence. The *Stubendiensts* complain, "We've city 'gentlemen' and, in general, fucking intelligentsia. We must teach them a lesson." The *Blockältester* agrees saying, "Yes, a good lesson. I don't want to have any trouble with them in the future."

Unlucky Pinek gets ten lashes. The bastards beat him over the head and on his rear. I, for being only partly guilty, get five. They beat vehemently. After the second lash, it feels as though my skin is being torn. Blood spurts from the wound. I am fortunate that the sentence was only five lashes. I don't think I could have endured any more.

After meting out the sentence, the *Stubendiensts* call all the newcomers outside in front of the barrack and announce, "For your own good, you lazy ones, you need some training. Follow our orders! March! Fall down! Roll over! Jump up!" The tempo of the exercises takes our breath away. Those of us who do not carry out the orders correctly are beaten with clubs. The beasts hit out blindly. We continue to exercise. Three cannot get up. Some *Blockführers* passing by remark with a laugh, "Very good, *mensch*!"

The *Stubendiensts* are pleased. They received some good marks. I have chest pains and cannot breathe. My sight is dimming. On the order "Lie down", I fall and cannot rise.

When I come to, I do not know where I am. I lift my head and open my eyes. My head throbs. The world is whirling. A group of people is nearby. Faintly, I hear the order, "Caps off!" The noises seem to get louder. Then everything is murky; I lose consciousness.

The second time I recover, it is dark, and I am lying on boards. My head feels unbearably heavy, and every inch of my body throbs with pain. I moan. I sense someone leaning over me.

"Quiet, Tadzek." It is Pinek's voice.

I slowly recall the day's events: our arrival, bringing the coffee, gymnastics, my fainting. Pinek begs me to go to sleep, but I insist, "What happened to me? Tell me Pinek! You must!"

When my questioning becomes too insistent, he becomes impatient and says, "You're lucky to be alive! During gymnastics you fell, probably fainted. Two bandits jumped on you and beat you over the head. It's a miracle they didn't fracture your skull. Of our group of eighty, only seventy-four are left.

"During the roll call, you were lying with the corpses and looked like one. That's all, more or less. The *Stubendiensts* wanted to leave you in front of the barrack with the corpses. They argued that, when the *Sonderkommando* comes in the morning, you'll be ready for them. Somehow we talked them out of it. There's no room for us in this barrack. They'll take us somewhere else tomorrow. Meanwhile, we must sleep two in a bed."

"Pinek," I say, "lie down next to me."

"No, Tadzek, I can't. It hurts. I'll lie on my stomach on the floor."

Our first day in Maidanek is over. I have a recurring thought: Fredzia and the others are lucky to have been left in Treblinka.

The gong sounds frighteningly. "Get up! *Kaffeeholen!*"

Pinek pulls me by the hand and says, "Get up! Yesterday they gave us a talk. If we don't obey orders instantly, they'll kill us. Rise quickly! They keep their promises."

I ache all over. My eye is swollen. Blood is clotted on my head and face. There is much confusion in the barrack as people jump from their bunks and dress.

There are several hundred prisoners in the barrack, Poles and Jews. Several Jews come over to us. One stares at me carefully, attentively. His face seems familiar. It is Dr. Tonnenberg, my father's friend. He looks strange in his striped outfit and shaved head. We shake hands. He has been here for four weeks and is in the road-building *Kommando,* but he has hopes of becoming the medic of the barrack.

When the coffee comes, we must stand in line; I say good-by to Dr. Tonnenberg. Pinek and I have to share a half a liter of coffee in a canteen. I take a sip, then Pinek takes one. We must drink quickly because the *Stubendiensts* are already shouting, "Roll call! Out!"

We run out. Hundreds of figures in striped uniforms are dashing to the roll call square. It is very cool and, judging from the grayness of the light, probably not later than half-past four in the morning. We are barefoot. One *Häftling*, an honest soul, consoles us kindly, "Don't worry, fellows. Raise your heads! The beginning is always hardest."

We are arranged five abreast by barracks. The *Blockältester* yells, "Straighten lines!" When the *Blockführer* approaches, the *Blockältester* shouts, "Quiet! Caps off!" and makes his report. As soon as the SS man counts the prisoners and leaves, the *Blockältester* shouts, "Caps on! At ease!"

The show is not over yet. Some high ranking SS officer on a motorcycle enters through the gate. Now the SS men stand in line. One with a piece of paper in his hand steps forward. Another yells, "Field 4, stand still! Caps off! Eyes right!"

The first SS man reports and salutes, *"Heil!"*

"Heil!" responds the SS officer and goes out through the gate.

"At ease!" shouts an SS man. Roll call is over.

"Form work *Kommandos*!"

Häftlinge run pell-mell, each rushing to where his group will start for work. We, the newcomers, return to the barrack. I am pleased. Maybe they will give us a minute to rest. No such luck! While the *Stubendiensts* prepare a breakfast with margarine and sausage sizzling appetizingly in the frying pan for "his highness" the *Blockältester*, the *Stubendiensts* have no such luxuries. They fix bread and marmalade for themselves. One of them turns to our group and says, "A volunteer to bring water to wash the barrack and to scrub the pots!" He points, "Here are the pots! There's the washroom!"

Pinek and I grab the pots and run to the washroom. Finally we will be able to drink enough water even though we know it is contaminated. I am aware of how dangerous it is to drink, but I do not think of the consequences. Come what may, I will get sick and croak! I remember the words of the *Sonderkommando* in Treblinka: "It will not make a hole in heaven."

In the meantime, I am drinking refreshingly cold water. Nectar from Paradise! I feel fine and must return. It does not matter if my head hurts and I cannot see straight. It does not matter if I walk stooped over like an old man and the skin on my rear end feels like fire. The most important thing is that, after so many days, I have been able to satisfy my tortuous thirst.

We bring the water. After the *Stubendiensts* hands us some rags and brushes and show us what to do, they add, ". . . but thoroughly! Understand!?"

We do their work, but since they have the "fucking" newcomers, let them work . . . the *Stubendiensts* organize the tasks. Pinek and I scrub the floor. Two others dry it. Some spray the woodwork. Others straighten out beds that were made incorrectly. About ten go outdoors to clean in front of the barrack. The water gets dirty fast. Pinek and I run to get fresh water. Each time we take advantage of the occasion to drink as much as we can.

Our bellies hurt. I ask a *Stubendienst* if I may go to the bathroom. He gives me permission and laughs ironically. My belly hurts more and more. I look for a latrine. By the wires between Barracks 6 and 8, there is a trench with a few boards across it. That is all. It stinks horribly. Several latrine cleaners are there. The prisoners lower pails on a rope, scoop up the liquid excrement, and pour it into barrels. Near the latrine, a *Häftling* with a club in his hand bars my way. "Where are you going?" he demands.

"I've a bellyache!"

"Don't you know you're not permitted to shit now?"

"Sir, I can't hold out. My stomach hurts—terrible pains!"

"Then shit in your pants!" he answers and beats me on the back.

Later I learn that, with the exception of the officials, *Häftlinge* here in Maidanek can satisfy their physiological needs only before roll call, during the midday break, and after the evening roll call. They do not want us to waste time during work.

I return to the barrack. The *Stubendienst* laughs, "Do you feel better now?"

Every minute my cramps get worse and I suffer terribly. I

cannot hold out any longer. Finally, the *Stubendienst* has pity on me. He is the same one who beat me yesterday.

He shows me a little spot blocked off by boards in the tool shed inside the barrack. It contains a portable commode for the exclusive use of the *Blockältester* and the *Stubendiensts*.

"Go there, but be careful. If the *Blockältester* catches you, he'll kill you!"

Luckily I am not caught. I feel better and can continue to work.

Pinek asks me a question, "What did you use for toilet paper?"

Surprised, I look at him and reply, "What do you mean 'What did I use?' I didn't wipe myself."

We finally finish our work and sit in front of the barrack to rest for a minute while several friends go with "Mr." *Stubendienst* to the clothes storage depot. They bring back wooden shoes, striped caps, numbers, and cloth triangles.

With difficulty, I find two wooden shoes that are the same size. They are very tight, and it is difficult to walk in them. I am distressed, thinking about what will happen when they send me to work. In the meantime, I sew the number on my jacket and pants. Under that, I sew two triangles, the red one below and the yellow one on top; together they form a Star of David.

In front of the barrack, several people post signs reading "Political Section". They sit at a table and take out forms. Each of us gets personal belongings: a piece of string and a little metallic tag with a number that matches the one sewn on his jacket and pants. One of the VIPs says, "Wear this tag around your neck. Whoever is caught without his number gets twenty-five lashes on his ass. Remember that!" We put on the numbers. The Mr. VIPs leave. From this moment on, we are registered citizens of this torture camp, Maidanek.

We get our midday meal at noon. Luckily for Pinek and me, they leave us alone. We still have bellyaches. Since we cannot use the toilet in the barrack, we wait impatiently for the signal to eat.

The *Kommandos* building the road nearby are coming. They are very tired and skinny and have black faces. I recognize Dr. Tonnenberg in the group. With his black eye, he looks like me. When he left for work this morning, he did not have it.

They are bringing our meals in steaming cauldrons. What an appetizing smell of cooked beets! The *Häftlinge* are excited. "We'll have some meat in the soup, won't we? Will it be potatoes or just cooked peels?"

The gong sounds throughout the camp. I am so excited at the sight of the soup that I forget about my cramps. It will be my first hot meal in many days and only the second in four weeks.

Pinek and I are near the cauldron. The *Blockältester* comes out of the barrack with a ladle in his hand, lifts the cover of the cauldron, and keeps stirring to examine the contents. No meat, no potatoes, only hard potato peels and uncooked beets are the main ingredients. I get to the cauldron with Pinek. The *Stubendienst* pulls the *Blockältester* by the sleeve and whispers "Mr. *Blockältester,* these two worked well today."

"Mr." *Blockältester* shakes his head understandingly. He dips his ladle deeply. Onto the dish falls a mess of potato peelings and beets. I step aside. The jealous eyes of my bunkmates follow me. "He's lucky! He got soup!" they whisper. I think of pigs whose food was tastier and much better.

In the meantime, a problem arises: what utensil to use to eat it. A *Häftling* comes over to me and asks, "Do you need a spoon, friend?" He pulls a wooden spoon from his pocket and says, "I'll sell you this for half a portion of your bread. Buy it. I'll come for the bread tonight."

His utensil is a necessity. I take it and agree. The majority of the prisoners sip the soup directly from the dishes. What is left on the bottom, they eat with their fingers. The *Stubendienst* rushes us by saying, "You peasants, gobble it up faster! We don't have enough dishes. The others want to eat also."

Dr. Tonnenberg sits on the ground next to me with his portion which is almost clear liquid. He pulls out his spoon, stirs the soup, and fishes out three pieces of beet and a few potato peels. He breathes heavily. Noticing my portion, he says, "Tadzek, don't think that the soup is always like that. I've been here a month and only once did I get thick soup."

I cannot express the sorrow I feel for this man. I give him almost half of my portion. Tonnenberg is happy. With tears in his eyes he thanks me and adds, "Maybe someday I can repay you, Tadzek."

Our midday pause lasts only half an hour and the time is running out. We must eat quickly.

Pinek, observing me through lowered eyelids, looks at me reproachfully and says, "You're an idiot! For the half a liter of thick soup you gave to him, you could have received a portion of bread and half a piece of sausage. For five spoonfuls, I bought myself a spoon with which to eat."

All the soup has been distributed. The *Stubendiensts* receive their portions of the good thick liquid which they hide under their beds. At night, they will sell it for bread. They scrub the cauldrons, pour the watery liquid into a container, and place the cleaned cauldrons in front of the barrack. As soon as they are in place, the famished prisoners pounce on them, reaching inside to clean the sides. They kick; they fight; they scream. It is a horrible, tragic scene. The *Stubendiensts* rush out with their whips and lay many heavy blows on the *Häftlinge,* but beating does not deter them.

Suddenly the gong sounds. "Form work *Kommandos*!" Wooden shoes clatter as the prisoners assemble into groups.

After the cauldrons and dishes are cleaned and the work *Kommandos* leave, the *Blockältester* gives a "pep" talk. "Tomorrow you go to work. I advise you to work diligently. Diligence is a seven mile step to freedom. Understand?!" What the *Blockältester* did not explain is that the freedom he is talking about is not the freedom found on this earth.

"And now," he says turning to one of the *Stubendiensts,* "give them a bit of exercise."

We put on our caps and line up in front of the barrack as we had done for roll call. The *Stubendienst* stands in front of us and barks out the orders, "Stand still! Caps off! Eyes left! Eyes front! Caps off!" At the word "off", we must slap our thighs hard with the palms of our hands.

In the beginning it amuses us. After an hour, the amusement is a little less. Finally the *Stubendienst* becomes hoarse and selects someone in our ranks who claims that he had been a sergeant in the army. The game continues.

After three hours, we have mastered the technique, but our hands are swollen from hitting our thighs. The *Stubendienst* declares that he is a human being and is stopping the cap exercise to teach us how to march.

"On your way to work tomorrow, you must pass through the gate with a sprightly step and in an orderly line, otherwise the SS man will beat you to death!"

We step through an imaginary gate. And once again . . . "Caps off! Eyes left!"

Trap! Trap! Trap! Trap! our wooden shoes clack on the stones. We exercise like that until nightfall and it is time for the evening roll call. One thing I cannot understand is where I get all of my strength. Only last night I was lying half-dead, beaten, and exhausted.

Tonight the roll call proceeds more smoothly. We return to the barrack relatively faster, line up five abreast in front of the barrack, and enter by two's for coffee, a portion of bread, and a piece of margarine. The bread smells delicious. I am extremely hungry. At a certain moment, somebody approaches and says, "Friend, do you remember? You bought a spoon."

With a heavy heart, I break my piece of bread. Pinek watches and is angry. That night he does not speak to me at all.

Dr. Tonnenberg comes over to me. I have no straw in my bunk, so we sit on the bare boards and talk. He tells me that Field 4 is the worst one.

"They finish us off here. Half the *Blockältesters* are bandits, and the *Stubendiensts* are even worse. They steal food and give us the liquid from the soup because they can exchange the thick part for cigarettes and vodka. When they cut and divide the bread, they take a piece from every loaf for themselves.

"Until two days ago, we had a punitive work assignment after the night roll call. Most of the time, we toil late into the night.

"We carry rocks from one end of the field to the other, and when we collect a good-sized pile, we take the same rocks back again, running all the time. The SS men, *Blockältesters,* and *Kapos* beat us with clubs. Often they hose us down with water from the hydrants.

"Every day about one hundred or more of us die. During the last few weeks, they made selections for the gas chambers in the women's field, only among the Jews."

While working on the road one night, Dr. Tonnenberg met his wife. The selections for the gas chamber took place the next morning. He has not seen his wife since. Six large trucks filled with women and children were delivered to the gas chamber. Their cries were heard in the barracks.

"Only German bandits and perverts are *Kapos*. On the job, they beat to kill, having been taught how to do this by the SS. They learned well. The *Lagerführer, Obersturmführer* Thuman, is a sadist, a beast. Anyway, you'll find out for yourself. If it doesn't end soon, no one will be left."

"Is there any hope that I can get into the health services and eventually become a medic?" I ask.

He smiles sadly as he says, "That will require much luck, Tadzek. They don't need doctors here. A few work in the health services in Field 1, but they are prisoners who've been here a long time. Medics work in the barracks. They've nothing in common with the medical profession, unless you call sending people to the other world, medicine. I was lucky. One week ago, an *Oberkapo* broke an arm; I improvised a splint for him. He was thankful and promised to talk to somebody. Maybe I'll succeed."

The gong sounds. "Everyone to bed!"

We say good-by. I lie down on my stomach; Pinek does the same. I am so weary that I cannot even think. I fall into a deep sleep.

"Get up!"

Already? Is it possible? I lay down just a minute ago! It is true. I see the bright sun through the barrack window.

My eyes are red and filled with pus; my entire body aches. I am hungry, but there is no time to meditate. They are bringing the coffee. I stay close to Pinek. He is in a slightly friendlier mood today as he says, "Just don't be a fool, Tadzek! Don't let them exploit you. Listen to me, and you'll be all right." We go to roll call.

"Form work *Kommandos*!"

We are chased to a place near the *Schreibstube* where we are told to wait and are reminded that, if anyone moves from his spot, he will be punished. Despite this admonition, Pinek runs to the water tap, opens the faucet, takes some water, runs back and says to me, "Wash your eyes." In the meantime, the *Kommandos* are leaving for work.

After a while, the *Lagerschreiber* arrives, counts us, writes something on a piece of paper, and disappears. He returns with an SS man. They have a short discussion and the decision is made for us to plant a lawn in the camp. The lawn in front of the *Schreibstube* is nice, but in the rear, near the kitchen, it is awful. The back area will be our project. There is still a sizeable pile of earth available for planting. Much work must be done.

Two Ukrainians, assigned as foremen, distribute the tools and divide us into work crews: ten to use pickaxes to break the clumps of earth, five to fill the boxes with soil, forty to carry these, and the rest to level the ground.

Pinek and I carry a box. I had feared that the job would be worse. I have the impression that the work is not too heavy even though we must continually run because the Ukrainians beat us as often as they can and my shoes are tight. When I mention my thoughts to Pinek, he looks at me as though I were insane and says, "Tomorrow, at any price, we'll change *Kommandos*. If you think it's easy or a joke, wait a few hours. You can't loaf here even for a minute."

Like executioners, the Ukrainians run around with their poised clubs. Woe to those who carry too small a load or don't move fast enough. In no time at all, the Ukrainians break several clubs over the workers' backs. Pinek and I get our share when I stop for a minute to put a leaf on my foot where the shoe is causing a blister.

After a while Pinek complains loudly that the soles of his feet burn. He has no alternative but to remove his shoes. Even this is bad. Glass and pebbles injure his soles, and, to make matters worse, my belly aches. This is all I need.

I soon discover that Pinek is right. I worked only a few

hours and this supposedly light work has become an unbearable torture. Oh God, if only the midday pause would come quickly! It is only eight o'clock in the morning or maybe half-past . . . still three and a half hours before we can rest.

We hear a motor. Thuman, the terror of the camp, arrives. The Ukrainians become wilder and shout, "Work, you sons-of-bitches! Tempo! Get going! Quickly!" We are scared. We forget our pains and run.

One of our group is the twenty year old son of a *shochet* (Jewish ritual slaughterer) named Pfefer. For as long as I can remember, he always pored over the Talmud and left his home only to pray in the synagogue. He is a typical example of a Talmudist: tall, thin, and pale. After surviving the experiences in the bunkers in Warsaw and in Treblinka, he looks more like a skeleton than a man.

When he notices the officer, he puts down his shovel, removes his cap and reverently approaches Thuman. In a whining voice, he begs to be assigned to different work. We watch the scene with fear in our hearts. What will happen?

A miracle occurs. Thuman smiles pleasantly, asks him what he did before the war and where he would like to work. We run around the unlucky boy with our loads trying to warn him of the danger he is in. Our efforts are in vain. We hear Thuman saying quietly, "So you want to work in the kitchen. Good. We'll see if you can do that kind of work. Come with me!"

Bewildered, Pfefer runs after him. We stop working. Even the Ukrainians are intrigued and pay no attention to us.

Just then, the cook appears with a metallic container of hot coals and throws them in front of the kitchen. Thuman orders Pfefer to take off his shoes and run over the burning coals. For a minute, Pfefer does not realize and cannot understand what is happening.

Thuman kicks him with the point of his boot and shouts, "Get going!"

Jumping wildly, Pfefer screams to heaven. With tears in his eyes, he runs to Thuman and begs to be forgiven and to be allowed to go back to his old job.

"Mr." *Obersturmführer* is furious. He orders him to undress. Pfefer does not hear. For a minute, he stands like a statue.

Thuman orders several cooks to tear off Pfefer's clothes and calls for more burning coals and wood. Turning to Pfefer, Thuman shouts, "Now roll in it!"

Pfefer screams like a bull being slaughtered. Thuman commands the cooks to force him to obey. They throw him on the hottest part of the fire. Then he demands that Pfefer be held by his hands and feet and be turned on his stomach and back—stomach and back.

Pfefer's screams are inhuman. His searing flesh emits a terrible stench. After a while, Thuman, with an iron poker, beats Pfefer over the face once, twice, three times. Pfefer has had enough; he screams no more; he is silent forever.

Thuman has had enough also. He goes to his motorcycle. We must salute at the order, "Attention!" He leaves to look for other victims.

The scene is so horrible that even the Ukrainians stare with hanging jaws, aghast. They have been in Maidanek for three years and have witnessed many crimes. They, themselves, have murdered, but they never witnessed a scene like that. For the next three-quarters of an hour, we walk slowly with half-empty boxes. When the Ukrainians finally recover and begin rushing us, the midday gong sounds.

The culinary news is that we have a good meal today with potatoes and pieces of meat in the soup. I get to the cauldron and look at the *Blockältester* who stirs and stirs . . . and pours clear liquid containing a piece of potato. I do not need a spoon today.

I search for Dr. Tonnenberg and do not see him. When I ask for him, someone says, "That one, he has luck! He was called to the *Schreibstube* when the *Oberkapo* returned from headquarters. He'll certainly become the medic of our barrack."

Pinek looks at me and says through clenched teeth, "Yes, Tadzek! You did the right thing after all when you gave that doctor your soup yesterday."

During the break, Pinek tore out the lining of his jacket, and I made a good bandage for him and for myself. When the gong sounds, we return to work.

We continue carrying soil. One of the Ukrainians looks at us. "You!" he finally shouts to Pinek and me. When we approach him, he says, "If you give us cigarettes or bread, it'll be easier for you to work. Tell that to your friends!"

The Ukrainians leave us for a moment. Everyone asks what is happening. When we tell them, they accept the foreman's proposition with enthusiasm. Our masters call us over and say, "So, what's the answer?"

"Harasho," I answer using one of the few Russian words I know. Pinek wants to exhibit his knowledge of Russian also and asks a very important question, "How much bread daily?" After thinking it over, they say, "One loaf every day."

After roll call that night, we meet and decide to select four good pieces of bread and then have each contribute a piece from his portion. The affair is thus settled. We can hardly wait until morning. It is not important if they do not take us to another field and we continue to sleep squeezed together on bare boards.

Finally it is morning. The weather is beautiful, not a cloud in the sky. Somewhere high overhead, we hear the drone of an airplane.

"Form work *Kommandos*!" does not sound so menacing today.

We run to the kitchen, form two lines, and wait for our foremen. Pinek is satisfied and says, "Light work is more desirable than food."

When the Ukrainians arrive, we give them the bread. They are somewhat dissatisfied that it is cut up, but we promise that, the next day, we will add a few portions of margarine. We talk it over and decide that nobody will stand still and we will be true to the principle of the camp: "Move constantly", but the containers will be almost empty. The foremen will look out for approaching danger. If they notice something on the horizon, they will shout, "Move!" Then we will have to work diligently until the danger is over.

"Get going, men! Work!", but this order is not so threatening. Once or twice during the day, the yell comes, "Move!"

That forces us to really work. This is living and not dying. Pinek is so happy that he can barely keep from shouting: Long live Maidanek!

Unfortunately, our luck is very short-lived. After three or four days of relative peace, we learn that we will be transferred to Barrack 8.

We are very uneasy. The *Blockältester* in Barrack 8, a true German from Warsaw who has been in Maidanek since the very beginning, is a homosexual and a sadist. He is hated by everyone: Poles, Jews, and Russians. When there were no Jews, he murdered Poles and Russians. Now his victims are exclusively Jews.

We receive our bread in the old barrack. The *Blockschreiber* then leads us to Barrack 8.

Our *Blockältester* is very pleased to have newcomers. He calls his assistant, Wanka who is Ukrainian and lived near Lvov. Of medium height, athletically built, and with the strength of a horse, Wanka is a hangman and delights in torturing Jews. When he sees us, his face twists into a wry smile. Only two weeks ago, there were one hundred fifty Jews in this barrack. All the places were taken. Now that seventy-three of us have arrived several beds will still remain empty. The *Blockältester* and Wanka can be proud of their talents as killers.

Before we enter the barrack, the *Blockältester* greets us with the usual big speech. He is obviously proud of his oratorical ability. Every once in a while, he addresses himself to Wanka. "Tell them, Wanka! Am I right? True?"

Wanka nods and laughs until his belly shakes.

The *Blockältester* adds, "I'm presenting my good friend, Wanka, to you! Do you know him? If not, you will, soon enough! True, Wanka? We're very friendly in Barrack 8. We don't yell. We criticize no one. If someone disobeys, we have means to deal with him. True, Wanka?"

Now his friend takes the floor. He stands with his arms akimbo. For a while, he delights in our miserable, frightened appearance. Then he says, "Today a lousy Jew complained to the *Blockältester* that I knocked out all his teeth. The louse was lying. He fell out of bed and hurt himself. I only helped him to get up. What do you think, you lousy Jews!? Whom do you think the *Blockältester* believed? Me, obviously me! The *Blockältester* and I are always right. Soon you will see how we punish liars. Get into the barrack fast!"

Wanka closes the entrance door and calls a number. A nineteen year old boy comes forward. His face and head are bloody and swollen. Wanka shouts, "Are you the one who went to the *Blockältester* and lied? Why don't you talk?" He hits him on the face once or twice. "Will you admit you lied, you louse?!"

The boy replies in a low voice, "I lied."

"Say it louder so everyone can hear!"

"I lied."

Wanka is nervous. "Louder, you son-of-a-bitch! They don't hear you in the back!"

The boy cannot get a sound out. He is bleeding copiously from his nose, and he stands in a pool of blood. He is getting weak. Wanka loses control and kicks him in the face with his boot. He wants to pound the boy even more, but *Blockschreiber* Janusz emerges. He pulls the thug to one side and says, "You've done enough for today, Wanka. Your nerves are getting the better of you."

The barrack is extremely quiet. No one dares to come close to the unlucky fellow who shows no sign of life. *Blockschreiber* Janusz comes from behind the screen, calls several prisoners, and tells them to put the beaten boy on a bed. He brings a bowl of water and a rag and asks them to wash the poor boy's face. But he is beyond help. Now he can ignore not only "Mr." Wanka and "Mr." *Blockältester* but even "Mr." Hitler who invented this "sanatorium", Maidanek.

The *Blockschreiber* comes out again, this time to assign us to our bunks. His head moves sadly as he tells us in a low voice, "Terrible times have befallen us. Keep together, boys. You'll witness even worse things. Those whose nerves break are lost." He extinguishes the light and then shouts loudly, "Now go to sleep quickly!"

We feel that he is a friendly soul. From behind the screen,

we hear the clinking of bottles, screams, and Wanka's drunken singing. The light is finally put out there, and the barrack is silent.

Again, the gong sounds. We awaken from a fitful sleep. After yesterday's scene, everyone's nerves are still frayed. Into what nice hands we have fallen! Pinek forgets the happy thoughts he had about Maidanek a few days ago.

The Jews in Barrack 8 are separated from the other *Häftlinge*. For coffee, for the noon meal, and for bread, they must stand at the end of the line and get the worst portions.

"It would make me sick to feed those lousy Jews well," says the *Blockältester* every chance he gets. But the *Blockältester* wants to stay healthy, so the Jews receive only half of what the others get. Since this barrack's criminal elements feel that they have authority on their side, they give vent to their hate and racism at every opportunity.

Silently and humbly, we stand in line for coffee. Pinek looks intently at the short figure in front of him. After a while, he whispers, "Father! It's you!" The elderly man turns around quickly. His face changes completely, and he almost shouts: My son, my son!

They cannot talk because that would mean a beating. We go out for the roll call.

Pinek's parents and their two daughters had been housed in a workshop in the Aryan sector. Two days before the Uprising, Pinek visited them and learned about their plans to escape. An acquaintance of his father's, a Pole, was supposed to have given the entire family shelter in a small castle outside of Warsaw. Pinek had great hopes that his loved ones would be saved. Now he meets his father in the barrack. The poor fellow will soon learn that his mother and two sisters were gassed during the selection a few days ago.

"Form work *Kommandos*!"

The *Blockschreiber* asks the *Blockältester* what to do with the new arrivals.

"Let the Jews go for turf!"

We join the others from Barrack 8 on this *Kommando*.

"Caps off! Eyes left!" Wooden shoes stamp the ground; hands slap thighs; heads turn left. We pass without trouble.

Our fellow prisoners tell us that we will bring wagons, that there will be twelve persons per wagon when we go to the field for turf, and that, generally, this work is not heavy, but the *Kapos* beat us and there is much running.

We arrive at the shed and pull out the wagons with the boards for the turf. As we tour the whole camp passing by Fields 1, 2, and 3, we look with envy at the glass windows in the first two fields. I sigh silently at the sight of the red cross painted on the windows of several barracks in Field 1.

Pinek and his father are engrossed in conversation, and nothing else in the world seems to interest them. I hear only fragments of what they say.

"I did not succeed, Pinek," whispers the older man. "Everything was ready. The next morning, we had planned to run with Mother and the children, but in the afternoon, the police came with cars. They ordered us to leave all of our belongings in the house and get into the vehicles. A few who tried to run, were shot. They took us to the Umschlagplatz and to the train. It was about fifty minutes before the scheduled departure. When we got here, Mother and your sisters . . . you know, son."

"Tadzek," Pinek whispers, as tears run down his cheeks, "we must avenge the shame of our women and the deaths of the innocent!"

"Amen," says his father.

There is little time to talk. We are at the work site where special *Kommandos* have prepared squares and rectangles of turf. We put them on the boards, then load the boards onto the wagons and return to the camp to lay the turf in front of the barracks . . . and run back.

The soil is already prepared in front of every barrack. The turf must be laid on the sides and in the corners. The camp will look very nice, even beautiful when they plant the flowers and flowering shrubs between the barracks. The paths will be covered with multi-colored pebbles.

I am worried about my feet. The blisters hurt; new ones

develop; my leg is swelling. I ask Pinek's father if it is possible to see the doctor, a Russian who has excused many people from work for the smallest complaint. Unfortunately, Jews have no access to the clinic and cannot be excused. They must work; that is why they came here. When they cannot work, they are struck on the back and head with clubs.

I decide to look for Dr. Tonnenberg after the evening roll call. Maybe he can help. We make our last run and finish spreading the turf in front of a barrack just as the gong sounds for the midday meal.

As usual, we are at the end of the line. Wanka, with a club in hand, supervises us. He has not started hitting yet. He says, "Oy, oy, oy! The Jews are hungry? Maybe you want fish? Maybe a roll with a some onion?" He is trying to remember the names of Jewish dishes. He thinks that he is very witty and laughs at his own jokes.

As we get closer to the cauldron, we notice that there are no dishes. Minutes slip by, but none of the personnel is bothering to pick up the empty mess tins—those are only Jews on line. Luckily, Janusz comes out and asks the *Blockältester* why we are waiting. The reply is, "We've no dishes for the dirty Jews."

Janusz turns and shouts, "Bring your empty dishes here! Quickly!" In a few seconds, we have an adequate supply.

Today we have grass for lunch: a few cooked roots, leaves, and peels. It stinks from far away, but for once, we get a full portion; hunger does the rest. There was a time when I was very picky about food. As an only child, I was spoiled by my mother. Now I swallow rotten smelling garbage with an appetite and even lick the dish. There are still a few minutes left. As I rest, I overhear a conversation.

"A terrible thing happened. Thuman caught one *Häftling* sleeping in the barn. Anyway, that isn't too important. What counts, is that the *Kapo* of the *Kommando* got twenty-five lashes on his back and the foreman received fifteen. But the most unfortunate part is that Thuman announced he'll punish the entire Field 4. We'll find out today after the evening roll call."

At the sound of the gong, I jump up quickly. Wanka, with his big club, is watching us carefully.

I find it harder to walk and think with despair that I will not hold out for too long. Pinek advises me to tear out the entire lining of my jacket and make a bandage for myself. It would be better than nothing. Maybe new blisters will not develop. With difficulty, I last until evening.

The *Raportführer* delivers his report during the roll call but does not leave. Instead, he announces that, as punishment for the sabotage perpetrated by a *Häftling* during the work period, *Lagerführer* Thuman has ordered our field to work an additional three hours immediately after roll call for the next ten days. Furthermore, twenty *Häftlinge* will receive special punishment. The *Lagerschreiber* calls the numbers. Twenty men step from the rows.

Two *Kapos* carry a wooden contraption shaped like a school bench from the *Schreibstube*. It has a long top on which the delinquent lies and, at the bottom between the bench legs, there are rings through which the victim must put his legs. The whole thing is designed so that the victim's body is arched and his behind protrudes making it easier to beat.

While the *Kapos* set up this ingenious contraption, the *Lagerschreiber* checks the numbers once more. The *Raportführer* reads the sentence.

"Twenty-five lashes for sabotage during work. For the second offense, fifty; but on the bare bottom. The third time, hanging. This applies to all *Häftlinge* in Field 4."

In the other fields, roll call is over. Here the performance just begins. When they call the first one, he lies down and stretches out his hands. Two *Kapos* secure his legs. One pulls his arms. Two SS men approach the victim with bats in their hands.

They beat steadily and hard. One hits from one side; the other, from the opposite position. Boom! Boom! Boom! The *Häftling* counts in a low voice, "One, two, three." When he gets to four, he counts louder. At seven his is screaming. At fifteen, he stops counting and gets the ten additional blows—

the executioners will teach him! Now he must pass in front of the *Raportführer* and click his heels. To the question: Do you know why you were punished?, he must answer: *Jawohl!*, then, on the double, run to his row.

They call the second victim. The SS men change—beating tires them. One of the victims is a Jew from Barrack 15. Wanka approaches the *Unterscharführer*, takes off his cap, assumes the basic position, and begs the *Unterscharführer* for permission to beat the Jew. That causes an outburst of laughter among the *Blockführers*. Even the *Unterscharführer* laughs and says, "Very well, Wanka."

Wanka has already prepared the handle of a shovel. With the victim's rear sticking out, he begins hitting so vehemently that every blow could probably kill an elephant. At the twentieth blow, the handle breaks. The *Unterscharführer* and other SS men are laughing uproariously. The *Lagerkapo* pats Wanka on the arm and supplies him with another handle. The show ends abruptly when the Jew dies. I think he expired after the fifth blow.

Next, next . . . and so, one after another until the very last. Then, "Form work *Kommandos*!" We go for more turf. My feet burn so much that I feel weak. I will not look for Dr. Tonnenberg tonight.

Work finally ends; the barrack is relatively quiet. Only Wanka, who has killed one Jew today and was praised for that by the SS men, has enough reason to celebrate. He drinks vodka.

The weather is changing. In the morning it rains. By ten o'clock, wind-driven rain clouds roll across the sky and the precipitation descends as if it were being poured from a pail. The elite in the camp, *Kapos* and foremen, wear plastic ponchos; we are soaked. Our jackets, then our shirts are so drenched that they stick to our bodies like cold compresses. We no longer suffer from thirst. Instead, we eagerly wait for the life-giving warmth of the sun.

Not everyone in the camp is affected the same way. The *Blockältesters* sit in front of their fireplaces while the *Stubendiensts* cook warm food for them. The *Kapos* pull their ponchos tighter and complain about their fate. With the rain beating on our faces, we suffer in the field as we follow our daily routine without a minute's respite.

It is time for the midday meal. In other barracks, the *Häftlinge* go inside, but ours is clean. This morning, our *Blockältester* was praised by his superior for its cleanliness so that he will not permit the dirty crowd to enter to mess it up. He would gladly keep us out all night.

Out in the open and without hope of getting into the barrack, we stand in line for watery soup. Finally my turn comes. It is nothing but water with a small piece of beet, but it is hot. I burn my tongue and esophagus as I swallow the hot liquid in big gulps. The life-giving heat courses through my entire body.

Pinek says, as he nudges me, "You had better speak with your friend, the medic. Maybe he'll manage to get us more food." I admit that it is a good idea and drag myself to Barrack 24.

This barrack houses only those workers who handle supplies: cooks, the transport column, only bigwigs. I hear no sound inside. The entrance door is closed. I am unaware that, because of the lice epidemic, Barrack 24 is hermetically sealed to outsiders. I learn that from a heavy-set cook who, with well-aimed blows, hits me in the face.

Meekly, I return to Pinek. He looks at me with pity and asks no questions. He sighs and says, "It's nothing, Tadzek. We'll hold out in spite of it all."

It is difficult to do this. The weather is not improving. The wind howls through the fields so that it seems more like November than May. We are soaked to the skin. With despair, I think about the work after roll call.

Some women carrying sandstone rocks in their arms walk by on the road to camp. Water streams from their striped uniforms. Women supervisors, who are mainly Ukrainian or German, prod them with whips to make them move faster. An SS woman walks behind them with a dog on a leash and a club in her hands. From time to time, she beats the women and sometimes turns the dog on them. The women supervisors are fat, heavy, well-fed girls who look at us with undisguised disdain. In passing, one greets the *Kapo* in a chummy fashion, "You've a nice *Kommando*! All cripples and skeletons. They're only good for the oven."

The *Kapo*'s feelings are hurt. He slaps her behind, and she giggles, very pleased with her joke. Suddenly, a piercing whistle shatters the air. It was the SS woman; she thinks that there has been enough joking. The *Kapo* jumps away from the girl, and she joins the other women. For the benefit of the SS woman, the female supervisors and the *Kapo* hit their victims to demonstrate their zeal.

At such a moment, Pinek remembers something incongruous and begins to laugh. Then he says with a smile, "Tomorrow's Sunday. We're free! We'll rest and maybe your feet will heal. My father and I will look around for someone we know who can help us."

As far as I am concerned, I am willing to work on Sunday in spite of the devilish pain in my feet and the terrible weather. To be under the same roof with Wanka is no pleasure.

It is Sunday; there is no work. In this camp, only two Sundays in the month are free, not out of regard for the *Häftlinge,* but for the SS men. Reveille is one hour later and there is only one roll call, at twelve o'clock.

However, my fear of Wanka proves to be groundless. Immediately after we have our coffee, we are chased outside, and we stand in the rain in front of the barrack until roll call. At about eleven o'clock, the weather improves. The wind blows the clouds away, and the sun comes out. We look horrible. We cannot even use the generally accepted method of warming ourselves by slapping each other's hands and backs. During the night, our clothes have had no place to dry and feel like sponges. Touch them lightly and a stream of water gushes out.

We could never even dream of the surprise they had for us this Sunday. After the rather short roll call, the *Unterscharführer* orders the prisoners to form a quadrangle around the upright pole in the square. Usually, at the very top of this pole is a serene-looking painting of a very red sunrise and a crowing rooster with a wide-open beak. Just below the picture is a horizontal board from which hangs a steel rail that is struck with an iron rod for reveille. Today, the rail and the painting have disappeared. Instead, at the bottom of the pole is a length of coiled rope. They will probably hang someone—who? and why?

An old *Häftling* tells us in a whisper that, not long ago, there were four such gallows from which they hung fifty or more people daily after roll call. The executions continued until late night with car lights illuminating the area while several *Häftlinge* played German military marches on trumpets and harmonicas.

Lagerführer Thuman arrives. A Jewish *Häftling* with his hands tied behind his back, is dragged from the *Schreibstube* to the gallows. The *Lagerführer* hands the *Raportführer* a piece of paper from which he reads in a loud voice, "*Häftling* number ______ will be hanged for trying to escape. This is a warning for everyone."

An SS man usually hangs the victim, but today is Sunday. All of them are dressed in their Sunday best and wear white gloves. The *Raportführer* whispers into the *Lagerführer*'s ear. Thuman nods his approval.

"Wanka! Wanka!"

As though projected by a catapult, Wanka leaps from the lines. With his cap in his hand, he stands before the *Lagerführer* in the basic position. As he listens to some remarks, his eyes gleam.

I am in the front line only a few meters from the gallows and can watch the monster. Wanka is an old hand at this. He started his career in our barrack where he hanged his victims from a rafter. When he acquired a certain amount of experience, he went public. He gleefully hanged Poles, Russians, and Ukrainians. Now he willingly offers his services to the Germans. In order to erase the blot from his conscience, he now hangs only Jews. In any event, he cares about no one. He is the *Lagerführer*'s and SS men's favorite.

The noose is ready. Wanka drops it around the victim's neck and drags him under the hook. The SS men call his attention to the little stool nearby, but he shakes his head.

He has his own system. He pulls the end of the rope over the hook, turns to his victim, and, in a terrible, hissing voice, says, "Dirty Jew! Get ready!"

Thuman goes to the condemned and asks, "Do you know why you're being hanged?"

"I'm innocent," replies the victim, "but someday you'll also hang!" and spits in the *Lagerführer*'s face.

The expression on Thuman's face changes. He slaps the condemned man's face three times and then yells to Wanka, "Hang!"

Wanka pulls the rope slowly. As the noose tightens around his neck, the victim's face turns red and his eyes open wide. Wanka pulls slowly, very slowly, one centimeter a minute. It is obvious that the sadist derives pleasure from this perversion.

I can hear the SS men and *Lagerführer* Thuman praise Wanka's expertise. He has pulled the victim a few centimeters off the ground. Suddenly, he releases the rope and loosens the noose. The poor man coughs and breathes with great difficulty. Taking advantage of the situation, Wanka punches him in the face, then tightens the rope and starts all over again. The victim is turning blue; his eyes express enormous suffering. Wanka whistles gaily. When the legs of the condemned man are twenty centimeters off the ground, Wanka finally fastens the rope, rubs his hands with satisfaction, and reports to the *Lagerführer* that everything is in order.

Thuman thanks him and then, turning to the *Raportführer*, orders, "The swine must be left hanging for twenty-four hours. All the Jews will have three hours of punitive exercise after roll call!"

The sun hides behind the clouds . . .

Field 4 contains three thousand Jews. We assemble in the roll call square where they divide us into groups of one hundred each. Several *Kapos* or *Blockältesters* and *Stubendiensts* or foremen are assigned to each group. Fate is kind to me. My unit of one hundred is under Janusz's orders. He tries to make a joke of everything, and does not allow us to be beaten harshly. He selects the easiest exercises: kneebends and rolling. Only when the SS men approach—they give up other delights for the pleasure of seeing Jews being tortured—does he change the tempo.

Finally, the gong sounds. In the square, are forty dead victims. Wanka is responsible for killing at least twenty of them.

We are exhausted and very hungry. We take out pieces of bread and sausage. I suggest that, in spite of the cold weather, we remove our wet clothes and drape them over the rafters. Perhaps they will dry by tomorrow, otherwise, we will, in all probability, contract pneumonia.

The barrack door opens. A figure calls, "Stabholz!"

I jump off the bed; it is Dr. Tonnenberg. As he hands me a small package wrapped in paper, he says, "I remember you, and I'll help as much as I can, but don't come to my barrack. You may do harm to yourself and me. I'll come to you."

I want to thank him, but I am so moved that I cannot utter a word. When he leaves, I crawl up to my bed and open the package. Oh God! Clean cooked potatoes and bones with meat on them! What a feast we have! We will keep the bread for tomorrow. As we eat in silence, I delight in every bite of warm potato and savor every piece of meat on the bone.

Loud voices come from outside. A laughing, drunken Wanka stands at the door and roars, "Hey, *Blockältester*! *Blockältester*! Do you know why I hanged a Jew today? Ha, ha, ha, ha! Someone put an old torn jacket without a red stripe under the Jew's straw pallet. Ha, ha, ha, ha!"

The food sticks in my throat.

Two harmonica players arrive in the barrack and there is much merriment. From behind the screen, the drunken hosts' wild shouts are deafening. The *Blockältester* and Wanka are celebrating a memorable day. During the exercises, they are singled out as the main heroes of the massacre. Suddenly Wanka remembers something. He stands in the middle of the barrack and yells, "Hey! Give me a singer, you Jews! Quickly!"

From a high bunk, one elderly man descends and says, I'll sing!"

He goes to Wanka's corner and, in a beautiful voice, begins

the song for the souls of the dead. For a minute, the drunken roars are silenced while Wanka listens to the plaintive melody. However, it is not to Wanka's liking. "Sing something Russian, you dirty Jew!" he shouts.

The first notes of *Volga, Volga* are heard. The harmonica players pick up the melody, and in a minute, the entire group shouts, "*Volga, Volga mat radnaya . . .*

The bastards are having a good time; the singing continues until late into the night. Raindrops tap-tap on the roof, and we think, with despair, that tomorrow we must work.

Once again it is a windy, gray morning. Dressed in our wet rags—they did not dry on the rafters during the night—we go to roll call without coffee. The *Blockältester* and *Stubendiensts* have overslept after their drunken revelry. We had to pull them out of bed at the last minute. They are in a bad mood, and we will pay for it.

During roll call, they make an inspection. This *Häftling* has holes in his pants, that one has a missing button, and another is not standing straight. They walk between the rows and hit us as often as they can. The *Blockältester* strikes me in the face several times because I am not shaved. It is not my fault. The barber for the barrack is supposed to shave us on Saturday night, but he somehow lost his razor. For "private" shaves, one must pay with bread. The week is starting badly, I think.

After the roll call, an *Arbeitseinsatz* comes to our *Blockältester* with a request for thirty *Häftlinge* to unload cement. I am among them. We wait in the square for the trucks. To keep us occupied in the meantime, they chase us to clean the latrine. What an unbelievable stink. I retch; they laugh.

"Look at him! We found a delicate one!" yells our foreman and kicks me with his pointed boot. Luckily, the work with shit does not last long.

When the trucks finally arrive with the cement, two *Häftlinge* climb up. Four are assigned to line the sacks against the walls of the empty barrack. The rest carry the bags. Two SS men and the drivers stand around impatiently. They are in a hurry. The foremen notice their impatience and beat us with clubs. The SS men, for their part, kick us as we pass by. We cannot catch our breath. Inside the barrack, two foremen watch us carefully to make sure that, after we throw down the sack of cement, we immediately run back for another. Some sacks have holes in them from which the cement leaks and gets between the wooden shoes and the soles of our feet, clinging to our wounds and causing them to burn. The first truck has not been unloaded as yet and more arrive. "Hurry! Tempo!"

A torrent of blows rains on our backs. The two prisoners on the truck are beaten to force them to pass the sacks to us faster. They pass the sacks to us in any way they can, as long as it is done quickly, and we bend under the weight of the badly placed ones. On one run, with a torn sack on my head, the cement runs down my face and into my nose and throat. I can feel the paper continuing to tear. When I stop for a second to adjust the load, I am struck on the thigh. At that moment the sack falls apart. I lose my equilibrium and fall. The cement covers me.

Faintly, I hear some laughter and feel a few blows followed by a loud, "Get up!" Is it an SS man yelling? I am half conscious and rise with difficulty. My thoughts are muddled. To die! Oh God, to die! What is all this suffering for?

Empty trucks leave; full ones arrive. "Work! Work! Keep moving, *Mensch*!"

During the midday pause, the *Blockältester* asks, "Who has swollen feet? Who has trouble working? Who has sores on his feet? I'm asking for socks and leather shoes."

Those words are heavenly music to my ears. Maybe I will get good shoes and socks, and my suffering will end. I think that, after a few more days in these wooden shoes, my feet will have to be amputated. I rush to the *Blockältester*. He writes my number on a piece of paper.

I search for Pinek, or rather for his father. This is such a wonderful occasion, and they are not here. They went for soup and they will miss their chance to get shoes. When they finally return, I tell them the important news.

Pinek's father looks at me as if I am insane. "Are you crazy or what?" he demands. "Don't you know this is a selection for the gas chamber? They're trying to catch those who can't work!"

Pinek looks at me intently and asks, "Tadzek, have you signed up?"

I admit it. Pinek grabs his head, scolds me, and calls me all kinds of names. He finally tells me to go to the *Blockältester* and beg him to remove my number from the list. "You!" he scolds, "you escape the hell of the Warsaw Ghetto! By a miracle you get out of Treblinka! And now, you willingly sign up to die?

I think Pinek is wrong and try to argue with him. The Germans are not ashamed of their crimes. Why must they use this ruse?

Pinek is furious with me. "Run to the *Blockältester*! Remember, in a minute it will be too late." He almost pushes me forcibly. His father adds, "Doctor, save yourself! Maybe he'll erase your number from the list!"

I become uneasy. I go to the *Blockältester* and beg him to remove my number. "I don't need shoes or socks! I can work! I'm strong!"

Instead of answering, the *Blockältester* turns to Wanka. "Wanka, throw out this half-dead bag of bones. What does he want from me!?"

Wanka grabs me by the collar with one hand and by the pants with the other. I fly through the air and land on my face. Pinek and his father despair. They try to think of some way to help me. As for myself, I do not believe that I have signed up to die.

After the evening roll call, the *Lagerschreiber* loudly calls the numbers registered at noon and orders those prisoners to stand to one side. The others return to their barracks.

We number approximately two hundred. They line us up in rows. The *Lagerschreiber* tells the Aryans to move to the left. The *Raportführer* comes over, looks at us for a minute, and orders, "Aryans, to the hospital! Jews, locked up in the barrack!"

Kapos and *Blockältesters* surround us. "March!"

I look back. Pinek and his father are standing at Barrack 24, probably waiting for Dr. Tonnenberg. I am very calm; I have been tortured enough. It will all be over shortly. I think of Fredzia; perhaps we will meet in heaven, and I smile to myself. Am I becoming childish in my old age?

Meanwhile, we go to the barrack where I worked earlier today. There are no beds, no wooden floor, only the ground. The place is empty except for hundreds of bags of cement piled up against the walls, the result of our efforts, our bloody work. The *Lagerschreiber* checks our numbers carefully as we enter one by one. I think: They count us as if we are valuable objects. And how do they treat us?

The door is locked from the outside; it is an unnecessary precaution. Who can run away? Where to?

We are about one hundred fifty resigned, completely exhausted Jews. Most of us have sores or wounds on our feet and are walking skeletons. The only thing the others seem to worry about is whether they will be fed before they die. Everyone is sure that we will be gassed. Minutes and hours pass, and it is growing dark. We will receive nothing to eat today; food is not wasted on the condemned. Let the one hundred fifty portions go to those who work. Personally, I agree.

I stretch out on the ground in the dark and try to think. I am surprised at how calm I feel. Some of the condemned are crying. Others loudly lament that they let themselves be duped so easily, so shamefully. I think of my approaching death with relief. Death is the only salvation, the only escape from this terrible torture. I was meant to die in Treblinka and, before that, many times during the German Occupation, but it seems that fate postponed my death for a while. What a pity I did not die with Fredzia!

We spend a sleepless night. Waiting for death is no pleasure. If they would only take us away . . . We hear voices near the barrack; our hearts beat faster, but nobody enters. The *Kommandos* go to work. We can hear a voice close to the barrack say, "They brought the *gamels* here yesterday."

A *gamel,* in the jargon of the camp, is a man unable to work, a man whose knees buckle under him from sheer exhaustion.

Maybe they will bring us something to eat now, perhaps a little coffee. We try to catch every sound from outside.

The sun is emerging from behind the clouds. It does so in spite of me. What a shame it is to die when the weather is so beautiful! Even I, who am the calmest one of all, feel a heartache. I realize how illogical and stupid it is. Some pray before dying; others angrily try to stop them. Their nerves are getting the better of them as they argue and insult one another.

I recall the Umschlagplatz. The comparison favors Maidanek. At least here, we are alone in the barrack and are not tortured before being killed. I am very satisfied with my reasoning and feel relieved. I become talkative. In a loud voice, I try to convince the others that it is not worthwhile to suffer any longer, that the war will be a protracted one, that we will not survive, and that the sooner we die, the better. I talk about parents. Then someone screams, "Shut up, you idiot!" I am silent again. I begin to think that I may be going insane. It is better that way.

The arguments and screams finally stop; the barrack is completely silent. Sounds from the outside reach us: *Mittagholen!*, footsteps—returning *Kommandos,* the gong. In a while, it sounds again. Once again we hear footsteps and voices as the *Kommandos* return to work. No one bothers with us.

In the Umschlagplatz and on the way to Treblinka, I thought of revenge. Today, I no longer think of it. I am tired, exhausted, mortally spent.

Again, hours pass. After a while, we hear beautiful music from the radio in the *Blockführerstube.* Damn it! I, too, was once a human being! Thoughts of revolt enter my mind, but not for long. I soon lapse into hopeless lethargy.

Once more there are voices and steps near the door. It is almost time for the evening roll call. But what is that gong? It sounds unusual. The staccato beats remind me of an air-raid alarm. No, no, that is no alarm. "Everybody out! Everybody out!" It is our turn.

I thought that I would take all those preparations to die calmly. Am I not completely indifferent, quite ready to die? Am I not very tired and unhappy? Did I not convince myself that death would be a relief? It is freedom from suffering!

Nevertheless, I lose my nerve. I revolt. A storm is brewing in my soul. I want to live! Yes, I want to live! I must live! I bite my fingers until I draw blood. Oh God, save me! Don't let me die!

The barrack doors are thrown wide-open; three trucks drive up. *Kapos, Blockältesters,* and SS men run into the barrack brandishing clubs and whips. "Undress! Move quickly! Quickly, you damn pigs!"

My bravado deserts me, and I am overcome by fear. My teeth chatter. My hands shake so badly that I cannot even take off my shirt. A few young boys cry for their mothers to help.

Wanka runs into the barrack with a club. Like a wild beast, he looks around and notices that I still have my shirt on. He runs to me and yanks it off with one jerk.

We are naked. They line us up according to our numbers. As each of us is called, he passes an SS man who checks the number on the tag around his neck, and the *Raportführer* crosses him off the list. The first truck in front of the barrack has a little stool on which to step up. Two *Kapos* "graciously" help each person into the truck.

When the first fifty are loaded aboard, two SS men jump on the back, and the truck takes off. The second truck pulls over. Soon it, too, is filled. I am among the last.

I do not know what is happening to me and I am sure that I am losing control of myself. Those in front of me are running to the truck. Suddenly, there is a commotion. An SS man standing there with a civilian, greets the *Raportführer* and hands him a paper. I hear my number being called. I do not understand what is happening. I want to run to the truck, but the civilian grabs my arm and asks, "Are you a physician?"

"Yes!" is the only answer I am able to give.

"You'll remain in the camp," he says, "and you will go to the hospital."

The last of the victims passes by. One of them waves in a sign of farewell. The last truck leaves.

My feet seem rooted in the earth. In my head I feel nothing. My head is a big vacuum.

"Well, pick out some rags and let's go!"

I am bewildered and obey the order like a robot. The SS

man and the civilian follow me as I leave the barrack. The civilian's armband reads: *Krankenbau Kapo."*

I am taken to the bath for a hot shower, given clean underwear and straw boots. In the "hospital", I lie down on a bed equipped with a straw mattress and a blanket. Two doctors come over and dress my feet. One bends over me and whispers, "Today the camp doctor is coming for a selection. Don't move from your bed. Our *Kapo* will handle everything. Do you hear?!"

I hear and do not hear. I look but I do not see. I am saved! Is it possible? I pinch my cheeks. I look at my bandaged feet. Enormously relieved, I start crying spasmodically.

Someone pulls my hand. It is the medic. He has placed a cup of coffee and a portion of bread with margarine on the table and then says, "You! Eat quickly! The camp doctor will come soon!" I barely manage a few gulps of coffee when "Attention!" is shouted from the doorway. The camp doctor enters accompanied by several SS men.

"All Jews come forward!" Remembering my instructions, I remain in bed. Thirty naked Jews file into the middle of the room, each bearing his hospital chart. Only two are sent back to bed. The others are chased to the front of the barrack by the SS men. I hear a truck engine roaring.

Now I am getting closer to insanity than at any other time. My head spins and millions of black spots dance before my eyes. I fall into an abyss.

When I wake the next day, it is dark outside. My surprised neighbor looks at me and says, "Congratulations, friend! You've had a sound sleep. You missed breakfast, the noon meal, and supper. It's night. Your food is under your bed."

I do feel hungry. I bend down and find two portions of bread and a ration of the midday soup. I feel better. My feet do not hurt too much. My neighbor wants to talk, but I feel my head whirling, and I fall asleep again.

* * *

The days pass quickly in the "hospital". I am recuperating,

but I try not to think. I lie in my bed with closed eyes and inhale the refreshing May air.

On the sixth day, I am discharged from the "hospital" and receive a new outfit, fresh underwear, and wonderful shoes with wooden soles but with cloth uppers. The barber cuts my hair and shaves me. All this enhances my well-being, and I feel regenerated. My brains are functioning normally, thoughts pass through my head. Who saved me? Dr. Tonnenberg? Pinek? Do they know that I am alive?

A large group of discharged prisoners return to Field 4. One philosophizes, "Such is life in this camp—one day on top of the wagon, another day, underneath. You can never tell." As to the accuracy of this statement, I receive tangible evidence on my own body during the next few months of life in the camp.

I return to Barrack 8. I am so sure of myself now that I am not afraid of the *Blockältester* or Wanka. I am eager to see their faces when they see me. The medic accompanying us hands our charts to the *Blockältester* who stands in the entrance and calls out the names. With my chart in his hand, he exclaims, "What?! How?! Stabholz?!!" He clears his throat and looks at me with dilated pupils. "And where did you come from?" He asked the right question.

"Yes, I'm back—from the crematorium," I reply lightly.

Janusz hears my name, runs to the door, and sees me. He stands right next to me, gives me a friendly pat on the arm, and shakes my hand as he says, "You're a lucky man. You probably will survive life in the camp, so help you God!"

I am so deeply moved that I could kiss him. When I enter, the first thing I notice is Wanka with a bandage on his head and his arm in a sling, sitting on a chair. He sizes me up and is surprised but does not say a word. I am puzzled by his appearance and very anxious to know who did this to him. I wait impatiently for the midday break. Finally, the *Kommandos* return and line up for soup. I see Pinek. He has changed in the last few days. His face is sun-tanned, but he is very thin. He is talking to his father and does not see me. Meanwhile, some surprised voices come from the line. "Look! Yes, it's Stabholz!"

Pinek turns his head, sees me, and, ignoring the *Stubendienst,* runs to me.

"Tadzek! You're alive!!?" He hugs me. Almost incoherently, he tells me about his talks with Dr. Tonnenberg and his conversation through barbed wire with Natek Remba. He also informs me that everyone felt sorry for me, but unfortunately, they could do nothing. Once again, we hug.

"It doesn't matter, Pinek. We'll hold out. But tell me what happened to Wanka?"

Pinek laughs, "The scythe finally hit a stone. Wanka had an argument with the cook. After the evening roll call, the cook came to the barrack, beat Wanka like a dog, and warned that, if he talked too much, there'll be someone in the camp who will stab him. For several days now, it has been peaceful in the barrack."

I am in an excellent mood. In the afternoon, I find part of a recent newspaper. The Allied Army landed in Sicily. The Russians are still quite a distance from Lublin. Nevertheless, I am full of hope. Mentally, I menace the SS men and their worthy pupils: Wait, you bastards! Your turn will come!

In the evening, Pinek describes in detail what happened while I was gone, and tells us about his talk with Natek Remba through the barbed wire. Shortly after being assigned to Field 3 Natek met a Pole, an acquaintance of his who was an old prisoner in Maidanek and has influence in the main *Schreibstube.* Thanks to him, Natek became a *Blockschreiber* and the brothers Tempelhof, *Stubendiensts.* Pinek has already received several portions of bread from them. The work after roll call lasted a week instead of ten days. Why?—nobody knows. In any case, while I was in the hospital, three hundred more Jews died. It is a miracle that Pinek and his father survived this hell. During the last few days, the situation in the barrack has worsened.

Pinek decides that, before the morning roll call, he will notify Dr. Tonnenberg of my safe return. Maybe he will prepare something to eat.

One thing remains unexplained: Who saved my life?

The next several days are quiet. Every day we collect turf.

The weather is favorable, and "Mr." *Kapo* is not beating. What is more important, the barrack is calm.

After the evening roll call, I go to see Natek Remba and talk with him through the barbed wire. He throws me a portion of bread and says that he talked about my case with his friend, the Pole, who promised to intervene with a higher authority. But now he sincerely admits that he was certain that I was lost.

Later that evening, Dr. Tonnenberg visits our barrack. His pockets bulge with potatoes. I share the food with Pinek and his father. Our hunger is satisfied, and we are optimistic.

During the night, we have a lightning and thunderstorm. The heavens open, and the water runs in streams. Pinek sighs, "If only it were bombs . . ."

After the rains, the morning is beautiful and warm. We do not carry turf today. Instead, the *Arbeitseinsatz* orders twenty of us to bring carpentry tools to the field. The shed for this equipment is quite a distance away. We march in the mud. At a certain spot, we come upon a big puddle, the remains of last night's storm. We avoid it. Suddenly, we hear a yell from one side, "Stop!"

Thuman, who had hidden behind a tree and watched as we approached, appears astride a beautiful horse. He holds a long whip. He calls the foreman, a young Pole of about eighteen who removes his cap and stands at attention before Thuman. The *Lagerführer* asks him why he spares us and permits us to avoid the muddy puddle. The boy does not understand German, and his face turns color. Enraged by the boy's silence, Thuman beats him several times over the head with his whip and tells him to join the line. The *Lagerführer* assumes personal command of our small group. He has us stand in Indian file—one behind the other—on the road and orders, "Lie down and roll!"

Back and forth, back and forth, we roll in the mud. The puddle is deep. We are soon soaked through and through and look like monsters. "Roll! Roll! Crawl!" But this is not enough for Thuman. Finally, he orders all of us to lie in the puddle while he, on his horse, rides over us. The horseshoes cause us severe injuries. I put my jacket over my head. With fear in my heart, I wait to be stepped on by the animal. After several minutes of this "game", the *Lagerführer* demands that we rise and "run to work!"

Of the twenty *Häftlinge*, only seven escape unscathed. Most received serious injuries; several have broken ribs. Pinek, his father, and I are fortunate. We look horrible. What can we do?! We must go to the carpentry shed for the tools.

Those in the shed have already heard about our misadventure. The carpentry *Kapo* is a nice fellow. He had prepared a barrel of water so that we could wash a bit. I made a few dressings for those who needed them most. Pinek begins to believe in miracles. He cannot understand how we ever escaped without a scratch. One thing that he does not know, is that this is just the beginning of our misfortunes for today. He will really have to believe in miracles, big miracles.

We are handed the tools: saws, hammers and shovels to bring to the *Blockführerstube*, we line up in fives, and the foreman reports our return.

The SS man looks at his watch and demands, "What took you so long?"

Someone in our group tries, in German, to explain the cause of our delay. He points to the injured, but the *Blockführer* does not believe him and shouts, "You're lying!" Another SS man comes over; they discuss the situation. One says, "Obviously the Jews are lying. We'll teach them!"

After we put the tools away, they chase us to a recently constructed five meter deep pond. Just two days ago it was filled with water. Pinek whispers, "Now we'll die!"

We are ordered to jump into the water; whoever resists, is pushed in. Pinek, his father, and I are among the first to jump. The water is warm enough, but it is uncomfortable with wooden shoes. I am a rather good swimmer, and this saves my life. I dive deeply and start to come up for some air. At that very moment, the SS men fire their revolvers at those who surface. I go down again and manage to swim underwater toward the steps with whatever strength I have left. God! How many meters more?!

I swallow water; I choke. When I have almost lost consciousness and think that the end is near and that I am surely going to drown, I reach the steps. With my last bit of energy, I climb up. Someone pulls me by my jacket and helps me. Half-conscious, I collapse on the grass and breathe heavily. Pinek and his father lie next to me. They cough; they spit; they choke. Only four others survive this "bath"; among them is our foreman, the Pole.

The SS men put their revolvers into their holsters. They had a good time. One offers us two cigarettes and tells us to divide them.

We take our tools from the *Blockführerstube* and enter the camp accompanied by one SS man. He tells the *Lagerschreiber*, "There was an accident on the job. Fourteen *Häftlinge* perished. During the midday break, find out their numbers and names! Understand?!"

We return to the barrack and do not work for the rest of the morning. Our *Blockältester* and Wanka already know about our experience and are very satisfied, especially Wanka. His head has already healed and his bandages have been removed, but his hand is still painful. Regretting that he was not at the pond, he says, "If I were there, not a single dirty Jew would have been left alive!" Of that we are certain.

Pinek says, "I held my father all the time. After several minutes, when we were about to sink to the bottom, I had to come up for air. The SS men shot at us; bullets whistled close to our heads. Nevertheless, I took a chance and swam toward the steps. I was fortunate to have saved myself and my father."

After all those events, we are physically and emotionally exhausted. Pinek's father thinks that death is not so terrible. He does not understand why he clings so tenaciously to life, especially after having lost his wife and daughters.

His father adds, "We can't expect anything more from life. It'll continue to get worse. When the final minute comes, we'll realize that all our suffering was for naught. We belong to the category of people who can be tortured and killed at will. For murdering a Jew, you gain the praise of the SS men and, sometimes, you may even get cigarettes."

Our good humor vanishes. We realize perfectly well the

hopelessness of our situation and the thousands of imminent dangers we face.

"Our verdict is already in," says Pinek. "We're only waiting for the execution. May God grant us a quick death with little suffering!"

The sun is almost warm enough to dry our clothes. After the noon meal, we are ordered to break the many rocks lying near the kitchen. Each of us gets a heavy hammer. The elderly foreman watching us is barely able to stand. When a *Kapo* or supervisor approaches, he yells, "Six!" which in camp jargon means danger. Then we really smash the stones with our hammers until the danger is over. "He passed by!"; the work tempo slows.

After the evening roll call, we are treated to a "show". A *Raportführer* calls ten numbers; ten prisoners come forward. Each will get twenty-five lashes. I am indifferent to the beatings and the screams. In the beginning it made an impression on me, but now I think that, because of these beatings, it will be late before I can stretch out in my bunk. I lived through many difficult moments today. Someone else's suffering cannot possibly rid me of my lethargic apathy.

A new victim is on the table; the SS men are whipping him. The poor fellow writhes terribly, but the SS men suspect something is wrong. They order him to take off his pants. The *Häftling* has padded his rear with several towels. For this fraudulent attempt he receives fifty more lashes. He loses consciousness, and they carry him off the table.

After the evening meal, I got a terrible bellyache. I obviously drank too much water in the pond. I am in a hurry and crawl down from my bunk. As I leave the barrack, I pass an SS man who has just remembered that he had to make an inspection. According to the rules, I must slap my hand on my thigh and turn my head in his direction. The SS man is not satisfied. He calls me over and smacks my face several times.

My belly hurts dreadfully. Saliva collects in my mouth. When the SS man finally releases me, I can no longer get to the latrine, and I soil my pants despite all my best efforts. I return to my bunk with a swollen face and no underwear.

It is still dark when I am awakened by Wanka's shouting, "Get up! Lice control!"

A Russian doctor is in the barrack checking our underwear. The lousy ones go to the bath. I introduce myself and offer my help. The work goes rapidly. There are relatively few people with lice in our barrack. I take advantage of this occasion to tell him in a few words of my experiences in Maidanek so far. Unfortunately, he cannot help me. If I wish, he will give me some ichthyol salve and a few bandages; these can come in handy. It is very difficult to get into the clinic, and for a Jew, completely impossible.

We leave together. He must still inspect a few barracks, but it is late, so he takes me to his quarters where he gives me the salve, a few gauze pads, and several bandages. I thank him profusely. He answers gently that he considers this his duty. I proudly show Pinek my treasure. He is overjoyed as he says, "You, fellow! Do you know what this is worth? Do you know how much you can make on it?"

We form a partnership. Pinek will bring me patients, only those who can organize and pay with something. I will apply bandages. What payment I receive, I will share half and half with Pinek. He will share his portion with his father.

The next day passes in nervous expectation. We have relatively easy work, digging another trench for a latrine. Immediately after the noon meal, Pinek runs through the barracks looking for patients.

After the evening roll call, two patients arrive, one with a big blister on his sole, the other with a large sore on his abdomen. After I treat them, one pays me with almost a whole portion of bread and the other, two cigarettes. Besides the paying patients, I make several bandages for no fee. My heart aches when I see the terribly neglected sores on those unlucky victims.

I crawl up to my bunk again. The patients bless me aloud. Pinek is furious with me, "When you're croaking, do you think anyone will help you? They'll probably kick you!"

He does not wish to work with me any longer. He finally reconsiders when I promise that I will go to the doctor tomorrow to ask for more supplies.

The food is getting worse. Day after day, they cook only grass. A *Kommando* of about one thousand *Häftlinge* strip the neighboring fields of all greenery and deliver it to the kitchen in huge baskets. Were it not for the honest patients who bring us something to eat, we would die of hunger like the hundreds who are dying daily.

I visit the doctor quite often. I tell him a very sad story of a non-existent younger brother who has a large ulcer on his thigh. Almost in tears, I beg for help. The doctor is a nice man and gives me dressing material in sizeable amounts. Pinek is almost satisfied as he says, "Even in a concentration camp you can organize your life. You only need to be smart."

One day, our *Kommando* goes beyond our field to dig a deep trench that will be the outermost limits of our camp. We are about ten meters from the heavily traveled highway leading to Lublin and we can see the cars, wagons, and people, free people taking advantage of the good weather, to stroll.

Women prisoners working next to us pick up stones, put them into baskets, and carry them into camp. Most of them are Jews from Warsaw. They look awful in their torn rags and short hair. With frightened eyes, they watch the haughty SS women who supervise them. Every once in a while, one of them finds a victim and beats her so mercilessly with her whip that blood spurts from her body. It makes no difference whether the victim is guilty of any infraction or not. They do it for sport or to frighten.

The fantasy that I created at the sight of the free world is shattered when I see the poor, horribly harassed, unhappy women prisoners. So overcome with helplessness, humiliation, and anger am I, that I want to scrape the earth with my nails; I want to bite the stones; I want revenge. I am furious. I look askance at an SS woman, I squeeze the shovel handle in the palm of my hand and think: "You creature from hell! I'll show you, you Hitler hero! You torturer of unarmed, helpless women!"

I take a few steps. In another minute . . . I fall; Pinek tripped me. He scolds, "Are you crazy? What are you trying to do?!"

I am so angry that I could tear Pinek apart. I call him all kinds of nasty names and make a lengthy speech. "How do you live? You only think of food and organizing. How do you differ from an animal? You live like one; you're treated like one, and if the animal could think, it would think like you!" I point to the women and continue, "See how the SS women mistreat our women! This is how they beat your mother and sisters who died in the gas chamber like Fredzia! Revenge! Revenge!" I scream. "I want to kill this SS bitch, the whore! It will repay only one millionth part of our retaliation to redress our wrongs!"

Pinek makes a fist as he comes closer to me. Just then, an SS man approaches us. He hits Pinek with the butt of his gun and kicks me. "Work, you pigs!" he yells. We make peace.

On the way to the noon meal I squeeze Pinek's hand as I say, "Forgive me, Pinek. I'm sorry. I hope you understand I didn't mean to vex you. I didn't know what I was doing. I was almost crazy."

Pinek returns my squeeze and says, "Listen! You wanted to kill the SS woman. Very nice! Do you realize you can only hit her once and for that fifty Jews would die? If you want to commit suicide, you're choosing the wrong method. I consider such an act a sign of cowardice. Maybe some of the Jews will survive the concentration camps and will seek vengeance for our mothers and wives, for our fathers and brothers. The Jews will make their voices heard and will expose this nation of murderers to the world for what it is. If all the Jews were to take their own lives, what do you think the result would be? Even so, ninety-nine percent of us will never know freedom again. In the meantime, we must live like animals and think like them. This outburst of yours today is only grist for the German mill. Hide your anger deep within your heart and think only of survival!"

We will not get our noon meal today. The returning *Kommandos* stand in a long line in front of the gate. As the SS men on each side let the *Häftlinge* through one by one, they are beaten and many fall. The corpses pile up in front of the *Blockführerstube.*

We do not get to the gate. Instead, we return to work, hungry. After the evening roll call, they bring the "table" from the *Schreibstube* and call out two Jews who will receive fifty lashes each for talking to the women. One spoke with his mother; the other, with his wife.

* * *

At night, I use the dressing material in a most unexpected way, for me. I am lying in my bunk as usual—it is the third one from the bottom—and turn to talk to Pinek when, suddenly, several of the boards give way. With a crash, I fall on my neighbor below, and together we land on the bottom bunk, and from there to the ground. In the process, I tear the skin off my thigh.

* * *

Pinek's talk leaves its mark. I conclude that there are three commandments. The first: If you think, think only of yourself. Secondly: The best idea of all is not to think. Thirdly: If you must do so, think of organizing for something to eat. This last thought is the healthiest, especially if it is realized in the form of a few cooked potatoes, a dish of soup, or a piece of bread.

Theory and practice are two different things. It is impossible to drive away the thoughts that stubbornly come to my mind, thoughts about the time when I had a home, a father and mother, a fiancée, and peace of mind, but now, in addition, I have this beastly persistent wish: To have something to eat!, and that is followed by: If, before I die, will I be able to go to sleep with a full stomach?

Wanka is almost his old self again. His hand no longer hurts; his voice is as strong as it was before. He roars like a lion and looks around wildly as he searches for blood. Once again we go to bed fearfully when we return from work. We are afraid to breathe. The barrack is silent.

During a violent storm one night, the wind tears the tar paper from the roof. Streams of water run into the barrack through the uncovered boards. I wake up to find that I am wet and lying in a pool of water. I want to go to Pinek's bed. It turns out that Pinek is coming to me. Meekly, we crawl down to find a relatively dry spot on the floor where we sit until morning.

* * *

When we return to our field for the noon meal, we hear screams and laughter from our barrack and sense that something is wrong. As we get closer, we see a cauldron of tar behind the barrack where they were fixing the roof this morning. Nearby are several SS men and Wanka with a brush in his hand. Some *Kapos* hold several completely naked Jews while Wanka dips his brush into the boiling liquid and paints the hapless men. The SS men laugh uproariously. Then Wanka has an idea. He looks for a certain sixteen year old Jewish boy. After ripping the clothes off the boy, Wanka dips him into the scalding liquid. A blood-curdling scream splits the air. Even Wanka pales somewhat and pulls the boy out. The SS men are so delighted that they give Wanka a pack of cigarettes. The boy dies in terrible pain.

I look at Pinek; he looks at me. We do not say a word. We clench our teeth.

After the noon meal, we return to dig the ditch. The soles of my feet are swollen and red and hurt terribly. I must get to the doctor at any cost. At night after the roll call, I ask Pinek to get my portion of bread while I go to the clinic alone.

I am one of the first. Patients come from everywhere. A few Ukrainians who notice my Jewish star, speak to the *Kapo* who stands at the door keeping track of what time each patient arrives. The *Kapo* approaches me, pulls me out of the line, and hits me in the nose so viciously that I am dazed and fall. Blood streams from my nose. At this very moment, the doctor appears in the doorway. He sizes up the scene quickly, calls a medic, and tells him to pick me up and take me into the emergency room. He then walks over to the *Kapo,* berates him in a loud voice, and smacks him in the face.

Everyone in the room looks at the doctor wide-eyed. They do not understand. Someone yells, "Doctor, it's a Jew!"

I am already in the doorway, but I turn my head to look. I notice that the doctor pulls the one who yelled out of the line and kicks him in his behind a few times. I hear the doctor speaking to the crowd in a loud voice. After that, he comes to me.

He carefully wipes the blood from my face, looks to see if I have a fractured nose, and takes care of my feet. Then he asks me to sit on a chair and offers me some homemade soup.

I eat with an appetite, but my tears are choking me. My conscience bothers me because I was fooling this man who has done so much for me. After I eat the soup and thank him kindly, I want to leave, but the doctor does not want me to go. He gives me a piece of bread with margarine and almost forcibly sits me down. Meanwhile, the medic changes the dressings of the other patients. I do not see a single Jew among them.

When the evening gong sounds, the doctor sits down and apologizes for the *Kapo*'s brutality. We talk. I tell him about my stay in Warsaw and Treblinka, and what I have gone through in Maidanek. He already knows. I feel that I cannot hide my secret any longer.

"Doctor," I say, "I have no brother. I lied to you to get dressing materials. I'm selling it for bread."

The doctor laughs and says, "It doesn't matter. Here, everyone tries to get along as best he can. It's better to get a piece of bread for a dressing than a pack of cigarettes for killing an inmate. Anyway, your appearance justifies everything."

With that, he hands me a mirror. I see a strange, unshaven, and terribly haggard face. Do I really look like this?

It is late when the doctor gives me a bottle of Burow's solution, bandages, salve, and gauze pads, and then escorts me to the barrack. In front of the door, he hands me a piece of bread. Patting me on the arm cordially, he bids me good-by.

Wanka, who is standing nearby, watches this scene with a dumb expression on his face.

When I crawl into my bed, Pinek is lying there with his father. They greet me joyfully; they were afraid that they would never see me again. Briefly, I tell them about my evening's experience. Pinek hands me my portion of bread, but I triumphantly pull out the piece that the doctor gave me and tell them to eat the other one.

Our pleasant evening turns out to be full of consequences. Wanka, who saw how amiably the doctor had treated me, stops harassing me. Even the *Blockältester* looks at me less viciously.

During the noontime meal the next day, the doctor enters our barrack and asks Wanka to call me. Pinek taps me on the back and says, "Leave the soup and run to your doctor."

He has encouraging news. He has talked with the *Lagerältester* about me. In a few days, I will be assigned as a medic of a barrack housing only Jews. I am very happy. Pinek jokingly worries, "Future medic, don't forget your poor friends!"

Meanwhile, I go to work with our *Kommando.* About one thousand of us are digging the trench which will encircle the camp. In general, the work is not too tiring; the *Kapos* are more interested in organizing than supervising. Suddenly, Thuman appears. He had been observing the progress of the work through binoculars. He writes down the *Kapos'* numbers and yells at the guards who were bribed. From that time on, all hell breaks loose and we are in trouble.

The *Kapos* and SS men watch us carefully; the whips crack; the *Häftlinge* scream; the *Kapos* roar, "Move quickly! Tempo!" The trench gets deeper; the earth is stonier; we throw it higher. As we become more tired, our strength is sapped. The work, instead of progressing faster, proceeds more slowly. Our supervisors do not understand that, or they do not want to. Shortly thereafter, several victims' skulls are crushed. This stony ground soaks up Jewish blood.

Pinek, his father, and I look in all directions. We are not as afraid of death as we are of becoming permanently maimed.

When a *Kapo* or an SS man approaches, the shovels fly as we work. But even this does not help much. No matter how hard we toil, we cannot prevent the whippings. Our torturers beat blindly just to frighten us. By nightfall, there are so many corpses and severely injured lying about, that the SS men must send for a cart on which to load the corpses before we can leave. Because this, too, must be done rapidly, we have no time to place the severely injured on top. "Shit is all the same, *mensch*—only tempo, just tempo!" comments our supervisor.

After the roll call, we get an unpleasant surprise. Our *Kapos* receive a warning from the *Raportführer* for being lax in the performance of their duties. They are not beaten in public. After all they are Germans even if they are common criminals and have green triangle insignias. As for us, the entire *Kommando* must work after roll call until nine o'clock at night for three days.

Because of the lack of time, all our plans to make dressings are foiled, and the specter of hunger threatens. I only hope it will not last long and that the doctor will keep his promise.

Two, three, four days pass. My back aches from the whip. My muscles are sore and I am in a state of exhaustion from the arduous work. We are so tired that the hunger pangs become unimportant. One cart is not enough for the corpses. At the very moment when I lose hope, salvation comes unexpectedly.

In the evening, the *Blockältester* tells me, "The doctor was here. Here's your chart. You're to report to Barrack 4."

I say good-by to Pinek and his father and add, "Don't be afraid. I won't forget you."

I want to walk in a brisk, spirited manner, but every step is excrutiatingly painful.

The *Blockältester* thinks for a minute and says, "No, you won't be my medic. You'll go on *Kommando* or you'll go back Organization had sentenced him to death. Only his presence in Maidanek saved him from being shot. Now, in this camp, he does not behaves much better than the German, Ukrainian, and Polish *Blockältesters*.

When he sees me, he breaks into a long hearty laugh, "This must be our medic. Ha ha ha ha! I'll die laughing. You look as if you need some help yourself." He pushes me slightly, but it is just enough to make me fall. He laughs for a full five minutes. Even the *Stubendiensts* consider me a funny sight.

"Look at his rags! What kind of shoes are they? He may even have lice!"

The *Blockältester* thinks for a minute and says, "No, you won't be my medic. You'll go on *kommando* or you'll go back to your old barrack. I'll discuss it with the doctor."

The bed that is assigned to me is the third bunk from the floor and contains neither a straw pallet nor a blanket. I lie down and think intently about the kind of people with whom I must deal, what they can possibly do to me, and the kind of tortures that still await me. I am very lonesome and quite unhappy.

After the morning roll call, I sneak out of the barrack without being noticed and run to the doctor. I tell him about the kind of reception I received from my new boss. The doctor is beside himself with anger, and together, we return to the barrack. He calls the *Blockältester* and says in a severe, sharp tone, "He must be your medic! Do you hear? If you treat him badly, you'll lose your position, you and your *Stubendiensts*! I'll see to it myself!" The *Blockältester* explains that he was joking, that he had nothing bad in mind, and that I will lack for nothing.

The doctor leaves without saying good-by to anyone, and I am left with people who would gladly tear me apart. The other possible candidate for medic, a husky fellow with the face of a bandit, is my worst enemy. Because of me, he must go on *Kommando* tomorrow. He vents all his anger on me and wants to beat me. "You'll go to the gas chamber! I'll see to it!!" he exclaims.

The *Blockältester* prevents him from attacking me and says with obvious irony, "Don't get nervous. Our new medic is a good fellow. He'll resign from his position of his own volition."

They take me galloping. "Scrub the floor! Sweep under the beds! Clean the *Blockältester*'s toilet! Bring the bread! Deliver the noon meal! Scrub the cauldrons! Return them! Clean the barrack after the meal!"

Whenever the cauldrons of soup are brought to the barrack, or when the time comes to distribute the bread, sausage, and margarine, they find an urgent job for me outside. I realize that my life depends on my position. In the evenings I undertake lice inspection and deliver my report to the *Blockältester*. At that time, I demand the liter of soup due me as a medic. The *Blockältester*'s face turns red; he blinks his eyes and twists his mouth as he says, "You'll get it . . . tomorrow. And I warn you, work better! Lice inspection I can do myself. I don't need you for that!"

I want to reply that, of all the personnel in the barrack, I work the hardest, but the *Blockältester,* it seems, is not inclined to discuss the matter with me.

The *Stubendienst* gives me a straw pallet with almost no straw in it and a short blanket stinking from urine.

After roll call on the following day, I look for Pinek. With despair, I tell him into what kind of hell I have descended. Pinek looks at me and says nothing. Instead, he shows me his red, swollen forearm. He was beaten yesterday; his father lost three teeth; twenty-five *Häftlinge* were killed. Finally he says, "You're lucky you're in another barrack. Hold on with your teeth and nails."

I face another day of hard work in the barrack with no time to rest or catch my breath. The *Blockältester* personally sees to it that the medic does not loaf. I crawl under the beds with a small broom to sweep the dust from every corner. Some spots have never been touched since the building became a barrack. When I am through, I must start all over again because when the *Stubendiensts* fixed the boards on the beds, a few straws fell on the ground. Now it becomes clear to me that they want to finish me off. I clench my teeth and do not utter a word.

That evening, a totally unexpected event occurs which changes the situation completely. After roll call we hear,

"All Jews forward!" I think that a general selection for the gas chamber is about to take place.

I notice that my *Blockältester* and *Stubendiensts* leave the row and try to mix with the *Kapos* and *Blockältesters* standing around. I want to drop out of line also. My *Blockältester* smacks my face and pushes me back. Instantly, we are surrounded by *Kapos, Blockältesters, Stubendiensts,* and foremen. No one can escape.

We hear a motor. Thuman arrives on a motorcycle to start the selection. With his finger, he points to the right, to the left, and to the middle. I see that Pinek runs to the right; his father is also sent to the right. I realize that Thuman sends people who are strong in that direction. Those who are somewhat weaker, are sent to the middle, and the very weak, to the left. Now it is my turn. I run to Thuman, click my wooden heels, and stand in the basic position. He sends me to the right. A minute later, I am in Pinek's arms. He cannot conceal his joy and shouts, "Transport! I heard it this morning! We're finally getting out of this hell! Nowhere can it be worse than here!"

Pinek is mistaken, and very much so! But for the moment, we do not know what awaits us. We radiate happiness.

There are over six hundred people in our group. After a while, we march to the barrack, the same one from which I almost went to the gas chamber a few weeks ago. But oh, what a miraculous transformation has occurred! There are several boards with straw mats and a pail available for use to satisfy our physiological needs. A few minutes later, we hear voices and the clang of cauldrons being taken off a cart at the door. They brought us supper. In addition to bread, we receive half a liter of soup. This is enough to make us optimistic.

I am happy, not for the additional soup, but in the knowledge that, before I die, I will see the world. That I will die in a concentration camp in one way or another, I have no doubt. There was a time when I liked to travel. During a trip, I enjoyed looking through the train window. Yes, I am happy that I will see the world before my life is over.

After the *Kommandos* leave for work in the morning, someone opens the door to the barrack and shouts, "Get ready!"

We gather at the roll call square. In the neighboring fifth field, we observe several SS men walking around naked women. Finally they are loaded on a truck. The *Raportführer* yells, "Take off! Move! Quickly!"

Another truck is parked in our field. We are ready. A few high-ranking SS men with Thuman in the lead move toward us. They look us over from every angle: front, back, and from the side. The few weaker ones they find, are ordered to stand to one side. And again, Pinek, his father, and I are lucky; we go to the right.

Pinek breathes deeply and says quietly, "Now I'm one hundred percent certain that we're going to work." When he sees my miserable face, he shrugs and looks disdainfully at me. "Nothing will ever satisfy you!" he says.

"On the contrary, only freedom," I retort.

About six hundred of us are left. Some "gentlemen" sit down at a table in front of typewriters to record our names and numbers. We ask them if they know where we will be sent. They tell us that they do not know, but that it is a good transport. Some offer us one hundred cigarettes to be included in our group.

My *Blockältester* walks by. I cannot refrain from saying menacingly, "Wait! We'll meet someday!" With an indifferent expression on his face, he pretends not to hear.

Once the formalities are over, we return to the barrack and the door is closed. It makes us a little nervous, but we are calmed somewhat when, instead of the usual six hundred we get eight hundred liters of exceptionally good potato soup even with traces of meat in it. We lick the dishes.

Immediately after the evening roll call, we are taken to the baths. We must wait a while because the women are inside. Some men become so vigorous after the good meal that the very thought of being close to naked women excites them. They tell pornographic jokes and laugh loudly. However, we seem to be waiting a long time. Rain begins to fall, and we gradually stop laughing. Instead, we long to get inside. When the door does open, everyone rushes to enter at once.

The SS men club us with the butts of their rifles. Two *Häftlinge* fall; their skulls are crushed. This upsets the count; two more *Häftlinge* must be brought from the camp.

It is late at night when I get into the bath. By some miracle, Pinek and his father were in the first group. They are lying on the floor sleeping the sleep of the just.

Dawn is breaking when we hear a hubbub among the women. In a little while, we hear the sound of their sandals as they are chased to the road by the SS men and women.

"Out!" an officer shouts.

We go, one by one, into the next room where we receive new striped uniforms, wooden sandals and, at the other end, supplies for the road: half a loaf of bread, a piece of cheese, and a slice of sausage.

We are almost at the road when we hear the gong in Field 4. Good-by Maidanek! May we find a better place! May we survive and avenge!

The clatter of our sandals resounds in the empty streets of Lublin. Here and there, a sleepy face peers out of a window. Frightened at the sight of the terrible procession, it withdraws quickly.

I breathe deeply. Oh God! We are passing through a town in which the residents live in freedom. Just the thought that there are such people who can move freely fills me with joy. I look at everything, and everything interests me: houses, stores, trees, posters. I begin to dream that this march is a hallucination, that I am obviously a free man who, after a sleepless night, is going into town to breathe unpolluted air.

"Keep going!" With that shout a rifle butt strikes my back and I return to reality.

"You're not paying attention! You behave irresponsibly!" scolds Pinek.

The poor fellow is angry and does not know that, in the last few minutes, I enjoyed a beautiful illusion. Just to have had those few moments, was worth my suffering for six weeks in Maidanek.

When we reach the freight train, we find that the women are already aboard. The SS men push us in, fifty in each car. A beautiful trip awaits us, almost a luxury ride with so few of us in the car. On the way to Treblinka, we were one hundred and fifty in much smaller quarters with lime on the floor.

The morning walk has heightened our appetites, and we start eating. No one thinks of how long we will ride and whether our supply of food will last. Bread and cheese are vanishing. After satisfying our hunger, we lie down on the floor; each of us gets as comfortable as he can and falls asleep. I am waiting for this moment to go to the window. We will move soon. Two passenger cars are hooked up to the rear of the train for the SS.

Steam hisses; several whistles blow; we are moving. I stand at the window and watch the fields and forests in the morning light. How beautiful the world is!

I hear women's voices in the car ahead of us. Like a nightmare, memories of Treblinka haunt me, thoughts of terribly difficult days and also happy ones with Fredzia. A protracted sadness grips my soul, and I lose interest in everything. Nothing I see pleases me, neither woods nor streams where children play. I lie down on the floor like the others and listen to the monotonous sound of the wheels. Eventually I fall asleep.

After several hours, I awaken. People are conversing quietly in the car. Optimism prevails. Maybe they are really taking us to work in some factory . . . they picked us so carefully.

We pass Denbice, a large railroad depot on the line between Lvov and Krakow. Several kilometers beyond Denbice, we stop unexpectedly at a small station where we remain for half an hour, two hours. Military trains pass us. Resignedly, I lie down and sleep fitfully. Once, while drowsing, I hear Pinek's voice and a locomotive's piercing whistle. I keep on sleeping.

Loud conversations in the car awaken me, and I rub my sleepy eyes. It is night. I call Pinek. He sits nearby and says, "You sleep like a horse. We rode several hundred kilometers and stopped for two hours in Krakow. Then we traveled farther. Now for a change, we haven't moved for quite a while. Maybe we reached our destination."

I look through the window. It is dark and I cannot see a thing. Everyone thinks that we are in Silesia. The majority believe that we will go to some factory or, at the worst, a mine. We wait impatiently, hopefully, fearfully. No one can sleep now, not even for a minute. It is a terribly long night.

Dawn comes at last. Little by little, the hidden forms and shadows become real. We are on a side track. On the right is a field with machine guns set up at regular intervals. On the left is a small railroad station displaying the sign: Auschwitz O/S.

4 Auschwitz II (Birkenau)

We begin a new chapter in our lives, or rather, of our suffering. Trucks pull over to the ramp. Several *Häftlinge* in striped uniforms march toward us and halt near the trucks while our transport *Kommandant* reports our arrival to an SS man who had arrived from the camp on a motorcycle. After they greet each other, the SS man turns to the *Häftlinge* and orders them to return to camp. The order seems to surprise them. We stand in the open door of the railroad car and are no less surprised. What does it all mean?

SS men arrange us five abreast prodding us with their rifle butts. Once we are in formation, we are counted and the number is confirmed. Ten are missing. They had jumped along the way, lucky people.

We march on a wide muddy road toward camp. If I thought that Maidanek was large, our new destination is immense. Endless rows of barbed wire, barracks, and guard towers stretch as far as the eyes can see. When we pass close to the large administration building, we are nearing the camp proper.

A gong sounds. People run out of some wooden barracks and some brick ones that are really horse stables as they were in Lublin. Women from their special section and men from theirs rush to the kitchen where they pick up full cauldrons and wooden barrels of the steaming morning drink.

We walk with sad expressions and bowed heads. Any optimism that we previously had, has left us. Occasionally someone curses. Somebody sighs deeply as he says, "What kind of place have we come to?"

They chase us everywhere: for new laundry, for new outfits, for more comfortable wooden shoes, and to the barrack!

There are no beds inside, only long tables at which *Häftlinge* in striped uniforms sit and record our answers to questions about our personal life and marital status on big squares of paper. When registration is finally over, all of them have mysterious expressions on their faces as they hand us new cards with our Auschwitz numbers. We ply them with questions, but they do not answer. Instead, they tell us to guard our cards as we would the pupils of our eyes. "You get twenty-five lashes for losing a card," and they walk out.

Several *Häftlinge* carrying lists and attaché cases enter our barrack. From the cases they remove ink and glass pens with wooden handles. Calling us one by one, they tell us to uncover our left forearm. I am one of the first to be called.

I go to the table and hand in my card. A *Häftling* grabs my forearm, stretches my skin, dips the pen into ink, and expertly tattoos my number: 126604. It hurts a little; I can bear it. Now I will have a souvenir for the rest of my life. The *Häftling* pats me on the arm in a friendly fashion and says in broken German, "Forget your name, fellow. From now on, you must remember your number."

I look for Pinek. He is walking away from a group around an elderly prisoner who is talking animatedly to the new arrivals. Pinek's teeth are chattering from fear. His appearance has changed so much that I do not recognize him. In those few minutes, he became an old man. I am curious to know the reason.

He shakes his head in complete despair and says, "Tadzek, you'd better not ask. We won't get out of here alive. It's the same as it was in Treblinka, except that, in Treblinka, there was no camp." He bends over and whispers in my ear, "Here there are four gas chambers, four crematoria, and several selections per month among the Jews. We're in Birkenau! BIRKENAU!!"

When they finish processing us around twelve o'clock, we stand outside the barrack waiting for the noon meal. Each of us receives one liter of watery soup. And now, "March to the barrack!"

We enter one of the several brick structures surrounded by barbed wire, the quarantine barracks. The *Blockältester* and his personnel are waiting for us. We expect a long speech, but here in Auschwitz, they have different procedures. The *Blockältester* limits himself to explaining certain rules, advising us to behave well, talk quietly, not to litter, and, for God's sake, no stealing. As we enter, I notice that the *Blockältester* has a Jewish star on his suit. One of the *Stubendiensts* is also a Jew. This does not impress me, especially since I have already learned in Lublin, that you cannot trust anyone.

The dark, gloomy barrack smells musty. After coming in from the outside, we must strain our eyes to distinguish things. We discover that the barrack is composed of four parts called *Stuben*, two to the left of the door and two to the right. A table, two benches, and an iron stove stand in the middle of the barrack.

A *Stube* occupies one-quarter of a barrack. Running down the middle of each *Stube* is a narrow corridor flanked on each side by tiers of triple bunks. And how are these built? At regular intervals perpendicular to the wall, thick projections support boards. The lowest level is simply the stone floor covered by thin straw mats. On this level and on the next, you have to crawl in to occupy your designated place. Where four should ordinarily sleep, they crowd twelve.

Pinek, his father, and I watch as the *Stubendienst* assigns the bunks. Despairingly, I think of what would happen if I should get a place on the lowest or middle level. We are fortunate. The first and second levels are filled. We are going higher. Happy, we want to lie down, but no, this is only a rehearsal. Instead, we must go outdoors to show the *Blockältester* how well we were drilled in the routine of camp exercises at Maidanek.

"Caps off! Caps on! Off—on—off—on!"

The training goes well. The fellows are hitting their thighs with their caps until dust flies out of the new pants. The *Blockältester* seems satisfied and wants to let us enter the barrack, but his second in command objects violently. "You'll see how much trouble we'll have at roll call with this shitty army. I have to train them well."

It is apparent that the *Blockältester* is a timid man. He allows his assistant to do whatever he wants with us. So we continue to take off and put on our caps. We march in the mud; we line up in rows. I do not know how long that game would have lasted if the *Blockältester* had not appeared in the doorway holding up his pants with his hands and shouting angrily, "You son-of-a-bitch! Why do you make so much noise?! You don't let me sleep!"

The assistant mumbles some obscene words under his breath and adds aloud, "Kiss my ass, you old pig!" But the exercises stop.

Threatened with a beating if we go beyond the limits of the quarantine area, we remain in front of the barrack waiting for the roll call. I take advantage of this quiet moment to talk to Pinek and to ask what other tragic news he has learned. But he is not in a talkative mood. However, he does say, "It's enough for you to know that more than two million Jews and over one million Poles, Russians, Frenchmen, and others have perished in Birkenau since 1940."

Today is the last day of June 1943. How many more people will die here before the war ends? And who among us will survive? The latter question I address to Pinek. He shakes his head, "Not I and not my father! You, as a doctor, have the best chance. But if you survive, avenge my mother and sisters. You must! Remember!"

At nightfall, we hear the gay sounds of an orchestra coming from the gate. We strain our eyes; we pull our ears. Maybe it is a hallucination?! Is this possible? Music?! Here, in Birkenau?!

The *Kommandos* are returning. Soon our sector is crowded with *Häftlinge* in bedraggled, striped clothes.

There are one thousand people in our barrack. Three weeks ago, four hundred Jews arrived from Salonika. Their trip took eight days. Of the five thousand who started, one thousand died en route. Of these fortunate ones, four hundred men and one hundred women were sent to the camp. The rest were sent to the gas chambers. A small group from Smolensk arrives.

Now that we are all here, we stand in line. The Russians are in front, then the Greek Jews, and we at the very end. I admire the *Blockältester*'s linguistic ability. With equal ease, he issues orders in Polish, Russian, and Italian. The Greeks are not conversant with German, but can understand all the Romance languages. The *Blockältester* must have said something funny because the Greeks are laughing loudly.

One by one, we enter the barrack after the short roll call. At the door, everyone receives a piece of bread and a slice of sausage except us. Were we not given some bread before we left Maidanek? This was supposed to have lasted for two days.

We crawl into our bunks. The mats have so little straw that we are virtually lying on bare boards. There are six bunks on each side of the corridor in my Stube. We have so little space that we are unable to lie on our backs, only close together on our sides. Sharp cries come from the lower bunks. People are choking. Even the devil could not invent a worse place for us to sleep, but this is only the beginning of our suffering.

In a few minutes, I start to itch and want to scratch, but it is very difficult because we are so close together. In any event, scratching brings no relief. I feel this unusual itch in several places on my body. Pinek and the others who, a while ago, were angry with me for moving and not letting them sleep, are also indulging in some fantastic contortions. Because we cannot move our hands freely, we rub our bodies against the boards and our neighbors. I am almost insane. I finally sit up, and without regard for anyone, I scratch energetically. Others follow my example.

By the glimmer of the night light, I see a solid mass of

crawling insects over my body under my shirt and shorts. Fleas, huge fleas almost as large as ants are so numerous that they almost cover our entire bodies. We itch so much that, if we could, we would gladly jump out of our red, swollen skins. It is impossible to fight off this parasite onslaught. In the straw mats, on the boards, and between the bricks are thousands, perhaps millions of these insects. Several occupants of the lower bunks stand in the corridor and vigorously shake out their shirts and shorts, but not for long. The night watchman, with club in hand, chases them back to the bunks, beating them without pity and yelling, "What?! You come here to shake off your fleas?! Here?!!

One of our bunkmates goes to the pail and returns with a bit of mint tea in a dish. It stinks slightly, but when we scrub ourselves with it, it is cooling. What a delightful feeling! We are very thankful to our comrade. Overcome by fatigue, we lie down and fall asleep almost immediately, but not for long. The fleas renew their attack; the mint tea no longer helps. In despair, we sit on our bunks and doze off for a little while before morning.

We are half-conscious when the night watchman shouts, "Get up!" and the first lashes fall on us. In the melée, we grab whatever shoes and jackets we can. We argue. More *Stubendiensts* beat us with clubs and belts. This only increases the chaos. We are finally presentable enough to stand in line for coffee. Each *Stube* has its own cauldron and the serving goes at lightning speed.

Soon the second gong sounds. *Kommandos* leave for work while the orchestra at the gate plays lively marches. In addition to our group of four hundred in the barrack, or rather, standing in front of it, are thirty Greeks, all young, strong-looking boys. They are very nervous and argue among themselves in a language unknown to us.

Meanwhile, the barrack is being cleaned. A few Greeks and one Russian help to sweep and scrub. After waiting for an hour, the *Blockältester* informs us that we will soon receive numbers which are to be sewn on our jackets and pants. He adds that he is dissatisfied with us; we make too much noise, and we will be condemned to the oven very quickly if we continue behaving in this way. What pleasant news so early in the morning!

While we are sewing on the numbers, several *Häftlinge* arrive and enter the barrack to talk with the *Blockältester*. They are doctors from the "hospital" who came to inoculate us against typhus. One seems familiar, but he has no time to speak with me. Altogether, they have four syringes and eight needles. Each doctor inoculates fifty persons with one needle.

We hear "Attention!" shouted loudly from the door. An SS man enters and asks the *Blockältester* about the Greeks. As the *Blockältester* reads off the numbers from a card in his hand, the Greeks tremble; their teeth chatter like people suffering from an attack of malaria. Arranged five abreast, they are marched out, followed by the SS man.

With the inoculations over, the doctors bid goodby to the *Blockältester* and *Stubendiensts*. At the door, one of them turns to the *Blockältester* and says, "If there's a doctor among the newcomers, send him to us after the noon meal."

I am excited. I share the news with Pinek who says happily, "You see, Tadzek, I told you! You'll be saved. You only have to take advantage of this opportunity."

I wait nervously until noon. We walk around in the small space in front of the barrack. What devilish earth this is! It does not appear to be clay, and it is not mud. Still, it takes quite an effort for us to pull out our shoes. Several of us want to use the toilet and ask the *Stubendienst* for permission. He moves his head knowingly and shouts, "Everyone who wants to go to the latrine, form a group because the next time you'll be allowed to go will be at night!"

Satisfying our physiological needs at a prescribed time is another restrictive similarity to Maidanek. I am among the first ten to go.

We often fall along the way. With these wooden shoes, it is almost impossible to walk in this deep muddy clay-like soil.

The *Stubendienst* consoles us by saying, "Don't be afraid! It's better now, here in Birkenau. You should have seen it a year and two years ago!" He shakes his head as he adds, "A Jew didn't have the right to live here for more than twenty-four hours. Only exceptionally strong ones survived for a week." In an attempt to comfort us, he quickly continues, "Not only Jews, but also thousands of Russians, Poles, and others died daily in this camp. Every day we pulled hundreds of people from this quicksand-like mud, not counting the ones who died in the gas chamber after regular selections and those who were killed on the job." He thinks awhile and continues, "Oh yes, it's better now, far better. Only Jews are being killed."

When I look at Pinek, he shakes his head understandingly. "He's right, Tadzek. That is how it was, and this is how it is. There's no possibility for survival." I revolt inwardly. Once again, the thought of the gas chamber comes to our minds.

For the noon meal, we get half a liter of grass soup with a few potato peels. I pay no attention to the food. With great impatience, I wait for the *Blockältester* to call the doctors, but he is in no hurry, and I am afraid to approach him.

Before evening, the *Blockältester* finally remembers and calls, "Hey there! Doctors, dentists, and medics report to me!"

I fly like an arrow to the *Blockältester.* I hear the clacking of wooden shoes behind me. Coming from the other end of the yard is some fellow, who appears better fed than I, whom I had not seen in Field 4 in Lublin, nor had I seen him during the trip here. We look at each other but say nothing.

The *Blockältester* asks for our numbers and names. The *Blockschreiber* brings our charts and, with a red pencil, marks: Doctor—at the disposal of the health service.

"When everyone goes to work tomorrow," says the *Blockältester,* "you will remain here in the barrack and will help the *Stubendiensts.* There are several Greek doctors who work well, and everyone is satisfied with them. You should follow their example. Now you may go."

My older colleague did not hear my name. I repeat it.

"Stabholz," he muses. "Oh, you're the son of the Director of the Czyste Hospital. It was your father who died so tragically. I knew him well. I'm Dr. Glatstern, Szymon Glatstern."

We shake hands. When I express my surprise at seeing him here, my new friend says, with a sad face, that he was unlucky. He had been a doctor in the German factory outside of the Ghetto. The day the Uprising took place, the SS seized the entire personnel of the factory, about one thousand five hundred Jewish workers together with their families and chased them to the Umschlagplatz. They were then loaded into freight cars and taken to Lublin. In Maidanek, he became a medic. Comparing his circumstances to that of others in the camp, he was well off.

One memorable evening, when the SS men had killed two *Häftlinge* in front of the bath, he was going to the *Schreibstube* with a report about the lice situation. It was after the gong had sounded. On the way, he met an SS man who refused to hear his explanation. He grabbed him by the collar and dragged him to the bath. Szymon is very distressed because he left a brother in Maidanek who will not know where he is and will probably die of hunger. He is helpless and has no one to help him. "Damn my cursed luck!" Szymon mutters.

Pinek and his father, curious to learn what the *Blockältester* said, come over to us. I introduce Szymek and tell them everything. Pinek congratulates us and is satisfied that he will go to work tomorrow. He will be able to look around to see if it is possible to "organize" anything.

We spend another sleepless night. As soon as we lie down in our bunks, the fleas begin their torture. We decide not to undress. Instead, we tie our clothes with a piece of string at our ankles and wrists making it just as tight as we can. Maybe, in this way, we can protect ourselves from the insects' attacks. Nothing works; the time passes slowly. Pinek whispers, "No sleep at night and work during the day—this will surely finish us off quickly. The devil with it!"

After the morning coffee, three groups go to work. I sincerely wish Pinek and his father luck at work and promise to help them to the best of my ability. Meanwhile, the *Stubendiensts* explain to Szymek the nature of our work. In the morning, we will check all the beds to see if they have been made properly and if not, eventually to fix them. We must scrub and sweep the floor. One of us will take out the garbage in the wheelbarrow while the other tidies up in front of the barrack. Then we will go for bread and the noon meal. After that, we will help the Greek doctors to wash the dishes and straighten up. Then we will bring the coffee. We must not loaf if we have free time, but we should find something useful to do for the barrack. "We don't work hard," says the *Stubendienst*. "Those on *Kommando* have a much worse schedule."

We begin. Szymek checks one-half of the beds; I, the other. We crawl into the niches and throw out pieces of dried mud. On the upper bunks, the ones we are able to see, we brush off the loose straw and straighten out the blankets. We are dreadfully tired from the sleepless nights and desperately want to sleep. While we are working, we hear a loud laugh behind us. Turning our heads, we see the *Stubendienst* and the assistant *Blockältester*, Frank Korasiewicz also known as "The Vampire of Birkenau" who orders us down from the bunks.

"If this is the way you work, you'll have a shitty death, you lazy bums! Even the Greeks work a hundred percent better than you!"

The *Stubendienst*, himself, crawls onto a bunk and demonstrates the speed at which we must work.

I get an idea and tell it to Szymek immediately. We will save time if we do the upper bunks first going from bed to bed, then descending to the lower bunks.

Our backs begin to ache from these contortions. Szymek suffers from chronic rheumatism which starts to bother him. He moans quietly. Finally, the beds are done.

I run for water instead of Szymek. The washroom is quite a distance, and the road is difficult. The *Stubendienst* slaps my face because it took me too long. We scrub the stony floor on our knees. After a few minutes, I have another thought: add a little lime to the water. The lime stings and burns our hands, but it does whiten the stone. The *Stubendienst* is satisfied and gives us a small piece of bread. He even apologizes for hitting me. He says that I should understand that he has been in Auschwitz for three years and that his nerves are so raw that he cannot control his actions. As we will discover later, people are not only nervous, they also kill, and this is all due to their extremely stressful duties.

"Now tidy up in front of the barrack!" He hands us two brooms. We pick up the garbage and sweep the puddles so that the ground will dry faster. All this is done quickly because the *Stubendienst* stands in the doorway observing us carefully. The amount of soup we will get at noon depends on how well we work.

The place looks so-so. The wheelbarrow is full of mud and garbage. Now I must empty it. To unload it, I must go to the second street where there are two wagons.

The wheel of the heavy wheelbarrow continually gets stuck in the mud up to its axle. I pant heavily as I push with all my strength, barely inching it along. Finally, salvation! I reach the garbage wagons and empty my wheelbarrow. Once rid of the load, I run back quickly. It is about time I did because, throughout the camp, we hear, *"Brot holen!"*

The Greeks bring out two open wooden crates with long handles. We go.

In the immediate neighborhood of the camp is a red building with a large high chimney and small, heavily barred windows. It is located in a small square that is surrounded by an electrified wire fence. Not a soul is to be seen. Fifty meters away is another similarly constructed building.

I point to one and naively ask what it is. The *Stubendienst* looks at me in surprise. When he realizes that my question is a genuine one, he laughs. "Greek," he says to one of the doctors in broken German, "tell him what it is."

The Greek looks at me pityingly and says, "The bakery."

Everyone considers it a big joke and laughs. I have been here for three days and I still do not know what it is. Where are my eyes? And where is my nose? Several hours after our arrival in Birkenau, a transport of four thousand French Jews arrive. One hundred fifty men and fifty women entered the camp. Three thousand eight hundred have gone to the gas chamber. The flames shot high into the air; the chimneys belched smoke for several hours. There was a terrible stench of burning bones and bodies pervading the entire camp. And I do not know a thing and simple-mindedly ask what that is! Did I truly believe that it is a bakery? They pat me on the arm, laugh, and say that I am quite a fellow.

As we approach the storage depot, the *Stubendienst* tells me to look to the side a little. "Do you see that small forest? Look closely, and you'll see two more bakeries."

Among the trees of the shabby little forest, I see two more red buildings. Each one features two chimneys. Since these are taller than the trees, the chimneys have lightning rods attached to them.

We stand in line according to barrack number and wait patiently. The bread distribution proceeds rather slowly because the barracks are quite large. Each one receives two hundred loaves.

Turning to Szymek and me, the *Stubendienst* says, "Be careful when they call our barrack! Then you," pointing to me, "grab one handle with me, and you," pointing to Szymek, "take the other handle with this fat Greek." We must get two hundred forty-four loaves or one hundred twenty-two into each big wooden crate. As soon as they are full, we must grab them and run, otherwise they will beat us mercilessly. Later on, we will be able to walk slowly. The most important thing is to get out of the place safely."

"Block 20!"

Our *Stubendienst* shouts, "Now! Let's go! Quickly!"

We run into the storage room and put the boxes close to the distribution point. Two *Häftlinge* throw the bread at us at a dizzying speed. In a few minutes our crates are filled. The *Stubendienst* hisses, "Now grab!"

Blood rushes to my head as I strain to my utmost, lifting the weight with great difficulty. I have the feeling that I cannot take another two steps.

"Faster!" I hear behind me. A fat SS man approaching with a club shouts, "What's the matter? Hurry a bit!"

My back is giving out. The handles are slipping away from me. I suffer terribly. Finally, two steps and we are outside! Szymek is gasping behind me. He had to stop twice inside the room and received several lashes on his back. Now he says wryly, "Isn't this a good cure for my rheumatism?!!!"

Crawling, one step at a time, we return to the barrack. In spite of the four of us handling each load, it is heavy. No wonder. One hundred twenty-two loaves weigh one thousand two hundred grams each plus the weight of the box—altogether it totals one hundred fifty kilos. For our combined strength, it is more than enough.

As compensation for bringing the bread, the *Stubendienst* allows us to rest until the noon meal, but the assistant *Blockältester* objects. "Franz," the *Stubendienst* says, "leave them alone. They almost shit in their pants picking up the bread."

We go with the Greeks to the darkest corner of the barrack. Two of them know German, having studied it in Vienna. They tell us their story which is almost as tragic as ours.

They are from sunny Salonika where they were very well-off. They owned beautiful villas, wonderful offices, and had families.

When the Germans arrived, they started persecuting the Jews: throwing them out of their homes, confiscating their possessions and wealth, and opening work camps for them. In the space of two years, thirty percent of the workers died because of the horrible conditions. During the winter of 1942, the Germans began deporting the Jews to Germany, and they ended up in Auschwitz. From December 1942 to the end of May 1943, nearly twenty transports arrived, carrying more than seventy-five thousand Jews. Seventy thousand of them perished in the gas chamber. Of the remaining five thousand, only half were still alive several months later. "Yes, friend, the climate, the conditions. . . . I lost my wife and little girl; they were gassed. Others, in addition to wives and children, lost parents and relatives."

He dried his tears. I want to tell him about the fate of the Polish Jews, but at that moment, we hear, *"Mittagholen!"*

Szymek and I go for the noon meal. On the way, we look at the crematoria and think of the enormity of this human tragedy.

Returning with the cauldron, we find the *Blockältester* waiting to inform us that the *Häftlinge*'s doctor has sent for us. We must report to the *Schreibstube's* health station. In a friendly manner, he warns us, "Keep your spirits up! He's a terrible man!"

We run to Barrack XII, knock on the window, and report to the *Schreiber.* He already knows about us.

"So, you're the new doctors?" he greets us before asking about our personal history. "Wait here a minute. I'm going to get Zenkteller."

Dr. Zenkteller, the chief doctor, arrives a few minutes later and scrutinizes us. He is a short, athletically-built man of about fifty who walks with a springy step and is the terror of the doctors and medics. "Couldn't you come any sooner, you sons-of-bitches?" he yells in a thundering voice. "Must I wait for you? Must I send people for you?! Wait, you bastards! I'll teach you!"

I do not understand what is wrong with our chief and want to explain everything. I start to open my mouth, but I notice a doctor behind him, making desperate signs. He puts a finger to his lips.

I am glad that I did not say anything, but the chief is screaming, "Do you want to talk, you idiot?! You'd better shut up and listen to me!"

After this introduction, he asks a few questions. "Studies? practice? where? specialty?" A short examination follows: a little internal medicine, a little physiology, anatomy, bacteriology, and surgery. This is Dr. Zenkteller's original system for eliminating charlatans.

He grimaces and states that we are poor doctors. Nevertheless, he orders the *Schreiber* to register us as physicians. "When I need you, I'll let you know. And now, back to your barrack!"

I look at Szymek, and he looks at me. "A nice chief we have, and we have the pleasure of working with him," I remark.

"We aren't at home," philosophizes Szymek.

At the barrack, it is long after mealtime. Our dishes contain a bit of soup, slightly more than a liter. "We had very little today," explains the *Stubendienst.* "Tomorrow you'll get more."

I am exhausted from the work and sleeplessness. I would gladly lie down for a while. The *Stubendienst* comes over with a proposition. HE wants to sleep. Szymek and I must stay in the doorway and watch in case some SS men or *Lagerältesters* come by. Should this happen, we must wake him immediately. "Have your eyes in the right spot, or you won't live long," he threatens menacingly.

Szymek stays with me. Together we remain at the door

and watch for signs of any possible danger. Loud snoring comes from the barrack, while we fight pervading sleep.

"Don't worry," I say, recalling the words of a friend in Maidanek, "the beginning is always hard. Heads up!" Szymek smiles wanly.

It is about three o'clock. Szymek, sitting on a stool, leans his head against the wall and, in a minute, is fast asleep.

There is movement in the barrack, and the *Stubendienst* comes out. "So, how is it, doctor?"

"Everything is in order," I reply. "I'm very sleepy."

"You'll sleep at night," he consoles me.

"The fleas bite like hell," I say, unconvinced.

"It used to be worse." He has an answer for everything.

The *Stubendiensts* begin cutting the bread as I watch. One slices the loaf into uneven parts. He cuts a piece from the larger section. Then he prepares four portions. The *Stubendiensts* get their rations in the form of slices which, when combined, are the equivalent of several loaves, and are eventually exchanged for fat and cigarettes.

"You, doctor!" calls the *Stubendienst.* "In the evening when we distribute the bread, don't hurry. You and your friend should be the last ones. We'll find the largest portions for you. You know that the loaves are cut unevenly and as a result there are larger and smaller pieces. Do you understand?"

He gives me two slices, one for each of us. "It's for you for watching."

Anger chokes me. You bastard! A slice cut from someone's bread is like stealing a piece of his life.

The *Stubendienst* notices that something is bothering me. He pats my arm and says, "Don't be an idiot. This is a camp. You must look out for yourself."

Szymek comes over to me. I give him a slice and tell him the whole story. He pats my arm and says, "Can you help it?"

No, I cannot. That is why I am so angry at myself, at the people, and at this mean, cursed world.

For a change, the possibility of a new job is on the horizon: *Kaffeeholen.*

The cauldrons here are even larger than the ones in Lublin. In a short while we are out of breath carrying them. I have an idea and announce, "Szymek! Let's go on *Kommando*!"

Szymek's face reddens. As he wipes the sweat from his brow, he looks intently at me and exclaims, "You're crazier than I thought!" To explain, he adds, "Did you think of the cold, of the selections?!" He waves his hand resignedly. "It isn't worthwhile talking with a fellow like you."

An orchestra of about fifty people carrying tubas, violins, clarinets, saxophones, accordions, and drums emerges from one of the barracks. The musicians sit on stools at the gate. One of the Greeks tells me in broken German, "Orchestra tra, tra, ta, but the people go to the gas chamber. Si, si!"

Immediately after we return with the coffee, the *Blockältester* calls Szymek and me to his corner. He tells us his name and asks us if it is familiar to us. What a surprise! The *Blockältester*'s father was one of the most important Polish Zionist leaders in the country and a member of Poland's legislature. I recall vaguely that his son had some difficulties after he graduated from school. He was accused of being involved in Communist activities, but news of the whole affair was suppressed, and he left the country.

Now I learn that he went to France where he studied at the Sorbonne. Later, as an idealist, he fought in the International Brigades against Franco. He was wounded twice and earned several medals. After the fall of France, he wanted to flee to Switzerland quickly, but he was caught at the border and sent to Auschwitz. He has been here for about two years. He wants to know about the conditions in Poland before the war and what happened after the Germans invaded the country. He listens with great interest while I tell him about the Warsaw Ghetto Uprising, Treblinka and Maidanek.

"Yes, fellows," he comments at the end, "you fell into a terrible trap. Not a single Jew will get out of Birkenau alive. Here, as in Treblinka, Birkenau is the last stop. It's all the same. We'll die in the gas chamber. It makes no difference if you're a doctor or a worker, *Blockältester* or *Stubendienst*. It's best not to think of anything. It's most important that we don't go hungry, and, if possible, to be among the last to be gassed."

He does not tell us how to do that. When we leave his corner and are in the doorway, he warns us about his assistant, "Watch him! He's a murderer."

In the corridor, we meet his pet with a full dish of generously greased potatoes, the first course in the meal for the *Blockältester*.

We join the Greek doctors and tell them of our conversation. They say with a smile, "Oh yes, the *Blockältester*! Perhaps he doesn't beat us so much, but he isn't helpful either. He's worried about food and his little pal with whom he has very close relations." I cannot understand what he means. "Oh yes, my friend, the *Blockältester* is a pervert like the majority of *Blockältesters, Kapos,* and our other supervisors. They all have this kind of boy who, during the day, serves them, and at night. . . ." He makes a grimace of disgust.

We switch to a subject of more interest to us. We complain about the plague of fleas that are eating us alive. Is there any help or solution?

"After a while it won't be so terrible. We got used to them. It seems that only the newcomers are attacked in such large numbers. In a few days the little insects become tame, and you won't even feel their presence."

We ask if he knows where they took the thirty young Greeks.

Sadly, our friend says, "The head doctor selected them, probably for some experiments. We aren't certain."

We hear noises outside as the *Kommandos* return from work. I look for Pinek. After giving him a piece of bread, I tell him about today's events and my idea of going on *Kommando*.

Pinek's response is similar to Szymek's. "Don't be an idiot. Hold on with your nails, otherwise you'll perish." He tells me that he worked in the neighboring section today and that there are seven similar ones as in Maidanek. One section marked with the capital letter "E" is occupied by Gypsies and their families. Pinek discovered that we will be transferred to Section D which is next to the Gypsies and that our place will be taken by women. Pinek did not work too hard today. He and others brought bunks to the barracks. The noon meal was not bad; they got one liter of soup.

During the midday break, Pinek learned more details about life in this camp. In the last few months, conditions for the Aryans have improved; even the sick are not sent to the gas chamber. Among the Jews, however, selections continue. Sick ones go to the crematoria every week. Once in awhile, a selection is made among the healthy, but when that happens, almost everyone ends up in the gas chamber. The Germans bring Jews to Auschwitz from all over Europe: from Poland, France, Holland, Belgium, Czechoslovakia, Russia, Greece, and Germany. "Let's talk about something more pleasant. How's the bread situation today?" he wants to know.

We learn about that after the evening roll call. There is margarine! Dealings begin in the barrack. The Greeks come to our room calling, "Margarine for bread! Bread for the margarine! Soup for margarine!"

Only the devil knows where they got dishes of hot soup. They stir the liquid with spoons to show that there are potatoes in it. "Good soup! Good!"

Lively deals are made. For half a portion of bread, one buys a dish of soup. The other one sells his bread for margarine. Someone buys an onion.

I sit on the bunk with Pinek and watch the noisy people. They use sign language and talk in some sort of international tongue. One's head can almost burst from all this activity. "Better not deal now," advises Pinek. "Maybe someday when we have more soup or bread."

When the light is extinguished in the barrack, the fleas remind us of their presence. I am not quite sure, but maybe they did become tame, or perhaps we are just too tired. A pleasant dizziness overcomes me, and I fall asleep.

On our first Sunday in Auschwitz, we work only until noon. The *Stubendienst* pulls shoes from a hole and hands us brushes, knives, and rags. Szymek and I are supposed to clean them well and bring them to the clothing storeroom tomorrow morning. It takes us until noon to finish.

By then it is time for the noon meal. This is an easy task: one thousand liters of soup in ten barrels of one hundred liters each. There are not enough people to carry it. Our *Blockältester* has an idea. He runs to the health station and borrows a cart used to transport lice infested laundry. We load six barrels on it, and the other four are carried. Slowly, carefully, we approach the barrack. Finally, we are there. The *Kommandos* are coming. After the short roll call, we have the noon meal.

Our barrack has five hundred two-liter tin dishes, one is shared by two people. We sit on the ground in pairs, pull out our spoons and eat, absorbed in the food. To swallow the liquid, we alternate: one swallows a spoonful and then the other. The potatoes are divided evenly at the end.

Our group eats rather quietly. Only occasionally do we exchange suspicious looks. Suddenly, two of the Greeks are embroiled in a violent argument. Their dishes fly through the air, spilling the contents on the clay ground. They kick, fight, and shout what seems like curses and vile language. The noise is so loud that the *Blockältester* must intervene. It seems that there was a piece of meat in the soup. One of them wanted to grab it before the other noticed it, but he had seen it. Both of them receive several whiplashes. After that, they make peace. They are hungry and look enviously at the others who still have a few spoonfuls left.

After the noon meal is distributed, several liters of soup still remain. The *Stubendienst* takes a number of dishes, and the rest are divided among the doctors. I get two liters of THICK soup. I return to Pinek and want to share it with him. He is more practical and thinks that, for such fine quality soup—he stirs it with his spoon and exclaims, "See how many potatoes!"—I can get at least half a portion of bread and maybe more for it. I give the whole dish to Pinek and ask him to sell it. All I want from the deal is a little piece of bread; he may keep the rest. Pinek is beside himself with joy.

I did not get the soup for nothing. Szymek, the Greeks, and I work together until nightfall washing the dishes. The Greeks put some of them aside and, before submerging them in the water, we carefully scrape the sides for traces of soup. These remnants are put into special "dishes". It is not an easy job. The hungry ones cleaned the dishes with their fingers and tongues. From several hundred of them, the Greeks manage to accumulate two portions of watery soup without potatoes, but still soup. I must admit that they are practical.

When I climb onto the bunk that night, Pinek proudly hands me a portion of bread. He admits that he took more than half for himself. In addition, he said that he pulled out a few potatoes from the soup and ate them on the spot. He also has a bone with a little meat for me. I think, "What a wonderful fellow this Pinek is!"

Days pass slowly. Each one is filled with the same tiresome, exceedingly monotonous work. I do not get a minute's time to talk with Szymek. I begin to feel extremely weak. Carrying the bread requires a great expenditure of effort. My heart beats wildly; I am short of breath; I feel faint more often.

Every day, Pinek beats into my head his opinion that I should consider myself lucky that I am working in the barrack.

"Do you know what is happening on *Kommando*?"

I do not know what is going on, but I see them dragging back several corpses every day. Those who have enough strength to return on their own, have wounds on their faces and bodies.

"The SS men here are worse than those in Lublin," Pinek complains one evening as he pats his wounds with a handkerchief. "The worst bastard of them all is *Unterscharführer* Schillinger. He's a sadist and the terror of all the *Häftlinge*."

In a few days, we are not so crowded. Two people from our bunk are gone. I bring Szymek there to sit and listen to Pinek's stories. Szymek nudges me with his elbow and says, "Are you still in such a rush to go on *Kommando*?!"

I reply that it is not exactly heaven here in the barrack and sometimes the work is even more difficult because we labor without a minute's respite. "If this continues, I won't hold out."

Someone in the bunk sighs deeply and says, "Doctor, I would gladly change places with you."

"I, also," adds Pinek.

The next morning they bring back the Greeks who were taken away a few days ago. They are very distressed. To every question they laconically answer, "*Kaput!* Greek *kaput!*"

The *Blockältester* is curious to know what was done to them. The Greeks lower their pants. The skin of their thighs and lower abdomen is the color of blue steel. Their testicles had been irradiated with Roentgen rays. They are very weak and have severe headaches. Every once in a while they vomit. In a few days they develop deep, smelly sores and enter the hospital. They never return.

* * *

One evening, the *Blockältester* gives Szymek and me additional work. We are to use the *Häftlinge*'s cards to find out what their trades are and to tabulate them. We finish our tasks around midnight. Before we go to bed, we walk in front of the barrack. Despite the cloudy night, it is very light. From the chimneys of the nearby crematoria, flames shoot several meters into the air. The wind blowing in our direction carries a putrid odor of burning flesh and bones toward us. I throw up my noon soup.

Outwardly, Szymek is quiet. In any event, he says nothing. When we return to our bunks, he covers his head with his blanket and his entire body shakes.

* * *

I try hard not to think of the past, but memories return in spite of my efforts to forget them. When I go for bread and see the women moving around in the nearby section, I feel burning pain in my heart and I recall Fredzia. Mountains evoke memories, too. Far beyond the wires, the beautiful, imposing Carpathians shrouded in mist appear near yet still unreachable. Memories! Memories!

"When the war is over, we'll go to the mountains, won't we, Tadzek?" It is Fredzia's voice.

I look around, stretch out my arms, and call, "Fredzia, where are you?!"

I hear laughter nearby. Half dreaming, I look around. The *Stubendienst,* Szymek, and the Greeks are watching and laughing uproariously at me. Szymek is of the opinion that I should have become an actor, not a doctor. My head feels empty; the world whirls; my heart beats fiercely.

Fredzia! . . . mountains! . . . my mother's face . . . bring the coffee! . . . crematorium . . . death . . . only death will bring salvation, a great overpowering peace.

* * *

"Hey, Doctor! What's happening to you? You look like a *muzelman*! Are you getting ready for the oven? Well, are you?"

The *Blockältester* stops me at the door and asks me these questions in a kindly manner. I do not know what the word *"muzelman"* means and what the *Blockältester* wants from me. I put the pail down on the floor anyway and breathe laboriously.

"Don't worry," the *Blockältester* reassures me, "the beginning is always hard." (I had heard those words before.) "Once I also worked. It was even worse then than it is now. Ha, ha, ha, ha!" he laughs heartily. "What does it mean 'worse'? Now it's a rest home compared to what it was a year ago." (This I also heard before.) "Do you think I became a *Blockältester* from the first minute? I'm at the end of my career and you haven't even started. Zenkteller is interested in you. If he takes you to Barrack XII, perhaps you'll have a chance to survive."

On parting, he gives me cigarettes for which I thank him warmly. I think about my fate and, if before I win, will I lose my life because I am just about at the end of my endurance?

I learn from the Greeks that, in Auschwitz jargon, *"muzelman"* is the same as a *"gamel"* in Maidanek; that is, a rag of a man, a skeleton doomed to be burned in the oven, a living corpse.

"What's Barrack XII?" I ask.

They smack their lips in ecstasy and raise their eyes heavenward. To get into Barrack XII is their unattainable dream; it is luxury. Doctors and *Häftlinge* worked for almost a month to build that barrack. It is a showpiece barrack for prominent doctors and *Häftlinge*. Medics, there, have their own room and their own beds.

I look at my scratched, sore-ridden, swollen body and think about a personal dish and, oh . . . a personal bed. If only fate would smile upon me!

I am scrubbing the table in the corridor diligently when I hear the deep voice that I know calling from the doorway, "*Blockältester!*"

The *Blockältester* puts his dish away and runs to the door. "Greetings, Doctor! And what do you wish?"

I overhear their conversation near the door. It sounds like beautiful music to me.

". . . So you send me those two characters today!"

The *Blockältester* comes to the rear of the barrack, nudges me with his elbow, and shouts loudly, "Did you hear, you fucking son-of-a bitch? You and your friend are going to Barrack XII. You've succeeded!"

Szymek receives this news with a philosophical attitude. "Everywhere you are is good, but it is still best at home. You'll be in XII, and you'll want to come back to 20. It won't be good anywhere in this camp."

I am angry with Szymek and try to convince him that he is wrong, but we must go for bread. The Greeks congratulate us for our unusual luck and distinction, and want us to remember them. Today, even the *Stubendienst* is friendlier to us, the future medics of Barrack XII.

Immediately after the noon meal, we receive our portions of bread. The *Blockältester* hands us our charts and the farewell ceremony begins.

"I think you had it good here," says the assistant *Blockältester*. "You've no complaints against anyone here. You were scolded and whipped, but you must understand it was only because we're nervous. And didn't you have enough soup?"

I agree readily and thank them cordially for their "protection", for their "soup", and for the "good treatment". I want to leave as fast as possible. Perhaps I will finally get to a barrack where I will recover from three weeks in the Warsaw

Uprising, the Umschlagplatz, Treblinka, and Maidanek. I am going to Barrack XII with a silent prayer in my heart.

"Hey! The millionaires have come!" the *Schreiber* of Barrack XII greets us happily. "Now, fellows, give me your charts and go to the bath. You aren't allowed on the ward the way you are.

We shower in wonderfully hot water. What a boon for our skins! The manager of the baths, a solidly-built peasant with an old number, brags, "We built it ourselves from nothing, from scratch. We gave away our own bread."

After we bathe, we are given clean laundry and some clothes in rather good condition. The barber shaves us and cuts our hair. Finally we cross the threshold of Barrack XII. "Good luck!" I whisper to Szymek.

Once again we hear, "The millionaires have come!"

Doctors, running from the clinic and dressing room, greet us in a friendly manner. To my great joy, I recognize one of them, Dr. Herman from the Czyste Hospital. When the Germans were approaching in September of 1939, he left Warsaw with his wife and fled eastward. He settled in a small place in the Russian occupied zone on the border of East Prussia, but he did not enjoy peace for long. The Germans arrived in 1941; deportations to Auschwitz began in the beginning of 1942. Of the three thousand five hundred people, three thousand two hundred went to the gas chamber; among them was his wife.

Someone else squeezes my hand cordially. It is Zbyszek Szawlowski, a wonderful fellow from Warsaw and a school friend.

All the doctors are curious and ask, "What do you hear from the outside? How long will the war last?"

We are in the camp for only two months, but, to them, it seems that we came from freedom.

"The Old One is coming."

Our conversation ends quickly. Someone had noticed Zenkteller in the area. The old "grandfather" enters the ward. He deigns to notice us.

"So you got here! Behave well! Work! In the meantime,

you're here as patients. For the smallest infraction, you'll be thrown out of here and will never come back. Understand?!"

"Yes, Doctor," replies Szymek.

I can only swallow my saliva. My voice is stuck in my throat. Finally the Old One leaves.

We study our surroundings. Barrack XII is worthy of its fame in Auschwitz. It is true that this barrack, like the others, is almost a stable, but its boards, its three-tiered bunks and the single beds are painted white, and its floor is cement. In the middle are two tables and a few stools. The whole barrack is divided into three parts. The first is the hospital where we are now. Glass doors lead to the dressing room. The third section is the ambulatory clinic.

The *Stubendienst* greets us and assigns us to the lower beds. We have two blankets and a pillow filled with straw. I look at Szymek. He moves his head knowingly and says, "Well, finally!" I think that we may be able to catch our breath now.

We are approached by two young Jewish doctors, one from Paris, the other from Belgrade. They say that they were lucky. The Yugoslav came to Auschwitz six weeks ago; the Frenchman, one day before I did. Both have been in the barrack for several days now.

They tell us about selections at the train station. The Yugoslav lost his parents, his fiancée, and other relatives, six people in all. They went directly to the gas chamber. The Frenchman lost his father, wife, brother and his wife and their children. Both men are very depressed and not willing to give us too many explanations. Their main obsession is their lost happiness. As they recall their dear ones, tears roll down their cheeks.

"You new gentlemen," says the *Stubendienst,* "will go for the coffee. The Frenchman will show you the way."

A familiar cart is in front of the barrack. We had loaded it with six cauldrons of soup only last Sunday. Now we pull it to the kitchen, but we do not have to stand in line. Two cauldrons of coffee are already prepared for the clinic. It is not much, not even one hundred liters.

"Roll call!" The *Stubendienst* counts the patients, and the medics stand in the clinic for awhile. It is wonderful. We don't even have to go outside. This is important, especially in winter.

As soon as the roll call is over, Dr. Herman and Dr. Zbyszek Szawlowski enter. "Come in friends! Help us work! We'll finish a little sooner, then we'll be able to talk for a while this evening."

We join them in the clinic. When the entrance door is opened, the first patients appear accompanied by the medic of their barrack. Every patient has a card bearing a number, name, and nationality. The card is divided into columns: date, diagnosis, treatment, signature (number) of the doctor.

The overwhelming majority of patients are surgical cases. The long neglected wounds and sores are purulent and smelly. When they can be endured no longer, the patients come to the clinic and are indifferent to their fate.

"To the hospital!"

"Good."

"To the gas chamber!"

"Good."

Surprised at their poor condition, I ask them why they did not come sooner, and why they neglected their wounds.

They all have the same answer, "I was afraid. I believe that the *Lagerarzt* looks through the cards from time to time and sends those patients who come to the clinic too often, to the gas chamber." This is true of the Aryans as well as of the Jews. Both reason the same way and have the same fear.

"You idiot! Don't talk so much! Work! I'll throw you out head over heels!" It is Dr. Zenkteller reminding me of his presence.

Zbyszek Szawlowski comes over to me, leans over, and whispers in my ear, "Watch the Old One. When he's on the ward, try to work fast, and may God help you. Don't talk to anyone, not even your own father if you should meet him here. The Old One is unpredictable. He beats; he kicks; he throws you into punitive company. He has finished off many doctors already. Be careful!"

I am thankful to Zbyszek for warning me of the danger and try to work rapidly. My hands are clumsy. They are swollen and thick, and my knuckles hurt when I bend them.

I watch the others for a moment. They really work very well. Attentively and in complete silence, they look at the wounds, take a gauze square, apply the salve with a spatula, than bandage and finished! Next! If there is some unusually difficult case, they take the patient to Zenkteller who works at a separate table.

Zenkteller delivers the sentence, "To the hospital . . . excuse from work . . ." The patient's life depends on Zenkteller's mood. For the *Häftlinge,* he is the highest authority and absolute ruler whose orders, right or wrong, easy or difficult, must be immediately and unquestioningly obeyed.

The most difficult patients are the Greeks with their scores of wounds and sores. Moreover, it is difficult to understand them. One of those unfortunates shows me a large sore on his right foot. I apply some antiseptic, place a gauze square, then a piece of cotton on it. I bandage him and call, "Next!"

But wait! The Greek murmurs something and takes off the other shoe. He has three sores: on the sole, heel, and ankle. With a faint heart, I discover Zenkteller watching me carefully and wondering why I keep this patient so long. My hands shake as I hurry to finish with the Greek. Finally I am done! "Next, quickly!" But it is not the end. The Greek lowers his pants. He has a purulent sore near his anus. Sweat pours from my forehead. I put some salve on the sore and want to be rid of him, but he shows me another one under his armpit.

Zenkteller screams, "I'm watching you, idiot! You're slow! You're good for nothing!"

My explanation that the patient had many sores earns me two punches in the ribs from Zenkteller. In a menacing voice he adds, "If you open your mouth one more time, you'll fly out of here!"

This entire scene occurs in front of many patients. I curse the Greek, Zenkteller, and most of all, my damned, shitty luck. From now on I work automatically. I am very surprised when I hear the gong. I feel happy and want to return to the ward, but I am prevented from doing so by Dr. Wortman who comes over to me. (He enjoys Dr. Zenkteller's confidence and is his right hand.) Wortman is a good fellow, but he assumes the airs of a chief as he demands, "Where are you going? Now you have to clean up here, and be careful not to break or spill anything!"

The Frenchman, Yugoslav, Szymek, and I divide the work among ourselves. Szymek and I clean the floor while the other two work on the stools. Luckily for us, the light is extinguished and we must stop our tasks. I go to the ward and pull the piece of bread from my pocket, and eat it dry because the coffee is all gone. We did not bring our belongings from Barrack 20. It bothers me that I cannot notify Pinek of my whereabouts. Unfortunately, I must postpone that until tomorrow.

My heart is heavy; I have fearful forebodings. I am in Auschwitz for such a short while and I am already in trouble with Zenkteller. What hurts me most is that all of his accusations are unreasonable, and I have no way to defend myself.

We see a light shining through the dressing room window; the door opens. Zbyszek Szawlowski enters and calls Szymek and me inside to meet the rest of the personnel. In general, they are young doctors, but old prisoners in Auschwitz.

They console me. Zenkteller has always been, and will always be, the same. The best way is to watch him carefully and, when possible, to get out of his sight. All of them have had difficulties with him.

They talk about the past almost taking pleasure in relating the horrible descriptions of what occurred in Auschwitz. During 1941 and 1942, the count was five hundred corpses a day. The bestiality of the SS men, the beatings, tortures, dirt, lice, typhus, gas, cold, hunger, lack of clothes, roll calls in freezing temperatures lasting eight to ten hours, took a heavy toll.

"We were forced to stand in the basic position. 'Caps off! No moving!' Like wild beasts, the SS men ran between the lines wielding iron pipes. If anyone moved, he was immediately felled with a crushed skull. The prisoners went insane from despair. In the morning when the electric current in the wires surrounding the camp was shut off, special *Kommandos* removed the bodies. At that time, doctors also went on *Kommando* and worked as ordinary prisoners."

Hundreds of people died before their very eyes, doctors among them. They were helpless, unable to aid their colleagues. They were fearful for their own lives. They have been in Barrack XII for only half a year.

For their first few weeks in Barrack XII, their work consisted mainly of carrying corpses. The chain of command was such that, when a *Häftling* was killed on *Kommando,* the SS men notified the *Blockführerstube*; the SS guard there notified Barrack XII. Then two medics carrying a stretcher would run, sometimes for two kilometers, to get the body. Very often they collected several corpses. The medics would carry these heavy loads running all the way with an SS man on a bicycle, chasing them. If he was kind, he would allow them to rest for a while, but if he was cruel—and that was the rule, he killed the medics. In this way, more than five hundred doctors and three hundred other health-related personnel perished in one year. To be a medic meant to live a few days more at best and sometimes only for a few hours longer.

I listen to their tragic accounts and am almost indifferent. It is well that the candle flickers out and they do not see the expression on my face. Even those stories cannot move me after what I have been through in the Warsaw Ghetto: hunger, disease, constant fear, the Umschlagplatz, deportations, the transport to Treblinka. Here is death; there was death. Here is suffering; there there was suffering. Here are the beastly Germans; there they were also.

I tell them about a January 1943 deportation, a story in which I happened to be the hero.

". . . One night as we lay in our beds, we suddenly hear a commotion in the hospital yard: boots tapping, weapons clanking, Germans shouting, and we see searchlights. We're panicky. Nobody expected it.

"My uncle, the hospital administrator, is in bed with a severe cough and a temperature of 40° (104°). He probably has pneumonia. Someone bangs on the door. It is the doorman. His whole body is trembling; all he can say is 'Deportation!' The hospital is surrounded. Yesterday the director went to the Aryan side to see his little girl and he isn't back yet. One of the higher ranking personnel must face the Germans, otherwise everyone will be killed. They give us five minutes.

"All of us in the house are fearful and quiver like a leaf in the wind. My uncle wants to dress. I pity the man and decide that I will go down.

"Fredzia throws herself at me, 'Tadzek! You won't go! They'll kill you!!'

"Kindly but firmly, I push her away and order everyone to go next door to Dr. Kaiser's apartment where there's a hiding place. I go downstairs alone.

"Several SS men are in the yard. I report to the officer; he looks at his watch. They are enraged and demand, 'Where's the head doctor?! Where are all the medical and nursing personnel hiding?!'

"I must tell them something or else they will blow up the entire place. I let them know that only the director and administrator live on the hospital grounds. The doctors and nurses are housed on the next street. At night, only the doctor on call and the night service are here.

"Seemingly satisfied with my answer, they give me five minutes to organize the personnel, bring out the sick patients and put them in the truck and cars in front of the hospital.

"I blow the special signal on my whistle: Men rush down! Within a few minutes, several nurses and doctors appear on the street. Speaking German, I repeat the SS men's orders, 'All the sick must be loaded in the cars and trucks!' In a low voice I add in Polish, 'Bring only the very sick. Hide the healthier and convalescent. Move quietly! No noise!'

"The SS men ask how many patients there are in the hospital. I'm unprepared to answer this question and say, 'I don't remember.' I receive several smacks in the face.

"Meanwhile Dantesque scenes occur in the hospital wards. Women go insane with fear, affecting the men. It's a hopeless tumult as people run to and fro like caged animals instead of listening to the nurses' instructions. Driven by this maddening fright, they run pell-mell down the stairs and literally fall into the hands of the SS men who chase them like cattle to the trucks.

"By the glare of the searchlights, I see the satisfied faces of the beastly SS men who think that so much noise is caused by the nurses beating and chasing the people downstairs.

"Several jump from windows; they don't get up. Only one silhouette is still crawling carefully toward the cellar. An SS man notices him and shows his companion the desperate figure. Both pull their revolvers from their holsters and shoot once, twice. After the second shot, we hear a scream; the figure no longer moves.

"I suffer through another hour of terrible tension. I think of Fredzia and the other inhabitants of the house. In my mind I curse the stupidity of people who expose themselves unnecessarily and fall victims.

"One of the officers yells to the chief of the transport, an SS man, 'How many Jews have we loaded?'

"'Three hundred twenty,' he replies.

"My heart beats wildly. There are about five hundred sick people in the hospital. So, some of them did hide. I think this is the end of the ordeal.

"Unfortunately, the officer asks me, 'Are you absolutely sure none of the sick are left?!'

"I'm not sure, but I take the risk and answer, 'Yes, no one is left.'

"Carrying flashlights, they surround me. We ascend the main staircase.

"Our hospital occupies a building that had been used to store tailors' supplies. We remodeled it and converted it into a hospital. Starting on the first floor, we enter the big rooms, look into the closets and the kitchen. Luckily no one is there. The same thing happens on the second and third floors. I feel a bit calmer.

"As we climb up to the fourth floor, I remember that there's a small operating room up there that is reserved for those

Jews who work outside the Ghetto. They are housed there also. Only severe cases that can't be handled on the spot in the Aryan sector are brought there. The Germans had ordered that those patients be separated from the others. On this ward are six men and two women, all fractures, lying in traction. My heart beats wildly. What could have happened to them? They cannot move and are at the mercy of others. We're already at the top. It is quiet and empty. We enter one ward and then the other. Nobody is there. There are two corpses in beds. We go back through the corridor to the staircase. I orient myself by the small blue light and notice that the medics have blocked the door leading to the fracture ward with closets full of dirty laundry. Next to these lie several smelly bedpans.

"We are on the stairs. I want to breathe deeply and heave a sign of relief when . . . a big boom, like an artillery shot, resounds through the empty building. The SS men pull out their revolvers and go back. They look around with their searchlights. Aha! They see it!

"They push away a closet and open the door. One of them turns on the light. In the beds are six young boys. A brick fell from one boy's traction apparatus, thus revealing the hiding place. Their faces display their terrible fear as they lie in their beds as though they are paralyzed. Women are sobbing behind a curtain. They know that their hiding place has been discovered.

"The SS men rub their hands with satisfaction. In low voices, they consult among themselves, then they ask me aloud, 'You're a doctor, is that true? Tell us if these people are able to work!'

"I guess what they're driving at and answer very carefully, 'Right now they cannot perform because they have broken bones, but they're basically healthy. In about two weeks, they'll be ready to return to work.'

"The SS men shake their heads 'sympathetically'. 'Tell them that the ones who can't work have no right to live, but those who can go downstairs unassisted we'll let live!'

"I don't have to translate. All of them understand German. The youngest, a sixteen year old boy, tries to move, but I notice that the slightest movement causes him unbearable pain. The others try but quickly give up.

"The SS brute takes out his revolver and approaches the first boy. The boy's eyes open wide in deadly fear. He stretches his hands in front of him. He wants to cry, but he cannot get a sound out of his throat. He wants to beg and holds his hands before him as if in prayer. At that moment a shot rings out. He gets a bullet between his eyes.

"Next. . . . The game lasts a long time. The SS torturers are in no hurry. They delight in human suffering and think it's funny that Jews are afraid to die. 'Papa and Mama are waiting in heaven!' say the Germans, trying to use the few Jewish words they know.

"There is a scream and the sound of breaking glass in the women's section. One of the patients with an orthopedic nail in her leg is attached to a heavy weight for traction. With superhuman effort, she had dragged herself to the window and broke the pane, but she cannot raise herself. The other is losing her senses and is only able to emit a long animal-like cry.

"I stand transfixed like a statue, unable to move. Two shots. Now it's my turn.

"One SS man says, 'You fooled us!' He repeats emphatically, 'You fooled SS men! I warned you that this means death! But because you are brave and wanted to save your brothers, we'll give you a choice: Treblinka or a bullet?'

"I decide quickly. 'A bullet!' I answer and think that Fredzia will know how and where I died. The Germans nod their heads in recognition. They will shoot me in the yard.

"'March!'

"We go downstairs slowly. Two SS men are behind me and one is in front lighting the way with a flashlight.

"I don't panic. After a minute of resignation, I force my mind to work intensely. How can I save myself? The situation appears hopeless. Suddenly, I have an idea. Like lightning, it illuminates my mind. Feverishly I make my plans.

"The stairs lead to the street level where there's a small corridor and a door to the yard. In the corridor, there is also a staircase that leads to an enormous cellar. It connects with the basements of the nearby buildings. We had begun erecting bunkers there and, in the process, we removed those stairs.

"I know what to do now. I walk slowly and quietly, measuring my steps in order not to betray the fact that I have plans to resist. From time to time I breathe deeply and emit long sighs.

"'Are you afraid, *mensch*?'

"'Oh yes!' I reply sadly.

"Now for the last few steps. . . . I tighten my muscles. Suddenly I push the SS man in front of me—the one with the flashlight, then turn around, and jump into the cellar. I'm bruised but, despite the pain, I run deeper among the ruins. I crawl from one cellar to another, first to the right and then to the left. I hear two powerful explosions behind me, but I'm safe now.

"I go home the next day. The deportation continues. Luckily, Fredzia and the others are safe in the hideout. When they see me, tears well up in their eyes. They thought that I had been killed."

At the end of my story, everyone is silent. Someone treats me to a cigarette. In a while, someone else proposes that we go to sleep. Tomorrow is another workday.

* * *

It is my first night in a bed. I have two blankets and I sleep alone. There are no vermin to bother me. It is paradise. My joy is clouded by an uneasy feeling: I keep seeing Zenkteller. I console myself with the thought that maybe it will work somehow if I try to avoid him. From the next bed, I hear Szymek's contented whisper, "Good night." He does not have my worries.

"Beginnings are always hard." That oft heard phrase comes to my mind. The next day I am angry. Will I always be a novice on whom they will unload the heaviest work?

I barely manage to bring the coffee with Szymek when I already have been assigned to worse jobs: to remove and scrub the bedpans; deposit lime in the barrel used by the less seriously ill to satisfy their physiological needs; make the beds of the severely ill; clean and scrub the floor (I crawl underneath beds again!); bring the bread; again the bedpans; noon meal . . .

On the way for the food, I remember that I have not had breakfast this morning. It is true that I finished my piece of bread last night so that I would not have had anything with my coffee anyway. But even the coffee alone would have been something. Two or three cups would fill my stomach and, for a short time, help me forget my hunger. My intestines growl.

We stand in front of the kitchen and hear that we have "potato peel soup and vegetables" today. With shining eyes, the Yugoslav says, "Today it's excellent. There are potatoes. We'll organize something later."

At first I do not understand what it is all about. Szymek is more astute. He looks critically at me as he says, "Why do you talk so much? You'll soon find out."

We load the barrels of soup and pail of potatoes on the cart and pull it a distance from the kitchen. The Yugoslav warns, looking in all directions, "Watch for Zenkteller!"

He grabs about ten potatoes from the pail and puts them in his pocket. The Frenchman does the same, and Szymek follows. My heart beats like a trip hammer when I decide to "organize"—this is the euphemistic word in the camp for getting something desirable—a few potatoes.

I put them in the pocket of my pants. The potatoes are very hot, and they burn. To justify himself and us, the Yugoslav says, "Other medics organize from the patients on the ward and from the clinic. They receive gifts from all sides and have enough to eat. We must help ourselves, otherwise we'll croak."

For the noon meal we get five potatoes and half a liter of soup. I am so hungry that I swallow the potatoes with the peels. The soup has a terrible taste and stinks from far away.

Each of our foursome has his benefactor among the older doctors. I have three saviors: Zbyszek, Dr. Herman, and Dr. Kleinberg who is from Kielce. When the dressing room doors open and we enter, I get fifteen potatoes and a full dish of soup. I breathe easier and plan to have my soup for dinner and to hide the potatoes and bread for tomorrow. Very carefully, I store all of these, together with the "organized" potatoes, in my bed.

An uproar erupts at the other end of the ward. The *Stubendienst* is beating a patient, a Greek who, as the *Stubendienst* explains later, suffers from a "wolfish" hunger. The victim swallows every spoonful of soup that the seriously ill leave, all the potato peels, and even gulps down the rotten, stinking potatoes that are fit only for the garbage pail. This time he was being beaten because he had dug a piece of completely moldy bread from the garbage and was consuming it with great relish. The bread was in a package that a Pole had just received. During the several weeks it had taken to arrive, the bread had become so moldy that the recipient threw it away.

The Greek sits on a stool and sobs, not because the whipping hurts, but because he regrets losing the bread. I look at him with disgust and anger.

The *Stubendienst* announces, "Bed rest!", but not for us. Now it is time to wash the dishes and cauldrons. I wash; Szymek dries; the Frenchman changes the water, and the Yugoslav puts the dishes away.

After the work is done, we sit on the stools next to the table and support our heads on our hands to rest awhile. Suddenly I hear sounds near the door. Zenkteller!!!

"Are you sleeping, you lazy bums?!" "I'll find some work for you!" he shouts, shaking his head.

I cannot restrain my anger, but his words make no impression on the others. They do not try to object. They are resigned to the fact that Zenkteller is always right, and we must listen humbly even to his most unjust accusations without saying a word.

We are curious to know what kind of work our chief will find for us. We have not long to wait. Szymek and I must load all the dirty clothes, laundry, and blankets on a cart and take them to be disinfected. There are so many of these smelly rags that we have to make three trips. The Frenchman and Yugoslav have a shorter but worse job. They must empty the barrel of shit. Brrrrrr!

As we load the material on the cart, the other two pass by with the barrel and tell us to look through the pockets before we load. Sometimes valuables are found.

The fellows are right. We find six pairs of scissors, several spoons, a few pieces of soap, some leather strips, and two mirrors. I share the loot with Szymek. We work hard all afternoon, but we are amply rewarded. I pray to God that I may have a few minutes tonight to run to Barrack 20 with these treasures for Pinek. He will make the best deal.

After roll call, I work like a machine in the clinic. Even Zenkteller, who watches me carefully, does not scold me. Fifteen minutes before the evening gong, with only a few patients in the clinic, I use the pretext of having to go to the latrine to escape from the ward and rush to Barrack 20.

I am lucky. Pinek is outside cleaning his muddy clothes. We hug. After telling him about the events of the past few days, I hand him the trophies and say, "Pinek, try to sell them for as much as possible. We'll share."

"Don't worry, Tadzek. Tomorrow night we'll have something to eat," Pinek says happily.

I fall asleep and dream of a slice of bread and a piece of sausage. I am fine, satiated with soup and potatoes. The thought that I will not go hungry until noontime instills confidence in me.

I can hardly wait until evening. I am not even worried that the noon meal was potato peels and that I did not get more than half a liter of additional soup from my friends.

After the noon meal, Zenkteller catches the Greek looking for rotten potatoes and crumbs of food near the garbage. The Old One is furious. He beats the *Stubendienst* about the face and scolds us, "Why don't you have eyes in the back of your heads? . . ." Menace, menace . . .

Before roll call, there is another adventure with Zenkteller. Fortunately, it does not involve our foursome. The chief caught some *Häftling* who came to visit a friend. Zenkteller threw him out by the scruff of his neck. The poor

Stubendienst got fifteen lashes in front of everyone on the ward.

After meting out the punishment, Zenkteller declares that it is our duty to see to it that no one from another barrack comes into the ward. We have the right to throw anyone out. If he catches us not fulfilling this order, we will be ousted.

We have much work at night: wounds, bruises, scratches, and fractured jaws, noses, and collar bones. We cannot keep up with the work load. It looks like the aftermath of a war or, rather, of a pogrom. The *Häftlinge* refuse to say how it happened or how they were hurt. All have the same answer, "On *Kommando*." It is enough to look them in the eye and fathom the deadly fear to understand everything.

I am so nervous that I cannot sleep but toss from side to side. I tell myself that, in the morning immediately after the coffee, I must run to Pinek. I catch myself with an alarmist thought: I am not so worried about him as I am that he might have lost all the supplies during the beating. I feel that I am blushing and am ashamed of myself.

In the morning, I tell the fellows my trepidations. Today all four of us must go for coffee and bring an additional cauldron of soup for the sick.

"You run to the barrack. We'll manage by ourselves," says the Frenchman.

Pinek is standing near the wires looking around. "You're here at last, Tadzek!" He calls his father. They hand me four portions of bread and three pieces of sausage. I want to share it with them, but they laugh. In the transaction, they received half a loaf of bread, a portion of cheese and then exchanged them for cigarettes. Today they will go to the women's section where they will exchange the cigarettes for bread and bring back a whole loaf because cigarettes are worth more among the women.

My head is whirling from all of this, and I wish them luck. Pinek begs me to try another transport. Perhaps they can sell it for even more.

Szymek looks at me wide-eyed as I hide the bread in my bed. "Where did you get all that, pal?"

When I tell him, he wants to give me all his treasures to sell. I tell him that I will attend to it in the evening, meanwhile we will share the bread and sausage.

Breakfast is over; the fellows are sweeping the yard. I am washing the barrack door when I notice a man in a striped uniform entering through the dressing room. The *Stubendienst* is not here. With a cleaning rag in my hand, I go over and demand that he leave immediately. He looks at me with disdain and says nothing. I yell at him. The newcomer retreats half a step and hits me on my chin with his fist. The blow is so powerful that, in spite of the daylight, I see stars, get dizzy, and fall.

When I come to, I see the character in stripes standing near a bed visiting quietly with a patient. At that moment Zenkteller enters. I rise with some difficulty and report the incident to him.

The fellow in the striped uniform turns around, listens to my accusations, greets the Old One and says, "Do you have any more idiots like this one? Isn't it funny?" Both laugh heartily.

I did not know that the newcomer was the *Lagerältester*'s lover. Obviously, all the trouble must be my fault.

This incident is cause for much laughter. In every barrack they tell the story of a *muzelman* medic who jumped on a "Mr. Paramour" and wanted to throw him out of the ward. Even Zenkteller is amused and, when he passes me, deigns to smile.

As the days pass, I feel that I am losing my humanity and am becoming a robot without a soul, just a machine. "Nurse, pass me the bedpan. Nurse, straighten out my bed. Nurse, give me coffee. Nurse, take the bedpan away." The upper echelon, who comprise the major part of the barrack, have no consideration for me. They do not let me rest for a minute. Then, of course, there are the usual chores: washing, scrubbing, coffee, bread, noon meal, dishes, and clinic.

When night comes, I feel weak and collapse on my bed. I hear fragments of conversations: Schillinger's latest abuses, other SS men's brutalities, the transport of Jews to the gas chamber. My brain stops registering this information. Slowly everything becomes a matter of indifference to me. One thought persists day and night, asleep or awake: food! Food! I am too tired to run to Pinek after work, and what I receive from my friends is not enough.

The Frenchman manages to get along. He found several acquaintances from Paris who were interned in Auschwitz for the past two years and work in *Kanada.*

Kanada is a gold-procuring *Kommando.* To get in, you need a great deal of influence or many gold dollars. *Kanada* works on the station ramp receiving the incoming transports, sorting the luggage, and cleaning the freight cars.

The Jews, who come from every corner of Europe, bring to Auschwitz their wealth, their most valuable possessions in their luggage and packages. They are convinced that they are going to a work camp and will need all of this. The Germans try to foster this belief. Why should they expose themselves to the eventual revolt of despairing people?

"You're going to work! But before that, you must take a bath and get deloused!" The method is the same as the one employed in Treblinka.

There is a market in camp: gold for soup and bread, champagne for shoes and a good place in a bunk. Little by little it becomes clear to me that those in *Kanada* smuggle foodstuffs and many valuable objects into camp. Now I understand where the watches and gold, dollars and diamonds, chocolate, sardines, champagne, and even goose liver come from. Some *Häftlinge* dream of getting into *Kanada* while others do not think about it much. I think of it with horror. It is true that *Kanada* has nothing in common with the *Sonderkommando.* They do not gas or burn people, but in spite of it all. . . .

One night the Frenchman brings a can of condensed milk and pours the thick sweet milk on his bread. I see it out of the corner of my eye, and my saliva runs. Lucky he, I think. A few minutes later I need to go to the latrine and relieve myself outside. From the nearby crematoria, flames shoot from the chimneys. The milk that the Frenchman is drinking belonged to those being burned.

A chill courses through my entire body. I am not envious about the milk. It would not have passed my throat anyway.

The day is nearing when we will be transferred to a new camp where I hope that I will be far away from Zenkteller. Every day several barracks are emptied and the people are moved to "palaces" in other places, other bits of earth encircled by electrified wires. In the meantime, we remain in Barrack XII. We will be the last to leave.

Every day after roll call, a small group of medics goes to the new camp to help out for two hours. It reminds me of Maidanek. The *Blockführerstube* is near the gate. On the other side of the wires is a green lawn flanked on both sides by two large kitchen barracks. A wide road extends through the camp with rows of barracks lining both sides. Each section is comprised of thirty-two barracks.

Much work is still necessary in the new camp. The *Kommandos* work feverishly bringing bunks into the barracks, digging ditches, laying drainage pipes, and planting. In the midst of this terrible chaos, *Kapos,* SS men, and foremen run around yelling and beating.

I carry a bag of instruments and look around. Maybe I will find a familiar face.

Somebody calls my name. I do not recognize him and look closer. Oh God, it is Pinek! He has changed unbelievably. He looks like a skeleton; his eyes are sunken; his cheekbones jut out giving him a peculiar, almost macabre appearance.

"I'm holding out, but not for long, I'm afraid. My father, please help him! He's waiting for the clinic to open."

I want to find out to which barrack he has been assigned, but a *Lagerkapo* is approaching with a big club. Pinek runs away.

We enter an empty barrack. After organizing a few stools, we lay out our things. I notice Pinek's father among the several hundred *Häftlinge* standing out front. A few are lying down exhibiting no visible signs of life. SS men and *Blockältesters* push through the crowd to maintain "order".

We start treating patients. I look at the poor souls one by one making the dressings as well as I can, but I realize that a paper bandage will not last long. My heart bleeds when I see the horrible wounds and sores. They are even worse than the ones I treated in the old camp.

Not long ago I looked like that. Now I am the doctor on whose conscience and resourcefulness depend the lives of many people. I too have lived through similarly tragic experiences and can well understand the plight of these poor people. I want to help them with all my soul. It is good that Zenkteller is not here. He is packing his treasures.

There is some commotion in front of the barrack. The *Häftlinge* remove their caps. Dr. Wortman hisses to us, "Attention, fellows! Schillinger!"

Through the open door I notice Schillinger in the company of a *Lagerkapo.* He stops in front of the clinic and looks at the waiting patients. The *Lagerkapo* explains to the SS man that those are the sick ones. Schillinger goes down the lines asking the patients to show him their wounds. He pulls out sixteen of them, lines them up on one side, and orders them to be watched. Then he enters the barrack and is greeted with a loud "Attention!".

Dr. Wortman reports, "Outpatient clinic at work!"

Schillinger waves his hand and laughs cynically, "I'm making your work easier. I've taken sixteen *muzelmen* out of this stinking crowd. Their sores are too smelly, and they would have taken up too much of your time. I'll take care of them myself." With these words he departs.

Dr. Wortman pales and stands motionless. He even forgets to shout "Attention!" Finally controlling himself, he breathes deeply and says with a sad voice, "Keep working, fellows."

I do not see Pinek's father. We finish our labors late at night and wrap our instruments. It is long after the gong has sounded, but work continues in the camp. The *Häftlinge* pay for the overtime with their lives.

When I return to the new camp several days later, I meet Pinek. In his eyes I see infinite despair.

"Tadzek! My father is dead. Schillinger killed him! He was among the sixteen he selected." One single tear runs down his blackened, emaciated face.

That evening when I return to Barrack XII, I learn that our fate will be decided tomorrow. Part of the personnel will go to several barracks which will serve as a hospital in Section F. The other group will be sent to Section D to work in an outpatient clinic. Where Zenkteller will go is unknown.

I share my thoughts with Szymek. He looks at me with a surprised expression and says, "Only yesterday you claimed that life is indifferent to you and that you would gladly die. Now you're interested to know if you'll still be under Zenkteller. There's a screw loose in your head."

Yes, Szymek is right. My thoughts are clouded, and I experience resignation, pity, vengeance, and a very great longing for what has passed and what will never be.

The next morning, the last group of *Häftlinge* leaves the old barracks in Birkenau. They will enter the new camp at night. The medics are divided among the empty barracks with orders to disinfect them. Every one of us has a pail of powdered white lime to sprinkle on the bunks and floor. As we work, we are attacked by ferocious fleas despite the thick protective layer of "Kuprex" and "Flit" that we spread on our bodies. In a few minutes we are ravenously bitten by the small vampires.

Zbyszek Szawlowski curses loudly. He calls Zenkteller an orangutan and says that all this work is for nothing. We finish late at night and have no place to sleep, for, while we were working, other medics took our beds and blankets.

Zbyszek has an idea to enliven our terribly sad life this last day in Barrack XII: to organize a talent show. Each of us will sing or present a monologue. The repertoire is truly outstanding. The performing artists, all amateurs, represent seven or eight nationalities. But the artistic evening ends abruptly. Zenkteller comes into the ward. He deals out several blows with his fists. He curses, scolds, calls us idiots and sons-of-bitches and. . . . Unfortunately, we must stop. What a pity! It was so nice.

After the morning gong, we load everything on the carts and take off. Szymek, the Frenchman, the Yugoslav, the dentist Aleks Baranek, Dr. Wortman, Dr. Reichmann, and I are going to Barrack 31 in Section D. The others are assigned to Section F. As our rotten luck would have it, Zenkteller comes with us.

Barrack 31 is not finished. Its walls and ceiling are constructed of rough-hewn, unpainted boards; the floor of tamped earth. Our new *Blockältester,* Modarski, is an optimist who states that, in a few days, we will fix our new barrack so that it will surpass Barrack XII.

It is a herculean task. We paint, clean, build, lay bricks and do carpentry. In general, Modarski is a good fellow but a little crazy. He has an obsession about his new barrack. He, himself, works like a bull but also demands much from us. As usual, the whole burden of the labor is on our foursome. We must carry hundreds of pails of water every day and run with the *Blockältester* to the depot for cement. Everything is done "in tempo". The *Blockältester* is nervous, and from time to time he beats us.

In the evening, I overhear the *Blockältester* talking with Zenkteller, "These new doctors are good-for-nothing. They work badly, especially the tall, skinny one."

This tall, skinny one is me. I truly work harder than anyone else, but what can I do? If, after two hours of running with cement, I sit down for a minute, the *Blockältester* sees me and shouts, "You're sitting?! You aren't doing your job! The others work like bulls!!"

Excuses do not help. The *Blockältester* does not want to hear them; he knows better. This is my rotten luck. I know very well that my only chance to survive is to work in the clinic. I realize very clearly that I would not last too long on a *Kommando* and that I would be consigned to the gas chamber without a rest? Do you know that I receive no packages from anyone? I don't organize; I live on a piece of bread and

"At the first opportunity, I'll throw him out head over heels!" says Zenkteller.

My throat constricts. I want to come out of my hiding place and scream in a loud voice, "It's unjust! It's unjust! I'm working more than my strength can bear. Do you know what tortures I go through to carry cement for two kilometers without a rest? Do you know that I receive no packages from anyone? I don't organize; I'm live in a piece of bread and soup. I don't eat as much as you do, you bastards! Do you know that my heart is failing?!"

I am helpless. A minute later I want to cry and beg for pity. Broken, I swallow my tears and return to my interrupted work. I can see Pinek's terribly emaciated figure and his infinitely sad eyes before me. Then I picture myself as I was in Maidanek, a skeleton whose body is ravaged with sores, a *gamel*, a *muzelman*, a rag ready for the gas chamber. And now I overhear some "excellent" prospects. Never! I clench my teeth. I make a firm resolve. I will fight for my life, for the right to avenge Fredzia, my father, and the millions of others. I will not stop fighting even if Zenkteller throws me out and sends me on *Kommando*.

* * *

From our blood and toil the new Barrack XII rises, this time redesignated as Barrack 31, the outpatient clinic of Labor Section D. The floor is made of cement. Everything is painted white in the barrack including the stone hearth. In the treatment room, the walls are gray and the ceiling, white. A screen of boards separates the outpatient clinic from the sick ward. This last is also separated from the dressing room.

I have the dubious honor to scrub the room in which Zenkteller and the *Blockältester* will live. I rush to work. Even Zenkteller notices it and remarks, "Maybe you'll amount to something after all, you idiot!"

Because our supervisors do not eat the *Häftlinge*'s food, we are getting a little more soup, three liters at noon and an extra dish in the evening. The four of us have enough to eat and we can save the bread for breakfast. As a result, I slowly become aware of camp life and begin to take an interest in what is going on.

Barrack 11 is the *Strafkommando,* the punitive barrack. A simple *Häftling* can survive there for only two to four days. If he is very lucky, he may live a bit longer. The S.K. has earned its well-deserved infamy. In the old S.K. barrack, the count was one hundred corpses a day. Of them, twenty-five fell under the blows of the barrack personnel who were *Reichdeutsche* brutes.

Almost any infraction is reason enough to be sent to S.K., for example, resting a minute during work, having a pair of scissors, organizing cigarettes, and, sometimes, even quite innocently. Our masters have to kill from time to time to adjust the number of inmates.

Next to the 11th barrack is the 13th; the *Sonderkommando* live there. Both are separated from the rest of the camp by a high wall. Only Jewish *Häftlinge* comprise the *Sonderkommando.* Against their will they are chosen for this monstrous job. When new recruits are needed, the order, "Jews come forward!" is generally announced after roll call. Then the *Arbeitseinsatz* and an SS man select the strongest people. All they are told is, "You're going to work."

They go to the bath and from there they enter the *Sonderkommando* barrack. Despairing does not help. Their only recourse is to commit suicide; many choose to escape that way. From the moment that they start working, they are doomed because, at certain intervals, they are liquidated.

"You're going to a different camp to work!" The former *Sonderkommando* are taken for a short ride—usually only a few kilometers—in freight cars that stop in the middle of a field where a company of SS men wait for them. There are a few screams and hopeless attempts at revolt, but a few salvos from machine guns and . . . the still warm, bloody bodies are thrown on trucks that return to one of Birkenau's crematoria where the newly selected *Sonderkommando* burn the bodies of their former comrades.

It is clear that the SS do not hesitate to use the most horrible and repressive measures to keep the secret of those death factories from reaching beyond their walls, but, despite all of their precautions, detailed accounts of the gas chambers reach the camp. These stories chill the souls of those who still live. . . .

* * *

We begin to hope that they may leave us alone. Maybe the hellish vision of the gas chamber embedded in our consciousness and subconsciousness will be replaced by the hope that, perhaps, they will start to be more considerate of the Jews.

We talk about it during the noon meal. Even the perennial pessimist, Aleks, has noticed that the chimneys have not spewed smoke for four days and that *Kanada* has been idle. Maybe . . .

All of our hopes are dashed. A few hours later there is a great deal of activity in the camp. *Kanada* goes to the ramp and the *Sonderkommando,* to work.

Two new transports of Jews arrive, three thousand from France and thirty five hundred from Sosnowiec. From these two transports, five hundred reach the camp. At a dizzying pace, big brown freight cars bring the human flesh to the gates of the gas chamber. The orchestra plays lively music in front of the *Blockführerstube.* During the night, flames shoot high from all six chimneys. Chocolates and French cigarettes appear in the barracks.

"To hell with it!" Dr. Wortman curses. Szymek congratulates Aleks for his "accurate" prediction.

* * *

In the evening Pinek is among a crowd of patients. Pushing himself toward me with his last ounce of strength, he asks if he can go to the hospital and, if he did, would he be gassed for that? I have no information about Section F and ask him to return the following day.

Pinek is not complaining; he is not lamenting. He states very calmly that his time to die has come. What meaning does life have when parents and siblings are gone? Even if a miracle happens, what will salvation be worth if one is always alone, alone until the end of one's life? He has only one fear. He is afraid of suffering in the gas chamber.

In the morning Zenkteller calls me, "You! I wanted to throw you out a long time ago, but lately you've improved. You're lucky. Starting tomorrow, you'll have additional duties. You'll be an attendant on the sick ward. Your chief will be Dr. Bejlin. You'll have to clean and scrub the floor, distribute the meal, and wash the dishes. The ward must be maintained in exemplary order. If I catch you committing the smallest deviation, you'll be kicked out!"

Everyone congratulates me for this honor. I still do not know whether I should rejoice or worry. Aleks takes me aside and whispers in my ear, "Don't be a fool! All the prominent characters will be in your section. They receive good packages from home. If you're clever, you won't suffer from hunger!"

In spite of the excellent prospects, I realize that, in the end, it would have been much better for me to work in the clinic, especially since Bejlin, to whom I am assigned, maintains that Zenkteller wants to finish him off. Now, since he is to be responsible for the sick ward, Zenkteller will always find a reason to criticize him. Bejlin is an old *Häftling* and Zenkteller cannot do away with him as easily as, for instance, me.

The *Blockältester* hands me several blankets and sheets with which to prepare beds. Bejlin enters the ward with me and shows me the ones I must make.

There is a small space with a table and two stools on one side of the ward between the beds. We sit down there while Bejlin, in a loud voice, instructs me in my duties.

Then he adds, whispering, "What I just told you loudly is for the benefit of the Old One. He has a habit of spying. Yes, it's a pity that Zenkteller is with us. He won't give us a minute's peace but will bother us at every turn. I've been with him in the old number XII and have known him for almost half a year. Once he accused me of not being able to diagnose pneumonia. I was of the opinion that it was typhus. Then after a week, the spots emerged. I don't know why, but from that time on he has hated me. He'd have sent me to the S.K. long ago, but I have many friends among the old *Häftlinge* in the camp. Unfortunately I can't help you. We're both marked by the Old One. I hope I prove to be a false prophet for I have the impression that neither of us will last long here."

His voice changes; he almost yells. I look at him as though

he were crazy. A minute later I understand. Zenkteller had sneaked into the ward as silently as a cat and is now addressing Bejlin.

"Did you give him instructions?! Everything must be ready! Tomorrow morning the patients will be here!"

At about noontime, the *Blockältester* sends me to Section F to bring the patients' charts from the other *Scheibstube*. It is the first time that I can venture outside of my section alone. My heart beats rapidly when I stand in the basic position before the *Blockführer* to report, "*Häftling* 126604 is leaving the camp."

It is not far to Section F. I walk slowly and look around. Birkenau is an immense camp, a mammoth one occupying the area of a big town. It has its own wheat and potato fields in which selected *Häftlinge* work. It is like a large rural enterprise and is well supplied with livestock and machinery. Birkenau is an almost self-sufficient camp. On the horizon I see the towers that form part of the outer chain of guard lookout posts just beyond the camp's limits. At night after the roll call when all the *Kommandos* have returned from work, the SS men leave the outer chain and man those set twenty-five meters apart next to the wires surrounding the individual sections. As soon as a *Häftling*'s escape is discovered, the SS occupy the outer chain and remain there for several days.

I can see only a small part of the camp. Thousands of *Häftlinge* work by the sweat of their brows tilling the soil and digging ditches.

Trucks are delivering boards for the construction of a third immense camp of several sections in Birkenau. This is Project Birkenau III. Maybe they want to imprison all of Europe in Auschwitz.

About twenty meters in front of me is a little shabby forest. Scrubby pine trees partially conceal the third and fourth crematoria. In front of each one is a square with several powerful searchlights set on high poles enabling the SS and *Sonderkommando* to process the transports at night. The buildings themselves have small windows and heavy doors.

A shed adjoins the main structure. These form the surface part of the gas chamber. In spite of the thick walls, the screams of the gassed can be heard from there.

I must finish my short walk and reconnoiter. In front of the *Blockführerstube* for Section F, I give the official password, "*Häftling* 126604 entering the camp."

I notice that everything is still being organized. Of the three rows of barracks, two of the smaller ones have windows, but those in the third row are like stables with bunks instead of individual beds. In the rear is the washroom with baths and toilets.

I meet Dr. Herman in the *Schreibstube* and tell him of my fate. "You'll manage somehow," he consoles me, "but you must try, at all cost, to stay there. The camp is . . . you know as well as I."

I remember my conversation with Pinek and tell him that I have a very close friend who is in a terrible state and wants to go to the hospital. "Is there any danger he'll end up in the gas chamber?"

Dr. Herman breathes heavily before he replies, "Unfortunately Tadzek, not only is there a danger, but it is a certainty. There is a special barrack for the Jews. Anyway, let's go. You'll see for yourself."

I have witnessed many horrible things in the camp, for instance, Barracks 7 and 8 in old Birkenau. But what I see now is appalling. It takes me a quarter of an hour in the fresh air to regain control of myself.

Filthy human skeletons lie crowded on the bare boards of the bunks. The stink is unbearable. As two German *Stubendiensts* pick dirt from the floor, they curse and hit the patients. Dr. Herman explains that all the diarrhea cases are sent to the Jewish barrack. This fearful camp disease finishes off even the strongest in a few days. Among the diarrhea cases are Aryans whom Zenkteller considers hopeless and, as such, are sent to the Jewish barrack for certain death.

"Yesterday they sent everyone to the gas chamber and today the place is full again!" complains one of the *Stubendiensts*.

A question comes to my mind, "Why the hell do they need

a hospital for the Jews if, after a few days, they take them to the gas chamber?"

Even Dr. Herman has no answer. Who can understand German logic?

When we are at the door, Dr. Herman tells me to turn around and observe the scene. The *Stubendiensts* are piling more skeletons on a blanket and, with one swing, throw the dead and dying on the top bunk where there already is an accumulation of corpses.

Noticing my state, Dr. Herman tries to comfort me. "Listen," he says, "if you want to hold out, you must get used to these sights." He changes the subject suddenly. "Have you seen the mountains?" indicating the direction with his hand.

On the horizon the Carpathian chain is illuminated by the bright sun. My heart beats wildly. MOUNTAINS! FREEDOM!!

The heat is almost unbearable. The SS men are in front of the *Blockführerstube* sunning themselves. The radio blares gay melodies through the open window. From one section come shouts, "Move! Move faster! Faster!" "How 'beautiful' is the world," I think as I repeat the required words, "*Häftling* 126604 leaving camp."

There is much activity in Section D. The *Häftlinge* dig ditches for the drainage canal system. Others are planting. The clay ground makes the task even more difficult. One group of prisoners carries railroad tracks. Others push empty wagons. The *Lagerkapo* runs around peering as intently as a hawk to see if anyone is not doing his job. Suddenly from behind a certain barrack come screams and sounds of a whipping. A minute later, some foreman drags a *Häftling* by the collar toward the *Lagerkapo*. Oh God, it is Pinek!

"*Lagerkapo*! This pig was relieving himself behind the barrack!"

The *Lagerkapo*'s facial expression changes completely. His face is red and his eyes almost pop out of their orbits. He throws down his whip, picks up a shovel handle, and approaches Pinek. Pinek explains that he has diarrhea and had permission to go to the latrine. Nothing helps.

I see what is coming and try to intervene. I introduce

myself as a doctor from the clinic and explain that this *Häftling* does have diarrhea and that he is being admitted to the hospital tomorrow.

"Away with you!" shrieks the *Lagerkapo* as he hits my back.

He may have broken several of my ribs. I have difficulty catching my breath. Now it is Pinek's turn. I do not look. I return to the barrack feeling quite depressed. For several hours, I cannot come to myself. Sometime around four o'clock, I escape from the clinic for a while and run to Pinek's barrack.

I ask the *Stubendienst* if he knows what happened to a *Häftling* who was beaten by the *Lagerkapo* before noon this morning. The *Stubendienst* leads me to the rear of the barrack. Just outside the door, Pinek lies naked in a pool of blood. His skull is horribly crushed. His number is written in ink on his chest.

Yes, Pinek, you got your wish. You did not die in the gas chamber.

"Why do you bother so much with this filthy *muzelman*?" asks the *Stubendienst*. "He's neither your father nor your brother."

* * *

On the following morning the four expected patients arrive. One is a *Volksdeutscher Kapo* from the *Kommando* of painters. An old *Häftling*, number 1080, he has been in Auschwitz for four years. Two other patients are Poles. The fourth is a Czech.

Aleks smiles and advises me to take special care of the *Kapo*. One can never tell; maybe someday I will slip and fall into S.K., then the protection of a *Kapo* will be very helpful.

Now I have additional work. Were it not for the slightly larger portions of soup I get, I would quickly join the *muzelmen*. I rise half an hour before the gong sounds, which means four o'clock. I wake the patients to straighten out their beds. I take the pail to the latrine and empty the bedpans. I sweep. I bring the coffee. The patients drink and eat. After breakfast,

I wash the dishes and sweep again . . . and then, scrub. When dawn breaks, I start to dust the rafters.

Bejlin enters the ward. Zenkteller has ordered that the patients' charts be kept in a very exact manner. It is ridiculous, but an order is an order. So we examine the patients every day. Thus we know that the *Kapo* came here just to rest. A diagnosis of the others is very definite: inflammation of the joints for the younger Pole, inflammation of the kidneys for the older one, and bilateral pleurisy for the Czech.

After the morning work in the clinic has ended, Zenkteller and the *Blockältester* enter the ward around nine o'clock. They start the inspection by checking to see if everything is in order and in place. They sniff in every corner. They look under the beds, into the pail and bedpans. They check whether the rafters have been dusted. Then they turn to the patients. With a pounding heart I await the verdict. When the *Blockältester* and Zenkteller leave, a weight is lifted from me. So today everything was all right.

As soon as the inspection ends, I run with a small pot to Section F's kitchen to bring a diet soup of thick buckwheat with fat-free milk. I am back on the ward in time to get the noon meal. After that, there is half an hour's rest for the medics, but I must clean up after the meal. Remembering Aleks's advice, I try to be very good to the *Kapo* who is quite demanding.

A few days pass. Then one day I witness something which does my heart good. Despite everything, it appears that there is some justice, that some higher force rules the world and avenges the spilled blood of the innocent. This time Providence points its finger at the *Lagerkapo,* that murderer who has on his conscience the slaughter of thousands of innocent victims.

In expectation of the arrival of several Jewish transports, the *Lagerführer* orders that the road to the crematoria be improved. Hundreds of *Häftlinge* are breaking their backs unloading and spreading gravel on the road under a hot July sun. The *Lagerkapo* reigns here as he does in camp. He saves his voice by applying the whip to the workers.

On this day, two trucks arrive with their trailers filled with gravel. Several *Häftlinge* with shovels are on top of the trailers ready to unload the gravel as soon as the truck is in position. The *Lagerkapo* thinks that not a minute should be wasted and that the workers should start unloading while the truck is still in motion. Wishing to encourage them in his usual way, he jumps on the running-board of the truck and is about to leap on the trailer when he loses his equilibrium and falls to the ground. He tries to shout, "Stop!", but the trailer's wheels slowly crush his stomach and chest. By the time I approach the accident site, the *Lagerkapo*'s husky body lies motionless with blood trickling from his mouth and nose. Your death, Pinek, and the deaths of many others has been avenged.

I return to the barrack in a fairly good frame of mind. I notice some new faces in the dressing room. Aleks explains that the new ones are spies for the *Blockältester*. They are: one elderly, possibly mid-fifty year old gardener named Kotarski who comes from the same town as the *Blockältester,* and a young boy of about twenty named Miecio who is from Warsaw and who will be the *Blockältester*'s and Zenkteller's lover. The *Blockältester* announces to everyone that Kotarski will be the manager of the dressing room and should be considered his assistant.

The "assistant" is a mean, old character as we will soon discover. He does nothing unless you call "work" scratching the earth in front of the barrack where he will supposedly plant flowers. He spends most of his time bothering us.

In the morning, he unmakes the beds which, in his opinion, have not been well made. He carefully dishes out the noon meal economizing on every spoonful of the stinking camp soup. This affects especially Szymek and me since we are the newcomers.

Also in the morning, I must hustle even faster on the ward because I have to endure an inspection by Kotarski who, like Zenkteller and the *Blockältester,* is never satisfied and likes nothing. He is even more demanding than they are.

Because our work load in the clinic keeps increasing, we return to the room after the evening gong to find Kotarski already in bed. He allows us to turn on the lamp just long enough for us to drink the coffee and swallow a piece of bread. Aleks Baranek, Wortman, and Reichmann keep a fire burning in the dental office and do not care at all about the Old One. We can only smell the tantalizing aroma of baked potatoes from a distance.

"You only eat and sleep!" Kotarski repeats every chance he gets. It is difficult for him to understand that someone may be hungry and be weakened from hunger. He receives large packages from home regularly. Moreover, his lover brings him preserves, bread, and pieces of sausage from the kitchen.

Meanwhile, life in Barrack 31 becomes more difficult with the arrival of new patients. We have several cases of typhus who are unconscious; one is delirious. I cannot leave the ward for a minute. This exhausts my remaining strength.

Finally, the *Blockältester* noticing my suffering promises to send someone to help me. "Remember," he says, "he's also a medic and is at your level. He'll care for one-half of the ward and you, the other."

The new medic, who is supposed to have the same rank as I, is a barber who shaves the *Lagerältester* and the VIPs in the main *Schreibstube*. He is very much aware of the important function he performs in the camp and takes advantage of it.

First of all, he never has any time. Immediately after the morning gong sounds, he scrubs the floor, straightens out the patients' beds on his side and, without a word, disappears. He returns at about ten o'clock to shave the medics. He has several kinds of razor blades. The best one is reserved for Zenkteller and the *Blockältester*. A good one is for Kotarski, Aleks, Baranek, Wortman, and Reichmann. A bad blade is saved for us, the newcomers; the worst one is for the patients. He always has excellent excuses to load all the work on me, for example, he is invariably looking for a razor strop or a sharpening stone. Sometimes he is busy searching for a new blade for the *Blockältester*. On other occasions, he must shave us and the patients. It is understood that I will always substitute for him.

It is true that the *Blockältester* said that the barber and I are on an equal footing. When he said that, he meant that I, a doctor, should not consider myself better than a barber. This is ridiculous. It is quite evident that "Mr. Barber" not only ignores me, but at every step he accentuates the distance that separates me, a half-*muzelman,* from him, the mascot of the mighty of this wire-encircled world.

As far as he is concerned, all the patients can croak. He said that loudly in front of everyone. The only thing that interests him is getting part of the packages that certain patients receive. I, who care for them unselfishly, am derided, mocked, and neglected.

Once the *Blockältester* hits me in the face because I had not managed to scrub the floor on time. When I try to explain that I have several sick patients whom I must feed, he replies that he does not care at all about them. The important thing is that the ward should gleam like a mirror. I have the distinct impression that Zenkteller is of the same opinion, except that he says, "The most important thing is to have a neatly written and up-to-date chart. The rest is nothing."

It is very difficult for me to grasp that. Aleks tries in vain to explain that once he was like me, but he changed, and that I, too, will have to do the same if I do not want to be thrown out and ordered to go on *Kommando.*

Zenkteller enters the ward. He sniffs and demands, "What stinks here, pig?"

Something certainly is not right. I check the beds and bedpans on my side. Everything is in order, thank God. I report to the Old One. Zenkteller crosses over to the other side of the ward and sniffs like a police dog until he finally discovers the cause. Some typhus case lying unconscious has soiled his bedding. I was at the other end of the ward and did not smell it. Anyway, it is on the barber's side and he is supposed to care for those four or five patients.

Zenkteller, however, has a different opinion. He scolds me, calling me an animal, a pig. He calls the *Blockältester* and shows him. After a short conference, they call the barber. Naturally he has an excuse: he had an urgent job in the *Schreibstube.*

I have to lie down for fifteen lashes; the barber gets only three. Moreover, the *Blockältester* officially warns me in Zenkteller's presence. He accuses me of being lazy and wanting to eat all the time, that the barber has too much to do, therefore, in the barber's absence, I must take care of the entire ward.

As they leave, Zenkteller punches me in the ribs and murmurs in an unmistakenly menacing voice, "You'll go to hell!"

When we are in the dressing room after work, no one says a word. My colleagues ignore the entire incident. Only Aleks murmurs something when he crawls up to his bunk. Even Szymek is not trying to console me. He says that, with such characters, there is no way out, and, to survive in the camp, you must be born a bandit.

I lie motionless in my bed in the dark. I hear the rumble of a train in the distance and, from the ward, the moans of the sick. The night watchman is calling them sons-of-bitches. I hear footsteps near the barrack. A minute later, the door opens quietly and the barber enters. He reaches his bunk by feeling for it. Then he pulls out several packages from under his shirt and puts them away. He goes to Kotarski's bed—the old fellow is not asleep yet—and whispers something to him. I overhear a few words.

"You'll have a good noon meal tomorrow, Daddy-O," says the barber.

There is no relationship between the barber and Kotarski. "Daddy-O" is a flattering expression in the camp.

"I've organized lard. I'll get potatoes tomorrow."

"You're a fine fellow," says the old man.

There is minute of silence. Then from his bed I hear the veiled voice of the barber, "But our Old One has given the Jew a few lashes that cracked his ass."

Kotarski sounds satisfied as he mumbles something. At the end I hear, "The skinny one won't stay here for too long."

A dark future awaits me. The vision of Maidanek returns. No one can help me; I can count only on myself.

Sleep brings no relief. I dream of my mother and see her frightened eyes as she says, "Don't go away, my son!"

In my dream I also see Fredzia high in a tree somewhere. I

am trying to climb after her. Someone pulls me down and yells. It is Zenkteller screaming, "You want to run away? You'll go to the gas chamber!" Someone throws me on a truck full of cadavers. I know that I am destined for the oven. I want to shout that I am alive. I cannot. We are going somewhere, but it is not Auschwitz. This is Treblinka. Yes, it is quite apparent that it is Treblinka. Fredzia, Sabinka, Dr. Stein are trying to say good-by to me. "You must go to the gas chamber, you poor fellow. We're returning to Warsaw."

I want to go with them but somebody holds me firmly. As the train pulls out, they wave their handkerchiefs. Fredzia calls, "Tadzek, run away! Come with us!"

The train travels farther and farther away. I cry and try to tear myself away. An SS man with a bull-like face beats me. I wake up.

Szymek is standing over me. "Fellow," he says, "why do you carry on? You've been screaming for an hour. Kotarski is threatening to throw you out of the ward."

For quite a while I cannot realize where I am as I wipe cold sweat from my forehead.

* * *

The camp is hell. The number of cases of typhus is increasing. *Lagerarzt Obersturmführer* Dr. Thielo and *Standortarzt* Dr. Mengele, the supreme medical officer, as well as *Obersturmführer* Schwarzhuber are so angry, they gnash their teeth. They are reprimanding Zenkteller, and he is taking it out on us. Everyone is nervous and excited. The rumor that the Germans will not bother to disinfect, travels like lightning throughout the camp. They will simply evacuate the *Reichdeutsche* and the *Volksdeutsche*. The rest will be gassed and cremated.

In this turmoil, I am forgotten. For the first time in a long while, I feel more secure. We are all facing the same fate, the same death. We are growing closer to one another. We are brothers.

A general psychosis prevails. Nobody wants to work despite Schillinger's savagery and the terrible blows from the SS and the *Kapos*. Why should we work? We are doomed to death whether or not we do. When nerves are strained to the limit, a numbness sets in.

This situation changes when a special *Kommando* arrives unexpectedly from Auschwitz bringing a truck with disinfection apparatus on a trailer. It looks like an enormous metallic bathtub which is set up between the two bathhouses with the help of *Häftlinge* from the Birkenau baths. Under the supervision of the SS men, the disinfection *Kommando* works feverishly.

A heavy load is lifted from everyone's heart. We Jews continue to be quite aware that the vision of the gas chamber is still very much before us and that our situation has not changed one iota. The implementation of our ultimate fate has only been postponed.

The *Blockältester* explains the general procedure. Every day three or four barracks will be fumigated. After the *Kommandos* return from work, they will spend a night outside in the Section because the barrack will be closed while the gas inside completes its work. At daybreak, the barrack inhabitants will undergo a general washing and their clothes will be disinfected. Every *Häftling* will throw all of his clothing into the bathtub which contains a solution of cyanide.

Noticing our surprise, he adds, "Yes, boys, tomorrow morning this tub that you are looking at will be full of water. An SS man will throw in *Zyklon*. Yes, the same poison gas they use to kill people."

While the clothes are being thrown into the bathtub, the barbers will shave the excess hair off the barrack inmates and the medics will wash the hirsute spots with a somewhat weaker solution of *Zyklon*. After that is done, the naked *Häftlinge* will run to the bath in the women's section.

We are shocked at this, so he explains, "If the women see them, it's unimportant. They're whores anyway."

There they will take a hot shower and, after that, the medics will examine the people for lice and nits. Then they will pick out their clothes and enter the barrack which, in the meantime, will have been ventilated after the fumigation of last night.

* * *

The next morning, and for the next eight or nine days, we do not have a minute's rest. Beginning at 5 A.M., the SS men, wearing gas masks, open the first containers of *Zyklon* and throw the blue crystals into the bathtub which is filled to the brim with water. The recognizable odor of cyanide spreads. We are ten meters away from the container and we are getting dizzy, but we have no time to worry about how we feel. The barbers have already shaved the first group, and the people are coming to us. We dip rags into the solution and wash the hairy parts of the bodies. Two SS men holding clubs carefully observe our work.

The people whom we treat can barely stand. After a full day of normal work on *Kommando,* they returned to camp and were forced to stand a whole night in the basic position in front of the barrack. this morning it is drizzling and cold; a strong wind blows in from the mountains.

Everything is progressing normally, "on the run". In the short interval between attending to the groups, I quickly go to the ward to empty the bedpans, give the patients a little coffee, and then run back.

The first group is returning from the bath. We make a lice inspection. Then the poor fellows must go to the tub to fish out their clothes and laundry from the bluish cyanide liquid. The rags are wet. As if spitefully, there is no sun. To make matters worse, those rags are emitting a poisonous gas. Every once in a while, a fellow carrying his clothes falls. I run to the first victim and apply artificial respiration slowly, systematically. However, my method does not please the SS man watching my work from a distance.

"You know nothing, you idiot!" he bellows. He knows better, and shows me his way. It is the same as mine except that he does it at a lightning tempo. The result is that the victim turns blue and remains permanently transfixed. The poison has a terrible effect. Others fall. By evening we have twenty fatalities.

When *Obersturmführer* Thielo arrives and learns of the unexpected results of the disinfection from a medic, he shakes his head and says, "It doesn't matter. The most important thing is to destroy the lice."

During the short midday pause, Szymek and I approach the bathtub where empty cans of *Zyklon* are strewn about. I want to take a closer look at the poison that has sent millions into the next world.

The blue tin cans are round and have a brightly colored label identifying the contents as *Zyklon,* a little flag, a simple design, several warnings including "careful—poison" and the explanation: "a cyanide preparation".

At night we suffer a new tragedy. Some "clever" *Häftlinge* in one of the barracks lit a fire in the oven and put their clothes near it to help them dry faster. Of the five hundred living in the barrack, only three hundred remain alive a few minutes later. Moaning loudly and exhibiting severe symptoms of poisoning, the living crawl out of the barrack to notify us of this terrible misfortune. It takes a long time for a medic wearing a gas mask to enter, put out the fire, and open the doors wide. Only then, can we begin emergency treatment. Help is too late for those who remained in the barrack. The only thing we can do is to try to save the other group, but in spite of all our efforts, another twenty die.

The rising sun finds us still at work. Our heads are in a whirl. We are close to losing consciousness and are so sleepy that we cannot see clearly. All we need is one hour of rest, but the gong sounds, and we must start our work again.

Two days after we finish the general disinfection, life in the camp returns to its old routine. At night we hear the whistle of the locomotive, the clickety-clack of the cars as they approach the ramp, the noise of the truck motors, and sometimes screams and shots. Truck headlights, focused on our small windows, illuminate the inside of our barrack. People are going to the gas chambers. From all the chimneys, flames lick the sky. "Tempo, *mensch*!"

New *Kommandos* are organized to lengthen the railroad tracks so that the freight cars can stop close to the gate of the crematorium. The work is rushed; whips crack. The beasts roar, "Always tempo, *mensch*!"

Always tempo. . . . Work makes free!

* * *

Several days of exhausting labor help to control my tense nerves. One evening after roll call when we are late finishing our work in the clinic, voices from the *Schreibstube* blare, "*Blockältesters*! *Blockältesters* out!"

What is going on? In any event, it is not good. Nervously, we await Modarski's return. He enters with an odd expression on his face, calls Zenkteller aside, and whispers something into his ear. The Old One's face changes. The *Blockältester* refuses to say a word.

Aleks leaves to get information from some people in the political department. He returns and goes into a dance. A list of people assigned to a transport to Mauthausen will arrive at the *Schreibstube* that night. There is even a possibility that Zenkteller may go. No one sleeps as we wait anxiously. Our *Blockältester* sits in the *Schreibstube*. At about one o'clock, the doors to the ward open and Zenkteller enters. We do not recognize the old bandit. He will leave at five o'clock. He is going to Auschwitz to say good-by.

Zenkteller is leaving. I cannot believe my ears. The words are as delightful as heavenly music. My heart is gay. I do not want to show how happy I am. He is saying good-by to me. He is actually shaking MY hand. It is unbelievable.

The farewell ceremony ends. A minute later we hear the door closing. He is off to the assembly point as dawn is breaking.

In the morning I almost dance as I work on the ward. I sweep under the beds; I scrub the floor; I dust. The pail of water somehow seems less heavy. Work and daily chores are lighter. It has been a long time since I was in such a good mood.

Around noontime we hear the news from Auschwitz. The Poles and Russians have almost murdered Zenkteller who escaped from them only with great difficulty. They wanted to pay him back for his brutality. We comment pleasurably on the news, and we wait. If only we had a report that the train left and that he would never return. . . .

The work in the clinic reminds me of the duties in a private hospital. No one screams; no one is beaten; no one is nervous. The patients, used to Zenkteller's continual terror, are surprised and thankful. I do not believe my good fortune and the good luck that we have had. Is it possible? Will the Old One really never come back?

The next evening the *Blockältester* bursts into the clinic like a bomb. The transport left, but Zenkteller remained behind. He will return tomorrow. The *Lagerarzt* rescued the Old One by convincing the higher authorities that Zenkteller was absolutely indispensable in Birkenau and that he performed his duties well.

So he is coming back. It's a shame. It could have been so much better.

* * *

A few hours after he returns, Zenkteller is punishing innocent people. The patients, who were spared his roars and beatings for a little while, stand quietly in line and look frightened. Even the *Blockältester,* who was the only one pleased at Zenkteller's return, makes a wry face. And when the Old One fells three Greeks by beating them simply because they do not speak German, and hits Szymek in the face because, in his opinion, he is not working fast enough, and the Yugoslav gets a few kicks because he tipped over a bottle of iodine, the *Blockältester* murmurs, "He's mad."

The *Blockältester*'s diagnosis is probably right. For several days, the Old One rages. He wants revenge for the hostile reception he received in Auschwitz. As always, the innocent suffer.

I avoid Zenkteller as much as I can. I rise at four in the morning and sometimes earlier.

The barber cuts hair and shaves the entire *Schreibstube* and canteen while continuing to neglect his patients. He says that he does not give a damn about the Old One. He is very sure of himself since he received several heavy packages from home.

Unfortunately, I have no influence with the camp's VIPs and do not receive any packages. From whom? Will they come from the other world? I feel very lonesome. At night despair grips me. I am too weak to do away with myself. I know that there is no place in the camp for people like me. I share the inmates' suffering too much and earnestly try to help them.

And so, in the midst of this continuous tug of war for life with its fear and drudgery, the Jewish High Holy Days, Rosh Hashanah, the New Year are approaching.

One evening I learn from Aleks that every Jewish holiday without exception had been celebrated with the mass extermination of the Jews. He is wondering what kind of gift the Germans will prepare for the Jews this time.

At night on the day before the first holiday, we hear, "All *Blockältesters* out!"

The Frenchman lifts his head from a wound he is cleaning and whistles. Szymek glances at me expressively, and my heart constricts.

A minute later we learn that there will be a general medical examination, and no *Kommandos* will go to work. Our fears are realized.

Among the several patients standing in front of me are a young boy of about seventeen from Sosnowiec and an engineer from Warsaw with his twenty year old son. Their bodies are covered with boils, sores, and purulent wounds, the result of scabies, dirt, lack of vitamins, insufficient nourishment, and general neglect. They know that they have no chance in tomorrow's selection.

"If only they won't torture us before we die!" the young man says to his father. This is his only wish.

As I dress the engineer's wounds, he thanks me and says, with a sad smile, "It isn't necessary, Doctor. Don't bother." After a while he adds, "I pity my son. I pity my child very much."

There will also be a selection in the women's section. Many of the men have mothers, daughters, wives, or sisters behind those wires. Feelings of pity, deep sadness, and utter helplessness envelop me.

What a sad, tragic night on the eve of the New Year!

Although it is daylight, the guards do not come down from the towers surrounding the camp. Immediately after the morning gong, everyone stands in front of the barrack. *Schreibers* with charts in their hands, and *Blockältesters* separate Jews from Aryans. Once more they check the names and numbers.

In the women's section, Mengele, Schwarzhuber, and SS men are examining naked Jewish women. Less than an hour later we hear terrible screams from these unfortunates as the SS men chase them to a barrack and from there to the gas chambers.

Meanwhile, the final preparations are being made for the "medical inspection" in our section. The *Lagerarzt* will probably visit our barrack. I clean the ward. I take the bedpans into the washroom to scrub them. One Jew from the punitive section is on our ward.

Laughing VIP SS men smoking cigarettes step out of three cars that stop in front of the barrack. They certainly are in an excellent mood. The *Lagerschreiber* approaches the SS men with a paper and pencil in hand. The "inspection" begins, and a deadly silence pervades the camp. Only from time to time do we hear desperate cries from the women's section.

The "inspection" proceeds rapidly. the *Lagerarzt* looks over a group of Aryans with lightning speed. Only a few are separated and will go to the hospital. In contrast, only ten percent of the Jews pass the selection.

At night we have the figures. Of the three thousand Jews in Section D, exactly two thousand six hundred fifty have been selected for the gas chamber, whereas, in Section F, of the eight hundred Jews there, only twenty-five are saved from death.

After roll call, Barracks 5, 7, and 9 are emptied. Their former occupants are replaced by Jews. The transfer of people lasts almost the entire night.

In our dressing room we hear the shouts and screams clearly. Aleks sleeps; nothing bothers him. Others pretend to do the same. In any event, they lie quietly and do not move. Szymek, the Frenchman, and I smoke one cigarette after another. We have traded our bread, sausage, and most of our clothes for these.

I know what those people are experiencing. Not too long ago I was in a similar situation. Szymek expresses the most optimistic idea. He thinks that our time will also come, and that we are idiots to wait until the Germans burn us, he further believes that not a single Jew will survive the hell of Auschwitz and suggests that we commit suicide to spare ourselves the needless suffering.

* * *

"*Blocksperre*! Close the barracks!"

The gong clangs continually. The barrack doors are slammed shut. The camp is full of SS men. Dogs bark.

"German *Kapos* come forward!"

My whole body is trembling. Someone gives me a cigarette.

Everyone in our barrack runs to the glass doors. Each holds his breath as he watches the tragedy unfolding outside. Starting with Barrack 9, a hundred naked figures race by accompanied by shouts of "Move! Faster!" as SS men kick and strike them with rifle butts, *Kapos* beat them with clubs, and dogs tear their flesh. SS men and *Kapos* chase their victims, one hundred at a time, to the third and fourth crematoria.

Rifle butts whack naked bodies. Clubs and whips crack. Barrack 9 is empty; now for Barrack 7. I do not care to look anymore and return to the patients on the ward.

Suddenly I hear a shout from the door, "Tadzek! Come quickly! Very quickly!"

I run to the window. Everyone seems transfixed by a horrible scene in front of Barrack 7.

Once the doors were opened, several Jews threw themselves on the SS men. A terrible fight ensues. Punching with their bare hands, the Jews also use their nails and teeth to scratch and bite. One even succeeds in grabbing a revolver from an SS man. Reinforcements arrive and the revolt ends except for two who fight desperately with a dozen SS men. The others are on the ground where they fell. *Blockältesters* and *Kapos* use their boots and clubs to complete the massacre.

Even Kotarski, who, until now, always remained indifferent as he watched "how they chased Jews to the gas chamber", is moved by the scene. Our *Blockältester,* Modarski, says, rubbing his hands, "At least the Jews gave them a few bumps!"

I do not understand what is happening to me. Although my heart is relieved, I am in a peculiar state of mind and feel a bit dizzy. I hear voices around me, but I cannot distinguish the words. My eyes focus on what is happening, but the picture does not enter my consciousness. My legs are buckling under me, and I hold onto the beds as I attempt to reach the dressing room. With my last ounce of strength, I plop on a stool. The world is whirling. I have hallucinations. "Maybe I'll die soon," I think.

The doors to the sick ward open and a figure appears. "Doctor!" he exclaims, "what is happening to you? Do you want some coffee?"

I revive enough to say, "Thanks, it isn't necessary. I feel better."

I take some water from a pail and pour it on my head. It helps.

In the clinic, the others are still standing next to the door. The men's barracks are empty. About twenty crushed bodies lie on the ground. Four Germans come to the dressing room; one must go to the hospital. Now it is the women's turn.

We hear screams and moans behind the barbed wires. Nearly two thousand naked women are being chased, all at the same time. Precautions are unnecessary as they run between two cordons of *Kapos,* SS men, and SS women toward the gas chamber close to crematorium II.

I pity them even more than I do the men. In this hour of their death, the Germans do not spare these women anything: neither shame nor humiliation.

Oh God, do you see it? Do you hear it? Why? Why?

At night the skies are scarlet as flames leap high from all the chimneys.

* * *

"All the Jews will go to the gas chambers in a very short while, maybe during the Day of Atonement."

Aleks brings us this pleasant forecast one afternoon while we are eating our midday meal. Is it not enough that our nerves are strained to the breaking point from the last selection, and now this?

Kotarski looks at us quizzically and clumsily tries to console us. "This one always brings the latest news. If they really wanted to finish off the Jews, they would do it all at one time."

"You'll see that the ones who are left aren't going to submit so easily," says Aleks turning to Kotarski.

Reichmann nearly chokes on a potato. Wortman, angry at Aleks for not letting us finish our meal in peace, scolds, "You idiot! You certainly chose the right moment to give us this information!"

Four days are left before the Day of Atonement. Life in the camp goes on as usual. There are no signs that Aleks's news could be true, but one never knows with the Germans. The day before the January deportation in Warsaw, Jews received a special treat of sugar, honey, and eggs.

Our nerves are taut. We run around the camp, our hair turning gray from worry. Our situation is analogous to that of a mouse caught in a trap; we are just as helpless and as powerless to escape. Our lives depend on a single order from someone higher up and it will be all over for us. They can shoot us, starve us, or beat us to death with clubs. How can we defend ourselves? How will it end? We saw it with our own eyes not too long ago. All that was left of a few brave boys was mush.

In spite of everything, I am convinced that we will defend ourselves for as long as we can, and we will make them pay for our lives. This will not change anything. In one way or another, it will be our death, and soon.

People react differently. Some organize something to eat. Others—and I belong to this group—smoke as much as they can. During the seemingly endless nights, I reflect about the past and once again—as I have done many times before—I prepare myself for death.

It is difficult to imagine the sunny days before the war when the world was good and people were not condemned to die in gas chambers. The horrible memories of the war years block out everything: home, family, my mother's kind smile; all that disappeared with the first explosions of the German bombs.

In my mind, I visualize an unusual series of superimposed pictures: German soldiers entering Warsaw, people being killed in the streets, the vandalizing and looting of Jewish stores, hundreds of thousands of people crowding together in the narrow streets and suffering from hunger and poverty, people disappearing from the Ghetto, corpses covered with newspapers lying in the streets, typhus rampant, cars with gendarmes shooting at passersby. Ever present is the spectre of death which suddenly, unexpectedly blocks your way and, with a bony finger, points: You! You! You!

The evil has no bounds. It looks as though it could never get worse, but it does, on the next day. When the first deportations started, we thought, almost nostalgically, of those terrible days of the past. And so it went, step by step, until the time came when living was worse than dying and men were too weak to end it all.

Now I recall the last days of the Ghetto, Treblinka, Maidanek, crematoria chimneys belching smoke and shooting flames skyward. Yes, even with the smoke blanketing the camp I clearly empathize with Fredzia's despair and hear her calling for help as she chokes inhaling the gas. She is crying bitterly.

My forehead is bathed in cold sweat. A curse passes my lips. To hell with this life! Yes, finally the end is near!

It is dawn again! Szymek lights a cigarette. I look at him bleary-eyed.

"If we could only survive in spite of it all," he says, "there'd be something to tell, but who would believe us?"

"If only one could remain alive . . ." A painful yet joyful shiver passes through my body. All of last night's thoughts of our terrible life surrounded by death and our salvation are rapidly leaving me. It is not true! Only death is horrible.

"A great day is approaching!"

Even Zenkteller, who has heard the news, leaves us relatively alone. I have the impression that our behavior is dignified and normal enough. In the morning, I make the beds even more carefully than usual, and continue my routine. The patients seem to know what lies in store for us. From all sides I receive discreet expressions of sympathy. During breakfast, they treat me to whatever they can.

Bejlin enters the ward. "So, Tadzek!! Any minute . . ."

He does not finish. We all know what he means.

One of the patients hears the words and says, "Hey there! Don't worry, doctors! Nothing'll happen! You'll see. Even if they take the Jews to the gas chambers, those sons-of-bitches will leave the doctors alone."

Aleks runs through the ward to some acquaintances who can give him information.

Life returns to "normal" in the camp. *Kommandos* go to work; so do the Jews. Despite everything, the day finally passes. We are under great tension and are prepared for every eventuality. Each of us has a knife.

When nothing happens after the evening roll call and the first patients arrive in the clinic, a stone is lifted from our hearts. The Yugoslav hides a long butcher knife in a box that was meant for food and curses the Germans in his own way. The saddest of all is Aleks whose information has been reliable until now.

"They've postponed the execution," he mumbles and crawls up to his bed.

* * *

Again, "normal" life starts, and once more, we listen to Zenkteller's usual insults and threats. New transports arrive: Poles from Warsaw, Jews from Silesia and France. The empty barracks are filling gradually. One week after the selection and the bunks are crowded again.

Hundreds of patients line up in front of the clinic. We cannot make much headway with the work. Only with the utmost effort are we able to continue to treat the patients.

Rumors reach us that Zenkteller plans to avenge the rather unfriendly reception he received in Auschwitz. The Old One walks around looking like an owl. Everything irritates him and makes him nervous. Woe to the one who crosses his path. He is just aching for an occasion to vent his anger. A storm is brewing.

Meanwhile, news from the outside world is wonderful. The British and Americans have landed in Italy. The Russians are pressing forward. Scraps of newspapers with front line communiques are being preserved as if they were priceless gems.

We become hopeful that maybe, just maybe a miracle will happen and we will survive this hell. It is foolhardy to believe it, to hold on and let another day pass, and yet let time rush on; it is like a ray of hope. In our most difficult moments when the spectre of death crushes our very being, then we can turn our eyes heavenward, and our lips, that have uttered so many blasphemies aloud, beg God for the victory of the Allied Armies and for freedom.

* * *

The Italians have capitulated. Mussolini is a prisoner. It is unbelievable! How did this news get through the barbed wires? Even the newspapers have not mentioned it yet.

In the clinic that night we discuss the situation in Italy and unanimously decide that it is a German provocation. We conclude that the Germans purposely spread misinformation through one of their agents, to punish us later when the rumor is denied.

The doors to the ward open and the *Blockältester* bounds in. As he pulls a folded *Voelkischer Beobachter* from his pocket he says, "Boys, this is sensational!"

So it is true! The item is on the front page in bold letters. Aleks reads aloud. We interrupt him from time to time with gusty hurrahs. The patients stand at the doors and share our elation.

We fall asleep hoping that maybe our suffering will end soon, and that even if liberation does not come quickly, the Germans, aware of the danger they face, will change their treatment of the *Häftlinge* for the better.

In the morning, last night's jubilant mood vanishes quickly thanks to Zenkteller. Immediately after the coffee, he calls us together in the clinic. Out of the clear blue he declares that, without exception, we are a band of good-for-nothings and pigs, that he has been observing us for a long time, and that, if we do not improve, he will make sure that we get more suitable jobs in the mines. To further vent his anger, Szymek receives a blow because his hair is too long, and I get kicked in the ankle because my pants are dirty.

I try to explain that I use these trousers to scrub the floor, clean the bedpans, etc., and that I do have a clean pair.

My explanation results in my being smacked in the face twice, and the Old One calling me all kinds of derogatory names, among them, dirty pig. He threatens that I will not even notice when he throws me out and sends me on *Kommando* and that he will remove my name from the list of doctors. He dismisses me.

I limp back to the ward and try to stop my nosebleed.

The next day, Zenkteller finishes off Dr. Bejlin, our ward chief, for committing a minor error. He is supposed to write the results of analyses on the patients' charts, but he made the mistake of recording findings of a routine urinalysis on another card.

Zenkteller has his own method of checking on the doctors. He goes along the ward, looks at the charts, and suddenly asks the patient, "When did you have a urinalysis?"

The patient does not understand and opens his eyes wide. Zenkteller hits him and repeats the question. Finally the patient answers that, as far as he can recall, he has not supplied any urine to be tested.

Bejlin explains that he obviously made a mistake. Anyway, there is no indication that a urine analysis was necessary in this case and that such tests are done only when it is absolutely essential because of the shortage of reagents.

Zenkteller is not even listening. He calls Bejlin a crook and a charlatan and slams the door loudly as he leaves the ward.

That afternoon, the *Blockschreiber* notifies Bejlin that he must pack his belongings immediately. On the orders of the *Obersturmführer,* he is being transferred to the gypsy section. He receives this news as if it were a death sentence. A typhus epidemic is prevalent among the gypsies. Bejlin has never had typhus. That fact coupled with his heart condition and the deplorable life style in that section, make his chances for survival, nil. Zenkteller is well aware of that.

Bejlin is packed. With no time to meditate, he says goodby to everyone. I accompany him to the gate. We worked together for a short time and became close friends.

"Yes, Tadzek," says Bejlin, "this is the end. I want to live. I have a wife in the Aryan sector."

I return to the barrack with a heavy heart and a gnawing feeling that I will not remain here for very long.

* * *

The boom falls sooner than I expected.

As Zenkteller moves through the ward, he smells cigarette smoke and declares that whoever is caught smoking will be thrown out. On the next day, a patient offers me a cigarette. I light up and go to the door to finish puffing it. With my hand still on the doorknob as I open the door, I find myself looking into the face of Zenkteller. He studies me from head to toe. I close my eyes expecting a blow. But no, the Old One shakes his head and says nothing momentarily. Then he shouts, "You idiot! Do you think I'll allow a bastard like you to disobey my order?!"

His voice is menacing. I want to explain, but the words stick in my throat. The old bastard turns and leaves.

For a moment, I am paralyzed. Now my turn has come. What can I do? I ask Aleks and Wortman for help. I want to run to the big hospital to see Zbyszek. Everyone thinks that I am hysterical. That Zenkteller caught me at the door is the surest proof that I was going out to smoke.

"Don't worry," says Aleks, "he'll forget by tomorrow."

It ends quite differently. At night the *Blockältester* comes into our bedroom and asks for me. "You! What have you done? Zenkteller is very angry with you. Tomorrow you must report to the SS *Lagerarzt*!" he tells me and leaves.

I hear people pitying me. Aleks is surprised at the turn of events. He did not expect that the affair would turn out this way. The Old One had threatened many times before, but mostly it ended only in a threat and a few blows.

"Don't worry, Tadzek! You can always count on us!"

Good fellows! They are trying to console me during this difficult period. Unfortunately, I know that as soon as I get out of here, they will forget me. It is only natural; it is a camp.

My feelings are most unusual. I thought that I would despair. Instead I feel quite calm. Very often, I have become very nervous expecting this moment, and now that it has arrived, I realize that nothing more dreadful can happen to me. If I want to survive, I must redouble my efforts. I want to think, to ponder my fate, but I cannot. My head is a void. I think with tenderness about my bed. Heretofore, I always had all kinds of complaints about it, but only now do I realize that my bed is soft and comfortable. At this time tomorrow, where will I be?

* * *

In the morning I clean up the ward and say good-by to my patients for whom I had cared until now. They are very sad and try to console me as best they can, urging me to hold out, secure in the belief that the war will end soon. Others curse Zenkteller aloud for sending me on *Kommando*. I receive several gifts: bread, sausage, cigarettes. Everyone is contributing so generously that I am embarrassed. Even in the worst of times, I was never a beggar.

The patients notice my predicament and say, "Doctor, don't be ashamed to take! We'll be lying comfortably in our beds and receive packages from home while you'll be dragging yourself in the fields somewhere."

I am deeply moved. How good they are to me! They do not think of themselves nor of the time of their discharge from the hospital to return to work in slaughterous *Kommandos*.

The *Blockschreiber* enters the ward and tells me to "Get ready! You're to report to the *Lagerarzt* in K.B."

Without saying good-by to anyone, I run out of the barrack leaving my box of food. I hope that I will have a moment to return for it.

The old medic from Barrack 20 is taking me to K.B. We join a group of *Kapos* and *Reichdeutsche* who, in all likelihood, are bound for the Front. *Obersturmführer* Dr. Thielo must examine them and, at the same time, settle my fate. We move slowly, and I think of the sentence I will receive in a very short while. Will he send me to the mines, S.K., or Barrack 10? Any of those eventualities means suffering for several weeks and ultimately death.

I am especially afraid of being sent into the mines, having heard a great deal about the horrible conditions under which the prisoners work there. I have seen healthy, husky, strong men who entered the mines and, in only three weeks, became skeletons covered with sores.

Barrack 10 houses a *Kommando* that works with a *Strafkommando* digging ditches in the fields surrounding the camp. They perform the same work and receive the same food and beatings as the *Strafkommando*, only Barrack 10 is the dirtiest and has the worst personnel: *Reichdeutsche* with green stripes.

The medic who is my escort, a Slovak, commiserates with me. He knows Zenktller very well and is also aware that, when he is angry at someone, death is a better choice than suffering from his chicanery.

We wait about ten minutes in K.B. for the *Lagerarzt.* He is walking down the wide street in our direction with Zenkteller, who does not come near our group. From a distance, I hear him asking Thielo for permission to inspect the washrooms and kitchen.

The formalities are short. The German *Kapos* are to remain in the hospital for several days under observation. When I stand before him and report in as strong a voice as I can manage, *"Herr Obersturmführer . . ."*

He stops me with an impatient gesture. "I know everything!" he shouts.

He thinks a while and then, turning to the Slovak, says, "10." This means that I must be taken immediately to Barrack 10. "Let him work a while. The *Blockschreiber* is to give me a written report about him."

That is all there is to it. Thielo leaves. I want to beg, to explain, but to no avail. Zenkteller has told him enough and described me the way he wanted.

The Slovak pats me on the arm and says, "Well, pal, let's go."

So it is to Barrack 10 for more suffering. And again I feel helpless and sad.

* * *

I bid my colleagues good-by.

"You'll come to see us here if you need anything. We'll always help you."

Without a word, Szymek forlornly squeezes my hand in a powerful grip. Aleks goes to the *Blockschreiber* to ask him to say a good word for me to the *Blockältester* of Barrack 10.

The *Blockschreiber* twists his mouth and shrugs his shoulders moving his arms. He promises to try, but Aleks knows this old bandit. If only I were transferred to a different barrack. . . .

The *Schreiber* knocks on the *Blockältester*'s door and enters. Through the window I notice them talking and pointing to me. After a while, the *Blockältester* comes out, looks at me, turns to the *Schreiber,* and says, "I don't like privileged guests very much. However, as long as you're asking me, I'll take care of him, but he'll have to go on *Kommando* anyway."

The *Schreiber* thanks the *Blockältester* loudly and shakes his hand. In saying good-by to me, he adds, "I've done what I could. Maybe you'll be treated a little better."

"Maybe better," I echo.

The *Blockältester* calls the *Stubendiensts* who slink out of a corner of the barrack. They appear to be three shrewd characters with bandit-like faces. The *Blockältester* points to me and says, "This is a doctor! Give him a good place to sleep!"

The *Stubendiensts* laugh uncontrollably and finally say, "We'll take good care of 'The Doctor'!"

They lead me along the entire length of the barrack to the last bunk where I know there is the barrel for people to relieve themselves. It is impossible to sleep there; it always stinks, and activity is constant.

I beg them to assign me to another place. They explain that the barrack is full and those who came before me have priority for the better places.

"If you'll give us something," they say, looking greedily at my package, "maybe we'll be able to find something else."

I open the package. They do not want bread. Instead they take my sausage, apples, and a few cubes of sugar . . . and all at once they find a better location for me on the third level. It is occupied by only five people while, on the other levels they crowd ten to twelve. The blanket is too short and in tatters. "If you get some cigarettes. . . ."

* * *

I stand in front of the barrack. The orchestra plays lively music at the gate. *Kommandos* are assembling. Nearby, the *Stubendiensts* are eating my apples. Motivated by the bribe I gave them for a better bunk, they are talkative and reason that I, as a doctor, will soon be transferred to a better *Kommando.*

"You won't last long here," they console me. "The work is horrible. Every day we end up with several corpses and our medic sends eight to ten *Häftlinge* to the hospital daily. What will happen when winter comes?"

Winter . . . this is what I am afraid of. It is early October and the weather is still quite good even if it is devilishly cold in the morning. In a few days the rainy season will begin in Auschwitz. What will happen then? I do not want to think about it.

The people returning from *Kommando* are dirty, tired, and in rags. We were lucky today; there are no cadavers. Roll call ends quickly. Immediately afterwards, several people leave with the *Stubendiensts* for coffee and soup.

Because they work eight kilometers away and the road cuts through marshes, it is impossible to bring the noon meal to them, so they fast the entire day, except for the *Kapos* who cook their food in their huts. At night, the people are given cold soup left from noontime, coffee, and bread.

At mealtime there is terrible turmoil. Wild with hunger, the inmates behave like criminals, so famished are they. To make matters worse, there is a shortage of dishes. People fight over one of these; they swear; they scream. The *Stubendiensts* beat them with clubs. It is hell. Broken, I drag myself to my bunk.

* * *

I lie there beside two Czechs, a Frenchman, and a Pole. I feel fortunate to have someone with whom I can talk.

In this barrack of four hundred *Häftlinge,* more than three hundred are Jews from the last transport, a few Czechs and Russians, and several Poles. My bunkmate got himself into this hellish place because he had an argument with a *Blockältester* who, out of spite, sent him here. He hopes that, as soon as he receives a good package from home, he will be able to change *Kommandos.*

"My brother, you can't last very long in here. Ten days ago, we were six hundred, and now, even though there are a few new arrivals every day, we are only four hundred. Yes, they kill people here terribly fast. It's well that the weather, at least, is bearable."

He lies down in his wet pants and uses his very muddy wooden shoes as a pillow. "To hell with it!" he exclaims. "You work in mud up to your knees all day, and when you return, there isn't a place to dry anything."

I cover myself with my blanket.

"We must sleep!" he continues. "I work like a horse and those bastard *Kapos* beat me mercilessly. Aha! If you've something in the package, hide it well because, in this barrack, they steal whatever they can lay their hands on."

"Get up! Move!"

We make our beds quickly. My new friend is cursing because his pants and socks did not dry overnight.

The second gong sounds. It is time to leave the barrack. Outside, it is cold and dark. Close to the wires, the lamps are still lit. I shield my head in my hands and raise the collar of my thin striped jacket.

As we march toward the gate, I look back. The doors of Barrack 31 are just being opened, and Mietek stands there with a pail in his hand. He is going to the washroom for water. Groups of patients led by medics start toward the clinic.

The orchestra plays a lively march; the drummer beats loudly. We move closer to the gate; the daily parade begins. "Straighten lines! With even step! Caps off!"

On the other side of the gate we are divided into groups of one hundred. *Kapos,* foremen, and a detachment of SS guards with dogs treat us with "tender loving care".

The good road ends quickly, and we are in a field. Our masters are well-off. They are dressed warmly and wear rubber hip-boots. We, in our wooden shoes, sink in the muddy clay ground. Only with great difficulty are we able to pull them out at every step.

We hear the first roars of the SS men, "Quickly! Tempo! Move!" The first blows start raining down on us. These SS brutes and their worthy helpers, the German *Kapos,* are cruel and sadistic.

Only God knows where they hurry. The *Kommando* works too far from camp even for Schillinger to get there. He cannot use his motorcycle.

To avoid the blows, I walk quickly. It is so difficult that, in a while, I begin panting like a blacksmith's bellows. The road seems endless. When I ask if it much farther, "We haven't even gone half-way," is the reply.

The march continues accompanied by beatings, screams, and other "encouragements" to walk faster. After two hours, we reach the work site, completely exhausted.

Then, after a minute's rest, we hear, "Move! Pick up your tools!"

The foremen distribute the picks and shovels. Our group of one hundred is divided into smaller units. A *Kapo* shows us a surface that has been marked out with driven stakes and says, "You're to dig out all of this, otherwise you won't get anything to eat."

My new friend, Jurek, estimates the work assigned to us and says, "If we work fast, we can finish by four o'clock."

He swings his pick and digs into the clay soil. I use a shovel; it is a nasty job. After a short while, so much clay sticks to my shovel that it is almost impossible to remove it in spite of my best efforts, and I cannot continue. Jurek notices, takes the shovel from me, and hands me the pick. "Let's see, fellow, if you can do better with this."

As the hours pass, the autumn sun warms my body pleasantly. I am surprised and cannot understand why no one watches us.

Jurek explains, "For several days we work with an understanding. If one group does not complete the job, on the first day they take away the bread, on the next the bread and soup, and on the third, the bread, soup and, as a 'bonus', everybody gets fifteen lashes." He smiles ironically as he continues, "Those sons-of-bitches have figured it out. Why must they run around in the mud and scream and supervise? Why should they get nervous? They're warm and comfortable in their huts. Over the last few days, they stole several loaves of bread and quite a lot of sausage."

The aroma of frying wurst coming from a nearby hut assails our nostrils, Jurek says, making a fist, "These are our tormentors. They're draining our blood! May they choke on it!!"

A red-faced *Kapo* comes out of a hut. He is rested. He comes close to us and watches us work. "Well, move! Get going!" he orders. "I'll take the club to you! The 'gentlemen' don't want to work? Eh?"

Jurek grinds his teeth and says, "I must get out of here at all costs. When the rains come, we'll be finished in a few days."

I am well aware of that. I have been working here for only a few hours in good weather and I cannot straighten out. My muscles hurt; my heart beats like a trip hammer.

The sun is at its highest point in the sky when we hear the gong in the camp signalling the time for the noon meal. Jurek pulls a piece of bread from his pocket, and I follow his example. Our co-workers jealously watch us. They had eaten their portions as soon as they received them last night.

After this scanty repast, I feel a little better. Now we must work more intensively, otherwise we will lose our bread. It seems as though new strength flowed into our muscles after we ate, but this is only an illusion. After several swings with the pick, my weariness is even more pronounced than it was previously, and my breathing becomes more labored, but I must continue to work. One prisoner watches the other avidly. We check each other. Our bread is at stake. OUR BREAD! It is truly a hellish punishment that our torturers have devised. *Kapos,* foremen, and SS men stand over us and laugh at our clumsy movements while gorging themselves on bread, margarine, and sausage.

One SS guard has a dog on a leash. A *Kapo* throws a piece of bread to the dog as many pairs of human eyes look with envy at the animal.

We finish the prescribed work a few minutes before the whistle blows at the end of the day. Others are not that fortunate. The *Kapos* write down the numbers of those in the groups who did not fulfill their quotas, seventy in all. This means seventeen loaves of bread and seventy portions of sausage. It is a treasure. The *Kapos* will exchange it for vodka and cigarettes; the prisoners will go to bed hungry.

We have one cadaver to bring back today; he died on the job. Even if we had a stretcher to bring his remains "home", we do not have the strength to carry him, so we take turns dragging him by his feet. The SS men find this very funny. One *Häftling* goes to the side of the road for a minute to relieve himself under a bush in the field. He had just pulled his pants down when an SS man shoots him. He was a member of our group, and it is my turn to transport him. Like the others, I pull him by his legs. From time to time I look back. There are streaks of blood along the ground.

I am completely exhausted, but I must drag myself to the barrack for roll call.

"Line up! Straighten out!"

People are falling from fatigue. The *Stubendiensts* do not seem to understand that. Quick with their blows, they are enraged because they have difficulty lining us up for a count.

Immediately after roll call, the orders *"Mittagholen! Kaffeeholen!"* are given. Because I am in the front row, I must go to the kitchen to drag the heavy cauldron. The *Stubendienst* is surprised that I look sad and says consolingly, "You'll get a double portion."

Despite the risk, I run to the clinic to speak to Aleks right after the soup and bread are distributed. Maybe he can think of a satisfactory solution for my tragic situation. I realize that, if I remain in this *Kommando* any longer, my days are numbered. I push myself through the crowd of patients.

"What's the matter with you? What's the rush?" demands the doorman, pushing me away from the entrance.

He does not recognize me. I wonder, have I changed that much in one day? I say something to him.

At the sound of my voice he turns in my direction and, with a startled look, says, "Tadzek! It's you?"

He lets me in, only asking me to watch out for Zenkteller. The Old One is still raging. I push myself toward the dental clinic, but I must wait. Aleks is very busy.

When I finally enter, I tell Aleks of my woes. Tearfully, I beg for help. Aleks is embarrassed and scratches his head.

He learned that I had been assigned to Barrack 10 by the *Lagerarzt,* himself, so it is a difficult problem with no apparent quick solution. I must suffer a few more weeks, then maybe something might be worked out.

Patients are knocking on the door. I must leave.

"When you need bread, come," I hear him say at the end.

I want to approach Szymek and other colleagues, but I notice their warning signals in the distance. Zenkteller is looking in my direction. I lose myself among the patients and retreat toward the exit.

Yes, I expected that. No one can help me. I must rely on myself.

By the time I return to the barrack, everyone is stretched out in the bunks. From the rear come complaints and moaning from those who received no bread. When it gets dark, the *Stubendiensts* light two lamps whose weak, yellowish flame creates an eerie atmosphere in our barrack.

I crawl up to the bunk; Jurek is not there. The Czechs explain that he finally received his package from home and ran to the main *Schreibstube* to arrange for his transfer. Although my eyes are closing, I wait for him. I am curious to know what he has arranged.

He returns at about nine o'clock in a very good mood. In a day or two, he will be transferred to an excellent *Kommando,* the clothing department. Sorting and distributing clothes are light work. It even provides opportunities to organize. Also, he will work under a roof where he will be protected from inclement weather. It cost him his entire package and, in addition, he ran up a debt of twenty Greek cigarettes. All he has left of his large package is one loaf of dark bread which he cuts and gives me two-thirds.

"Hide it! You may need it!" he warns.

* * *

Jurek left the next morning. Several days later, his place is taken by some filthy, lousy Ukrainian who stinks unbearably and appears to be looking for something to steal. I must watch myself. He has already discovered that I have a piece of bread among my treasures.

The bread Jurek gave me stands me in good stead. Shortly after his departure, we fail to fulfil our daily work quota, and our "reward" is taken away. As a result, we are so weak that we produce even less on the following day and lose our bread and soup.

The weather is becoming stormy. A strong wind brings rain clouds. In the morning, it starts to rain. The road that is difficult enough to traverse in dry weather, is almost impassable now. The clay sticks to our shoes, and our feet sink deeper into the cursed mud. We are coatless, dressed for summer in short-sleeved shirts, undershorts, striped uniforms and wooden shoes. These are our clothes for Fall as well. Before we reach our destination, our uniforms are sopping wet from the rain. However, the *Kapos,* who wear rain ponchos, enter their huts and light a fire in the stove.

Our only salvation is hard work. It requires much effort. Our strength is waning. Streams of water from our soaked striped caps flow under our collars. We stand in mud over our ankles. Every time we strike the ground with our shovels, mud splashes on our clothes and faces. Our misery seems limitless. There is no place for us to go for warmth. If only we had some heat even if only for a minute, blessed heat from a hot oven. . . . The less hardy lose control of themselves. Screaming wildly, they throw themselves on the ground and roll in the mud waiting for a bullet. Several of them remain down. The SS men call the *Kapos.* Horrible scenes ensue. People refuse to stand; they beg to be shot. Beating and kicking do not help. They do not get up, but beg for death.

Not a single group has fulfilled its work quota. In spite of that, we all receive bread and soup for overtime, for dragging fifteen corpses and twenty-five half-dead bodies back to camp.

Inside, the barrack is cold and water runs into the bunks through holes in the roof. It is bad enough that we have no place to dry our clothes or something with which to wipe ourselves, but now we must also lie on wet straw mats and cover ourselves with wet blankets. During the night, a barking cough resounds through the barrack. I feel a worrisome pain in my left side. I am very cold and cannot sleep during the entire night. In despair, I finish the rest of the wet bread. I dare not think of tomorrow when I will not have a piece of bread to eat at work. Maybe heaven will help me so that I will not survive the night.

The rain continues. A rush of cold water splashes on my head. I am shivering. Oh God, how long will this suffering last?

Our *Kommando* is melting. In the morning about twenty people cannot rise. The medic finds that all of them are running high fevers. He has no thermometer, but it is sufficient for him to touch their hot foreheads to confirm this. Camp regulations do not recognize the possibility of sudden sickness during the night. Only those who requested an appointment to see the doctor the night before may visit him in the morning. The ill are chased on *Kommando,* but they run away from the lines and drag themselves to the clinic where they fall and do not move. Nothing helps, not even the *Kapos'* screams, roars, and merciless blows.

The rain continues. It is a sad, gray sky, but our life is even more forelorn. Instead of two hours, it takes us four hours to drag ourselves to work. What does it matter that the guards and *Kapos* are hurrying to get to their huts and warm stoves where they are protected from the rain? What can they do to us? Beat us? Please do! Our frozen bodies are insensitive to the heaviest blows. Shoot? Please! We are awaiting a bullet for salvation. Take our bread? It's all right. We feel no hunger; our stomachs have shrunken. Food does not get past our throats.

I stopped thinking. Nothing interests me. I belong in the other world. I do not even go to the clinic; I have already forgotten about that possibility. Instinctively, I find my way to the barrack, stand in line with the others, and passively let the *Stubendiensts* place me wherever they wish. At the order "Caps on!" or "Caps off!" my hand automatically executes the prescribed motion.

After roll call, I drag myself for bread and soup as does everyone else. I become aware that others wait for my dish, and I must hurry. Like an animal, I gulp my soup from the bowl. I lost my spoon; perhaps it was stolen.

Sometimes the soup is hot. Then I gulp it down in big quaffs and quickly run to my bunk, take off my rags, and cover myself with the blanket. Occasionally, I succeed in warming up.

* * *

Several days have gone by; I do not even know how many. I have simply lost track of time. It is rainy and cold and I feel miserable. People fall; others come to fill their places. The new ones die; we drag the cadavers through the mud.

One night, I suddenly hear someone calling my name from the doorway. I do not care; let them scream. The voices are nearer my bunk now. I can make out the *Blockschreiber*'s voice saying, "The doctor is lying there on the third level." In a lower voice he adds, "He's a complete *muzelman,* good for the oven."

Someone climbs in. It is Aleks. Szymek and Wortman are there also.

"Tadzek! We hoped you'd answer! We've been looking for you for an hour."

Someone pulls the blanket off me. I am cold, my teeth chatter, and I curl up.

Aleks's strong voice enters my subconsciousness. "Get dressed in whatever you have. Come with us at once!"

I execute several routine movements to dress. Getting the wet shoes on my feet is difficult, but I finally succeed and descend. They help me to the clinic and into the dressing room. Oh God, it is warm! A fire crackles in the stove. I was once in this paradise. Tears fill my eyes; I cry. I am ashamed, but I cannot help it.

They observe me from every angle. Even Kotarski is scared by my ghastly appearance. "Is he run down!" he exclaims.

I do not object when Aleks fills the bathtub with hot water and tells me to wash. I look around uncertainly, fearfully. "Maybe Zenkteller will come in," I protest.

"It's none of your business! Do as I tell you!"

They change the water twice. The barber shaves me and cuts my hair. I am given clean laundry, a sweater, a new striped uniform, and shoes. I sit at the table and Szymek hands me a dish of warm potato soup and a piece of bread with margarine. I am reviving. My brain starts working. Emotion chokes me.

"How will I ever repay you for this?"

"Stop making a fool of yourself!" says Aleks angrily, or maybe he just pretends.

When I finish my third dish of soup and can eat no more, they scold me. Why did I not come? Why do I look so bad? Why do I neglect myself? Do I want to go up the chimney with the first selection?

They are good fellows, but why do they ask those ridiculous questions?

It is late; I must return. Aleks begs me not to lose hope and to conserve my strength. They know that this *Kommando* is very difficult. They tried to help me, but without results. In the *Schreibstube,* they promised Aleks that they would give me a better *Kommando* as soon as they are able. Maybe even Zenkteller will forgive me, and I will go to some barracks as a medic.

I have no adequate words to thank them for all they did for me as I shake hands with everyone.

Aleks accompanies me and we enter the barrack. The *Blockältester* is asleep, so Aleks calls the *Stubendiensts.* They become angry at being disturbed so late, but when they see Aleks, their attitude changes. Respectfully, they ask what he wants.

Aleks puts his hand into his pocket and pulls out a few packages of cigarettes. He points to me and says, "He has to receive two good blankets that you'll always have to watch so they aren't stolen. He must get good soup and not be required to stand in line. And I will pay for your services."

Soon after Aleks leaves, one of the *Stubendiensts* brings me the blankets, another one takes me to a different bunk in the barrack.

"Here the roof's been repaired. It's not leaking."

I develop cramps from all the good food I ate and go to the barrel. By the light of the small lamp—the only one in the barrack, the night watchman reads a newspaper—the latest edition of *Kattowitzer Zug*. I notice the date on it: October 16th, my birthday.

* * *

I am hopeful and confident. I do not mind the mud any longer even if my new outfit and shoes are soon soiled. The idea that I am not alone, that someone thinks of me, and that I will find help in time of need, warms my heart. I decide to fight.

I recall the times in Maidanek when I had a little medical practice and think that perhaps I should start one here. I run to Aleks and explain my idea.

"I like that," he says, pleased with my decision. "I've also lived through some difficult times. Always keep your chin up. Don't let yourself go."

The next day, I receive a box containing various salves, a flask of iodine, several gauze bandages, and some adhesive tape. The fellows included a chunk of sausage, half a piece of bread, and a few cigarettes.

I find no willing patients in my barrack, but two foremen from a neighboring barrack ask me for help. One has a sore on his thigh; the other, a blister on his foot. In a few days they are healed and I am given two portions of bread, a piece of sausage, and four cigarettes.

Despite the laborious work and the bad weather, from the 16th of October, I feel reborn and new strength seems to be returning. My appetite is wonderful. Even with the two liters of soup I receive since Aleks's intervention, I would still suffer from hunger were it not for the additional food I receive from my practice. I remember, with terror, the days not too long ago when I lay in the bunk like a homeless, abandoned dog. I realize now how close I came to death. I vow that never, even if I suffer more grievously than I did before, will I ever lose control again, but I will fight until my last breath.

A few days after I take this oath I encounter a test of fire.

I am applying a dressing during a visit to one of my patients in Barrack 4 when somebody grabs me from behind

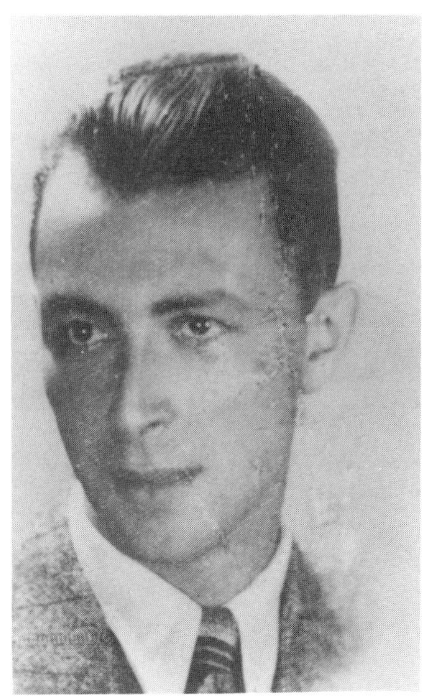

Dr. Stabholz circa 1938

Dr. Stabholz today

One of the schoolhouses in the Umschlagplatz where Jews were held while waiting for the train to Treblinka. It survived the war and is now an office building in Warsaw.

r. Stabholz in front of the granite monument about 200 yards
om the Umschlagplatz in 1988

plaque on the front of office building in photo #3

Treblinka. Symbolic cemetery of 17,000 rocks. 130 rocks are engraved with the names of places from where the victims came. Ten large rocks represent the countries from which the murdered Jews had come.

Treblinka. Polska (Poland) and part of Czech rock.

Entrance to Birkenau. The building housed the Gestapo, Drs. Thielo and Mengele, etc. The SS guard were under the glass top. At the very top is the siren that sounded the alarm when a prisoner escaped. (1988)

Birkenau. A general view of "Abschnitt A", the quarantine section.

Birkenau. Ruins of gas chamber Crematorium II. (1988)

Ruins of Crematorium II. 1985

Ruins of gas chamber Crematorium III. (1988)

Birkenau. In lower right corner is a railroad track.

View of Birkenau. A close look at the lower edge, one rail of the track leading to the ramp of Crematoria II and III is visible

Plaque in Birkenau. The inscription is written in many languages

and lands several punches to my face. It is the medic of the barrack who, justifiably I must admit, vents his dissatisfaction with me for entering a barrack not assigned to me to care for his patients. He threatens to report me to Zenkteller. Only after I leave him all the supplies that I obtained with so much difficulty, does he decide not to tell the Old One.

I am left with no resources. The extra bread that I earned from my practice has been cut off and hunger returns. I must look for help from my friends in Barrack 31.

Late at night, when work in the clinic is over, I knock on the dressing room door. No one is there, but I hear guitar music coming from the ward. That must be where everyone is. I know that I should leave, but it is so warm. . . .

The doors to the sick ward open. ZENKTELLER!! He looks at me for a second with a terribly angry expression. "You came to steal, you hoodlum! Eh?!" he thunders and approaches me with clenched fists. "I don't ever want to see you here or in the clinic again!" He delivers one blow to my mouth and another to my belly. As I retreat, I see Aleks's pale face through the open door of the ward.

* * *

Aleks has an unpleasant incident, and I experience difficult days again. The *Blockältester* found several pieces of gold in his storage bin. It could mean S.K. With great difficulty, he managed to get out of his predicament, but it cost him a great deal, and he ran up a debt. He regrets that he will be unable to help me.

The other doctors in the clinic are living only on their regular ration. With several hundred patients from the new transports flocking to the clinic, they have so much work that they have no time to even think of organizing.

I write a letter to Zbyszek Szawlowski in the *Krankenbau* asking for help, but I receive no answer. I cannot even find the fellow who delivered the letter for me. My only other alternative is to contact Bejlin. I stand near the wires separating us from the gypsy section and learn that he is very ill with typhus.

The *Stubendiensts* demand more cigarettes. They will not continue to give me a double portion of soup indefinitely. My two good blankets disappear; in their place I find a short, tattered rag. Hunger stalks me more often, cramping my intestines. The situation looks hopeless, but I decide not to succumb. My mind is occupied for a whole day in trying to find a solution. In the end, an idea takes shape.

In the barrack, an immense container used for satisfying physiological needs has to be emptied two or three times a night. The watchman awakens four men to take care of this unpleasant job. It is truly distasteful to leave a warm bunk just to carry this stinking load.

I look up a husky Russian and explain my plan: The two of us will carry and empty the barrel. The watchman must wake us whenever the barrel is more than half full. We will manage between us. We will ask for a portion of bread from the four who usually perform this job. We will thus earn half a portion of bread.

The Russian eagerly accepts my proposition. Immediately after the bread is distributed, we go to the foursome who are supposed to be roused at night and talk with them. They agree, and we get our bread. Now, in addition to our usual work, we have a night job.

When I notify the night watchman, he is also agreeable and satisfied that he will not have to fight with the people. There is only one unpleasantness: I must change bunks and sleep near the barrel. Moreover, the light is always on, the odor is extemely unpleasant, and people are constantly coming and going all night long. However, what can one do about it? I am proud of myself; I have begun to fight for my life.

* * *

The first night we are awakened twice; the next, three times. The night watchman is very satisfied with us and, in recognition, he gives us a few potatoes. One night he offers us a partnership. The *Kapos* and foremen give him their clothes and shoes to clean and pay him well, but he has too much to do. He needs our help and offers to give us bread.

I am elated. Naturally, it's a deal.

The work lasts late into the night. In the morning, our eyes burn from lack of sleep, but we have a portion of bread in our pockets, a FULL portion.

It rains constantly. It is true they gave us striped overcoats, but these do not help very much. The Russian, who is very astute, organizes several heavy, cement paper bags from somewhere. While I clean shoes and clothes, he makes some ingenious raincoats.

We become friends and work in the same group. In the morning, we go to work in a heavy rain. Once we pass through the gate and are in the field, the Russian takes two sacks from under his arm. As he hands me one, he says, "Put it on, *Tovarich*!"

Since I have difficulty in getting it on, he shows me how, and I follow his example. The opening at the bottom of the sack is for the head; two holes on each side, for the arms. Although motion is somewhat restricted, it is unimportant. We laugh at the rain all day long.

The SS men and *Kapos* notice our new uniforms. Since they are in a good mood, they allow us to wear them.

That night the Russian gets several orders for his "raincoats". As payment for one, he will receive one and a half portions of bread and sausage. Everything would be fine, but he cannot find any more sacks.

"You," he says to me, "maybe you have friends. You bring me cement sacks. I'll work, and we'll divide the loot."

Although it is late, I run to the clinic that same night. Briefly, I tell Aleks the whole story. This dear fellow is very depressed because he has been unable to help me, but when he learns of my need, he jumps off the stool and runs to the road construction *Oberkapo*. A few words are exchanged and. . . .

"Tomorrow morning before coffee, you'll get . . ."

Early in the morning I report to the *Oberkapo* who takes me to a corner of the warehouse where there is a supply of empty sacks. "Take as many as you want and disappear. Move!" he orders.

I grab as many as I can carry. The Russian is as happy as a child and exclaims, "Wonderful!"

We go to work in a good mood even if it is raining and our teeth chatter from the cold. As usual, the *Kapos* and SS men hide in their huts. We hear hoofbeats and several revolver shots that shake us up. A moment later Schillinger appears tightly wrapped in a rubber coat with a gun in his hand. He roars at the SS men and the *Kapos.* An *Unterscharführer,* guards, and the *Kommandant* try to explain. It is of no avail.

Schillinger yells for the *Kapos.* Sport. . . .

Our hearts are joyful, and we rub our hands with satisfaction when we see the fat bulls rolling in the mud. Before Schillinger leaves he yells something. The *Kapos* stand in a line and shout, *"Jawohl, Herr Raportführer!"* as water runs off them.

The *Kapos* pick up their clubs and shout, "Work! Faster! Tempo!"

We had had a few quiet days. Now we are paying the bitter price for them. Blows land often as the *Kapos* make us suffer for their humiliation.

". . . Schillinger killed three *Häftlinge* and severely wounded two!" This is the news that circulates among the groups.

The Russian clenches his fist and shouts, "Only let Father Stalin come! The SS men and *Kapos* will be hanged! The sons-of-bitches! The murderers!"

* * *

The make-shift raincoats protect us quite adquately. We are the objects of envy and admiration.

Immediately after the evening meal is distributed, we start working. I clean shoes and clothes; Ivan makes raincoats.

We work late. We hear the locomotive's whistle and the sound of freight car wheels and truck motors at the railroad ramp. Another transport arrived with human fodder for the gas chamber.

The next day the report is received by a new SS man. Schillinger has disappeared, gone without a trace. The entire camp is excited. Everyone is curious. What could have happened to him?

We learn what occurred only after several days have passed. The *Sonderkommando,* who bring all the news into camp, are enthusiastic. Schillinger has been killed.

One memorable night, a transport of Jews with passports and visas to South American countries arrived for the gas chamber. They were detained in a temporary camp in Vitel on the Swiss border and were supposed to have been exchanged for Nazi spies. Only a few were lucky. Ninety-five percent of them were sent to Auschwitz "for convalescence".

They brought a sizeable amount of wealth with them. Schillinger ran from the ramp to his house as though possessed. Robbing was not enough for him. When the victims were close to the crematorium and only a minute remained before they entered the gas chamber, the pervert noticed a beautiful young girl. In front of everyone he called to her in a loud voice, promising that he would save her from death in the gas chamber if she would come with him for a while to a side room. She objected vehemently. Schillinger pulled out his revolver and was ready to shoot. He did not succeed. The brave girl wrested the revolver from his hand and, with two well-aimed shots, killed him. She used the third bullet on herself.

Schillinger, the executioner of Auschwitz, died at the hands of a woman. "Rejoice, brothers!"

At night the weather improves. By that time we had sold all of our raincoats and have a backlog of orders to be filled. We collected so much bread that we do not know what to do with it. The Russian suggests that we exchange it for cigarettes since they take up little space and can always be traded for food.

After Schillinger's death, the general situation worsens. The Germans, afraid to relax their discipline, treat the prisoners more brutally. The SS shoot at every occasion; even without a reason. It is a massacre.

My Russian friend has enough of this. On the way back from work he tells me of his plan. "Tonight I'll go to the *Schreibstube* and give all my cigarettes to the *Schreiber*. We must get out of here. They'll finish us off very soon."

I remind him that Aleks promised to pull me out of this hell if it is at all possible. I would ask Aleks to help him, too.

"You've been here so long and haven't learned a thing! Before Aleks fixes anything, we'll have several holes in our heads. We'll probably get out of here through the chimney if we wait any longer!" scolds Ivan, shaking his head.

Immediately after the roll call, I give Ivan my cigarettes and the two of us go to the *Schreibstube*. Ivan enters alone; I wait. He talks with someone, gesticulating in a lively manner. Then, looking around carefully, he deposits the cigarettes into the man's hand. The fellow in the *Schreibstube* writes something in a notebook. Ivan's face is radiant when he comes out.

"It's beautiful! In two days we'll be 'free'. He promised to reassign us to an excellent *Kommando*."

* * *

We count the minutes and seconds that separate us from the blessed moment when we will leave for the new *Kommando* because the situation grows more tragic every day. The rain his constant; the road, impassable; the mud is up to our knees. We lack the strength to walk. The SS men and *Kapos* chase us like cattle, yelling, "Faster! Faster!" Every minute another victim falls. All this affects us. Ivan looks at me and sobs soundlessly.

On the day after Ivan's conversation with the fellow in the *Schreibstube*, we return to camp late at night. We are barely able to stand and are desperate.

"He's fooled us, the bandit, but I'll show him!" shouts Ivan, hiding a piece of a shovel handle under his arm. "I'm going to kill the bastard!"

In vain I try to restrain him from taking this crazy step.

"I'll kill the bastard! KILL!" he repeats, stubbornly.

He pushes slowly through the crowd waiting for soup and coffee. Just at the very moment he approaches the exit, we hear a loud voice from the entrance calling our numbers. We cannot believe our ears, but it is true. Help has come at last!

"Pick up your belongings and march to Barrack 16!"

On the way there, we speculate about the kind of *Kommando* we will get. The barrack is silent; everybody is sleeping. The night watchman collects our charts and assigns us to a temporary bunk where we rest on the bare boards without blankets and with ten other people.

Ivan says confidently, "Everything will be all right tomorrow morning. I still have a pack of cigarettes."

So we are on a new *Kommando*. Despite my earnest desire to have a job under a roof, we are assigned to a *Kommando* that is building a railroad track from the ramp to the crematorium. The construction of this line for the SS is contracted out to a private company from Berlin that is eager to make as large a profit as possible; the opportunity is there. They have been working on the project for a long time, but the results are negligible. It is no wonder. The job is huge, and there is a lack of even the most primitive tools so that everything must be done manually. There are enough people, rather, there is enough human flesh.

A few days ago, a commission came to the building site and noticed the unsatisfactory progress. As a result, several hundred *Häftlinge* have been assigned to work day and night. The *Kapos* have received new instructions on handling them.

I am discouraged. My friend Ivan is in an excellent mood.

"We got out of the swamp. Now we'll revive. There are many Russian foreman here so we'll get an easy job. The road to the *Kommando* site is short and not tiresome. The barrack is good. When the transport reaches the gas chamber, you'll find that much will be thrown away, and we'll have enough to eat," he says, all in one breath.

The work is no bed of roses for me. I do not want to see my brothers chased to the crematorium. I do not want to pick up the things they throw away. My friend Ivan does not meditate much about these details and walks away, whistling happily.

Before we begin working, some character in a leather jacket with the party insignia on the lapel, delivers a short talk. "The administration is dissatisfied with your work. Such poor performances will not be tolerated. Everyone must give everything he has, otherwise it will be bad for you. I'll be watching. Woe to the one who tries to sabotage orders! Do you understand?!"

"Jawohl!"

Ivan and I are ordered to unload two freight cars filled with planks at the ramp. We begin by carrying the heavy boards two at a time and placing them along the newly prepared ground. A few minutes later however, our "guardian angel" arrives with a club and orders us to carry planks one at a time and faster.

"Move!" he shouts and hits Ivan on his back. Luckily I avoid a blow.

For a long time we run like mad. The pile of boards grows. It does not matter if several people fall because they cannot continue the tempo. It doesn't matter if blood flows from noses and mouths. Building a side-track to the crematorium is more important. "Move! Work! Tempo!"

The character in the leather jacket is finally satisfied. He shouts something and leaves. Let others take over; he sets the tempo.

When I meet Ivan again, I examine his ribs. He is fortunate. Everything is all right. He menaces the Germans by invoking the powers of "Father" Stalin and the Red Army.

At last I am able to beat some sense into Ivan's head by convincing him that Stalin and the Red Army are far away while the Germans are here. We must save ourselves. We think of what we can do as we go for another board.

Ivan has an idea. He disappears without a word. I meet him during the noon break. He is triumphant; he has settled it. Some Russian foreman took him to the highest-ranking *Oberkapo* who, for five packs of cigarettes and a few other small objects, assigns us to sort screws and hooks, a very easy job. Ivan gave him one pack of cigarettes on account. He will give him the rest when the first transport arrives . . . and maybe the *Oberkapo* will forget.

We pass the days buried among iron, sorting screws and hooks. Ivan lights a small fire and bakes potatoes. From a distance we hear the *Kapos* and SS men roaring, the thumping blows of their clubs, and the cries of the beaten. For the time being, we are safe.

* * *

We are reassigned to the night shift. Simply put, we do not return to the camp but continue to work except for short recesses for roll call and the evening meal. In addition to our regular portion of bread today, we receive an extra piece of sausage. "For good work," the man in the leather jacket explains.

Ivan winks knowingly and says, "So, *Tovarich,* we've worked hard for those bandits and sons-of-bitches! Wait for "Father" Stalin and the Red Army!"

This time Ivan talks more about "Father" Stalin and the Red Army and dwells longer over the tortures they will inflict on the Germans.

We work by the light of regular lamps. At about ten o'clock when the powerful searchlights near the railroad ramp are turned on, we hear the roar of a motorcycle and some voices.

Ivan jumps from his place and shouts, "You! Transport!"

Trucks are arriving, *Kanada* is coming.

We hear the panting locomotive and then its whistle as it pulls into the Auschwitz station. A few minutes later, the powerful lights focus on a small locomotive pushing many railroad cars. Soldiers jump out of two passenger cars and take up positions around the train. All the lights illuminate the ramp. It is almost as bright as it is in the daytime.

We hear the sound of hammers as the freight cars are opened and, "Get out! Get out!"

Though we are several meters away, we are close enough to clearly see the horrified human faces. We hear the terrified cries of the children and the desperate calls of families. Above all these sounds, the overpowering voice of some SS man on the loudspeaker is heard, "Silence, you dogs!"

As more freight cars are emptied, the chaos on the ramp increases. I cannot tell what language they are speaking, but I get the impression that they are Jews from Holland. All of them are neatly dressed and carry valises, rucksacks, and packages.

Another order is issued over the loudspeaker. "Men to the left! Women and children to the right!"

How well I know those words! I still remember them from Treblinka. My heart pounds violently.

The families defy the order and stay together.

A small passenger automobile arrives, and the *Lagerführer* and *Lagerarzt* step out. They stand to one side, light cigarettes, and look indifferently at the terrible tragedy being played out before them. When the SS men notice these authorities, they become wild, use dogs, beat with the butts of their rifles, kick, and forcefully separate families. The people's screams must reach heaven.

When order is restored, the SS men and officials walk by the group, select one hundred men and command them to stand to one side. Then they approach the women. They laugh and point with their fingers as they look them over. Finally they separate fifty women from the entire group. These one hundred fifty will go to the camp.

There are twenty-five freight cars on the ramp. On each one, the figure "120" is printed in chalk. It is simple arithmetic. Twenty-five times one hundred twenty is three thousand. Of these three thousand human souls, one hundred fifty will be sent to the camp. It is exactly five percent.

The performance is about to end. Those who were chosen to stand aside are taken to the camp by SS men. The rest will leave in trucks. Eight large freight trucks are filled to capacity. SS men on motorcycles escort the noisy trucks while the rest of the people wait on the ramp for their turn.

Kanada goes to work. They enter the cars by twos to throw out the valises and packages and to pull out the corpses.

The trucks return; another convoy departs. And so it continues for several more times. On the last trip, the living go with several corpses. Everyone will be cremated.

Kanada finishes its work loading the luggage on trucks, and returns to the camp.

SS men inspect the freight cars carefully with flashlights, looking underneath especially around the wheels and inside the caboose. Then, slowly the searchlights on the ramp are extinguished. A small locomotive draws up and pulls the empty cars away.

I am deep in thought and do not notice Ivan's absence. He returns in the morning with bulging pockets.

"And you, stupid, sit here and do nothing?!" is his amiable, accusatory greeting. "All the *Kapos*, SS men, and *Häftlinge* have everything and you wait here for me to bring you things?"

I try to explain. Ivan laughs.

"You don't want to take," he says, "so croak with them in the gas chamber. We're alive and need to stay that way and . . . it's all the same!"

Ivan eats some chocolate and then salami and cheese. As he drinks some condensed milk, he mocks me.

The gong sounds in the quarantine camp. We finish our work.

Ivan gives me a few things saying, "If you don't want to organize, at least help me pass something through the gate." I agree to do that although the risk is great. What else can I do? We leave.

We are lucky. . . .

As soon as we get to the barrack, Ivan gives the *Stubendiensts* chocolate and cigarettes. We are assured good blankets.

The daytime *Kommando* leaves for work. Musicians play at the gate. Flames leap from the chimneys.

With a broad smile on his face, Ivan hands me a pair of warm socks, shorts, a sweater, and half a loaf of bread.

I am dizzy; my head is in a whirl. Oh to sleep, to sleep even for just a short time to forget the horrible reality!

The knocking, noise, and turmoil are so great that one cannot close one's eyes. A stream of water falls on my head. Ivan curses and menaces the *Stubendiensts* who clean the barrack. Finally, the *Blockältester* interferes and demands silence. I am surprised that I managed to sleep for two hours.

On that day we sleep very little. We have our noon meal followed by inspection. After that, there is the distribution of bread and then, roll call.

I find two cans of shoe polish on my bed and decide to give Aleks this modest gift. I sneak out of the line for a moment and run to the clinic. The fellows are pleased to see me. "What's happening to you? You haven't visited for such a long time."

Aleks brings some bread from his corner. I thank him and proudly offer him MY gifts.

* * *

Winter is coming. It gets quite cold at night and I am grateful to Ivan for the warm clothing. I cannot imagine how I could possibly survive a night without it. When I thank him, Ivan is pleased and says, "You wait. We'll have plenty of everything when more transports arrive."

In spite of my wishes to the contrary, Ivan's prognostications come true. Not a single night passes without the arrival of two and sometimes three transports. Activity on the ramp is frantic. Thousands of people are condemned to the four crematoria. I am distressed and almost deafened by the cries. The searchlights blind me.

Like crows on a battlefield, the SS men, *Kapos,* and some *Häftlinge* hunt for loot. No one watches anyone else. Only one motive fascinates our superiors: greed. What did the Jews bring? How much gold can be stolen or seized? The Jews are going to die and will not need any valuables.

Angered by my helplessness, I moisten my burning lips with my tongue. Through my half-closed eyes I catch a glimpse of a woman with a child in her arms. Oh, she throws away a rucksack, and several persons immediately run after it.

Ivan is furious with me as we return to camp. He had organized several rings and watches. At the gate there is such strict control that he is forced to throw everything away. SS men find money on five members of our *Kommando* and kill them as a warning.

"Obviously, all of this is your fault. You won't organize anything. You don't even want to help. You exploit me!" Ivan complains.

I refuse to respond to Ivan's accusations. I resolve to separate myself from him at the first opportunity.

Someone suggests that I give him my night shift. He offers to pay me a portion of bread for every night he works. Moreover, he will also share part of his booty with me. I am happy. I would gladly change even without compensation because, though I try to control myself, my nerves are frazzled from watching the nightly scenes on the railroad ramp. I do not mind if I must work day and night.

I carry railroad tracks. I push carts of gravel. Sweat pours from me in streams. I have difficulty in breathing. From time to time some "helping hand" hits me on my back. It does not matter. It is worth anything not to hear the desperate screams and the children's cries, not to see those faces going insane from fear.

Ivan has a tragic end. It came faster than I expected. One night he walked out feeling very happy and full of hope. As he left, he looked at me with disdain and spit on me. In the morning they brought him in on a few boards, an improvised stretcher. He was dead, but blood was still trickling from several holes in his head.

Someone said that Ivan got into an argument with a foreman about some loot, a small leather wallet which was said to be filled with dollars. The two of them screamed; they harrassed each other. An SS man approached, shot them both, and took the wallet. The one relating the story comments, shaking his head, "What a pity!" He forgets to add whether his lament is for the man or the money.

* * *

Hunger is my lot again. The fellow with whom I changed shifts gets his regular portion of bread at night, so obviously, he does not give me any of it. Work during the day is heavy.

I must look for a way to organize some bread to make up for what I lost on the night shift. I do not want to beg from the men in the clinic any longer.

I report as a volunteer to bring the noon meal. At about eleven o'clock every day, eight people go to the camp to carry two one hundred liter barrels of soup for our *Kommando.* Two carry a barrel for a kilometer, then they alternate. Sometimes we must run back when the kitchen is late. After each of these trips, our normal breathing is impaired for an hour, and our hands . . . I'd better not talk about that. The joints in the arm, elbow, and wrist, ache. It becomes chronic. For this labor, we receive an additional liter of soup which we can keep in our canteens until evening or, depending on the quality of the soup, exchange it for one-half to three-quarters of a portion of bread.

I try not to think . . . only to kill time from roll call to noontime, and from then, to evening . . . until I change shifts.

Once again I am on the night shift. For a week I am assured that I will have bread again. Sometimes my "benefactor" gives me a few cigarettes. This is also good, for it is difficult to find a way to receive the minimum amount of food and not die of hunger. On the other hand, there is always the danger of becoming apathetic which is tantamount to a death sentence.

In the barrack one night, we hear someone shout, "A singer! Is there anybody here who can sing?"

"Oho, maybe I'll get something!" I think. I throw off my blanket and run to the *Blockältester*'s corner where a party is in progress. Someone there is playing a harmonica emitting some hoarse, asthmatic sounds. Since there cannot be a party without songs, I must save the situation. Something in my being laughs at those in whose company I find myself.

I try to buoy my confidence by telling myself, "Calm down, Tadzek! It's easier to sing than to carry soup."

For my guest appearance, I decide to open with the best song in my repertoire, *The Tales of Karlowicz,* a haunting, nostalgic air of lost childhood. I try to sing with feeling and as loudly as possible while watching their faces for the effect.

"Today I remember my childhood with nostalgia. . . ." The words of the song are flowing. . . .

The *Blockältester* hides his face in his hands and dries his eyes with a dirty handkerchief. "Aha, it has moved him." I am glad, and I am touched, but unsentimentally. "Maybe he will give me a portion of bread or perhaps more. I must concentrate so that I do not forget the lyrics of the song."

When I finish, there is a moment of silence, then applause. The *Schreiber* opens his box, cuts a piece of bread and smears it thickly with fat. I thank him sincerely and start to put it into my pocket, explaining, "I'll eat it at work tomorrow."

The *Schreiber* will not hear of it and insists, "You must eat it right now. You'll get more at work."

What a heavenly taste! I would prefer to chew it slowly and savor every bite, but the company is impatient.

The *Kapo* is German and does not understand Polish. He maintains that the most beautiful songs are French. A discussion ensues. The *Kapo* cuts it short. "We'll see! Sing something in French!" he demands.

I do not know French, and French songs, even less. However, an order is an order. In despair I recall a few French words that I heard as a child. The melody is less troublesome and I sing, *"J'attendrais le jour et la nuit . . ."*

As I try to imitate the popular singer Tino Rossi, I think to myself, "All this is rather comical. I hope no one here understands French." Finally it ends. The effect is unbelievable. I must repeat it!

The party lasts until the wee hours. I run to my bunk with a pack of cigarettes and half a loaf of bread under my arm and fall asleep. In a dream that night, I see my mother's smiling face.

* * *

It is snowing. I trade a pack of cigarettes for a pair of beautiful fur-lined gloves and a very warm ski cap of brightly colored cloth. I am protected against the cold and, generally, not too badly dressed for my first winter in the camp. The fact that I am managing for myself is reason enough to celebrate.

Others are falling. Cold and hunger take their toll.

* * *

Every Sunday, we have lice control. During one inspection a few of the insects were found. In the beginning of December, there is talk about a new delousing program. Zenkteller wants to demonstrate his ability and zeal to the SS. One day en route to the noon meal, I see him conversing with the *Lagerarzt.* As he explains something to Thielo, he gesticulates in a lively fashion. Thielo nods his head approvingly.

Now I am sure that there will be a general delousing. Given the winter conditions in the camp, it means the death of several hundred *Häftlinge.*

My fear becomes reality. While returning from work as usual one bitterly cold day I think morosely about standing in line for roll call. In the distance we see signs of our impending disaster. Our straw mats are spread out in front of the barrack and the blankets are tied together in bundles in the corridor. Coffee is unavailable. There was no time to deliver it. Roll call is protracted. An icy wind blows in from the mountains. Our teeth are chattering. We feel despondent. Our situation seems utterly hopeless. So as not to lose a valuable day's work, the first two barracks go to the baths that night after roll call. We await our turn.

"Caps off!"

Finally, we start. The *Stubendienst* loads a heavy, poorly-tied bundle of blankets on my head. I have difficulty handling this unwieldy material and, consequently, it takes me longer to reach my destination.

The new baths are said to be beautiful, but, unfortunately, they are not finished. "Unfortunately" . . . in a short while we will learn what this "unfortunately" really means.

About eight hundred of us from two barracks wait in the bitter cold. Brrrrrr! We are frozen, but we have no will to warm ourselves by slapping or massaging one another. We stand stooped over. To avoid disorder, the SS men permit us to enter in groups of one hundred. From time to time, the doors open and another hundred go in. People push, trying to get inside as quickly as possible because the SS beat us with their clubs. Many of their victims fall and never rise.

I am one of many candidates for entry into the "paradise". I push myself sideways, using a minute when the doors are open. A human wave pushes me into the room.

We enter the "dirty" side. The place is immense; it could easily accommodate all eight hundred of us. But why should the SS men and the bath personnel exert additional effort? The cattle can wait outside. Let them freeze. Who cares?

"Undress! Hang your clothes on a wire behind the screen! Go to the steam room!"

Inside it is warm; it feels heavenly. I stretch with pleasure as the steam hisses from the pipes. Much too soon a whistle is blown and then, "Go to the barber!"

They chase us into the cold, window-lined corridor; not a single pane of glass is intact. We stand in line. In one minute we descend from paradise into hell. Oh God, what torture! Why do the barbers work so slowly?

We are moving at last. We are soon in the shower, under the heavy pressure of jets of hot water. The burning sensation mingles with the delightful feeling of warmth. Would that it could last forever!

A whistle is blown. The *Kapo* shuts the faucet. Another whistle, "Move! On the double!" We are chased to the clean side. It is as large as the dirty area, the only difference is that it is icy cold. The pipes for the central heating system are cold. A frigid wind continues to blow through the paneless windows.

My body that came alive in the heat, is now seized by the terribly painful cold. My teeth are chattering like a man in the throes of a malaria spasm. I hope to get my clothes soon.

I am trying to recall how enjoyably we bathed at home in winter in the "olden times". Mother would knock on the bathroom door and asked the little boy if he were cold and if he would like an electric blanket on the bed.

"It's well you can't see this, Mother," I think with despair.

The first of the uniforms arrive in a cart. There is no trace of mine. I am naked, but I must wait until morning for my clothes. When they finally arrive, I hurry because roll call is about to start. We will leave for work soon.

They stole my gloves; my bread is gone. I am freezing and hungry. If I could only thaw out a little, if only I had something warm to drink. . . .

As I push the wheelbarrow full of stones, I suddenly notice something shiny in the ditch. It is a can of conserves. I open it with my primitive knife, cutting myself. My blood spurts, but I feel no pain, anyway, it doesn't matter.

There are meat and vegetables in the can. I look around. When the supervisors do not see me, I begin eating. I would like to save something for later to exchange for bread, but I do not have enough will-power. I finish it all and lick the can. It tastes good.

Only after a little while, when my stomach starts to digest the food and my hunger is appeased, do I try to think where this can came from. Oh wonder, my conscience does not bother me.

* * *

Several days after the bath, I suffer from a severe headache at noontime. With difficulty, I hold out until evening. Immediately after roll call, I run to Aleks for aspirin. It does not occur to me that I could be sick. I must be healthy! I must survive in order to avenge!

I exchange a portion of sausage for a little boiled water, then crawl into my bunk, cover myself with blankets, swallow the tablets, and go to sleep. I wake in a pool of sweat. The aspirin has had its effect. My shirt, sweater, blanket, everything is wet. The gong in the quarantine barrack sounds; in fifteen minutes, it will be time for reveille. When I get out of the bunk, my teeth chatter. The barrack is as cold as an ice-house. I use a piece of paper that I found in the garbage to wipe the sweat. Maybe my shirt will dry by the time I return at night if I leave it in the barrack. My throat tickles; I develop a hacking cough. I try to minimize the seriousness of my condition by convincing myself that it is nothing. So what if I have a cold? I go to work with the *Kommando.*

The weather is beautiful with not a cloud in the sky. You can see the mountains as clearly as the palm of your hand. It could be a bit warmer, but the December sun warms my back delightfully.

Work goes slowly. The world is beautiful, and the rays of the winter sun. . . . Maybe the eternal beauty of nature will affect our "masters".

"You! Do you want to bring the noon meal?!"

I am gazing in the distance at a pleasant view: a train going by with passengers looking out of the windows.

"So, are you going or not? Will you honor me with an answer?!"

"No, I'm not going!" I finally reply.

"What a funny character," I think. "What does he want from me? Why would I want to carry the cauldron? Isn't it better to stay here?" I feel pleasantly dizzy. The sun is warm; I no longer feel cold; I am fine.

Before evening, I feel a sharp pain in my side. I take my pulse; it is very rapid. I reason that it must have been caused by the walk, and if I rest, it will slow down. If I do not feel any better tomorrow, I will go to the clinic. The fellows will help me. Then again, maybe tomorrow my condition will improve. Others have been in worse shape and did not visit the doctor. Just to be sure, I will go. If only my side was not so painful. . . .

I do not wait for the coffee, not even for bread. I hurry to the bunk. For a portion of bread, the *Stubendienst* lends me two heavy blankets. I undress completely and pull the covers over my head. For a while I shiver violently, but then I seem to feel all right.

Why is it such a short night? The lights are turned on in the barrack; people are moving about. Someone pulls me.

"Hey, you! *Muzelman!* Maybe you'll get up! Must we send you a special messenger?"

"Good morning, *Stubendienst,*" I greet him in a Warsaw accent.

Everything seems so simple, so easy. The world is whirling a bit. My knees are buckling. Amid all of these feelings, only one thing bothers me: Who is poking a hot iron into my side?

"Hey, friend, why don't you go to the doctor?" I hear someone ask, but then I lose track of it.

"Move! Get going!"

Suddenly it is dark and cold. I stretch my hands in front of me. I hear someone laughing nearby. It takes a few minutes before I realize that I am outside. I hear music in the distance.

Someone hits me in the neck and shouts, "Can't you take off your cap, you idiot?"

Aha! We must be marching by the gate. I start to cough; I cannot hold out. How it hurts! The hellish pain brings me back to reality. I find myself pushing a wheelbarrow full of gravel, but I do not know how I got here.

My cough is worse. I run my tongue over my parched, cracked lips. I must have a drink and grab some snow. I lick the snowflakes from my collar. It finally occurs to me that I am sick and seriously so. My heart beats wildly. I must get to the hospital, otherwise I will die. I recall how indifferent I felt. It is clear to me now that I was feverish. I clench my fists, determined not to succumb to the fever. My mind works furiously. What shall I do? How can I save myself?

I think of begging Zenkteller to send me to Barrack 12. How absurd! The old bastard will not neglect the opportunity to send me to the gas chamber. But I do have friends in K.B.: Zbyszek, Dr. Herman, and others. Oh God! Oh Mother! If only the work would cease! If only we were back in camp!

An SS man walks toward me. I grab the wheelbarrow, but do not know where to go nor do I remember what I must do with the contents. I have an idea: to go straight ahead. The road is hard and well-beaten. Pushing is easy. I try very hard not to cough.

A horn sounds. Two open freight trucks containing naked bodies pass near me. Maybe they are corpses from K.B. No, I hear some moaning. SS men standing in the freight trucks club someone from time to time. I watch the trucks for a moment.

They pass through the open gate on the road to the second crematorium. After the SS men jump off, the trucks turn around and back into the opening. The platform is tilted, and the people roll down. I do not hear the cries. To think that this is being done in broad daylight where everyone can see it! What a pleasant prospect! Maybe it's an hallucination caused by my fever. I pinch my ear. Unfortunately, it is true and just as real as the pain in my side when I cough.

I pour out the gravel and return with the empty wheelbarrow. Fortunately no one noticed my absence. People are headed for the noon meal. So, half a day has already passed.

After I eat, I feel as though I am losing consciousness. I am certain that, if I succumb to that sensation, I will fall. Then I will either freeze to death or some *Kapo* will finish me off.

I rub my head with snow and bite my lips until they bleed. I scratch my face with my nails until finally—oh heavenly moment!—a sharp whistle, and we assemble.

We are almost at the gate when the siren on the *Kommandant*'s house wails. But this is not an air raid; it is a signal to the chain of outside towers that a prisoner has escaped. I think, "What cursed luck I have! Who knows how long roll call will last now?"

"Caps off!"

Why the hell does it take so long? Are they crazy? Our shaved heads offer no protection against the bitter cold which penetrates the skull to the brain and nips the ears.

At the gate, we can hear the *Lagerführer* roaring.

Ten *Häftlinge* in one *Kommando* have escaped. SS men are in pursuit. For punishment, we must stand at attention with our caps off until they return. *Blockältesters* and German *Kapos* are responsible for the proper execution of the order.

As night falls the searchlights on the wires are turned on. SS men and *Kapos* armed with clubs, run around like ghosts. Woe to the one who puts on his cap!

I sob quietly in my helpless torture. It seems as if my time has finally come. Everything is hopeless. I lack the strength to fight; death is the welcome solution. Once again I fall into a blissful state. Just a minute or even a second is enough to give up the struggle and fall, and end my suffering.

With a superhuman effort I regain control of the situation. Oh God, what is the limit of human suffering?

The night drags on endlessly. Perhaps daylight will never come. Thirst, coughing, and cold plague me. I must be having a nightmare, but why can't I wake up?

The gong sounds. "Go for coffee!" So we did stand all night in the bitter cold without our caps!

I think of only one thing: Get to the clinic! I turn in that direction. My legs are stiff and move like pieces of wood. The rest of my body is as unresponsive as if it were made of stone or ice.

I wait a few minutes in front of the door. Zenkteller is still asleep. I look for Wortman and see him in a corner talking with someone. I approach him to complain, but all I can manage are some unintelligible sounds. Somebody sits me down and puts a thermometer in my mouth. As if in a fog I hear, "41" (105° F). I laugh. He must be crazy; I am only twenty-eight. Someone holds me under the arm guiding me somewhere. It is cold, so cold.

I hear a voice urging me, "Hold on a while longer."

I am in a bath in the washroom. My suffering will soon end. I cough. Oh, how it hurts! Someone throws a blanket around me and again I walk, but not far. Some doors open; a blessed warmth envelops me. I lie down on a bed and get under the blankets. It is heaven, and I experience nirvana. I open my eyes for a minute and hear Zenkteller, "This one has typhus for sure—to Barrack 12."

"Not that!" I scream and move from side to side.

Someone places a hand on my forehead. It feels good. A voice next to me says, "Tadzek, it's me, Zbyszek. Calm down. Nothing will happen to you here."

* * *

I cannot cough; I am choking. I cannot breathe; I am suffocating! I am lying in water. Help!

Some friendly hand is removing my shirt. I open my eyes before I realize where I am and what is happening to me. It takes me but a moment to become oriented and to recognize that it is Dr. Stern, the chief doctor of this barrack who is standing beside my bed. He is pleased as he says, "I thought that you would die." Then he calls the *Stubendienst* and tells him to notify Zbyszek again.

I am as helpless as a newborn baby. Stern tells me that I suffered from bilateral pneumonia and that for seven days I was unconscious with temperatures above 41° (105°). "If it had not been for Zbyszek who gave me injections every day . . ." It is easy to guess the rest.

I look at my hands and legs. I am skin and bones. It is a miracle that I did not develop serious bedsores.

"Congratulations, Tadzek! You'll survive the camp. Such pneumonia! But let's not talk about it," says Zbyszek, handing me a package containing white bread, sausage, sugar, and several apples. "This is from my holiday package. Eat! You must get stronger!"

Herman, Dr. Schor, and others visit, bearing food and whatever else they could get. Tears well up in my eyes. The fact that, in this hell, there are people who remember me kindly, moves me deeply.

* * *

With Christmas near, a fir tree appears in the barrack. The patients make decorations from boxes and paper which they hang on the tree. Letters and packages also arrive.

Letters . . . I envy no one more than those who receive these letters. Oh God, what do I live for? What can I expect after liberation? What awaits me? No one will rejoice that I am free, just as no one will lament my death. Anyway, who will ever know? Number 126604 ceased to exist. All I have left are memories of Mother, Father, Fredzia, and a beloved, holy home.

In three days, I gain back enough strength to rise from my bed and drag myself to the doctor's scale in the barrack. A while ago a *Stubendienst* weighed a *muzelman*. He weighed fifty kilos. I step on the scale and find that I do not even weigh that much. As for my height of one hundred and eighty-two centimeters . . . I must fatten up at all costs, otherwise I will be sent to the gas chamber in the first selection.

I have enough to eat. At the insistence of my friends, the *Blockältester* gives me two liters of soup daily. In addition, the fellows supply me with bread. I gain six kilos in one week. I am on the road to recovery and regaining my strength. I would like to stay in the *Krankenbau* for as long as possible, if only Zenkteller. . . .

The *Blockältester* announces the forthcoming visit of the Old One. I immediately try to compose a speech that I hope will convince him to extend my stay in the barrack. Maybe he will assign me somewhere as a medic.

Zenkteller's visit is short. He stands in the middle of the ward, looks around suspiciously, notices me, and shouts, "Out with him! I don't want to see him anymore!" He slams the door, and that is that.

Nevertheless, I remain in the hospital for another two days. There is a higher power. There is no clothing in the depot. I use the time to organize a few warm rags and to converse with my friends. I want to be transferred from the labor section to K.B. Zbyszek Szawlowski shakes his head as he says, "It's bad, Tadzek. Unfortunately it's impossible now. A few days ago, the *Lagerarzt* examined the medic situation and came to the conclusion that there are too many of them. He discharged fifteen to barracks and promised a further reduction."

What can I do? I must be satisfied with Zbyszek's promise that he will bring me into K.B. at the first opportunity.

Fifty of us return to camp, fifty *muzelmen*. We can hardly drag out feet. We are given some fantastic child-sized garments from the K.B. clothes depot. My pants barely reach my ankles. My jacket is so tight that it makes no sense to talk about buttoning the jacket. I have two left shoes: one is made of leather; the other, of wood. The cigarettes Zbyszek gave me on parting will help me a lot.

I noticed that, in my career as a *Häftling*, "dress maketh the man". This popular adage has never had a more practical application than here in Auschwitz where there is a special method of judging people. Intellectual qualities mean nothing. You may be the most learned man in the world, the most famous one, but if you are not dressed nicely, no one pays any attention to you. You may be dying of hunger and no one will offer you a bread crumb. The most important quality one may possess is the ability to organize. When someone meets you for the first time, he appraises you from head to toe, noting your suit, shoes, and cap. Then he asks what you want and, finally, who you are.

We are divided among three barracks. I go to number 18. Following the usual procedure of *Blockältesters,* they are painting, and things are in disarray. We are not allowed inside. How unfortunate it is for me!

I run to the clinic. Through the window I see Zenkteller and I cannot go in. It is too bad that the doors to the clothes depot are closed. I must wait until nightfall.

Tonight is New Year's Eve; tomorrow is the beginning of the New Year. Maybe they will want someone to sing. It is true that I am still too weak and my voice . . . but I hope that I will be able to sing soon.

The sky is turning gray. I hear music at the gate. The *Kommandos* are coming, and it is time for roll call. After that, the chief *Kapo* announces in a loud voice, "*Blockältesters* out!" We assume that the *Raportführer* will deliver a New Year's speech, or maybe he will offer us additional food. In any event, we do not expect anything bad.

Having received their instructions, the *Blockältesters* return with enigmatic expressions on their faces. They answer no questions. I sense that something is in the air and I become uneasy.

Immediately after the bread is distributed, we hear the gong and shouts throughout the entire camp.

"*Blocksperre!* Close the barracks!"

The *Blockältester* emerges from his corner and stands on a stool to announce, "Attention! Tomorrow is a workday. Everyone except the Jews will go on *Kommando.* The *Blockschreiber* will stand at the door with charts and will make a note of everyone who leaves."

The *Häftlinge* are restless and talk in loud voices. I am so stunned that I cannot move or utter a sound. A selection! To hell with it! You can go insane.

Barrack 18 has sixty Jews among its *Kommandos.* They have low numbers and are good sturdy fellows, organizers. They form into a group and discuss their situation.

Reasoning objectively, I know that my chances are nil. Not only am I a *muzelman,* but I have also been removed from the list of medics. I intend to keep my promise to myself that I will fight until the end, although I do not know how I will manage right now.

That night I do not close my eyes. I smoke one cigarette after another. In the morning the pack is empty.

The gong sounds. I am anxious to find out what the day will bring.

The *Schreiber* stands at the door with his list; the Aryans leave one by one. He checks the chart once more to see if, by chance, a Jew has escaped. We are left alone.

The mood is funereal. No one talks. Everyone has his own thoughts. My only regret is that I smoked all of my cigarettes, otherwise nothing intelligent comes to my mind.

Once again the gong sounds! The *Schreiber* runs into the barrack shouting, "Undress! Be ready! The commission is here!"

Through the half-open doors I see Thielo and Schwarzhuber accompanied by *Blockführers.* A group of naked men run from the first barrack. The action is fast. Half an hour later, our turn comes.

"Get out!"

We run outside in front of the barrack and wait. The temperature is minus 20° C. We shiver terribly. Why the devil did they not allow us to wear our shoes? When will they come?

The *Blockältester* arranges us in two lines. Try as I might to be near the front, I do not make it. I am the very last in line. The commission approaches.

"Attention!"

Thielo with a pointed stick in his hand and the *Raportführer* with his notebook stand side by side. The parade begins normally enough. "Show your tongue! Turn around!" Now one word is spoken, either "away" or "number".

"Away! Away! Away!" Three words, three people saved.

"Number! Number!. . . ."

It is my turn at last. I wish to make a good impression and try to run. Unfortunately, I am too frozen to move quickly.

Thielo calls, "Number!" in a friendly voice. The *Raportführer* writes 126604. He checks again; he has made no mistake. He even smiles farewell.

I enter the barrack and dress in my rags. Nearby, the fortunate ones who passed the selection are laughing and celebrating. Twenty of us are marked; our lives have ended. Poor and forgotten, we stand quietly in a corner.

To prepare to fight for my life, I decide upon a plan of action. I will run to Aleks immediately after the commission leaves.

Without knocking, I enter the dressing room. All I can manage to say is, "Aleks, save me!"

He understands and puts on his jacket. We go to the *Schreibstube* where Aleks speaks with Kazik, the *Lagerschreiber.* Kazik nods understandingly, but, unfortunately, he cannot do a thing. He has not yet received the list of those destined for the gas chamber.

We return to the clinic, and Aleks gives me cigarettes and bread. He exhorts me to bear up while he tries to do everything in his power to help.

I have confidence in Aleks and return to the barrack. But I still am bothered by a nagging thought: Can he succeed?

After roll call, the *Schreibers* convene a special meeting. I know what that means: They will get the official list and, a while later, we will be taken to the special barrack.

Everything is happening as predicted. The *Schreiber* returns and calls all the numbers. Then he double checks everything and orders everyone to be ready to march. We will go to Barrack 27. Those Jews who were lucky enough to pass the selection gather around us and offer us cigarettes. As the Poles distribute bread and fat they say, "Eat, fellows, before you die!"

I am one of five hundred victims standing in a snowstorm

in front of Barrack 27. Some appear quite healthy; in fact those men look good. I crawl up to a bunk near the entrance. Maybe some help will come.

Someone screams, "They'll exterminate all the Jews in one way or another. Why suffer anymore?"

Another voice suggests that we fight.

From the other end of the barrack someone laughs mockingly, "Aha! Self-defense!! You'll sit here for a few days in the cold without food. You'll pray to God that they take you, and you'll stop thinking of self-defense."

One joker remarks, "You'll bother the Germans as an angel and even more as a devil."

It is frigid, and I lie curled up. I am lucky that I have cigarettes. I exhale big puffs of smoke and wonder: Has Aleks succeeded? Can he possibly accomplish anything?

Somebody wants a drink; another feels weak; one has pains. The entrance and exit doors are blocked from the outside. The wind howls through the wires. The barrack becomes silent.

It is daylight again, the second day of 1944, perhaps the last one of our lives. I gradually lose hope. If Aleks was successful in arranging something, if he had some possibility of saving me, he would have let me know by calling from the outside.

I have no remorse. I fought as hard as I could, holding out through many difficult moments. You only die once.

I am surprised at my calmness and learn that many others react in the same way. Two boys lying next to me in the bunk are only seventeen years old, but they look like old men. A shiver passes through me. I think of vengeance . . . when? on whom?

The sun shines through an upper window. In the distance I hear the familiar shout: "Out! Move!"

Someone observes, "It's a nice day to bid farewell!"

"If only they'd given us a good lunch for a last meal."

"They'll give you gas, you idiot!"

"God, if there were only a little bit of snow! I'm dying of thirst."

"Die, so you won't choke in the gas chamber!"

I rub my eyes. I pinch my ears. What are those people talking about?

An elderly gentleman in the next bunk is wondering aloud, "Will anyone in this world know how we spent this New Year's Day?"

"So many are dying from bullets and bombs, and you, old man, are wondering if anyone will pity shitty characters like us!"

My frayed nerves are getting the better of me. Arguments ensue in the barrack. Cries for reconciliation do not help.

The orchestra begins playing. The elderly man in the next bunk sits up and listens attentively as though he would like to take the melody with him to the other world and says, "My son plays in the orchestra. Does the poor fellow know that I'm going to my death?"

It is night again. I lie motionless on the bare boards of the bunk and think of nothing. A feeling of paralytic helplessness pervades my body from my feet to my hips and spreads to my stomach. I am certain that when it reaches my heart, I shall die. A tranquil sensation overwhelms me. Then thousands of small pins prick my feet, my legs, and thighs. Hordes of hyperactive worms crawl over my body. I want to sweep them away, but I cannot move my hand. Maybe Aleks will come. I try to go down. Oh God, what is happening to me?

There is a noise at the door. They are coming for us. I raise my head as several figures enter the barrack: the *Raportführer,* the *Lagerältester,* the *Lagerschreiber,* and Zenkteller.

The *Lagerschreiber* holds a card from which he calls several numbers. He repeats. No, I am not mistaken; my number is among them.

Exerting great effort, I go to the *Lagerschreiber* and show him my number. Zenkteller glares at me with hostility as he says, "Go to the clinic, you moron, and wait for me there."

Once more I escape death. When I get to the barrack, Aleks is waiting for me outside. He grabs my arm and pulls me to the clinic.

When Zenkteller returns, I am already washed, shaved, fed, and practically dressed. He looks in his notebook and says, "You'll go to Barrack 24! You'll be a medic there, and, because you haven't been punished enough for your lousy behavior, you'll have to work an additional four weeks as a night watchman. Understand? Disappear!"

Aleks accompanies me. As we walk, I thank him as heartily as I can. I am fully aware that there are no adequate words in any language to express my gratitude.

"Nonsense," he says shaking his head, "there's nothing to talk about. It's over. Now you must concentrate on settling down in your new barrack as comfortably as you can. *Kanada* came there yesterday. It shouldn't be too bad for you."

The new barrack is as active as a beehive. Of its four hundred *Häftlinge,* one hundred fifty belong to *Kanada.* Business is booming. Aleks takes me to the *Blockältester* who is very pleased. "Now I'll finally have peace," he says. "The *Stubendiensts* were on duty day and night until today; then they almost rebelled!"

Aleks whispers something into the *Blockältester*'s ear.

"Don't worry, Aleks," he replies, "*Kanada* is in the barrack. He won't have it hard."

On parting, Aleks urges me to organize as much food as I can. To be a medic and a night watchman is really too much. If I do not feed myself well, I will not last long. I realize this quite clearly.

The evening gong sounds. The light is extinguished, and I take up my position at the end of the barrack next to the toilet barrel. Voices can be heard from the *Kanada* bunks.

"Night watchman! Hey, night watchman! You!"

I am handed several pairs of shoes to clean. "Make them shine! And here's something for you so you don't die of hunger! If we're satisfied, tomorrow you'll get more."

I am given several portions of bread with margarine and a few cubes of sugar. "It begins well," I think, and I start working.

It is after midnight. The barrack is so quiet that I can hear the sleeping *Häftlinge* breathe. The noises made by the guards outside are clearly audible.

I am terribly tired. I wrap myself in a blanket to protect myself from the cold and hunch over a stool.

Suddenly, from the gate, I hear the noise of a motorcycle

and the sound of boots tramping on the frozen ground. The shouting of orders seems to come from nearby.

"Get up! Quickly! Out! Get going! Move! Tempo!"

There are screams, yells, cries, chasing . . . commotion.

I break into a cold sweat as I run to the door. Yes, there is a large detachment of SS guards in the section, and the door to Barrack 27 is open. I was there only a few hours ago.

This morning there are no sick ones for the clinic. I feel that I have earned a little rest and I want to lie down. I crawl into a bunk.

Suddenly, somebody pulls me down and punches me in my neck. It is the *Stubendienst.* "Your highness wants to sleep?! And who will clean the barrack?!"

Blood rushes to my head. What does this animal think? Is it not enough that I just came out of the death barrack and, without rest, immediately assigned to night duty? I punch him in the face.

This *Stubendienst* is a husky fellow. He grabs me by the neck with one hand and beats me with the other. I want to call for help, but I cannot. I can only make a gurgling sound. One minute more, and I will be done for. At the last second, another *Stubendienst* pulls the hoodlum away from me. Blood runs from my nose.

The second *Stubendienst* explains my situation to my torturer. At first he refuses to listen. He tries to grab me and beat me again, but, after a minute when more explanations have penetrated, his cruel face undergoes a change, and he becomes more human. He walks toward me with his hand extended.

"Excuse me. I didn't know you had been there, and, in addition, you're a medic. Don't be angry. You see," he clumsily explains, "I'm a bit nervous. I've been here for two years, and I've lost my entire family."

I hesitate for a minute as he stands with outstretched hand looking at me. We finally shake.

He squeezes hard and hugs me. "You're a hell of a guy. From now on I'm your friend. If anyone wants to harm you, he'll have to deal with me, Garbatka!"

I get the impression that he may be a man whose mind is

warped, but I am too tired and mistreated to pay much attention.

To demonstrate the sincerity of his feelings, my newly-acquired friend throws a pack of cigarettes and a piece of chocolate in my bunk. "Go to sleep. We'll talk tonight," he adds.

I believe that I slept only for a minute when somebody pulls me and shouts, "Roll call. Get up!"

My feet are twisted. I do not know what is happening to me. Outside, the cold air revives me and I am alert again.

With roll call over, I step in front of the line with a paper in hand and ask if anyone is sick. Only one patient comes forward, and I take him to the clinic.

When I return to the barrack, a dish of hot soup is waiting for me, the work of my new friend. He brings over a stool and encourages me to eat. Meanwhile, I learn about Garbatka's life.

Garbatka is not his real name, but a nickname by which he is known throughout the camp. This pseudonym is derived from a village not far from Radom where he lived for all of his life. Garbatka is, or rather, was a peasant, one of the few Jews who tilled the soil in Poland. He does not look Jewish. "The sun and wind lightened my hair and eyes," he says in the peasant dialect of the region. He tells me his sad story, one of many such tales.

Near his village, in the neighborhood of Radom, someone killed a *Volksdeutscher*. During the night, gendarmes surrounded the village and chased all the inhabitants into a field. Women and children were separated from the men. Garbatka saw them stab his wife with a bayonet and crush his three small children under their feet. Half of the three hundred men were shot. The rest, one hundred fifty strong, were sent to Auschwitz. From the entire transport, he is the only one who remains alive after two years. The memory of his wife and children is always with him, and he still remembers his wife's murderer. He must survive to avenge them!

Two other *Stubendiensts* join us. They, too, are Jews. One, a young man of twenty, named Chaskiel, comes from Pomerania. The Germans caught him with five of his friends and jailed them for smuggling food into the Ghetto. A few days later, the Germans erected six gallows and ordered all the Jews to report to a square in the Ghetto to witness the execution of Chaskiel and his friends. Chaskiel was lucky; the rope broke. The Ghetto *Kommandant* pardoned him and sent him to Auschwitz. He has been here for more than a year.

The other *Stubendienst*, Zygmunt, smokes a cigarette in silence. He is deep in thought. He has an honest face.

It is late. We must begin our duties. I have shoes and clothes to clean.

"You! Don't let them exploit you!" Garbatka advises me.

* * *

An additional two hundred people are assigned to our barrack, young Dutch Jews between the ages of twenty and twenty-five. The Germans told them that they were going to work in a factory. They are very surprised to learn that they are in Auschwitz. They had heard about gas chambers and crematoria, but they did not want to believe it. Until now, they were interned in work camps in Holland where they received packages from home, were all right, and were not beaten. Their morale is high. They are in a fighting mood and hope to survive.

Two days later they have diarrhea. I had been emptying the barrel once a night; now I must evacuate it every hour. Before, I had only a few patients to take to the clinic; now, I have a large group of them. The boys are deteriorating before my very eyes. Their original fighting spirit is vanishing and complete apathy sets in.

I show the Dutchmen how to behave in front of Zenkteller. I beg and ask them in the most friendly way, but I cannot teach them camp discipline. The Dutchmen think that I am inventing a story or propagandizing. They cannot understand that a doctor would beat patients and that he should be feared. They regard me suspiciously.

One morning one of them complains about a small sore on

his heel. He asks Zenkteller to excuse him from work for several days.

The Old One kicks him in the stomach. I get slapped in the face and chewed out. He calls me a moron and says that I do not know how to teach people to behave properly. Zenkteller adds that he regrets pulling me out of the gas chamber selection and that, on the next occasion, he will see to it that I perish miserably.

As I learned from experience, I stand silently.

The night work is terribly exhausting. Although I have enough food, I feel unbearably tired. Nighttime is torture for me. Sleep during the day gives me no rest, but I realize that the position I now occupy offers me a ray of hope for survival. I clench my teeth.

On a night when I am unusually sleepy, I hear a voice next to me. "Night watchman, the barrel is full!"

"All right! All right!" I answer. I lack the energy to wake the people and go out in the snow to the latrine.

A thin figure without pants approaches the barrel. Excrement runs out of the poor creature's behind. He sits on the edge of the barrel. Suddenly, he loses his equilibrium, screams hoarsely, and falls in.

As though jabbed by a needle, I jump up. I wake the two fellows in the closest bunk, and together we pull the poor soul out of the smelly mess. I do not know whether to laugh or cry. And so the nights pass.

The barrack is full. Thirty Greeks arrive from Auschwitz I. They steal whatever they can. I dare not close my eyes even for a minute; I am always on guard. When I hear a noise in a bunk, I run with my flashlight to find out what is happening. Garbatka and Zygmunt appreciate my ordeal and pity me. At every opportunity they get, they empathize with me. They also see to it that, during the day, there is silence in the barrack so that I may sleep even if only for a few hours. They share the noon soup with me which they prepare themselves from what *Kanada* brings. I occasionally see Aleks and Szymek. They are satisfied that I do not suffer from hunger and that I am adequately dressed. They maintain that eventually I will get used to the night work.

* * *

At noon on the 18th of January, I am awakened by an unusual commotion. A medic returning from K.B. a while ago brought alarming news. All Jews on the infectious and surgical wards have been moved to Barrack 12. Their charts were taken to the *Schreibstube* and from there were sent to the political section.

What can that mean? Is it a selection? Is it the general extermination of every single Jew without exception? Less than three weeks ago we were decimated during the New Year selection. Our nerves are frazzled. We have the most dreadful foreboding.

The *Blockältester* announces the sad news that night. Tomorrow, the Jews will remain in the camp for a medical inspection that will take place in the barrack. I must light the fire early so that the barrack will be warm.

One Greek *Häftling* goes insane. He climbs on the stove and, in a terrible animal-like voice, screams, "Today I live! Tomorrow, crematorium! I burn!! All burn!!"

Garbatka tries to pull him down. He bites and kicks and will not let anyone near him. Zygmunt and Chaskiel run to help. The three of them manage to get him down but only with great difficulty.

Kanada is also in a funereal mood. Until now, *Kanada* never experienced a selection; they usually went to work. Today they have no instructions. Their *Kapo* runs to the *Schreibstube* and back as if he were mad.

Around midnight, Aleks knocks on the door, enters, and whispers in my ear, "Try to be the first one, or at least among the first few in line for the selection. Don't wait for Thielo's verdict! Run away! Remember, don't wait for his sentence!"

I know what Aleks has in mind. I thank him for remembering and promise to heed his advice.

Kanada went to work in spite of everything. An *Unterscharführer* came for them and led them away.

Around eight o'clock, the *Blockältester* announces that the commission is here. We must undress. There are about two hundred twenty of us present for the selection.

I hear a few shots close by. Kazik, the *Lagerschreiber,* enters the barrack and asks to check the charts. He wants to know if everyone is present. In one barrack three Jews hid under the bunks. When they were discovered, *Obersturmführer* Schwarzhuber, himself, had the honor of shooting them.

We are curious to know how this selection will proceed and if a large percentage of us will be sent to the gas chambers. The *Lagerschreiber* is not saying.

"Attention!"

Fifteen SS men enter the barrack with the *Lagerführer* and the *Lagerartz.* "Let's begin! Move!"

I am the first to run. I stick out my tongue, turn around, and, as Aleks instructed me, run without waiting for the verdict. An SS man leads me to the *Blockältester*'s quarters.

Through a crack in the door, I watch the progress of the procedure in the barrack. I hear Thielo's monotonous voice, "Show your tongue! Turn around!" It is getting crowded as more people join me. Zygmunt, Chaskiel, and Garbatka are not here. The Dutchmen are bewildered. They do not understand what this means and ask me if the SS man wrote down my number. I pretend not to understand what is happening. To tell them would be cruel.

I cannot calm down. My heart beats wildly with emotions.

Here come Zygmunt, Chaskiel, and Garbatka now. Luckily they passed. They embrace me, and we hug and kiss. I ask how the selection is going. Zygmunt cradles his head in both hands in anguish.

A minute after the commission leaves, Aleks comes to the barrack. "Now it's perfect," he says, squeezing my hand and runs back.

At night we learn the results. In our barrack fifteen Dutchmen and two Greeks passed, in addition to the four of us. Ninety percent are going to the gas chambers. In other barracks, the results are the same. As yet, we do not have the figures from the women's section.

We are unhappy at our salvation. It is apparent that our days are numbered. The camp is surrounded; guards are armed with rifles and machine guns, assisted by dogs. The order "close barracks!" is final. If you stick your nose outside, you get a bullet in your skull. Soup, coffee, and bread are unavailable. The barrel of excrement overflows.

The doomed ones have been placed in four barracks. Our *Blockältester* informs us that, from our section alone, over two thousand people are condemned to be gassed.

We four lie in a bunk. Garbatka tells us gloomily that, in the two years that he has been here, he has never witnessed anything like it. He is under the impression that the Germans are finishing us off and that the selection is a tactical maneuver on their part to prevent a revolt. With that, Chaskiel jumps from his place and brings with him, several knives used to cut bread which he procured from the storage area.

"Here, boys," Garbatka says, dividing the sharp utensils among us. "Each of us will take care of one *Schwab,* at least. I guarantee that I'll take care of two!"

We can hear the roar of the truck motors through the closed doors. Today it lasts a long time, much longer than usual.

When the doors open in the morning, the camp is empty and very quiet. One can see an occasional Jew walking slowly with an expression of terror on his face.

There are changes in our barrack. Our old *Blockältester* is transferred to the *Schreibstube,* and the one from Barrack 9 takes his place. He brings his own medic with him and throws me out to go wherever I choose. Of the three *Stubendiensts,* only Zygmunt remains. Chaskiel and Garbatka go on *Kommando.*

In a camp, one can never adjust to the place or the people. I am transferred to Barrack 22. Since a medic is there already, I do not know what my function will be.

I don't want to go to Aleks. The poor fellow is overwhelmed. He lost his girlfriend and several "good" patients in the last selection. It is apparent to me that, if I had been selected this time, no power on earth could have saved me. I would have met my end in the gas chamber as thousands of others have done.

Meanwhile, I try not to fathom the futility of life in the camp. I have some bread, good shoes, clothes, and two packs of cigarettes. What is most important, however, is that I will remain in the barrack and not go on *Kommando.* Anyway, after the last selection, I developed the same psychosis as have all the other Jews. I expect my end on any day, at any time.

The *Blockschreiber* tells me something quite important. He has some compassion and spent the whole night trying to find a proper function for me. He knows that I am a doctor and that the shitty intelligentsia is not used to heavy work, but one must toil in the camp even if only a little. Thus, every morning I will go for the coffee; at noontime, for the midday meal and bread; in the evening, for coffee again. To prevent boredom in the interim, I must wash the dishes. The *Blockschreiber* thinks that I should be very satisfied with these assignments.

The *Kommandos* in my new barrack work in the camp proper so that they eat their noon meal in the barrack. The advantage of this arrangement is that I do not have to drag the cauldrons by myself. On the other hand, I must wash about three hundred dishes after the noon meal all by myself during the short interval between the noon and evening meals. The *Blockältester* and *Stubendiensts* bestow upon me the "honor" of giving me their own greasy, burned pots to clean.

I never considered dishwashing as heavy work and that it would require an expenditure of so much effort on my part. It is quite possible that the same chores in a private home or restaurant, where the appropriate supplies and equipment are available, may be an easy task, but here it drives me crazy.

Only one pail is available for dishwashing. Before I put the dishes into it, I clean them of all remnants of the potato peel soup. After immersing eight or at most ten dishes, the water looks like spittle and is impossible to use. Every few minutes I run to the washroom to scrub the pail and to get clean water. I smell of potato peels, and the pungent odor stays with me day and night. I only have to look at the soup and I become nauseous. I want to get out of here at any price. Aleks promises that, as soon as there is an opening for a medic, I will be transferred. In the meantime, I must continue.

One night I share my troubles with Garbatka and Zygmunt. Garbatka has a brainstorm. He advises me to scrub all the food remnants from the dishes and to keep them in a separate pot. After the evening roll call, I should bring the pot to him. He will show me how to make gold out of shit. I never heard of this sort of alchemy, but I heed to the advice of this man who has had more experience in camp life than I.

I collect so much soup that I need a special container. I estimate that I have at least eight liters. As soon as he returns from *Kommando,* Garbatka cooks several potatoes. I bring this liquid concoction which he divides evenly. In this way, we get four portions of thick soup. Of course, we have many customers. Garbatka, who is also a very good salesman, exchanges the "good thick" soup for bread and, sometimes, even for cigarettes.

"You see, you moron," he says jokingly, "we've bread and cigarettes. You'd have poured it all down the drain."

In our daily conversations, we also speculate on how many days of life we have left.

After awhile, Garbatka is in a better mood. It is the end of January already, and our fears have not been realized. There were six Jewish transports and one-third of the occupants entered the camp. It seems to be a good omen.

I begin thinking of the possibility of escaping. Everyone looks at me as though I were crazy. Each asks, "Now, in winter?" I am asked if I have forgotten the sight of SS men in the camp on Christmas eve. Of course I remember that fateful day when ten Poles fled a *Kommando* and we were forced to stand outside through the night after roll call. All ten were caught. Four were shot. With their heads propped up by shovels and huge signs on their chests that read: "Hurrah! *Ich bin wieder da*" (Hurrah! I'm back), they were placed on chairs in front of the gallows on which the remaining six were hanged.

* * *

One day, the medic of the barrack returns in a very happy mood. In a loud voice, he announces the happy tidings that the K.B.'s *Lagerältester* is sick and Zenkteller is named as his successor until he recovers. The sick are being treated by Wortman. It is wonderful. The Old One has so much work in the hospital that he comes to the clinic for only a few minutes.

I jump from the stool as if I were pricked by a needle. Maybe this is my opportunity to retire from the "restaurant" business.

On the way to the clinic, I meet Aleks. He was just coming to see me to tell me that I can become the medic in Barrack 7 because the former one developed pneumonia and went to K.B. He also warns me that the *Blockältester* is a *Reichdeutscher* named Fritz who is an old bandit, and that I will have to be careful. In general, he advises me to think it over before I accept the position.

I do not want to think it over and assure Aleks that I will manage somehow. A few minutes later I leave for Barrack 7.

When I knock on the *Blockältester*'s door and introduce myself, Fritz looks me over carefully and tells me that he was very satisfied with the former medic even if he was no doctor. Then he lays down his rules. I must remember that being a doctor gives me no privileges. When I have no medical duties to perform, I must work in the barrack like a regular *Stubendienst.* If necessary, I will scrub the floor, sweep, and take out the garbage. It is understood that I will go for coffee, bread, and so on. I agree readily. I understand, of course, that the regulations that the *Blockältester* outlined must be rigorously followed, and that I will fulfill all the conditions.

The *Stubendiensts,* three Poles and one Jew, all very pleasant fellows, receive me cordially and ask about the *Blockältester*'s speech. They laugh heartily when I repeat everything. Then they explain that the *Blockältester* is a very heavy smoker, getting through as much as four packs a day. They offer him a gift of cigarettes every week. Woe to the person who does not manage to organize cigarettes. The old fellow is a professional bandit and has a way with those who disobey his orders. He has, on his conscience, the deaths of hundreds of *Häftlinge.*

I remove from my pocket, the two packs of cigarettes I received, thanks to Garbatka's alchemy, and knock on the *Blockältester*'s door.

"Mr. *Blockältester,* I don't smoke. Maybe you. . . ."

The old bandit says with a smile, "So, if you don't smoke. . . ."

I am assured of peace for a few days, but I soon regret that I came to Barrack 7 and think of the "restaurant" with nostalgia. The sick, frightened by the old rumors, do not present themselves at the clinic just now when Zenkteller is not there. Come what may, I must stay in the barrack.

It soon becomes apparent that I have not given enough cigarettes to Fritz; he is after me. The *Stubendiensts* would like to spare me from the heaviest jobs as often as possible, but it cannot be done. Early in the morning, the *Blockältester* checks my work.

One day he orders me to scrub the floors under the bunks. He wants me to dust the rafters. For two hours I must perform miracles. "Cut the wood! Clean the square in front of the barrack before roll call!" In addition I am to "go for bread, coffee, and the noonday meal"; these are my "real" duties.

My strength is fading alarmingly. I have not adequately recovered from my bout with pneumonia.

In difficult moments even friends often fail me. I must admit that they, too, are experiencing difficulties. Zygmunt must work very hard under his new *Blockältester* and he receives nothing for it. Everything *Kanada* brings, the *Blockältester* takes for himself and his two lovers. Garbatka is on *Kommando* and must concern himself with organizing for himself. Chaskiel works on *Kanada,* but he has to turn over all his "wealth" to his "Mr." *Kapo* for this assignment and is left with nothing. He must still risk his life to smuggle prohibited items past the guard for a long time to pay off his debt. In the clinic, all I can get is a dish of soup; there are no patients. The fellows are living on their regular portions. To make matters worse, I have no way of getting cigarettes for the *Blockältester,* resulting in the old bastard being dissatisfied with me. Not only does he find the most disgusting jobs for me like scrubbing the excrement barrel, but he also beats me quite often. I am so desperate that I think of volunteering for the *Kommando*. I realize that, because of the cold and my serious weakness, this would be a fatal solution, but I see no other way out.

One morning, after a sleepless night, I decide to go to Aleks to ask him for help, but at that moment something happens that makes me really believe in miracles.

The *Blockältester* calls me to his corner. I find him sitting awkwardly on his stool with a razor in his hand ministering to the little toe on his right foot.

"Hey, you medic! I don't get much help from you. You don't do a day's work. Maybe as a doctor, you'll do something for me. I'm suffering from bunions."

I adopt a serious expression. Using all of my will-power to hide my great satisfaction, I carefully examine his foot. He has a corn the size of a pea on his little toe which he has probably treated with his razor many times. The toe is red, swollen and no doubt very painful to the touch. I warn him of the danger of infection if he continues to dig into the bunion with dirty instruments. I promise to help him on the condition that he follows my instructions.

First, I prescribe a twenty minute bath in hot soapy water. This is essential. The *Blockältester* screams with pain, but he obeys. I bring surgical scissors and some dressing material from the clinic.

My heart pounds, and I count on my lucky star when, after twenty minutes of soaking, I start the procedure. I carefully manipulate my scissors. After cutting through a few layers of skin, I find a small purulent abscess. the *Blockältester* screams to heaven and threatens to kill me. I assure him that all his suffering will be over soon. One more delicate move and the pus spurts out. I am pleased with the result and apply a sterile dressing. I tell him that he must stay in bed until the next morning and then come to roll call without a shoe.

I am on my way to the barrack with the coffee when I meet my master in high boots. He says with a smile that reaches from ear to ear, "Medic, come to see me when I return."

A weight is lifted from me. The operation on which my fate depended is a success.

A few minutes later I learn from Fritz that he is very satisfied with me. He had been suffering from bunions for a whole year and was given all kinds of salves, all to no avail. Only I was able to cure him and in a very short time. On the table are bread and margarine. "This is for you, medic!"

I look offended and say, "I did it for you, Mr. *Blockältester.*"

The lie almost chokes me. The *Blockältester* is pleased with my behavior. He puts the bread away and announces that, starting tomorrow, I will be excused from heavy work. "A doctor is always useful in a barrack," he adds.

Through the door that night, someone calls for the medic. It is the lover of the *Oberkapo* of the *Kommando* of masons. The *Oberkapo* has corns on his toes. It is rather obvious that Fritz has bragged about his medic's ability.

Although I am angry, I am even more amused. Dear God, what else will I have to do in this camp? But there is no time to wonder. The *Oberkapo* is demanding help.

I prescribe the same cure: before anything else, soaking. I return in half an hour. The "operation" is also a success. I am given a piece of moldy black bread. The *Oberkapo* is a German, and Germans know how to be generous.

Apparently, cutting corns is a very lucrative job. As my fame spreads throughout the camp, my patient load increases. Sometimes I return late at night. My wooden box is filled with food; I have cigarettes in my pockets.

* * *

"*Stubendiensts* out!"

The fellows have gone for coffee. I am alone in the barrack.

"Medic, find out what's going on," Fritz orders.

The *Raportführer* and *Lagerältester* are standing in front of the *Schreibstube* and shouting excitedly, "Move! On the run! Quickly!"

We number about twenty from the nearby barracks. Others are running in the street, but the *Raportführer* does not wait for them to arrive. He orders the Jews to step forward and the Aryans to return to their barracks. We are four. When he demands that we move toward the gate, we become fearful. What in hell is happening? What kind of an affair is this? What can we do?

We stand in front of the *Blockführerstube* and wait. I silently cursing Fritz and my rotten luck. I had enjoyed several days of peace. However, it looks as though it is no longer meant for me.

SS men lead several Jewish *Blockältesters* from the quarantine section. In a few minutes, a group of women from the female section arrives. The *Raportführer* arranges us into two lines, and again, we wait. After a quarter of an hour or so, an elegant limousine stops near us. Both fenders display black flags with silver lightning bolts—SS.

The doors open. *Obersturmführer* Schwarzhuber comes out first, followed by an SS general.

"Caps off!"

The general receives the report from the *Raportführer,* smiles pleasantly, and tells us to put on our caps, adding, "It's cold today."

Schwarzhuber enters the SS building with the SS man. After a while he comes out and, with a rather friendly gesture, invites us to enter. We never expected anything like this; we were awaiting the worst. Meanwhile the murderers behave like sheep. Schwarzhuber takes us to his office where the general sits behind a desk smoking a cigarette. He excuses himself for bothering us and for taking us away from our work, but it is an important matter. He hopes that we will be able to understand his intentions and that we will be helpful.

Our consternation surpasses all limits. We are dumbfounded. Even the *Lagerführer* has an idiotic expression on his face. He tries to cover it with an embarrassed smile.

"Listen carefully to this," the general begins. "A Pole sold a cow to a Jew in Litzmannstadt."

"Maybe he's crazy," I think to myself. "What does he want from us?"

". . . Yes, he sold the cow, and for gold, for GOLD! As all of you know, we opened special sectors for housing Jews in the territories occupied by the victorious German Army. Naturally, we did it for the Jews' own good, to protect them from the unfriendly local people. In some localities, like Litzmannstadt, the Jews had to be moved quickly to a new place for technical reasons. As a result, they had to leave all their belongings. In other areas, the move took somewhat longer." The general smiles sweetly as he continues, "Gentlemen, just as we know that the Pole sold a Jew a cow in Litzmannstadt, we know other things. We know of Jewish wealth that is hidden in walls or has been entrusted to Poles for safekeeping."

The general's intentions become clear. We begin to guess at what is going on. Standing beside me is the medic from Barrack 12; he, too, is a doctor. His face is turning red; he clenches his fist. "The bastards, the bandits, the hoodlums, the sons-of-bitches, the creatures from hell!" he whispers in my ear, his entire body is trembling as the general continues to talk in an amiable manner.

"We're asking for your cooperation. It will benefit us and you. In ten days you will conduct a search among your fellow Jews and will write down the exact information. We want to know:

1) Who had money, furs, clothes, materials, or valuables?
2) Where? Give the place very exactly.
3) Please note the place, the kind of transaction, and what kinds of objects have been turned over for safekeeping or sale. We are interested in objects worth more than one thousand Reichmarks."

There is a moment's pause while the general lights the second cigarette. Now comes the heart of the matter.

"Business is business. You'll gain from this as well as will those who have hidden the wealth. For your cooperation, you'll receive two percent and the owner will get ten percent. The money will be paid in *deutsche* marks on the day you leave camp."

The general hopes that we understand what he is talking about, and he wishes us luck before he says, "*Auf wiedersehn!*"

Schwarzhuber leads us out of his office and turns us over to the *Blockältester* who then takes us to our respective sections.

In front of the *Schreibstube* during roll call, hundreds of eyes peer at us with curiosity. For some time we are surprised, irritated, and amused, but we cannot grasp what is really happening except for one thing: It is the matter of Jewish money. I ask myself, "How can the Germans demand that people doomed to die in the gas chambers, deliver their families to their executioners? How can we give our worst enemies our wealth, should any exist and remain hidden?" The SS men's logic and reasoning is a mystery to me.

An order is an order; we must begin working. Above all, we try to give this event as much publicity as possible. Did not his highness, the general, tell us to do so, and to do everything we consider appropriate?

That night, the camp throughout its length and breadth has an excellent subject for discussion and laughter.

We deal with the formal aspects of this problem in a very simple way. We divide the barracks among us. At night when everyone is present for roll call, we announce the general's wishes.

"Is anyone willing?"

No one!

"All right."

We go to the next group. In two days we are ready. Nobody has anything to declare. In the *Schreibstube,* the report is written in impeccable German. We wait several days longer to give our work the appearance of thoroughness. Then, in a dignified manner, we submit the report to the *Raportführer* in a sealed envelope.

* * *

During the month of February, no major changes take place in the camp. I have enough bread and cigarettes. Excising corns becomes a fashionable procedure among the prominent. It is even considered sophisticated to say to a friend during the course of a conversation, "Oh yes, I got rid of my corns." It is true that I have competition, but there is enough work for all.

"The waiting for death syndrome", as we call the depression period after the second January selection, is leaving us, thank God. For the nth time the camp is filling up. Transports arrive from all over Europe, but the majority of persons comprising them are still Jews.

The crematoria are working, but the brisk wind blowing in from the mountains dissipates the smoke. The snow melts under the rays of the sun. Once again the longing for freedom returns. It does so in spite of every reasonable thought, in spite of all our enemies' preparations foreshadowing a short life for the Jews. Zenkteller is back. He has worked off some of his abusiveness during the weeks he was on K.B. For a time he even beats less.

Garbatka brings a newspaper he found on *Kommando*. It has been a long time since I saw one. Among the photographs and articles praising the valor of the Germans, the descriptions of the triumphs of certain divisions and the great losses the enemy suffered, the real truth is evident. I read that the Allies have made great progress on all fronts. The Russians are approaching the Bug River. The Anglo-Americans are pushing forward in Italy.

"But the Ruskies are still far from Auschwitz," worries Garbatka.

Although the mood here is not conducive to the development of political interests, we calculate how many kilometers the Russians can advance on the average per day, and how long it will take them to reach us. That night we are greatly buoyed for no one could have imagined the possibility of a quicker end or an imminent evacuation.

While we revel in imagined pictures of victory, Chaskiel tells us about the trainloads of Jewish wealth and worldly goods that leave Auschwitz for the Reich. He works in *Kanada*'s main warehouse, a large building near the station ramp. After a transport arrives, everything that they confiscate from the Jews, ends up there and is sorted by *Kanada* under the supervision of the SS.

"You have no idea of the sort of treasures that are found. The Jews, thinking that they are going to work in the East, bring their best with them: furs, suits, materials, cameras . . . everything of value. Every few days, we load the freight cars which are dispatched to the Reich for the personal use of the dignitaries, their wives and mistresses. Jewish clothes, with specialty labels removed, are sent to the stores. The warehouse is always full," Chaskiel says, smiling wanly.

This Saturday afternoon, the weather is twenty degrees below zero. The camp orchestra is at the gate one hour earlier than usual to play for the SS. As we stand next to the kitchen waiting for coffee, six freight trucks with trailers pass by roaring along the road heading for the third and fourth crematoria. A figure in a striped uniform leans out of the last truck. SS guards on motorcycles escorting the convoy yell at him, and the figure disappears. Cries come from the wooded area, but they do not last long.

We pick up the coffee and carry it to the barrack. A few minutes before we came, six new Jews arrived in the section. They were among five hundred others in the freight trucks. As they stood naked and prepared to die, Schwarzhuber arrived. He was drunk and in an excellent mood. From the entire group he selected six. They went to the bath and are now here in our barrack.

One of the six is from my transport to Maidanek. I remember him as an athletically-built fellow. Now I see a skeleton with gray-violet colored skin. I make room for him beside me in the bunk and offer him bread and a cup of hot sweet coffee.

At night we have a long talk. Abram Braverman tells me of his fate. In the Fall they sent a newly arrived Jewish transport directly from the railroad ramp to the coal mine. He was working nearby. It was his extreme misfortune that several Jews in the transport had died from heart attacks or suicide, but that part is unimportant. What mattered was that, when the transport was about to move, the quota still needed to be filled. The *Oberscharführer* grabbed several Jews working nearby, wrote down their numbers, called the *Schreibstube,* and sent them out with the transport.

Abram describes his work. With gas escaping from the mine, he worked stooped over and knee-deep in water for fourteen hours a day. If they did not fulfill their quota of coal, they received no bread. People died very quickly. At night, the Germans sent full truckloads of living corpses to the crematoria. Finally, a catastrophe! The mine supports gave way. Fortunately, it happened during the change of shifts, and both groups returned to camp. On the next day, before they were loaded in freight trucks, they were told that, because they had done such a good job, they were being sent for convalescence while the mine was being repaired and. . . .

"The rest, you know. Do you have a cigarette?"

* * *

Zbyszek in K.B. sends me a letter to tell me that they will soon build a barrack for convalescents that will probably be ready in six weeks or, at the latest, two months. He will be the chief doctor there. He remembers me and sends me cordial greetings.

Oh God, to go to K.B.! Although it is true that my latest business of cutting corns is profitable and I am relatively well off, the general activity in the barrack is affecting my nerves: the constant commotion and noise, "closing doors", roll calls sometimes lasting late into the night, and Zenkteller. The Old One is becoming violent again.

* * *

It is March. The snow is melting; the sun is radiant behind the clouds. The mountain peaks are illuminated by the sun as they emerge from the morning fog.

In the camp there are more escapes; the sirens wail more often. The *Kommandant* is angry; the *Häftlinge* are pleased. Because some get away, the remaining *Häftlinge* must stand for hours in the roll call square. We think, "May the escapees succeed! May they have good luck! May they tell the world what is happening in Auschwitz! Perhaps then, help will come sooner!"

Yes, may they have luck escaping. It is not so easy to flee Auschwitz. After two to three days, ninety-nine and nine-tenths percent of the time the escapees end up in Auschwitz again. If they are still alive, they stand in front of the gate and hold up a sign with both hands that reads: "Hurrah! Back in Birkenau!"

Very few are returned alive. The corpses are placed on stools in comfortable-looking positions. This sight is meant to be a warning to the returning *Kommandos* who pass and look.

A report circulates in the camp: A *Blockältester* in the Czech section has run away. . . . Days pass. The camp is quiet. Police dogs have not caught him. Thousands of mouths whisper softly, "Good luck!"

* * *

What in hell is happening in the Czech section? The gong is pealing; *Blockältesters* are shouting. From our barrack we see them arranging the families in the square.

The *Kommando* of roofers returns from the Czech section with mysterious expressions on their faces. When we ask them why there is so much turmoil among the Czechs, they just snicker. What is going on?

The Czechs, or rather, the Czech Jews had arrived six thousand strong in two transports from Teresienstadt. They came willingly! As compensation, they have their own section, Section B, where they live with their families and are not sent on heavy *Kommando*. The only thing that they must do is to write letters to Teresienstadt about how well off they are. They received stationery a while ago. Everything would have been all right if the *Raportführer* had not delivered a speech in which he said that the letters must be dated the 14th of April, or almost one month ahead. He explained, "There are difficulties with the mail. The enemy is bombing the post offices more frequently."

The next morning, frightening events occur. The gong sounds in the Czech section for roll call. The roars of the SS men are heard throughout the camp. Women and children scream. The gong is heard again. "Close barracks!" Two small groups of men and women leave the sector. Two hundred fifty men come to us; one hundred women go to the women's section.

An hour before noon, the *Kommandos* return from work. A strong detachment of SS surrounds that section. At dusk, trucks arrive. From the Czech section we hear desperate voices of hopeless despair mingled with the noise of motors, howling dogs, and roaring SS men.

The faces of the several Czechs in our barrack express their deep anguish and helplessness.

After a very long night every minute of it stained with blood, the sun shines once more. Among the Czechs there is silence and emptiness. The children's playground is deserted; the carousel is abandoned. Nobody sings merry songs. The smoke, belching from all four chimneys, obscures the sun.

In the near future, someone in Teresienstadt will receive a letter from Auschwitz dated April 14th. "Come! Come! It is very good here. Don't believe the horror stories!"—a letter from the other world.

But one cannot spend much time in the camp meditating on "minor matters". What is the extermination of twelve thousand Czech Jews? It is like a drop of water in the ocean compared to the millions who have died in Auschwitz.

* * *

The German Army enters Hungary. Auschwitz is preparing to receive Hungarian Jews. *Kanada* is building new, more spacious barracks.

* * *

"All Jews out!"

We had roll call long ago. Most of the Jews are already in their bunks after a hard day's work.

"All Jews out! All Jews out!"

I call Abram. He has a long Finnish knife that he hides under his arm. "Yes, this must be the end," he whispers.

I run toward the clinic to get some information, but a German *Kapo* blocks the way. "Back, you pig!" he shouts.

Oh you crazy heart, why do you beat so violently? You should be used to the horrors of Auschwitz.

Abram looks around. In a muffled voice he shares his observations. "The section is not surrounded. The guards are in the towers as usual. There are no additional guards!"

So the time is not yet. But why worry? We will find out soon enough.

Lagerschreiber Kazik and two SS men come from the *Schreibstube.* I recognize one of them, the *Raportführer.* But who is the other? It is almost dark; I cannot see too well.

"Attention!"

The three come closer. I study them carefully, and my knees start to buckle. A minute later, I lose my self-control. Were it not for Abram's strong arm, I would drop. My teeth are chattering; I shake like gelatin.

After the inspection is over and after the "commission" writes down several numbers and leaves to go somewhere else, only then do I revive. It is well that it is dark so that others do not see the expression on my face. Abram is intrigued, but he asks no questions.

Life goes on in the barrack. There are screams and noises. The inmates are satisfied that it is not a selection. It is a while before I regain my composure sufficiently to tell Abram what this event means.

The SS man who accompanied the *Raportführer* and who, in passing, listed the numbers of the strongest fellows, is none other than the chief of the *Sonderkommando* and the crematoria, *Hauptscharführer* Moll, who is one of the worst beasts and sadists in the world, the extent of whose cruelty only the *Sonderkommando* is aware. In muted voices, horrible stories circulate of tortures that Moll inflicts on selected victims destined for the gas chamber.

Obviously, Moll was choosing people for the *Sonderkommando.* Now I remember . . . Auschwitz is preparing to receive Hungarian Jews.

The selected ones do not realize the gravity of their fate. I say nothing. May the unlucky be spared.

* * *

The barrack doors burst open. Like a projectile, Garbatka dashes into the room with a wild look in his eyes. He is a picture of despair.

"Tadzek! Tadzek! Where are you? Help!"

He beats his head against the wooden bunks. I jump down from mine and run to him. Chaskiel and Zygmunt enter right behind him. They want to take Garbatka with them. He will not go and tears himself away. Suddenly he suffers a spasm and cries like a child who has been punished unjustly.

"Tadzek! Tadzek, because I once hit you . . . it's certainly for that!"

I look questioningly at Zygmunt who shakes his head knowingly and points to the number tattooed on his arm.

I understand. I guessed it from the first moment. Moll signed up Garbatka for the *Sonderkommando.*

Garbatka's appearance and behavior causes a sensation in the barrack. A group of people surround us, and a heated discussion ensues.

One fellow, whose number was taken down by Moll, asks Garbatka why he is so despondent. He glares at him with a wild look in his eyes and howls in an almost inhuman voice, "Tadzek! Friend! Poison! Give me poison! The devil has written down my number for the *Sonderkommando*! Tadzek! Poison!"

There are more shrieks and moans in the barrack.

Poor Garbatka! For him to be assigned to the *Sonderkommando* is catastrophic! It is even more calamitous than going to the gas chamber as a *muzelman.*

To pull the gassed from the chamber, to remove the gold teeth from the cadavers and to work near the oven . . . there is no salvation from this job, only suicide.

* * *

There is activity in my section. The S.K. is leaving Barrack 11 for Barrack 9 in my area. Barracks 11 and 13 are enclosed by a wall and form a unit that will serve as housing for the enlarged *Sonderkommando.*

I write a desperate note to Zbyszek. I have definitely had enough of camp life and want to get on K.B. at any cost. The reply comes that same evening: "The barrack is not finished yet. There is no paint. Be patient. I remember."

The next morning, even before the gong sounds, the *Lagerschreiber* comes to the barrack to announce that all the numbers that were written down are to remain in the barrack. A minute later, Garbatka comes running. He has calmed down a bit. His eyes are gleaming. He has a plan. In the meantime, he cannot divulge that secret . . . maybe in the future. We say good-by.

* * *

It means nothing that the Russian Army is already on Polish territory and has been for some time now. It is of little consequence that the Americans and British are nearing Rome. It is not important that the invasion day is getting close. It is no great news that German towns are being destroyed.

Auschwitz is preparing to receive the Jews, those remaining in Europe. We expect great activity. A fence of pine branches has been erected to hide the four crematoria and to camouflage the railroad line that leads from the ramp almost to the doors of the gas chambers of crematoria II and III. All is ready. Several hundred people from the new *Sonderkommando* engage in some secret work in the field. Auschwitz is getting ready.

* * *

One evening I receive a visit from Garbatka. The *Sonderkommando* are forbidden to leave their barrack under the threat of death, but Garbatka has certain privileges. After all, he is one of the oldest interned Jewish *Häftlinge* in Auschwitz.

Garbatka is as elated to see me as if I were his own brother. "I couldn't hold out any longer, Tadzek. My skull is bursting. I must talk it over with somebody, otherwise I'll go crazy."

I ask no questions. It is unnecessary. In a minute I will hear the most horrible secrets of Auschwitz from an eye-witness.

Garbatka talks very quickly. His words pour out as if he is anxious to be rid of a heavy, insupportable load, as if he is afraid that someone will stop him at any moment.

"Before us we envision monstrous pictures, too horrible for the human brain to conceive. It's hell, living hell!

"The gas chambers for crematoria II and III are built for comfort. Wide steps lead down to the underground waiting room.

"The *Sonderkommando* has two faces: a polite smile for those who don't know, but for those who do and from whom they can expect resistance, a club, a roar, and help from the SS.

"'Please undress for the bath,' the *Sonderkommando* encourage the unfortunate souls. In the crematoria's waiting room, are several SS guards who observe the *Sonderkommando* carefully. Woe to anyone who utters an unpleasant word!

"'The bath's waiting.' The *Sonderkommando* lead the way. It's an enormous hall with some unusually heavy steel doors that have wheels attached for hermetic closure. The place is very warm with shower heads in the ceiling, hundreds of them, but if you look closely, you notice that they are made of wood. The pipes that are supposed to bring the water are also made of the same substance. But who pays attention to these small details?

"The immense hall is low and dark. In the center and equidistant from one another, are three columns. Who among the victims realizes that these columns are connected above ground with openings into which an SS guard will soon empty the gas? No one pays any attention to the thick metallic net that fences off the column's opening near the floor.

"'Where does the door on the other side of the hall lead?' The polite *Sonderkommando* has an answer to that. 'To the clean side of the bath.'

"It would be more difficult to explain why the door is so heavy and built of steel, but generally, nobody asks.

"More trucks keep arriving. More people walk down the steps. The 'bath' gets crowded. *Sonderkommando* line them up one behind the other, one next to the other and order, 'Silence, the *Lagerarzt* will come soon!'

"People are surprised. Didn't they have a little inspection on the railroad ramp? But then they realize that they've come to a camp where some unusual customs may prevail. Some want to satisfy their natural biological needs, but the door is far away. They have to push themselves through the crowd.

"They call the 'Bath Supervisor' who answers them very politely. 'The *Lagerarzt* is here already. Inspection will start immediately. You'll be free in a short while, but if you can't hold it, you can urinate in the many drainage grooves criss-crossing the floor.'

"Someone yells from the entrance, '*Sonderkommando,* attention!'

The 'Bath Supervisors' quickly squeeze through to the outside. SS men close the door and the lights go out. There's fear and havoc in the hall as we hear the first screams of bewilderment and despair. Now they can scream.

"Downstairs, an SS man pushes the button that sets off an electric bell. An SS man on top puts on a gas mask before opening a can of *Zyklon* B, the deadly cyanide gas. He quickly goes to the first opening, drops the can into it, closes the flap, and runs to the second and third openings. Three cans of gas for three to four thousand people . . . how economical! When they have all been dropped, the SS man on top rings twice.

"The gas spreads slowly through the net at the bottom. People start to choke. Through the thick steel doors come screams so horrifying that even the most hardened criminal could turn gray in a minute.

"SS guards, listening quietly to the sounds emanating from the chamber, are unaffected. After all, there are only Jews in there, 'only' Jews.

"To satisfy their sadistic impulses, high-ranking SS and Party officials sometimes come to see for themselves. Then the SS attendant throws a switch and the one thousand candlepower light brightly illuminates the Hall of Lost Souls. The dignitaries peer through a little ten centimeter thick window in the entrance door. There they may comfortably observe the final agonies of their dying victims whose blood oozes out of their mouths, noses, and ears, and who bite their fingers and hit their heads against the wall in their death throes.

"The gas spreads slowly through the hall. The lucky ones are those who are close to the emission points; they suffer for a shorter time. Those farther away have to wait fifteen minutes or longer for the salvation of death.

"Finally it is quiet. Huge exhaust fans start drawing out the poisonous air. At the opposite end of the hall, the steel doors open onto the 'clean side'.

"The *Sonderkommando,* in rubber boots, wade through clotted blood up to their ankles and load the gassed on carts that are then brought up an elevator to the actual crematorium located at the surface.

"Before the bodies are thrown into the oven, 'dentists' extract gold teeth, and 'barbers' cut women's hair, which is needed for mattresses."

Garbatka is silent for a minute. He pulls a second pack of cigarettes from his pocket. I sit silently in the bunk. After a moment, Garbatka, remembering something especially terrible, clenches his fists and utters menacing curses. He talks about Moll's assistant, a young, perhaps twenty year old SS man.

"He surpasses his chief as a callous sadist. The *Sonderkommando* have nicknamed him 'The Vampire', but this is far too mild to adequately describe the full scope of his infamy.

"Vampire and Moll not only indulge in orgies with selected people from the transports, mainly young women on whom they inflict inhuman atrocities, but Vampire also serves another 'important' function. He's the Gestapo's representative in Auschwitz. On behalf of this murderous organization, he extorts information from people who have already undergone interrogation for several weeks in Auschwitz. To achieve this end, the Vampire has, at his disposal, an instrument that has been perfected and used by the Gestapo for quite a while. It's 'the dental chair', a mild name, a benign word.

"The victim sits in it as he would in a regular dental chair, but this one differs from the real one in that it has many belt attachments. The Vampire straps the victim so tightly that even the slightest motion is impossible. The head is also immobilized by special devices.

"When the performance starts it does not matter if the victim knows what will happen and clenches his teeth, a powerful jaw opener negates this resistance. The drill's hum is low. The Vampire smiles sweetly as he asks, 'Which tooth would you like me to treat?'

"In a minute the nerve is exposed. Very often the victim admits to being guilty of the most fantastic infractions just to be freed from the unbearable torture, but the sadist usually keeps drilling a little deeper just to satisfy his inhuman craving for inflicting pain.

"The 'confession' has already been prepared and is on the table for the victim's signature. With a polite smile, the Vampire thanks the poor soul, excuses himself for the unpleasantness he has caused, and with an elegant gesture, shows the tortured one to the door, behind which waits an SS man with a revolver equipped with a silencer. The muffled shot destroys the skull as the victim falls dead. The method is quiet and often bloodless.

"Lately, the murderer has been quite busy. He's become quite adept."

The barrack is silent. We hear the sleepers' heavy breathing and the ticking of the night watchman's clock.

Before he leaves, Garbatka reveals another detail—the secret work being done by some of the *Sonderkommando.*

"It's in a sixth gas chamber that is outside of the camp in the area behind the new baths. This building is rural in appearance, like a peasant living at the entrance to Auschwitz.

"When the present gas chambers and crematoria were being built, they gassed hundreds of thousands of people whom they then burned in ditches which were dug not too far from the 'house'. Now that place has been remodeled and is encircled by a beautiful fence that hides the view not only of the 'house' but also of those trenches made by the digging *Kommando*.

"I forgot to tell you, Tadzek, that a wide road leads to this 'house'. Every several meters along the road, signs have been posted in every language possible, indicating the number of meters to the bath. Yes, Tadzek, the Hungarians are people of a friendly nation. That's why the Hungarian inscription is written in large letters and placed right after the German text. Now bye-bye. We may meet again."

* * *

There is an unusual amount of turmoil and confusion in the nearby Gypsy section. The beautiful Gypsy girls, tearfully beg their admirers for help for themselves and their loved ones.

That the Gypsies will share the fate of the Jews has been accepted for a long time in the camp; however, nobody paid any attention to those rumors. Now the poor little Gypsy children are crying near the wires. The old are tearing out their hair. The men form small discussion groups and talk in loud voices.

During the last two days of April, the Gypsy section reminds us of the Czech one, not too long ago. There are hourly roll calls; SS men go from group to group. The decision is finally made. Several hundred leave, supposedly for Auschwitz I. A group of two hundred women are sent to the female section.

We enjoy several days of peace. The Gypsies drag themselves around in the designated area. The young women, aware of the fate that awaits them, talk sadly with their lovers at the wires.

One night, despair hangs like a pall over the Gypsy section again. Cries and screams gradually cease as the trucks leave with their living cargo and disappear in the darkness on the way to the gas chambers.

It is morning. Once again there is a GREAT SILENCE

where not long ago we heard children's voices, harmonica playing, and choirs singing sad Gypsy melodies.

While human souls soar to freedom in the smoke rising from the chimneys, crews appear with disinfecting apparatus on their backs, trucks arrive from the clothes depot, and workers load the colorful gypsy rags that were left behind. Auschwitz is preparing to receive the Hungarian Jews. Elien!

* * *

At the railroad station, a *Kommando* of electricians is installing powerful lights on high poles. Other *Kommandos* are working at a feverish pace to complete barracks in Birkenau's third section. Part of the *Sonderkommando* is moved permanently near crematorium III. The administration expects the transports to arrive any day.

I sit with Zygmunt and Chaskiel until very late in the evening. When I return to the barrack, I find Abram in the bunk. Everyone is discussing the same thing: the Hungarians and the likelihood that, after their demise, those from Lodz will follow, and then it will be our turn.

There is a persistent rumor that Auschwitz will become an exclusively Jewish camp with Jews coming from all over Europe so that, at any given moment, all of them can be disposed of. We have no doubt whatsoever that, with the present advanced state of German technology, the remainder of European Jewry can disappear from the face of the earth in a few days. That is why our conversations are tinged with sadness and we so very rarely smile. To die?! Good! We will depart this earth without sorrow, but please let the torture of waiting not last too long. We are aware that no miracle will help us and that we will not go peaceably. Our knives are ready.

* * *

The expected transports are not arriving although everything is ready for their reception.

It is Spring. The sun is warm; birds are singing. Grass in the nearby fields is turning green. Even a few dwarfed trees growing close to the crematoria are budding. A ray of hope enters our souls and maybe . . . just maybe?

A locomotive's screeching whistle shocks us back into reality and all of our hopes are dashed like papier maché dwellings before hurricane winds. Cattle cars approach the ramp, and the drama starts again. They try to pull people to the crematoria by every means possible: to two, three, four, and five, and the little peasant house on the beautiful road with its ornate signs announcing in many languages, "One hundred meters to the bath".

One train leaves; two others have already unloaded their human cargo. The old gypsy section is crowded with prisoners talking a language totally incomprehensible to me.

The newcomers have no idea where they are. They look wide-eyed at the smoke and flames coming from all of the chimneys and deep ravines. The stench spreads through the entire camp, permeating the barracks. The smoke obscures the sun.

The Hungarians look, but do not trust their senses. They search for their relatives who are no longer alive. They accuse the older *Häftlinge* of lying when they are told the horrible truth. The Germans told them that women, children, and old people are going to rest in a special place only a few hundred meters from the ramp. The newcomers want to see their families and try to follow them, but fall under the blows of the *Kapo*'s and *Blockältester*'s clubs.

Hurrah for the Hungarians! What good things you bring: salami, buillon, goose fat, Tokay wine! The camp has a full supply of food. Only wine and fried goose have a special value.

The smoke is choking. Food does not pass the throat. Oh how warm the sun is! How thick the smoke everywhere, everywhere!

I receive Zbyszek's letter from K.B. notifying me that the barrack is ready and that I can come right away. But I have doubts, and I am afraid of Zenkteller.

At the first opportunity, I join the sick transport and go to K.B. Zbyszek laughingly remarks, "You can be sure that the Old One has nothing to say in this matter. He can only kiss your ass. Understand?"

I get a card from the *Schreibstube* telling me to report to K.B. early the next morning.

That evening I am visited by Garbatka. He, too, is leaving the section for new housing near the crematorium, and wants to say good-by . . . forever. Garbatka has changed so much that I hardly recognize him. His hair is gray: he resembles an old man.

"Why do you look at me like that, Tadzek? Have I changed that much?" He is silent for quite a while, then, suddenly, his eyes gleam. "It won't be long, Tadzek," he says, "it won't be long! You'll soon witness some curious events. Have a little patience. The right moment is coming."

He becomes a bit more animated when he talks about women and children being thrown alive into the flames and of thousands upon thousands of people dying daily in the gas chambers.

"The day of reckoning is almost here, Tadzek. When it comes, think of Garbatka! Stay well!"

* * *

I say good-by to Abram and Zygmunt and leave the barrack at dawn to run to the clinic. Aleks is not sure. Nevertheless, he tries to bolster my courage and helps me to resolve my doubts. He wishes me all the best. I receive several packs of cigarettes; they will help me start on K.B.

I report to the *Blockführerstube* about leaving and show my assignment to K.B. to the guards. They do not permit me to leave. I must wait until the transport passes.

Hundreds of young and old carrying rucksacks go quietly to the gas chamber. They are unaware. At the gate, members of the orchestra tune their instruments; the musicians play the lively march *Vienna Remains Vienna* while smoke rises high.

The SS man finally allows me to leave the section for K.B. When I arrive, Zbyszek greets me cordially. After acquainting me with the barrack personnel, he leads me to my living quarters. My first surprise is the sight of a special room for the medics with clean beds, good blankets, a table in the center, chairs, and windows.

The sick ward is divided into six sections with each one having its own doctor. There are more than four hundred sick people here. I have sixty; their charts are waiting. Zbyszek pats me on the back as he says, "Move! Work! During the noon hour we'll talk." He has several important things to tell me.

It is difficult for me to believe the good fortune that has become mine. With every hour that passes, I feel better. I laugh when Zbyszek characterizes the personnel in the barrack. He warns me about the big-shot, Zimmer, a bloodthirsty anti-Semite.

I am elated. The barrack is peaceful and quiet. My colleagues, the doctors, are polite and even cordial. The *Blockältester,* Engineer Prendowski from Warsaw, is a man of unusual qualities and character. The *Schreiber,* Julek Ganzer from Krakow, is honest and is one of the leaders of a literary group of which Zbyszek is the pillar and driving force.

In this atmosphere of relative peace and mutual understanding, all the horrors which we witnessed at such close range, do not evoke as horrible a reaction in us as they do in the rest of the camp.

Our barrack is for convalescents, the majority of whom are Russian prisoners who were sent to Auschwitz from the Flossenburg quarries and are in terrible shape. I recognize several patients from my former section among the few Poles in my part of the barrack. One treats me to a cigarette.

Zimmer notices it, runs over, tears it from my hand, and shouts, "You came to smoke the patients' cigarettes, you dirty Jew! I'll teach you!"

He smashes me in the face. I seethe with anger and would like to grab him by the neck and choke him. With great effort, I restrain myself and leave without a word.

I knock on Zbyszek's door and tell him the story. He is angry and runs to the ward, calls Zimmer from the other end of the barrack and, in the presence of all the patients, harshly reprimands him.

Zimmer is enraged. He accused Zbyszek of defending Jews. Zbyszek grabs Zimmer and wants to beat him. In the commotion that ensues, the *Blockältester* comes over and separates the combatants. As Zimmer leaves, he throws a hateful glance in my direction and threatens to finish me off in one way or another. Zbyszek consoles me and asks me not to be upset. While he is in the barrack, not a hair on my head will be touched.

To spite Zimmer, Zbyszek brings a Jewish barber, Josek, and a Jewish friend, Moniek, to the barrack. Boiling with rage, he bites his lips until they bleed, but not wishing to get into trouble with Zbyszek, he says nothing.

The camp is hell. Day and night, processions lead to the hidden entrances to the gas chambers. People enter and disappear into the dark void as into the jaws of a mythical monster. Only the flames leaping skyward from the chimneys are mute testimony that the demon has annihilated his victims.

I try not to think; I work without stopping. I examine the patients; I write up the charts. I help clean the barrack; I volunteer to help build a sport field. I return very tired and crawl into my bed and sleep as though drugged until the morning gong sounds.

I have enough to eat. My superiors appreciate my work and compensate me with additional bread. The patients are thankful for the care I give them, and they treat me to some of the food from the packages they receive from home. Even Zimmer slowly changes his hostile attitude toward me.

At times I cannot find any additional work in spite of all of my efforts, and I go to bed earlier. I listen to my neighbors' conversations about their dreams of home, family, peace and of the future when the world, after this war, will be better, happier . . . and a soothing balm seems to assuage my aching soul and wounded heart. I think that, perhaps someday, I shall be happy even if only for a little while. Josek gossips with Moniek in the lower bunk discussing crazy plans for the future: of Palestine, of a festively-prepared Friday night table.

Away with such thoughts! Away with happiness! I am alone in the world, all alone. The scarlet flames shine through the windows. Those with whom I could have been happy, have become the innocent victims of this kind of fire. I am pleased when the sun rises and I can begin my daily work again.

With great difficulty, I organize a little medicine for several of my patients with scabies and place a can of thick oil on a night table. This is to be rubbed on the patients at bedtime.

By the time I am ready to start the treatment after roll call, the container has disappeared without a trace. Several *Stubendiensts* and I search everywhere, but in vain.

Late at night, the watchman pulls me from my bed because several patients are stricken with terrible cramps. I run into the ward. The problem is clear. Lying next to the patients writhing in pain is bread thickly spread with the oil. "Excuse us, Doctor," explains one old Russian, "I thought it was honey."

* * *

Sad news spreads throughout the camp. The present *Lagerältester* will be transferred to Auschwitz I, and Zenkteller will take his place. Everyone is worried. For me, this news is especially tragic, and again I curse my misfortune. Even Zbyszek is not too elated when he tells me that Zenkteller will assume his new position in two days.

I am prepared for the worst. The Old One will certainly want to avenge himself on me because I was transferred to K.B. without his permission. But what can I do?

Meanwhile, a mysterious epidemic whose symptoms are terrible vomiting and diarrhea is raging throughout the camp. I suspect that it is caused by the Hungarian goose fat that was smuggled into the camp in large amounts. I, myself, swallowed one bite of bread smeared with this fat and now, for several hours, I have had a foul aftertaste in my mouth. We have to save fifty patients in our barrack who are diagnosed as suffering from food poisoning.

On the day that Zenkteller is expected to arrive, I rise earlier than usual. I bring all my patients' charts up to date, and when the announcement is made from the door that the Old One has begun his rounds and will soon be in our barrack, I leave through the rear door. With Zbyszek's permission, I rush to the pharmacy for medicine.

To my great surprise, I meet Garbatka there. He had accompanied the doctor of the *Sonderkommando* to help him transport medicines.

I start to greet him, but he signals me not to approach. Behind him is an SS guard brandishing a club. I hear some animal-like growling, "Move! Go away!"

Miraculously, I avoid a blow. I recall that, under the threat of death, members of the *Sonderkommando* are not allowed to talk.

It takes half an hour for the doctor and Garbatka to load the medicines and leave the pharmacy. Two SS men, armed to the teeth, follow them. The whole group approaches the exit.

Suddenly Garbatka is seized with a severe coughing spell and spits toward a bush of beautiful flowers. One of the guards scolds him. As Garbatka is explaining to the SS man, he signals me with his hand, and points to the bush.

While the pharmacist is preparing my drugs, I leave the barrack and move toward the bush Garbatka indicated. I am looking. . . . Yes, there it is . . . a small piece of paper covered with saliva. I unfold it. It contains only a few words: "I am living in hell. Do not buy fat, it is human. Vengeance is near. Good-by. Regards to friends."

Zenkteller's visit in the barrack is over. He limited himself to a short conversation with Zbyszek. After the noon meal, he will make the rounds through all the barracks and will acquaint himself with the personnel.

Immediately after we distribute the meal, we line up: doctors on one side, *Stubendiensts* on the other. Here comes our master. After greeting the *Blockältester* and Zbyszek, he pulls out a notebook from his pocket, looks into everyone's eyes, and marks down the number and name. A deadly silence pervades the barrack. When my turn finally comes, I feel like sinking into the ground. This is worse for me than a selection.

"And this one, where does he come from?!" Nobody answers. He repeats the question. "Where is he from? Eh?!!" he screams.

Zbyszek volunteers a muddled reply. The Old One shakes his head and scornfully looks in my direction.

At night, Zbyszek calls me to his room. "I've settled with him for now, but you must watch yourself, Tadzek," he cautions.

Two days after seeing Garbatka something occurs that helps me forget the Zenkteller menace. While we are taking advantage of the short noon pause to sun ourselves—especially since the wind changes direction and blows the smoke from the chimneys toward the field—we hear shouts from the third crematorium. We do not pay too much attention because we have often heard cries of despair from that direction. Suddenly, a tremendous explosion shatters the air. Flames shoot high. Several figures in striped uniforms run to the road screaming defiantly, "Down with Hitler! Long live freedom!"

SS men from the *Blockführerstube* try to block the road. We hear a short blast of machine gun fire, and SS men are falling.

Oh God! Our people have arms!! They are running toward the outside towers! The siren is wailing loudly. Helmeted SS men on motorcycles are racing everywhere. In the camp, gongs are sounded and "*Blocksperre!* Close the barracks!" is shouted. The entire camp is surrounded by reinforcement patrols. We hear cannon fire from the field. Crematorium III is in flames. Despite the closing of the barracks, the words "Revolt! *Sonderkommando* revolt!" spread like wildfire through the camp.

So this is what Garbatka had in mind. May God help him to escape the clutches of the beasts!

After several days the details of the revolt reach us. Crematorium III is burned to the ground. The Vampire was thrown into the fire alive. Eight SS guards are dead; ten are seriously wounded. Of the three hundred who revolted, two hundred ninety-seven have been killed. Three have escaped. SS patrols have been sent in pursuit.

Three have escaped. Maybe Garbatka was lucky . . . maybe? Who knows?

* * *

The news from the camp is that three hundred Jews have been selected for the *Sonderkommando* to replace those killed in the uprising. In the space of two days, they bring fifty fatally poisoned, newly-chosen *Sonderkommando* to K.B. They had committed suicide.

* * *

"Medics come forward!"

Zenkteller is delivering a speech. He is dissatisfied with us. The barracks are dirty. The patients' charts are not up to date, and what is more important, the medics' beds are not made up well. All of us realize the absurdity of his accusations, but what can we do? The Old One is the master of life and death here.

Zenkteller is establishing the reign of the iron fist in K.B. Every day several medics go to the labor section with a note on their charts: "For heavy work". For all practical purposes, it means labor in the coal mines, or a death sentence.

Neither at night nor during the day do we have a peaceful moment. From his various hiding places, Zenkteller pounces like a wildcat ready to attack. The mood is depressing and full of unidentifiable threats. This one man has the sadistic ability to terrorize the entire camp. He has frightened all the *Blockältesters, Stubendiensts,* doctors, and the sick. "Attention! Zenkteller!" Those two words uttered by a special guard are enough to stop every conversation and eradicate a smile from a face.

I know in how much danger I am. For a Jew to be sent to the camp at this time means to be automatically assigned to the *Sonderkommando.* I rise before the gong. My bed is made in conformance with all the rules of the camp. I examine my patients daily, and enter on the fever charts, all the camp's laboratory tests that are available. I check until late at night so that the Old One can find no pretext to brutally harass me. However, as the adage goes, if you want to hit a dog, you can always find a stick.

One of my patients is a famous Polish scientist, a professor of physics at the University of Lwow named Tolloczko. He is more than seventy years old. Were it not for the help he gets at every turn, he would not survive in Auschwitz.

As Zenkteller enters the ward, the professor is smoking a clumsily rolled cigarette. Zenkteller is not sentimental. He punches the old man in the face and shouts for the *Stubendienst.* When the *Stubendienst* tries to explain that, after all, this is the professor and that. . . . Zenkteller kicks him in the abdomen with his pointed boot. He doubles over.

"Where's the doctor on this ward?"

I jump from my stool, put away the chart on which I am writing, and report.

"Of course! Who else would it be?!!"

I do not dare open my mouth in my defense.

Zenkteller punches me on my jaw with such a powerful blow that he knocks me out. When I revive, I feel as if my skull is cracked in many places. I see triple; my head aches. Far away, three Zbyszeks are smiling at me. They talk to me. What is being said penetrates my mind with great difficulty.

"You've succeeded once more. Your punishment will be, loading cadavers for three nights."

Someone changes the cold compress on my head. So I succeeded . . . all is in order, but my head is bursting. I close my eyes.

"Get up!" One of my colleagues is nudging me. "Get up! You must report immediately to carry cadavers."

Where have I heard that before? It takes me a while to fully realize what is happening. I rise from the bunk and do a few exercises to make sure that I am still alive and normal.

Moniek lends me an old, dirty, striped outfit, and a minute later, I report to the *Totenkommando.* I meet another unfortunate friend, Dr. Libermann who came to K.B. only a few days ago.

One of the *Totenkommandos* takes us to the morgue, a small hut adjoining the Jewish Barrack 12 where we find today's dead. These come from K.B. and Section D. Other sections have their own morgues.

"You're lucky. There are only a few corpses today."

"A few" means one hundred twenty mostly skinny, horribly dirty, and unbearably smelly bodies that we must take out to the road. When the truck arrives, we are to load them as fast as possible because the SS driver is very nervous.

For a pack of cigarettes, we each borrow a pair of thick rubber gloves and a long rubber apron. We begin.

The *Kapo* arrives, takes one look, and yells, "What in hell!! The truck's coming and the bodies are still in the morgue!!" He threatens to complain to Zenkteller.

In the beginning we both carry one body. Later at night when we expect the truck at any moment, each of us drags a body by the legs. Libermann is terribly nauseated. I nearly faint from the stench.

Someone shines a flashlight on us, and we hear a low laugh. Zenkteller is watching.

* * *

"Invasion! Invasion!!"

One of K.B.'s great political commentators, Maks Weinryb, comes running from the washroom to our barrack with the *Kattowitzer Zeitung*. This newspaper arrives at a time when the situation in the section sorely tries the limit of our endurance because of the Old One's reign of terror.

Libermann and I continue talking and bemoaning our fate. We will soon leave for our third night of loading corpses.

Joyful shouts come from the barrack. Zbyszek calls to me, "Come see this, Tadzek! Maybe your work with cadavers will be lighter after you read this news!"

With every word and every phrase I read, hope, pleasure, and happiness flow into my destroyed, burned-out, Auschwitz soul. I keep reading and cannot tear my eyes from the short communique: "Last night after a heavy bombardment by air and artillery . . ."

Unrestrained joy grips the camp. People are dancing and singing. Even on the miserable faces and in the sad eyes of the very sick, a ray of hope glimmers. Along the streets of the camp we hear a song whose lyrics were composed by a home-spun poet in the camp:

> A new era begins today,
> And let Zenkteller go to hell.
> A new era begins today,
> And everything will be swell.

Every minute, someone else arrives with the most fantastic news. "The Allies are near Paris! The Allies are near Hamburg!" I could listen all night long. Libermann, standing nearby, rushes me, "Let's go to work!"

The *Totenkommando* use a stretcher in the morgue to carry cadavers from the hospital wards. Usually, we are not allowed to use it without special permission. Today is a holiday. They are not watching us and we can do as we please. We put five to six emaciated corpses on the stretcher—how much do these skeletons weigh? The work goes faster and we do not seem to feel the load.

From the barracks, shouts and songs; from the crematoria and ditches flames shoot upward. The elevator is functioning; the locomotive is whistling; new transports are arriving. From the camp come screams and the beastly roars of the SS men—the Auschwitz symphony.

A drunken *Totenkommando* chief appears holding a bottle of Hungarian slivovitz. He remarks happily that our work is over and adds, "Drink, boys!" as he hands us the bottle, laughing merrily, "Hahahaha! You're better carriers than doctors. Hahaha!" Apparently satisfied with his joke, he stands a while, then slams the door shut to the empty morgue, and leaves. We hear his hoarse voice singing, "A new era begins today . . ."

* * *

The one person least satisfied with all of these historical events is Zenkteller. The old bandit knows that an Allied victory means a noose around his neck.

The situation in K.B. is worsening. He must have heard the words of the song. With a ferocious look on his face, he runs through the barrack sniffing, sniffing, sniffing. One day he calls all the medics together and announces a forty percent reduction in personnel. "You have it too good here! Your life is too easy!"

Zbyszek is my last hope. Anyway, I do not have to ask him.

Our barrack is K.B.'s show-place. If a high ranking dignitary visits Auschwitz, the *Lagerarzt* shows off Barrack 18. Moreover, Zbyszek, the *Blockältester,* and Julek the *Blockschreiber* receive good packages from home. Their friend, Moniek, is a fine cook. Zenkteller knows this. Using the pretext of an official visit, he enters the barrack in the evening. There is great activity and confusion in the small kitchen. Bacon is grilled on a small stove. Julek removes the goodies from the packages and yells to Moniek to hurry and cook food for the old wolf.

Before each of Zenkteller's visits to our barrack Zbyszek convinces several people who receive packages from home to give up some food. He organizes ham, herring, fruits. . . .

"Maybe I can silence the Old One," he says musingly to console himself.

Those nights, more pleasant aromas emanate from the kitchen. Zenkteller sits for a longer time than usual. We hear glasses clinking and a whispered, *"Prosit!"*

Meanwhile, the doctors and *Stubendiensts* wait in line in front of the barrack as they did at other times. Zenkteller arrives after the party, takes out his notebook, and writes diligently. From behind his back, Zbyszek carefully looks in my direction and smiles discreetly.

Before nightfall, the slip of paper with the sentence comes from the *Schreibstube.* Three Russian doctors are sent to the labor section. A famous Polish neurologist, Dr. Krzeminski from Lodz, and I remain in the barrack. Zbyszek is not affected; he is the chief. Seventy-five percent of the *Stubendiensts* must leave their comfortable beds for ones in the labor section.

To replace the Russians, two Jewish doctors join us: Libermann and a young physician from Krakow, Edwin Bieberstein. The number of *Stubendiensts* is not increased. The doctors must help to scrub the floor and bring the meals.

I am happy because I do not have a minute's respite. I am so absorbed in what is happening in the barrack and in what must be done, that I have no time to think of what is taking place around me. The only diversion that I allow myself is a talk with Maks occasionally. I feel somewhat safer now, but, like all the Jews, I continue to doubt the possibility of salvation. With one news report following another, I have the deep satisfaction of learning that the Germans are being beaten in Paris, Rome, and Lwow. In the west, the war is nearing the frontiers of the Reich. The Russians are closing in on the Vistula.

It is Sunday; life in the camp remains the same. Two transports wait on the ramp until there is room in the gas chamber. Flames leap forth from all the ditches and chimneys. On the sport field a big soccer match is in progress: Section D vs. Sauna. In the washroom, a hundred Jewish children from Lithuania have been locked in a narrow space for the past twenty-four hours and are dying of thirst, and no one can do anything about it. Their terrible cries are drowned out by the noise from the sports field.

Somewhere far away, a siren is wailing. It must be a locomotive. Can it be an air-raid on Auschwitz? Nonsense . . . no one can even think of such a possibility. The game continues; it is sensational. Sauna is leading 2 to 1. The fans in the camp are yelling loudly for a goal.

Suddenly we realize that it is an air-raid. The siren blares nearby. A near riot occurs as the SS men run down from the towers helter-skelter and hide in the grass. We hear airplane motors and raise our heads in defiance of the guards' orders to seek shelter even though they threaten to fire at us.

There! High among the rays of the sun we see small shiny objects. Here! Here! More of them in the sky! All are flying toward a synthetic rubber factory. Over Brzezinka and the fourth crematorium, the roar of the engines is exceptionally loud and menacing. Oh God! It is a whole squadron flying low, very low—so low that we are able to see the American star on the wings and tail.

Zbyszek grabs my neck and we improvise some crazy dance. Others scream delightedly, wave their shirts, and jump in the air. We hear machine guns and anti-aircraft fire and see small patches of white smoke bursting around the vanishing planes.

The barrack shakes from much greater and louder explosions: bummm, bummmmmm bumm, bummmmmm bum bum. Windows fall out. The artillery shoots madly. Shrapnel hisses through the air; no one pays any attention to the danger. The wind brings sounds of unusual activity from the city of Auschwitz: fire truck bells ringing and ambulance sirens wailing.

Only when we become hoarse from shouting and our hearts begin to hurt from the effort, do we return to the barrack. Half-alive, we fall on our beds. It is the first air-raid by American planes on Auschwitz! Long live the U.S.A.!!

During the noon meal on Monday, gratifying news comes "through the wires". Seventy-five percent of Buna has been bombed. In Auschwitz, a bomb scored a direct hit on the SS housing. On Tuesday, one hundred twenty caskets are ready for funerals.

* * *

It is the beginning of the end. Often, at night, there are blackouts on the wires surrounding the camp. Sirens sound nearby. Warsaw is threatened; Lodz is in danger. The Germans are ousted from France.

Edwin Bieberstein crawls into my bed and tells me about his mother, father, sister, and fiancée in a concentration camp near Krakow. He hopes that they are still alive. His father, a doctor, occupies a high post in the camp's hospital. Edwin is the only son. He realizes now that sometimes he did not behave properly toward his parents and sister. If he survives, he will know how to cherish a family and home.

Libermann says, looking skeptically at Edwin, "So old and so dumb! You hope you'll get out of Auschwitz alive and you're making plans for the future? You're dumb! The better the situation is in the outside world, the worse it is for us. Every military advance by the Russians or the Western Allies brings us a step closer to our end."

It is true. I agree with Libermann, however, I think that he should not proclaim it so loudly.

Edwin is extremely angry. He scolds Libermann for saying that he wants the Germans to win, and for being afraid of the Allied victories. It seems as if a lengthy discussion will begin, but it is cut short by Josek who drenches us with water. Unhappy that his sleep is being disturbed, he slipped out of the room and brought in a pail of water.

I move to Edwin's bed. Poor Libermann is forced to sleep in a wet bed. No one likes him because of his defeatist attitude.

* * *

Our last hope for the miracle of our salvation peters out. The gossip of the July 20th aborted bomb attack on Hitler's life comes over "the wires" of the camp even before it appears in the newspapers. It excites us and raises our hopes but, unfortunately, only for a short time.

A certain uneasiness, visible even among the SS men for several days after the attack, is disappearing. Our hopes had buoyed our mood for several days, but now that the Führer is safe, it is a terrible blow. Over the loudspeakers and radios in the *Blockführerstube,* we hear martial music and the usual communiques from the Front.

The first Polish transports are leaving Auschwitz. Some Hungarians, who had passed the selection on the ramp and were admitted to the camp, are also going. Everyone thinks that they are on the way to a new, immense recently activated crematorium near Auschwitz.

The first transports arrive from Lodz only to discharge the people, in overwhelming numbers, for the gas chambers. The remaining Slovakian Jews are arriving in Auschwitz in large groups from various labor camps in East Prussia. As the Russians occupy more Polish cities, Jews are arriving from factories and warehouses. They are the "last of the Mohicans".

When Maks comes into our barrack with a newspaper one night, Libermann deliberately turns his back on him. In lieu of good-night, he murmurs, "Instead of reading newspapers, prepare yourselves to die."

* * *

The evacuation of the Lodz ghetto, the departure of the Aryans, the concentration of Jews from other camps near Auschwitz alarm me. It is quite evident that we must act, otherwise. . . . Many others are of the same opinion.

More frequently our *Kommandant* "weeps" and the siren wails, announcing the escape of *Häftlinge*. From the reports reaching the *Schreibstube*, it appears that ninety percent of the escapees are Jews, but almost every attempt to flee from Auschwitz ends tragically. Two to three days after the alarm, they are back with bullets in their heads. A small number die on the gallows.

Despite all of this, I am thinking of running away and send a letter to Abram that I want to see him. The next day Abram, who has guessed what I want to discuss, comes to K.B. with the *Kommando* of drainage ditch diggers. For the past several weeks, he, too, has been thinking of escaping. Even without my letter, he wanted to see me to suggest that we flee. Almost everything is ready. It is true that he could have many partners in his section, but he trusts only me.

Abram is aware that our days are numbered and that only escape can save us. It seems that the best time to go would be when the Russian soldiers are nearing Auschwitz. He tells me of his plan.

At present, the situation is as follows: On an enormous field near the main railroad line is a cemetery for damaged airplanes. Every day, trains arrive with cargos of wrecked planes. Abram worked for several weeks on a *Kommando* of several thousand *Häftlinge* that dismantles these downed machines. The usable parts are sent to factories in Germany. In such a huge crowd, one can disappear several times a day without being noticed. Abram chose one wrecked transport plane and crawled inside through a window. Hidden from view, he broke through the floor with his shovel and began to dig a hole. It is so deep now that it can accommodate not only two people but also all the necessary supplies and equipment. Abram managed to obtain sacks to protect the walls of the bunker so that it will not get too cold in there at night. What is more important, he brought and threw around the plane, many sharp-edged metal sheets to camouflage it and make it impossible for people to get too close.

My job is to gather food supplies, enough to last from four to six days. It will be best to secure cans. Abram will bring water in special containers that he found in the planes. When everything is in readiness, I should ask to be transferred to Section D, then report to the *Kommando* and meet Abram. We will remove the metal sheets and enter the bunker by crawling through the window. Before we do that, we will spread lime around so that the police dogs will be unable to track us. According to Abram, we must sit in the bunker for several days until the SS, who will be searching for us, call off the hunt. Then, in the middle of the night, we will leave, watching at every turn for thousands of possible dangers. This is our only way to elude capture and to escape.

Abram's plan is good. The weak part is that we are unfamiliar with the terrain. He will have to search through the wreckage for a good compass.

I return to the barrack feeling proud of myself. I look, almost with disdain, at my companions in misfortune who moan and complain but do nothing to fight for their lives.

On the first day of August, news reaches us of a Polish uprising in Warsaw. Communiqués from Poland report that the Russian offensive is halted at the Vistula.

I send an urgent letter to Abram asking him to meet with me for another "war council". He reports that everything is prepared, and that even the bottom of the bunker is lined with bricks so that our feet will not get wet if it rains. I tell him that, in my opinion, we should wait until the Russians renew their offensive. I think that it can only help us if we take advantage of every distraction that the approaching Russian Front offers.

Abram agrees with me completely. I give him several cans and a few drugs to deposit in the bunker. He proudly shows me a lighter and says that there is enough gasoline in the area. Should we find it necessary to camp out in the woods at night, we will be able to have a fire. Before I say good-by, we agree that we should communicate every once in a while. In case of danger, he will run to me, and together we will enter our hiding place immediately.

* * *

I continually consider various new ways and means of improving our escape plans. It occupies me not only during my free time, but also at work and at night. I am not even afraid of Zenkteller. Zbyszek opens his eyes wide when he hears me answer the old bandit boldly when he asks me something. It turns out that this is the best way to handle him, because now, after so many months of persecution, he finally leaves me alone.

In the meantime, the arrival of massive transports has ended. The ditches are being covered. The greater part of the *Sonderkommando* are taken elsewhere by truck. Nobody doubts that it is to their extermination; the slaves have done their work. The ramp is empty. We can finally breathe relatively fresh air.

One morning we see a small locomotive pushing three open cars filled with wood. The remaining *Sonderkommando* climb onto them and unload the big pieces. Other *Häftlinge* place the wood next to the fence of crematoria II and III. After a week, the space in the square is so limited that the *Sonderkommando* place the wood on the road leading to the peasant house. Naturally, this material is for us. . . .

"Tadzek, now you can select the piece of lumber that will get you to heaven," says the defeatist Libermann.

I look at him disdainfully and say, "I'll try not to die in Auschwitz and certainly not in the gas chamber."

Libermann does not know what I am talking about and is surprised. He tries to talk with me, but when he sees that he cannot elicit any information from me, he goes to the wires that separate K.B. from the women's section to talk with his brother's wife, the closest person to him in all the world. They do this every night.

The medics take advantage of the fair weather to go to the sports field in groups. The main topics of conversation are the approaching end of the war and our quick extermination. All this has a very depressing effect on me. I decide to run away regardless of the probable consequences.

On the following Sunday, I visit Section D with a group of medics to conduct a thorough lice inspection. While I am there, I take advantage of the occasion to have a long talk with Abram. He has better control of himself than I. He shows me a newspaper in which there are reports of Russian reconnoitering and slow advances. The distance between Auschwitz and the Front grows shorter every day. In any event, everything is ready for our escape. All I need to do is to come to Section D, and on the following day . . . we are on our way to our hiding place.

I must admit that he is right. There is nothing left to do but to wait.

* * *

There is a selection in Barrack 12. Thielo and Mengele are in an excellent mood despite the rain as they walk among the skeletons whom they have chased outside. Thielo has a new method. He deceives those he selects with a laconic gesture as he points to the barrack. The *Schreiber* waits and marks down the numbers of those who enter; these will go to the gas chamber. Thielo kicks the others and orders them to do exercises; they will remain. Zenkteller stands to one side with a satisfied smile on his face.

We are standing in the doorway and can overhear Mengele telling Thielo a story. An hour ago, Mengele made a selection among Jewish children up to fifteen years of age who were in a barrack in the Gypsy section. Mengele has a kind heart and has pity for the children. He wants to save them.

On two poles, he placed a bar about one hundred seventy centimeters (67 inches) from the ground. He ordered the children to line up in single file and pass under the bar. Those who were taller than one hundred seventy centimeters were saved. Unfortunately, only two of the three hundred fifty children reached the bar.

Was that his fault? Mengele wanted to do something, but the Jews are a degenerate people and too short. This is not true of the German race. Both he and Thielo laugh loudly.

* * *

It is a gloomy, rainy, cold September night. Zbyszek returns from the *Schreibstube* with very bad news. In several days, more than ten thousand Aryans, men and women, will leave the camp. The transports must be accompanied by medics from K.B. Thielo has already given the orders to Zenkteller.

In the middle of the night we hear distant claps of thunder and are surprised to hear it in such a cold rainstorm. However, we do not think about it; our minds are occupied with thoughts of being transported and wondering where they might take us. Suddenly the doors to the medic's room fly open.

"Up, you sons-of-bitches!" It is Zbyszek's voice. "Up, you SOBs! You sleep like logs, and out there the artillery is pounding!"

I am half-conscious and sleepy, but I get out of bed. I trip over a stool and hit my head on the door. Regaining my equilibrium, I run after Zbyszek to the sports field where I witness a most unusual sight: *Blockältesters* in nightshirts, Zbyszek in colorful pajamas, Julek in shorts, all of them straining their necks and cupping their hands to their ears, trying to catch the sounds in the distance.

"Now!" whispers Zbyszek.

Boom! Boom! Boommm! Boommm! The louder, clearer booms are the German artillery; those that sound like echoes are the Russian replies.

Zbyszek improvises a wild dance as we did on the day of the first air-raid on Auschwitz by the Americans. The barrack is in turmoil. The sick do not know what is happening, but look and wonder why the chief doctor is hopping around the barrack followed by the *Blockältesters* and *Schreibers.* Everyone seems to be in an excellent mood.

Instead of good-night, Zbyszek shouts into the ward, "We hear guns! Our imprisonment will soon end, fellows!"

They reply with triumphant shouts of *bravo.* Quivering with excitement, I crawl into my bunk. I cannot wait until morning.

At daybreak I run to the gate. Abram must have heard the artillery. He should come to me.

Abram is approaching K.B., but not with the labor *Kommando.* The medic of Section D is leading him and other sick ones. Abram is vomiting and holds his head. He sees me, smiles weakly, and says, "I'm sick, very sick."

After three days Abram is transferred to Barrack 12 and then to Barrack 9. He has typhus. All is lost! I break down. Obviously I am not destined to save my life.

Libermann sees my sad face and says by way of explanation, "It got to you? Don't worry too much. All of us face the same fate."

Abram lies unconscious. I organize food and injections for him. The fellow merits it.

The camp is being emptied. Transports leave every day. Even small groups of Jews are leaving. It is generally believed that the Jews are to be exterminated and the Aryans will go to work.

Dr. Krzeminski, the famous neurologist is going. All the *Stubendiensts* too. We must use patients to supplement the personnel.

Abram feels a little better. He still has fever, but at least he is conscious. After listening to his neighbors' conversations, he knows what is happening in the camp. He is desperate. I try to console him, but I am not very good at it.

Abram is silent for a while. I think that he is asleep and wants to leave, but no . . . I hear him whisper, "Tadzek, we'll never know. Maybe it's better this way. Our escape could have failed."

I have no answer to that. I return to my barrack in the rain. The mud sticks to my boots. The water cools my burning head and the wind seems to blow Abram's words into my ears, "Maybe it's better . . . maybe it's better . . ."

All the Aryans, including Zbyszek and the *Blockältester,* are ready to move. They are waiting.

It is obvious that Zbyszek is avoiding me. I understand that. In this situation, nothing can help me, and consolation is absurd. Everyone knows it.

with those Aryans who are too ill to be moved. We cannot interpret as a good sign, the fact that the chimneys have not been in use since the last selection in Barrack 12 because we can see that the tops are being cleaned of soot every day. The artillery sounds farther and farther away and then stops completely. The camps comprising Auschwitz: Buna, Jawiszowice, Swietochlowice, and others, are being evacuated systematically. All the Jews are concentrated in one camp, Birkenau.

In this "happy" mood, I celebrate my birthday in Auschwitz once more. Only Libermann knows this. Edwin is politicizing with Maks in the washroom. I have the impression that, despite everything, they are hopeful. I tell Libermann about my unsuccessful attempt to escape. I am glad that I can talk openly with him; my mood is a little brighter as a result.

Edwin tells us that he discussed the situation with Maks. They have some theoretical solutions, but they want our opinions.

I look straight into his eyes and say, "Edwin, we won't let them push us into the gas chambers alive! We'll fight. We'll propagandize so that the others will join us in the struggle!"

Edwin and Libermann shake my hand. It is agreed. We have made a pact for life and death.

* * *

"All medics out!"

I am at Abram's bedside. I notice, with great satisfaction, that he is quickly regaining his health. I must run quickly to the *Schreibstube*.

"Don't forget to let me know what's going on," Abram requests as I leave him.

I am one of the last to join the group when Thielo arrives.

"Jews to the right! Aryans to the left!"

Six Aryans step to the side and are ordered to return to their barracks. Thielo looks us over carefully for a while. Then he calls Zenkteller and whispers something in his ear.

Zenkteller brings the general list of medics from the *Schreibstube* and reads several names. Those who are called step forward and return to their barracks just as the Aryans did. Only a handful are lucky: the pharmacist, two surgeons, two internists, and a radiologist.

Zenkteller marks our numbers on the list. We hear a truck coming. Several SS men arrive from the *Blockführerstube* and . . . "March!" We go to Section D. They did not even allow us to bring a piece of bread.

Near the washroom in Section D, a group of several hundred *Häftlinge* are waiting for us to arrive.

After a short medical inspection, we march to the sauna and bath. Then we are given some tattered rags. Fortunately, they let us bring our leather shoes.

They chase us to the ramp from where we see a line of freight cars in the distance. We pass near the clinic; Aleks and Szymek are standing by the wires.

"Good-by fellows! Thank you for everything!" I shout to them.

Edwin and Libermann are near me. The final minute is approaching. With seventy to a car, they are filling up quickly.

"Full!" The doors close. Three of the four windows are sealed. Someone opens one. This act is followed immediately by a shout, "Close it!"

We hear loud noises on the ramp and the clickety-clack of wooden shoes as other cars are filled.

All this looks very suspicious. Usually, before a transport leaves, armed SS men are posted in the middle of the car with food for the trip. Now there are neither guards nor food. Meanwhile, it is getting dark.

"There's a new crematorium not far from Auschwitz." Someone at the other end of the car offers this bit of unsolicited information. Nobody protests; no one is nervous.

Edwin nudges me with his elbow and whispers, "You remember?"

I do. I remember very well. It looks as though everyone is prepared for the worst. Small groups are forming and whispering secrets. Those SS men will not have an easy time with us.

A rumble passes from car to car. Steam hisses. Another locomotive is added, and once again, there are sounds of steps on the ramp. This time they are of boots with taps on the soles.

Our car doors open and five SS men enter. A *Häftling* hands them stools. We hear the locomotive's prolonged whistle and its asthmatic panting as if the engine has trouble dragging the load. In a few minutes, we are moving.

It is dark. Through the cracks in the doors, we see the last lights on Auschwitz's wires. The train picks up speed. Someone whispers, "Don't sleep! Watch!"

Minutes pass; tension rises; the wheels roll . . . where? Where? And again, some light enters the car. One *Häftling* gets close to the door and looks; we hear him call quietly, "Kattowitz." Despite all of our calculations and planning, a faint, dumb, bewildering hope is kindled in our hearts. Perhaps?!

Sachsenhausen

We are moving very fast now. Three guards are snoring loudly; two others are awake. They look around with flashlights from time to time and yell, "Lie down!"

Only the threat of a beating makes us obey. We are not allowed to get up even if our bones and muscles ache unbearably from lying on the hard floor of the cattle car.

After a seemingly endless night, the gray dawn is visible at last through the cracks.

Someone risks a question, "May we urinate?"

The guards consult and finally reply, "Yes! Go one by one through the crack in the door!"

Intestines growl. We have been without a piece of bread for twenty-four hours. Anyway, no one thought of eating when we were preparing to fight.

Taking advantage of the darkness, Edwin slips a pocket knife from his boot and bores a hole in the car's wall. Maybe we can orient ourselves and learn in which direction we are moving.

The train seldom stops. We take turns looking through the hole. We yearn to see people, cities, fields, life. During our long stay in Auschwitz, we saw only flames.

The train is slowing as it approaches some large city. We see a sign, "Lignitz-Schlesien" through the opening Edwin made, and realize that we have traveled too far to arrive at a crematorium near Auschwitz.

The fellows are stretching out on the floor as best they can and try to sleep. I find half a handful of bread crumbs mixed with dust and the stink of disinfectant in the pocket of my coat. The crumbs are tasty and I share them with Libermann and Edwin. After this "excellent" snack, we follow the example of the others. The monotonous drone of the wheels lulls us to sleep.

After a while I awaken, but it takes me some time to realize where I am. Looking through the hole, I discover that we are passing the city of Kottbus somewhere in the vicinity of Berlin. All my doubts disappear; I am blissful.

* * *

So we really got out of Auschwitz alive! Views of the monstrous gas chambers have disappeared. I feel fine despite the hunger and cold. What can be worse? Optimism overwhelms me. I fall sleep again.

I am awakened during the night by wailing sirens and the sounds of unusual activities. We are somewhere in a field. The guards stand at the open doors ready to jump. Outside, we see some bluish lights. A menacing voice orders the SS men to remain in the car, and, if any *Häftling* raises his stinking head, he is to be shot at once. In a while we hear the same words from a greater distance. The person is obviously going from car to car.

The sirens stop; it is deadly quiet. The guards are not exchanging "witty" remarks on their usual theme: They should have finished off such garbage as we in Auschwitz, and not have to drag us to the devil knows where.

We hear a roar high in the air. What is going on? It suddenly becomes even brighter than it normally is during the day. Our eyes hurt from the glare. Is the sun coming out at night?

Planes are parachuting incendiary bombs. Our guards

stand up to talk among themselves. I can detect fear and anger in their voices. They seem to be incensed at their superiors for telling them to remain in the car with Jews in the face of such imminent danger.

The air is filled with terribly loud whistles. Somewhere near us, devastating detonations burst one after another causing our entire train to rise, and then fall back on the track with an awful crash of the wheels.

Fires from the bombs are being extinguished slowly, but many still illuminate the entire area. Aside from the detonations, we can distinguish cannon, anti-aircraft, and machine gun fire. Fragments hit the roof of the cattle car. The guards curse and leap to the ground. Before the last one jumps, he threatens us with certain death if anyone tries to run away.

The cannon fire lasts a long time. Finally, the noise from the airplanes fades; the anti-aircraft guns are silent. A screeching siren signals "All clear!" The guards return and nervously smoke cigarettes and pipes.

My thighs hurt from being slapped. Each time a bomb explodes, Edwin expresses his elation by hitting my thighs with his heavy hand. However, the great joy and feast for our eyes we experience on the following day.

After such a stormy night, a bright, golden-red sun rises. Electric trains hum next to us. Through the half-open door, we see the skyline of a large town in the distance. Our locomotive's whistle blows; we are moving slowly toward Berlin.

Columns of workers line the tracks, repairing the destruction wreaked by last night's bombers. What is even more important is that we are in Berlin. The good news of the city's destruction had reached us in Auschwitz, but no one hoped to see it. It was our unrealizable dream, like being free. For us, the miserable prisoners, this is a visible sign that, in spite of it all, justice prevails in the world, and that the spilled blood of the murdered innocent ones has its avengers. The judgment of Heaven is imponderable.

Our train crawls over an elevation at a snail's pace. Our guards remain near the open door and gaze at their ruined capital. We take advantage of every crack between them to let our eyes and minds greedily absorb the sight of every ruined building and bombarded factory . . . and there is plenty to be seen.

We have been circling the city for more than two hours. On one of the streets the houses are in ruins; only chimneys remain standing. Against this background, some people with baskets and sticks in their hands dig among the ruins.

We bite our lips; we clench our fists; we choke. From our innermost being, a cry of triumph and joy almost escapes and we think, "You got it, you murderers! You really got it for our suffering!"

One Greek, a longshoreman from Salonika, cannot hide his satisfaction. His face changes; he mumbles something in a mixture of Spanish, French, and German about his whole family being gassed in Auschwitz. In a while he points to the town and emits a horse-like cry, "Hooray! Viva America!"

With the speed of lightning, the guards jump from the door and attack the daring man. One SS man smashes him in the stomach. The Greek falls. As he lies there, another SS guard beats the poor prisoner's head angrily, sadistically with the butt of his rifle. He smashes so hard that the bones of the Greek's skull crack and his brains and blood spurt out onto the wall and floor.

At the same time the other three SS men organize a punitive action in the car. They remove their belts and lash out blindly with the metallic buckles. The massacre lasts a long time, but no one utters a cry in spite of the blood flowing from noses and lips. We do not want to give the sadists the satisfaction.

The train stops at a small station where the guards are given food: a hot soup in bowls. The delightful aroma of boiled meat pervades the car. It is not too difficult for the bastards to correctly guess that our intestines are twisting from hunger.

They gulp loudly, delighting in the taste and looking appreciatively at the pieces of meat in their spoons. After a short while their bread arrives. They cut thick slices, spread grease on them, and top it all with slices of sausage. Savoring every bite, they exclaim, "Excellent! Very good!"

It is almost dark when the train starts to move. The ride is short. We recognize a familiar sight: a well-illuminated barbed wire fence. What concentration camp is this?

Meanwhile, some peculiar things are happening. From the side of the locomotive we hear shouts, "Move! Get going! Tempo!" . . . followed by footsteps. The locomotive hisses and crawls forward for a few meters, and again, "Move!! Get going! Tempo!" . . . and footsteps.

Edwin whispers in my ear, "What the hell is going on?"

I do not expect anything bad, and I remain calm. This is confirmed in a few minutes.

Because there is no ramp for the trains in the new camp, the cars pull up one at a time to a primitive gate in the yard. *Häftlinge* in striped uniforms place a wooden bridge in place for the SS men to step down first, and we follow on the run. Despite my assurances, Edwin is restless, but we have no time to ponder.

"Move! Tempo!" We rush down to join a sizeable group of prisoners from the other cars. They have already managed to get some information. We are in Sachsenhausen, a quarantine concentration camp on the grounds of the Heinkel airplane factory.

SS men and some *Häftlinge* arrange us in groups of five. Half an hour later, all the cars are empty and then the order, "March!"

We move down a wide hard-topped street until we see the outline of a huge building in front of us. Despite all assurances that this is a quarantine camp, we are suspicious and look carefully about, but doors open and the first five pass over the threshold into an enormous, brightly illuminated hall.

Just by looking around, we realize that this cannot be a gas chamber, but a very modern, albeit very damaged, factory building one hundred and fifty meters long, eighteen meters wide, and about twenty-five meters high. Most of the windows are broken. In the center are bunks four or five high. Although there is no trace of a blanket or straw mat, we dream of being allowed to lie down, but no such luck!

We are counted and arranged in groups of one hundred.

Every once in a while, someone enters the hall: a *Lagerschreiber, Arbeitseinsatz,* or *Arbeitsdienst.* Each one counts and writes something down.

The wind howls through the enormous hall; it is definitely worse than the railroad cars. We begin to feel the full effects of hunger, cold, and exhaustion. This is the third night since we left Auschwitz.

It is still dark outside. Finally we hear the gong. Maybe they will pity us and let us have a little warm coffee.

Instead of the coffee we hoped for, we have roll call. This time it is supervised by three SS men. Afterwards, we are compelled to stand, but still nothing happens. The sky turns gray outside. The first rays of the morning sun shine into the hall, and still nothing occurs. Obviously, they have forgotten us. We look around. The hall looks good. It is too large and too cold, but we hope that we will not be here for too long.

In the meantime, somebody pushes open a large partition from the outside. Several men in striped uniforms enter. Their armbands read: *Lagerpolizei.* This is something new. They look us over for several minutes, whisper among themselves and . . . leave.

Through the open door, we see barbed wires, towers, and behind the wires, a railroad track. A passenger train is going by.

Edwin is as happy as a child. "Tadzek, you see what compensation we have for looking with disdain into the eyes of Death. We've a very pleasant place." He stops talking and looks at me with a peculiar expression on his face. After a while he says, "See if you have any more bread crumbs in your pocket."

I do not have time to find out, for, just then, camp dignitaries appear surrounded by *Lagerpolizei,* and again they start counting. After an entire hour of this, they divide us into six groups of two hundred each. We are told that we must wait until the camp administration assigns *Blockältesters* to us.

From the lines come meek requests for bread and coffee. It is four days since we have had anything in our mouths. They respond by telling us that they are very sorry that we are hungry, but as long as we have held out for so many days, we can bear it a little longer. The *Blockältesters* will arrange everything.

Libermann looks critically at the man who spoke and turns to us saying, "That son-of-a-bitch certainly had a good breakfast. It's easy for him to say 'wait a few hours.'"

Our *Blockältesters* are here. A few *Häftlinge* bring tables and chairs, and each *Blockältester* takes his place in front of his group.

Each of us in turn goes to the table to get a colored chip that assigns him to a barrack. There are Black Barrack A and Black Barrack B, Green Barrack A and Green Barrack B, Red Barrack A and Red Barrack B. Once again we stand in line while the *Blockältesters* carry large colored shields to the bunks and fasten them there. Now we know exactly in which corner we will sleep.

We accept these arrangements with mixed feelings. On the one hand we are frustrated that we have to remain in this hall, and on the other, we admire the organization. Above all, we curse everything and beg Heaven for a Moses or a miracle to give us some sustenance.

One "optimist" remarks that maybe the Germans ran out of *Zyklon* B and want to use hunger instead, to finish us off. This unknown's analysis may not be too far from the truth. People, weak from hunger, begin collapsing, and two drop dead.

For a change, the *Blockältesters* give us important information.

"First of all, regarding air-raid alarms. At night when the sirens in the hall sound, don't hesitate a minute, but run from your bunks to the yard," which he indicates through the open door. We must "stay there until the 'all clear' signal sounds. Whoever remains in the hall gets a bullet in his head if he is discovered by the SS."

What protection the yard offers, he does not say.

Then the *Blockältester* wants to select an assistant and several *Stubendiensts* from among us. The assistant organizes the *Kommando* of food haulers. "We will go for the straw mats and blankets after the noon meal."

Even before he finishes his last words, a noisy row starts. As if shot from a catapult, several *Häftlinge* jump from every line. They want the "honorable" positions. I, Edwin, Libermann, and Maks Weinryb, who also joined our group, stand open-mouthed. Before we realize that the positions can earn an additional portion of soup or bread, the new functionaries get their armbands.

"Yes, fellows," says Maks, "we intellectuals aren't fit for life in a camp. The best place for us is a nice warm spot in the gas chamber."

Edwin disagrees. With great assurance he says that this is untrue, that he is brave and only knows that we are in quarantine for a short time. He did not want to push himself with the others.

With their armbands secured with a piece of wire, the new *Stubendiensts* immediately exhibit unusual energy. "Get out! Get out! Get some fresh air! We want to clean the hall."

Their decision to do this comes at a very inopportune time; it is raining. We do not mind; we want to study our surroundings. We discover that our camp is very big. The terrain is overgrown with trees and bushes. At a certain distance in the midst of the trees, we see a whole line of buildings like ours. Throughout the length and breadth of the camp, there are hard-topped roads. We want to explore further, but unfortunately barbed wire and *Lagerpolizei* bar our way. Cut off from the rest of the camp, we must postpone our explorations and walks until another time.

A group of people leave to get food. In half an hour they return dragging a wooden platform on which—Oh God! —are cauldrons of soup and racks of bread. They leave the valuable load and go back. To bring food for one thousand two hundred people is no easy job.

Finally the long awaited moment comes—NOON MEAL. The people are as hungry as wolves. With burning eyes, they watch every move the *Blockältester* makes as he dips the ladle into the cauldron.

"He's cheating! He isn't giving a full portion!"

Those are the first voices of protest. With cold, cruel eyes, the *Blockältester* looks at the lines from which the complaints originated. He blows a whistle. The police enter the hall, about twenty well-fed characters wearing insignias. They are a nice group, all professional bandits. The chief of police asks the *Blockältester* what is wrong.

"Aha!," he says and barks a curt order, "Sport! Lie down and roll over!"

The hall is large enough for punitive exercises. But the *Blockältester* has a "good" heart. He intervenes in behalf of those who are punished while we observe the scoundrels with bitterness.

The meal is "excellent": marinated snails from the fields in a gray sauce. Actually, it is dirt which, despite our terrible hunger, barely passes our throats.

After this "rich" meal, we have a pleasant distraction: marching across the entire camp to the clothes depot for straw mats and blankets. Along the way, we see buildings that are almost completely destroyed. We are especially pleased by the sight of an underground air-raid shelter whose three meter thick roof has not withstood the devastation of the bomb. Once we arrive at the clothes depot, we stand and wait for them to give us our "bedding".

Not too far from where we are, old-timers in striped uniforms are digging a ditch for lime. Several sneak into our group, and we learn a few interesting things from them. We discover that they were the first Jews to arrive here. They have been in this camp since 1942 and thought that there were no more Jews left in all of Europe. It is very flattering to hear that, but we try not to show it.

Our informants are two Dutchmen and one Pole who tell us that the last air-raid on the Heinkel installation occurred in the middle of August when American bombers attacked at noon; the raid lasted two minutes. "When the dust settled . . . well, we can see the immensity of the damage."

In the underground hall, *Häftlinge* were assembling powerful four-engine bombers that have the capability of flying from Berlin to New York with a full load of bombs without refueling. The underground crew, who, for safety reasons, had the special protection of three meter thick reinforced cement, were killed on the spot. The bomb penetrated the bunker with such unbelievable ease that the emergency squads could not separate pieces of bodies from the machinery. Three hundred *Häftlinge* died, but the establishment, Goering's pride, has virtually ceased to exist.

On that same night, the British added their contribution. One bomb fell on a hall and killed several *Häftlinge*. That was the origin of the crazy order for us to run into the yard during a night air-raid. The informer adds with a smile, "Because more people die from shrapnel than from the bomb, we must remain in the yard for the entire night in the rain and the cold. To hell with the Nazis!"

He offers another piece of information about a most important subject, food.

"It became hellishly worse ever since new transports began arriving from other camps. We get snails for the noon meal every other day. It's impossible to organize. It's bad, fellows! We may meet again. Good-by."

Every other man gets a straw mat with very little straw and two blankets. One is full of holes and should serve as a sheet, and the other, only slightly better, for a cover. On the way back we think about why they did not give each of us individual bedding. Will we have to come back again? Our fears are unfounded. The *Blockältester* announces that we will sleep two in a bed because more transports are expected soon.

It is raining again. Under such circumstances, it is, of course, always better to be under a roof. So despite the strict control, we shrewdly delay bedmaking until after the evening roll call.

With roll call over, we get bread, and then we must make our beds on the run. Amid screams, shouts and beatings, everyone fights for a bunk on the first or second levels because to climb a ladder to the top is not easy. Once again the police enter the hall, and once more we stand in line.

Under the watchful eye of the *Blockältester,* places are assigned. This time it is just. As their turn comes, every two people are assigned to a bunk.

Edwin and I are in the highest one, underneath the ceiling. It is very uncomfortable for us since we are both very tall and, in spite of our loss of weight, even our bare bones require a bigger surface. It is entirely possible that, while we sleep during the night, one might kick the other unwittingly, causing him to fall. What can we do about it?

We undress quickly, putting boots and clothes under our heads. We remove the blanket from the straw mat and cover ourselves with it, then put our coats on top. Finally, after suffering for three days and three nights and undergoing many hardships, we are in bed. I look down and try to estimate the height. As if from a distance I hear Edwin's comment that six years ago he had a more pleasant sleep with a pretty girl. I cover my head with my coat . . . may the world fall apart.

Woooooooooo! Wooooooooooooooo! Wooooooooooooooo!

The siren screeches in our ears filling the whole hall with its unbearable wail. Our eardrums are bursting. The lights go out; it is completely dark. From below we hear the police roaring, "Get up! Move! Tempo!"

The confusion that ensues in the hall is truly impossible to describe. Aroused from deep sleep, the people are totally disoriented. They do not know what is happening or what to do. The loud siren drowns out the police orders. Someone falls out of bed. Boards are breaking as one pair of *Häftlinge* drops on top of the ones below and, they all fall even lower.

Edwin and I are relatively calm. There is a question of our getting dressed in time, and we decide that the best thing to do is to stay where we are. We spread our blankets on top of the straw mattress, crawl under, and lie on our stomachs, putting our hands next to our thighs in case of an inspection to decrease the possibility of being discovered.

Somewhere in the distance, anti-aircraft artillery goes into action. From the doors we hear the sounds and voices of those leaving. I risk poking my head out from under the straw mat. The hall is dark and empty; we can sleep.

On the next morning we hear some very interesting news. There was a tremendous air-raid during the night. Several bombs scored direct hits on ammunition depots located a few kilometers from the camp. Shrapnel killed eight *Häftlinge* in the yard.

Edwin looks at me a mischievously as he asks, "Did you sleep well, Tadzek?"

After the morning roll call, the *Stubendiensts* try to restore order in the hall. We must stay outdoors in the fog and cold. The hours drag by. Our only diversion is hitting one another to keep warm. Maks delivers an occasional political speech telling us that, although the situation on the front is exceedingly favorable, we are in a very precarious position because we are in the heart of the Third Reich. Furthermore, even if we are freed, we will be the last ones . . . and who knows what we can expect in the meantime.

We are all mulling over our situation. We indulge in fruitless discussions, but even the worst pessimists among us cannot imagine that what we will face will be as horrible as our stay in Auschwitz.

Although we are not working, being outside for several hours is quite distressing because the weather is terrible. The morning fog changes to low lying clouds that turn into unpleasant rain. We must get under a roof at any cost. I have a brainstorm—at least I think so. I consider it best to get some work inside the hall: washing cauldrons, dishes, whatever . . . no sooner said than done.

For a change today, we have snails for our noon meal. The *Blockältesters* do not even cheat; they give us a whole liter of "soup". Edwin is desperate. I think of oysters, and somehow the food becomes tolerable.

Now, quickly . . . through the intervention of one of the *Stubendiensts* who was my patient in Auschwitz, I attain the high position of cauldron washer. Maks finds a friend from Krakow who gives him several fat snails. The dignified Libermann declares that, as long as he can stand on his feet, he will not do that kind of work but, of course, if someone forces him. . . .

Edwin and I drag cauldrons to clean them under the faucet. We must hurry because those who bring the food are waiting to return the empty cauldrons to the kitchen. Edwin remarks, with a sad face, that the sides of the large receptacles are scrubbed so thoroughly that he can see the scratches on them.

Since the cauldron washing cannot last forever, we are unemployed a half hour later and must leave the hall. This presents Edwin with another reason for his discontent. He complains that it is not enough that the cauldrons were empty and that we had to scrub sticky goo from them, but that, after all of our work, we must go out into the rain.

We spend the next few nights in this camp without any sleep. The sirens signal the approach of enemy planes, and we run to the yard. The rain is heavier, and the scrawny trees offer no protection.

One night Edwin breaks down. He is almost in tears as he moves his hands resignedly and says, "How can we hold out here, Tadzek? During the day we're outside and at night we're also outside. If we don't get out of here soon, the devil will take us."

A broad-shouldered figure visible from a distance interrupts Edwin in a melodious bass voice. "Why do you complain, colleague? You didn't come here for a vacation. Be satisfied you don't have to work."

Colleague—the use of the word and the ease with which the person speaks confirms that we are dealing with an intelligent man. Curious, I move closer to him and start a conversation. As we talk, I discover that he is Dr. Sawczyc, a good friend of my father. I had not completely recovered from my surprise when we suddenly hear a deafening crash, and, as an unknown force knocks me to the ground, I dig my nose into the sand. It is a long time before I revive. I have the impression that my eardrums have burst.

I call to Edwin and Sawczyc. Luckily they survived without a scratch, but we hear calls for help nearby. How can we even think of securing aid when all of the anti-aircraft guns hidden in a nearby wood start firing at the same time? We hear the metallic whistle of shrapnel and the meancing sound of diving planes.

Luckily for us, the pilots, as if they have knowledge of our presence, unload their bombs beyond us. But the shrapnel!! We are fearful when we hear it whistle overhead. Before the pieces fall to the ground, we experience unusual emotions: Will they score hits or won't they, and if they do, on whom?

The splinters land quite often, judging from the growing number of cries for help. After several hours, the long eagerly awaited "all clear" siren finally sounds. The lights come on. Ten are killed and more than twenty-nine are wounded. It is "not bad" for one night.

It becomes apparent that the Germans want to keep us in the open even though covered trenches criss-cross the camp and offer good protection from shrapnel.

We crawl up to our beds and barely manage to undress when we have a new surprise. Near the wires we hear the chug of a locomotive, and, after a while, the familiar orders, "Move! Quickly!"

The lights in the hall are turned on, and *Häftlinge* enter through the open door. In a few minutes we recognize old friends from Auschwitz, Poles who left that camp one day after us. They are very surprised to find us here. After our departure from Auschwitz, rumors circulated that we were taken to the nearby woods and shot.

I come down from my bunk and find a patient whose life I saved when he was very sick with pneumonia. He is happy to see me and, to celebrate our meeting, he treats me to a pack of cigarettes. I accept it with some hesitation. A pack of cigarettes in this camp is the equivalent of gold. For several days at least, I am assured a double portion of soup.

When I crawl up to my bunk again after an hour, I find Edwin there, smiling. He has organized a piece of bread and a little bit of sugar. When he notices my cigarettes, he utters a cry of triumph. We will improvise a feast: bread, sugar, and for dessert, a cigarette. What does it matter if we must climb down from our bunk to find a light? The future seems less bleak.

In the middle of the night I am awakened by a mysterious noise near my bunk. I open my eyes and see a figure climbing down the ladder. In a second he disappears between the beds. I have a bad premonition and feel my pocket. The cigarettes are gone. With a shout I awaken Edwin, but it is too late. The cigarettes have disappeared and with them, my hope for a double portion of soup. The ghost of hunger haunts me again.

We are in the worst possible mood when we rise at the sound of the gong. With about two thousand people in the hall, it is very noisy, and it takes about an hour before we are ready for roll call. Meanwhile, our bosses are worried about providing us with "entertainment". It is finally decided that part of us will register with the political section and the rest will go to the baths.

A large group of us are going to the baths. We have nothing with which to dry ourselves and must cover our wet bodies with our rags because others are waiting. Outside, it is snowing for a change. As we walk quickly to our "home", an *Arbeitseinsatz* stops us. He is accompanied by two SS men.

"You're taking a stroll?! I have work for you!"

Several fellows want to run away, but the SS guards reach for their revolvers and fire several shots at the fleeing *Häftlinge*. Humiliated, they return. They receive a few kicks and follow us.

We are taken to the other side of the camp to a tall building with a large chimney. Freight trucks loaded with charcoal briquettes are arriving. We stand in line, single file, and put our coats on backwards. In this way, they serve as sacks, we fill with charcoal which we must carry up a winding staircase and throw into the burner.

A flame shoots out of the furnace; it is pleasantly warm. Unfortunately, we must go in and out quickly. I get an idea. I look around the place carefully and, when I am going down for the second time, I cleverly take advantage of the inattention of a boilermaker and hide behind some lockers that are in a corner of the room. I try to make myself inconspicuous. I am warm. I close my eyes for only a minute. . . .

When I awaken, only two boilermakers are there. I am afraid; cold sweat forms on my forehead. Who knows for how long I have been sleeping? Maybe roll call is over. I must act. I smear my face with soot—there is plenty of it in the corner where I slept so comfortably. Silently I crawl out of my hiding place, take two jumps to the staircase, and run.

It is dark outside. I look around trying to orient myself, and study the terrain. I have it. I am running quickly, as fast as my strength will allow. I dash into the hall, literally at the last minute. The *Blockältester* is already reporting to the SS guards that one *Häftling* is missing.

One of them kicks me in the rear. The *Blockältester* corrects his count, and the whole affair ends happily for me. I feel fine. At least I slept in a warm corner, even if only for a little while.

After roll call, I tell Edwin that I will ask for an additional piece of bread for my "heavy work". Edwin cannot keep from laughing.

I am standing very humbly in front of the *Blockältester* as I say in as tearful a voice as I can, "They kept me working a whole day, Mr. *Blockältester.* They didn't give me my noon meal."

The *Blockältester* looks at me and my blackened face and hands. He hesitates.

"Yes, Mr. *Blockältester,* they didn't give me any food during the whole day," I repeat stubbornly with tears in my eyes.

The *Blockältester* makes me wait. In a little while I have a full dish of soup with potatoes and meat and, in addition, a piece of soap.

"Eat! And don't forget to scrub yourself right away!"

I eat until I am stuffed. I leave a few tasty morsels for Edwin. Satisfied and sated, we go to sleep.

Damn it! That cursed siren again! We are angry at the British. If they would only attack during the day. . . .

Edwin declares that he has to go down only because he has cramps after eating my soup. I crawl underneath the straw mat. In the meantime, Edwin is ready to go, and I ask him to cover me well. The last footsteps are fading. The lamps go out, and I fall asleep.

Suddenly, loud voices fill the hall. The lights come on. What in hell is happening? Is it after the "all clear"? It is impossible! The siren did not sound.

I hear German voices. Very quickly, a thought comes to mind, "It's a hoax! A German trick!"

Through a small slit I see SS men and *Lagerpolizei* with long sticks. Someone is climbing my ladder. I flatten out as much as I can. He is already checking the bunk below mine. My heart pounds wildly from fear. May he not hear it! Soon my turn will come. I hold my breath. He jumps on my legs; I can barely suppress my cries of pain.

From below I hear someone saying in German, "Be careful, Hans. You'll fall."

From the next bed, a laugh, "I'm careful."

From the other end of the hall, a shout, "You bastard!" followed by whipping and shrill cries.

The guard passes over my bed quickly and goes down. Meanwhile there are more beatings and screams. I think the Germans made a good catch. Then I hear orders, shouts, sounds of a struggle, some preparations, and silence.

The sirens howl again. The people reenter the hall and find five *Häftlinge* hanging. Attached to each corpse is a hand-printed sign: "We have disobeyed the orders of our superiors."

I carefully crawl out from under my straw mat. With an apprehensive look on his face, Edwin climbs up and finds me sitting in the bunk with a pale, but smiling face.

* * *

"Jews out! Poles remain!"

The *Lagerältester* issued the order immediately after roll call. Edwin and I are walking calmly as if the order did not apply to us. Nothing remains of the tragedy that took place a few hours ago. The hanged had been cut down and removed. In the middle of the hall is a table with a few chairs around it. At about ten o'clock, several cars arrive in front of the hall. A number of civilians in leather coats and an SS man enter and occupy seats at the table.

We hear a low whisper from among the Poles, "They came to look over the merchandise."

The civilians open valises and remove various tools. The SS man stands up and yells, "All locksmiths, here!"

One by one they call plumbers, mechanics, metal workers, and others. Each one is subject to a short test and if he passes, the SS man writes down his number on a list.

Edwin proposes that we announce ourselves at the table, but I do not want to take the risk. In the last few hours, I have lived through enough.

That same night, the Poles leave the hall and once again

we are alone. I hope that something will start for us. Within two hours after the Poles depart, new transports arrive, bringing some six thousand persons from the concentration camps of Grossrosen and Leitmeritz.

The next day is filled with unbelievable turmoil that is especially noticeable during mealtime. Finally, toward evening the command that we were expecting is shouted, "Jews come forward!"

We go to the baths once more. As I learned from previous experience, I stand but do not open the shower faucet, and so I get out only with wet feet. Others who really bathed are now cursing in despair when they must put clothes on their wet bodies.

Contrary to our expectations, we do not return to our hall. "In the morning we march," explains one of our escort policemen.

We end up in a demolished theater; every window is broken. A howling wind blows through the building. I pull Edwin toward the stage and find a dark corner where we hide behind colorful decorations. This has an advantage; there is no draft.

Even before the gong sounds, the *Lagerpolizei* chase us to the sports field and arrange us in groups of one hundred. They keep counting. In the end, progress is made. The *Lagerältester* reports the results to the SS men who order, "With even step, march!"

Stamping our boots on the hard asphalt road, we approach the exit.

"Caps off!"

With a parade step and hands close to our thighs we pass the gate. We have so much experience in marching that we could form an honor guard for any army in the world.

Two companies of SS guards equipped with machine guns ready to shoot, wait for us outside the gate. We do not lack pessimists who insist that the Germans will finish us off in a field or forest where nicely prepared graves await us. But I have already gained some experience in camps, and I try to console the worried, telling them that this is how every innocent march appears.

Our biggest worry now is that winter is here. The cold

nips our ears as we march down a good wide road and across a bridge over a four track railroad line. Through the fog, we can see the silhouette of Berlin's skyline in the distance.

Traffic increases on the road. Apparently, we are approaching a major center. After marching for several minutes, a large yellow sign reads: Oranienburg. As we continue, the number of homes increases. Inhabitants peering out of windows look at us indifferently, showing no signs of pity. A woman throws an apple core into the ditch. Our people immediately jump to grab this valuable treasure. The SS men beat them with their rifle butts. Several young girls watching this entire scene with great interest seem to enjoy it, for they laugh loudly.

I clench my fist in helpless anger. Edwin looks at them askance and murmurs, "You German whores!"

Upon entering the town, we see, at every step, huge posters urging enlistment in the Home Guard. Mostly women stand in long lines in front of the stores.

Now we have reason to be satisfied. The Germans must be desperate because they are accepting grandfathers into the army.

We turn into a wide street. A few hundred paces more and we come face to face with barbed wire. A sign picturing a skull hangs nearby announcing that this is the boundary of a concentration camp and that entrance is strictly prohibited. We pass alongside a five meter high wall on top of which are electrified wires—we can glimpse porcelain insulators. The head of the column stops.

"Caps off! Straight lines! Maaaaaaaaaarch!"

At least ten members of the SS and a few high-ranking officers at the gate count us carefully as we enter the camp of Sachsenhausen. We are in a large square with loudspeakers in the center and barracks arranged in a semicircle. The barrack walls facing the square bear the slogan:

WORK MAKES FREE

"Halt!"

Several of the SS accompanied by well-dressed people from

the *Schreibstube* rapidly divide us into small groups. A sharp whistle sounds followed by the order, "*Blockältesters* out!" Shortly thereafter, our group of thirty stands in front of a nice barrack marked 11.

Our *Blockältester* wears a red insignia, so we know that we are dealing with a political prisoner. It starts well. In general, we like it in this camp. The barracks look good. They have windows and lawns and trees in front of each one, and, what is more important, a pleasant aroma wafts from the kitchen.

As is the custom in every camp, the *Blockältester* delivers a speech. Fortunately, it is short and we enter the barrack. With pride, he shows us how the place is arranged as he explains, "Every barrack has two wings. Each has its own dining and sleeping areas. In the corridor are washrooms and toilets, separate ones for each wing." Our admiration reaches its peak when the food haulers place the cauldrons of food in front of the barrack: goulash and potatoes.

The gong sounds; the *Kommando* is returning from work. One hundred people with great suffering visible in their faces take their places in the dining areas. In front of each of us is a dish of goulash. Close at hand are five to six potatoes. We wait. It is understandable that the workers are the first to be served.

From conversations at the tables we learn that, for several weeks, our friends in the barrack have had the unpleasant experience of walking around in tight shoes. We certainly would not have guessed this. One *Häftling* notices our surprise and explains that their job is to break in boots for the soldiers.

From time to time shipments of shoes arrive directly from the factory and are meant for the soldiers at the Front. The boots are uncomfortable; the leather is hard; the soldiers could damage their feet. Since the *Häftlinge* have nothing better to do anyway, they must walk in those boots until the authorities declare that they are comfortable enough to be worn by the brave soldiers of the *Waffen*-SS.

"The noon meal was excellent," the *Blockältester* tells us good-naturedly, "but unfortunately, there's no more." We observe the truth of that statement later in the afternoon. A person enters and carries away a full container of goulash in exchange for a pack of cigarettes which he leaves on the table for the *Blockältester.* We have no control over the situation.

Loudspeakers in the square blare a lively march as the *Kommandos* return from work. We learn that there is only one roll call a day in Sachsenhausen, in the morning. Better and better. . . .

After the bread is distributed, they assign us to places in the sleeping area. It is overcrowded; two must sleep together. That is no problem. The straw mat is full and the blankets are good.

During the morning coffee, the *Blockältester* announces that, after breakfast, we will go to work with a *Kommando* that breaks in shoes. A new shipment has just arrived.

Inside the clothes depot, six *Häftlinge* and two SS men stand beside the boxes filled with shoes. They look with a trained eye at our feet and throw a pair of shoes to each of us as we approach. There is no appealing their decision even if the shoes are too small and hurt unbearably. The old-timers know that and do not complain, but a few newcomers dare to protest and are beaten so badly that they must be taken to K.B.

Edwin and I are last. The *Häftling* distributing the shoes looks knowingly at our big feet and points them out to the SS men. All of them burst into uncontrollable laughter and pull some enormous boots from a box. It cannot be helped if they are too big.

Once the *Kapos* arrange us in lines, they order, "Mark time!"

For the first half hour, Edwin remarks in a satisfied manner, "It's better to walk than to dig ditches, for example." After a few minutes he realizes the idea and exclaims, "We're breaking in shoes so that the Germans will be able to run faster!"

A little later, Edwin loses his desire to talk and joke. The boots are so large that they fall off our feet and require a great effort just to keep them on. Our tendons are strained so severely that they soon cease to function properly. This torture is unbearable.

One of our group whose boots are too tight leaves the line for a minute to loosen his shoelaces. One of the two *Kapos,* who conducts the game and has a bat in his hand, curses and brutally beats the fellow over the head. To a passing SS man, the *Kapo* calls the hapless prisoner a saboteur. The SS man nods understandingly and continues on his way.

"Sing!"

Edwin and I take advantage of the order by moaning loudly to our hearts' content. We pray to God that noon comes soon, maybe we will find some solution. Meanwhile, time moves at a turtle's pace. I lose count of the number of times we traverse the square. Our only distractions are the various orders that are barked.

"With even step, March!"

"Mark time! March!"

"With even step, sing!"

The *Kapos* watch to see if anyone is tinkering with the boots and not obeying orders. Punishment is meted out by the head *Kapo.* We witnessed it with our own eyes a while ago. Just when we are taxing our energies to the limit and can hardly stand straight, the saving gong sounds.

Helping one another, we stumble to the barrack. We do not feel like eating. We organize a few rags and stuff them into the toes of the boots. Of course it feels much better immediately, but it is too late. Our feet are swollen at the ankles and hurt agonizingly.

"Tendosynovitis," Edwin declares with a funereal expression on his face.

We must return. The torture starts again.

At night we find a new use for our blankets. We roll them up, place them under our feet, and apply cold compresses.

We decide to report sick immediately after roll call. Unfortunately, there are many others who want to do the same. In anticipation of a massive desertion, the *Kapo* comes to our barrack, tears up the medic's card on which he marked our numbers and, using a bat, forces us to march. And so another cursed day begins.

"With even step! Mark time! Sing!"

As the people try to protect themselves from the bats, the

Kapos become nervous and threaten "sport". Once again we summon up all of our strength and march for fifteen minutes. Finally the column stops. Even the bats are ineffective. People fall and cannot move. Even with the rags that Edwin and I put into our boots to make it easier for us to walk, we are barely able to stand. The *Kapos* finally capitulate.

With slow steps, we go to the rear of the camp and rest between the barracks. The fellows take off their boots. Most of them have terrible blisters and sores on their feet. The *Kapos* will have to look for others; these poor souls are finished.

In the midst of all this activity, we lost our own good leather shoes, the only valuable part of our wardrobe. They just disappeared. In their place we find a worn-out pair of wooden shoes. Edwin tries to complain, but the punch in the face he receives from the *Kapo* shuts him up.

The afternoon is free. We sit in the dining section and enjoy the heat coming from the red-hot stove, but not for long. A messenger from the *Schreibstube* enters the barrack and announces, "New arrivals! Everyone to the sports field!" We must leave.

All the SS are on the field, waiting. They begin counting. The *Schreiber,* with a list in his hand, calls out names and divides us into groups. Before I realize what is happening, Edwin and Libermann are on the other side. A short order and their group marches toward the gate. Edwin and Libermann wave good-by and shout, "Until we meet again! Until we meet in freedom!"

I am dumbfounded. I got used to Edwin. He was the only human being close to me. Now we are separated. Who knows, maybe forever.

Someone taps me on the shoulder. It is Sawczyc. "I see you've a sad face," he says gently. "Is it because your friend left? But don't let it upset you too much. Who knows who is better off?"

The loudspeakers announce the latest communiqués from the Front. The German Army has inflicted heavy losses on the enemy. Because they do not name any cities, we cannot tell where the battles are taking place.

"The most important news," says Sawczyc, "is that they are retreating. The report that they are inflicting heavy losses is only to bolster their morale."

My feet hurt excruciatingly. I would like to return to the barrack, but here, seemingly for spite, we wait and wait. It seems as though there is no place for us anywhere. Four transports are waiting at the ramp. As long as we are leaving, it will do no harm if we stay outside for a few more hours.

Finally someone remembers us. We are led to a barbed wire-enclosed field between two barracks. They give us some bread and . . . good-by. The gate is closed and we are alone.

It becomes colder. I look with envy through the window into the dining area where the *Häftlinge* are drinking hot coffee and warming themselves at the stove. Sawczyc finds a wooden box, places it near the barrack wall, and invites me to sit with him.

"At least you'll be protected from cold drafts," he says in a half-resigned tone.

The voices and the clatter of dishes cease behind the wall. Lights go out. It is night. Someone offers us two cigarettes for a place on the box. Sawczyc laughs and calls him crazy.

The searchlights blink like lamps in a lighthouse. There is no protection against the icy wind. Our teeth chatter. Our striped overcoats are lined with frigid air.

"Yes, my dear, this is how it is when you come to someone as a guest, but I hope when we finally get to our own camp, it will be better. Be patient," says Sawczyc for goodnight. He turns up the collar of his coat, pulls up his knees almost to his chin, and, in a while, I hear his snoring which, eventually, lulls me to sleep despite the unpleasant conditions.

When the morning gong releases us from the arms of Morpheus, it takes a long time before our frozen extremities and muscles start functioning. Someone shouts through the barbed wire for us to get ready for roll call. A small group of prisoners stands next to two *Häftlinge* who show no signs of life; they froze to death during the night.

After an SS man takes the roll call, two figures emerge from the fog. One asks if anyone is sick and, without waiting for a reply, they both disappear.

It is obvious that we will get no coffee because we are like homeless strays for whom no one cares. Happily, we see the *Lagerschreiber* who checks our names again and declares that we are leaving right away.

"Right away" lasts several hours. We spend the time warming up and dreaming about our new camp which we hope will be better than the Heinkel factory or Sachsenhausen.

The long awaited moment finally arrives. We march. And again, the SS men surround us. Judging from their heavy rucksacks, we guess that we are in for a long ride.

The transport's *Kommandant* is a young *Unterscharführer.* Across his chest, a brand-new machine gun is suspended on a leather belt. He is as proud as a peacock and continually runs from the front to the back of the line and back again yelling and playing with his gun very often as though he would like to try it out on us.

A ten minute march brings us to a side track where the train is waiting for us. We enter, fifty to a car. The walls are covered with subversive writings and drawings executed in chalk by some very gifted *Häftling* painters. We laugh until we hurt. Our mood improves even more when we see the truck with provisions coming from the camp.

6 Dachau XI (Bauunternehmung L. Moll)

It is evening. Despite the warning that the provisions must last two days, not one of the fifty people in our freight car has a crumb left of his half of a loaf of bread. It is true that Sawczyc decided to keep one piece for the black hour, but the temptation is too strong. Every once in a while he breaks off a piece. Soon he, too, is out of bread.

As our stomachs begin rumbling, we come to the conclusion that metabolism is not a mere invention. We clearly feel life-giving heat spreading throughout our bodies.

"Long live calories!" murmurs Sawczyc.

We sleep with slight interruptions until ten o'clock in the morning. Through the half-open doors, we see a deep snow-covered hilly landscape dense with trees. The sun shines brightly. It is lovely winter weather.

Passing through Nuremberg at about noon, we are pleased to see the ruins, but, as we learned in Berlin, we do not show our elation.

"Keep your mouths shut!" advises one *Häftling* with satisfaction from the other end of the car.

During the night, the cold penetrates our bodies, but we

have no way of protecting ourselves. The wheels are switching tracks.

The train stops; we hear the screech of metallic bolts being opened in nearby cars. When one of our guards opens our door, we learn that we are in Munich.

Someone risks a remark that the Germans may be taking us to Switzerland. The guards do not understand Polish, but, hearing the word "Switzerland," they guess that we expect to go there. From their conversation it is evident that we are mistaken and that the only suitable place for us is a crematorium.

Meanwhile our stop seems interminable. Even the SS men become impatient and curse the conditions on the German railways. At last we can hear the locomotive being attached.

The train is moving again. We have visions of warm barracks and dishes of hot soup. Some optimist in the car consoles us by saying, "They certainly know that we haven't had anything warm to eat for three days."

The trip is interrupted by short stops, but it does not last much longer. With a loud grinding of brakes and a spasmodic jolt passing through the cars, the train comes to a halt beside a wall. We have reached our destination. The guards open the door and jump into the field.

It is pitch dark. We are surprised not to see any trace of light from a camp because, before we left Sachsenhausen, we heard that we were bound for Dachau. The direction of our trip indicated that. However, we did not know that Dachau has many satellite camps. Our destination is undoubtedly one of those.

We suffer increasingly from cold and hunger. Added to this is the uncertainty: Where are we? What is in store for us? We wait anxiously for daybreak.

In the gray dawn we see snowflakes driven by a powerful howling wind. The guards keep us in the cars. The spectre of death from hunger and cold haunts us again.

The weather changes. Now the wind is driving the clouds away, allowing the warm sunshine to break through, relieving our deadly stiffness. Some SS man goes from car to car banging on each door with his rifle butt and yelling, "Move! Get out!"

The guards jump out first. Only then are we permitted to leave our prison, but not before we pull two frozen bodies from a corner of the car. We realize that, under such conditions, none of us would survive for more than a few hours.

We stand in snow up to our knees while the SS men count us. This procedure seems to last for a terribly long time and is quite unpleasant, especially after such a long trip. However, it does give us an opportunity to study our surroundings. We see a few railroad tracks, a dense forest, and, within that forest, several barracks and a number of figures in striped uniforms. There appears to be no trace of a camp.

The SS men order us to toss several corpses into the freight car, then to stand five abreast. The order to march is finally given.

We start . . . tripping over railroad tracks and rocks. The snow gets deeper.

Meanwhile, there is nothing as yet to indicate that there is a camp nearby. After wandering for an hour, we cut across a wide road lined with large trees. We cover another several hundred meters and halt in the center of a clearing. A dense forest hides the view from us. Thick smoke above the treetops leads us to believe that we are close to our destination.

The *Kommandant* of the guards speaks to several SS men and they enter the forest together. Half an hour later, we overhear a lively conversation emanating through the trees as our guards return in the company of an *Obersturmführer* who, judging from his appearance, seems to be unhappy at our arrival. Why? We will soon find out.

As we march farther, the road to the camp is blanketed with snow. The SS guards walk easily in their high boots, but we. . . .

We stop near two green barracks: the SS kitchen and SS guardhouse. The kitchen's chimneys are belching the thick bluish smoke that we had seen on the other side of the forest.

Judging from the discussions among those at the head of our column, it appears that they can already see the camp.

Meanwhile, we are suffering tantalizing tortures induced by the aroma of food coming from the kitchen.

Finally the order is given, "Caps off! With even step!"

The head of the column turns. Our wooden shoes are beating rhythmically. Our hearts pound.

After a short while, when we turn to a curve in the road, we find ourselves in a clearing with a few unfinished barracks . . . our camp. Is this all there is? No, not all. We enter some sort of roll call square. Behind a few barracks we notice many mud-covered roofs. It takes us a long time to orient ourselves and to realize that these underground huts are meant for us.

I stand dumbfounded. Sawczyc's knees are buckling. Even in our most nightmarish dreams we never encountered anything like this.

A happy voice behind us says, "You fellows expected to arrive at a luxury hotel and now you're disappointed. I expected something much worse. I must tell you that I'm satisfied with the reality. In the winter those huts are wonderful. It's warm underground." It is Maks. He relishes a half-rotten potato and laughs at our expressions.

Our attention is drawn to what is happening in front of us.

The *Lagerführer* arrives and is greeted with a loud "Attention!" Several *Häftlinge* stand around him in the basic position with their caps in their hands. One of them says something to the *Lagerführer*.

Nodding his head knowingly, Maks says, "Soon we'll have our *Blockältesters*."

He is correct. We hear the *Lagerführer* shout, *"Jawohl!"*

A few minutes later the *Lagerältester* introduces his team of co-workers. Ninety percent of them are veteran prisoners from Auschwitz who are never lost in any situation. In the next quarter of an hour, we have our *Blockältesters, Stubendiensts, Schreibers,* and a whole staff of cooks and their helpers. Among the last group I recognize my friend, *Stubendienst* Zygmunt from Auschwitz.

The *Lagerführer* orders the kitchen personnel to run to the unfinished kitchen and begin working. We wonder where those people get their strength. Maks, Sawczyc, and I can barely stand. Every once in a while someone collapses near us.

We conclude from the arguments reaching us from the kitchen that we cannot expect a hot meal for at least several hours. They need professionals to assemble the cauldrons.

The *Lagerführer* leaves; the guards take up their positions in the towers. A suspicious-looking character, our new *Blockältester,* comes over to our group of fifty *Häftlinge,* counts us, and orders us to follow him.

We stand in front of one of several mud huts and wait while the *Blockältester* and *Stubendienst* disappear inside. Just as the kitchen is unsuitable for cooking, this hut is unfit for habitation. But there is no escape. We must enter, or rather, jump in one after another.

I have a personal reason to be "satisfied". Maks, who expected conditions to be nothing worse than they were before, stands transfixed. He can only whisper, "Horrible! Horrible!" He needs only this little push to bring him back to reality.

Maks is on the verge of a breakdown, and no wonder. The Germans have the insolence to put people who have suffered for so many days in a cold freight car without food, into a place which makes a pig-sty look like a palace.

Our new barrack is simply a hole in the ground dug five meters long, seventy-five centimeters wide, and one meter deep. On both sides, a few rough-hewn boards extend through the entire length of the hut and serve as our beds. Other planks, arranged in an inverted V, form the ceiling inside and the roof outside. The latter is covered with mud. Two sides of the barrack are made of boards with holes for windows, but there is no glass in them. Another wall has openings cut out for a door and a window; there are no panes in this window either. A stove in the middle is equipped with a pipe protruding through the roof. This is all. There is no light, no straw, no chamber pots, absolutely nothing . . . only emptiness, hopelessness, despair and tears.

Our *Blockältester* is enterprising. He goes outdoors with the *Stubendiensts* to organize some wood and lights a fire in the stove. For the first time in a long while, we feel a little heat. Everyone tries to get close to the stove. It seems quite evident to me that, if they do not install a regular door and windows, it is useless to heat the barrack. I pull Maks and Sawczyc by the sleeve, and we go out to organize.

The camp makes a sad impression. Everywhere are examples of quick, haphazard work. Among the unfinished barracks are bricks, frozen cement, carts with rocks and half-uprooted trees.

I recall the expression on the *Lagerführer*'s face when he first saw us. He appears to be an honest fellow who showed his dissatisfaction with his superior's order to send people to a half-finished camp, but there is no time to think. We wade through deep snow and trip over rocks, stones, tree trunks, and railroad tracks. After all, we came to organize building material.

We find a barrack similar to ours, the only difference is that it is constructed of cement. The doors are closed with a lock, but this does not deter us. We are convinced that there is something inside. Our hunch is correct.

Although we think it is meant to be a bathhouse, we find many tools, several mounted windows complete with glass and a door. Sawczyc takes the door; Maks brings glass for the windows. I keep searching. In a corner I find a can containing several potatoes. Among the ashes in the fireplace are some half-baked potatoes. I put all these treasures into my pocket, grab a window frame, and run after Maks and Sawczyc.

Our return elicits joyful shouts. In a twinkling of an eye, we install the door and the window. After our success, several *Häftlinge* decide to forage for wood. In recognition of our productive exploits, the *Blockältester* gives us a place next to the stove. Naturally we take Sawczyc with us. I dare not pull out my potatoes because the *Blockältester* and *Stubendiensts* would probably take them away.

It is almost dark. We wait in vain for bread and coffee. We use our coats and jackets to improvise some kind of bedding and then lie down to rest. In some respects it is better than the freight car. It is warm and we can stretch our legs. One thing is certain: were it not for the heat from the stove, the majority of us would not live through the night.

Maks and Sawczyc are not talkative; they cover themselves with their coats. I remove the treasures from my pocket and divide them evenly. We hold a short council at which we decide that we will eat the potatoes as they are because, if we were to bake them in the fire, it could very possibly provoke a riot in the barrack.

My share of the booty is three potatoes, one baked and two raw. I clean the skin on my pants and eat. I never thought that raw potatoes could taste so good, almost like nuts.

We are awakened by the penetrating cold. The windows are frosted over; the stove is cold. We dress quickly, even if it is only to go out to satisfy our physiological needs.

There is activity in the camp. O.T. men are running around in their green uniforms decorated with a black swastika on red armbands. Two bulldozers bite into the frozen ground. In other barracks, fires are burning; black smoke rises from their chimneys. Our *Blockältester* is cursing the world. With so many of these Germans around, it will be impossible to organize wood.

Help comes from Sawczyc. Without a word, he goes outdoors and returns in a few minutes. He pulls two boards from under his trousers; they reach all the way to his neck. He is almost two meters tall so he can get away with such a manoeuvre. Once again a blazing fire crackles in the stove. It is our only comfort.

The *Blockältester* smooths out his uniform before he goes for information. Fifteen minutes later he returns with good news. The soup is almost ready, but we must go to the kitchen to get it since that is the only way we can be fed. There are too few dishes and utensils.

As the *Blockältester* predicted, one hour later we hear, "Barracks report in numerical order for soup!"

Obeying this "in order", results in an unbelievable turmoil. The starving people push and leave their lines to get in front of the kitchen. Screams are heard everywhere. Several SS men arrive with bats and disperse the crowd. Several *Häftlinge* are killed and are left where they fall.

We wait until dark for our first meal, half a liter of watery soup and a portion of bread which we eat by the light on the guard towers. If they had given us the soup in the barrack, we could have crumbled half the bread into it and made it thicker, but, conditions being what they are, and with the agitated voices of the starving behind us, urging, "Eat faster! We, too, are dying from hunger!" we gulp it down and pass the dishes as quickly as possible.

Once more we return to the barrack and to hopelessness.

Leon Sztajn joins our group. He is an ex-*Kapo* from Auschwitz, but a truly friendly chap. Leon has no shoes, or rather, he does have shoes, but they are worthless. He is desperate. He could have had a position, but w-i-t-h-o-u-t decent shoes, it is tragic. Despite that, he is optimistic and tries to console us.

"It's only the beginning. In a few days, all will be organized and in better shape. The important thing is that we aren't in Auschwitz. Here we may die a natural death from hunger or disease, and, comparatively speaking, that is good."

It is still dark when the gong wakes us up.

"It's surprising," mumbles Sawczyc, "there's no food, no light, no straw, no blankets, but there's a gong. Where did the sons-of-bitches get it?"

To dress in the dark is difficult and unpleasant, but we must get out because the gong is tolling furiously. In single file we march to the roll call square. We are lucky; it is cold and dry.

Each *Blockältester* rounds up his group of *Häftlinge* and keeps it together. As each barrack is called, the *Blockältester* shouts the numerical tally.

Our *Blockältester* notices that there are only forty-nine in our group. One is missing.

They shout, "20!"

Our *Blockältester* calls, "20, here!"

He re-counts. It does not help. The *Blockältester* finally has an idea. He sends the *Stubendienst* to the hut. Perhaps someone is still asleep.

The *Stubendienst* returns in a few minutes dragging the laggard by his feet. The poor soul fell asleep, a sleep from which he will never awaken.

Leon looks to heaven as though in a trance. He forgets about his shoes and says, "Fellows, look! What a beautiful sunrise, maybe the most beautiful one in Bavaria and on earth!"

It really is a magnificent sight. A small section of visible sky over the forest changes colors: scarlet, silver, and a pale red.

Very few of us are in a mood that is conducive to marveling at the wonders of nature. Maks scolds Leon, calls him an idiot, and tells him to find out why they woke us up at a quarter of five in the morning.

The answer to this comes not from Leon, but from Sawczyc. "The bastards think that the *Lagerführer* may have something important to communicate at nine o'clock."

Sawczyc's guess is partially correct. We must listen to a speech, not by the *Lagerführer*, but by the *Raportführer*, the former *Kommandant* of the guards who escorted us on the trip from Sachsenhausen. His speech is not scheduled for nine o'clock, but for ten. After standing for so long, we are almost frozen.

He speaks for almost an hour, most of the time, incoherently. He talks about obedience. ". . . It will be better if we, ourselves, help to build the 'houses'. . . . The food will improve. . . . When the two-week quarantine period is over, we'll be assigned to the enterprise, to an enterprise that assures the victory of Great Germany. . . ."

Maks is arguing with God, complaining that all the curses we invoke against the *Raportführer* are ineffective. The *Raportführer* keeps on talking.

At the conclusion of his monologue, the *Raportführer*, certain that his words have had the desired effect, calls for volunteers to work. Because no one steps forward, he announces that there will be no coffee this morning and that we will be forced to work.

Several SS guards immediately block our escape route to the barracks. We stand in place waiting for the O.T. men.

The O.T. *Kommando* is late, arriving at about noon. It is almost time for the midday meal. The chief of the O.T. *Kommando,* a square-shouldered German, holds a brief conference with the *Raportführer.* They agree that labor is more important than food. Anyway, the meal will not run away.

Maks, Sawczyc, and I are assigned to a group that carries sinks, pipes, and similar items for the washrooms in the camp. The job is rather easy, but we lose the opportunity for assignment to a permanent *Kommando.* Those *Häftlinge* without designations become food haulers, kitchen aides, and so forth.

We work without interruption until evening. The noon meal is cold and extremely bad. At night we feel itchy all over. Shouts echo out of the darkness, "Lice!" It is no wonder. After a trip of several days, we have had no opportunity to wash. In the entire camp, the only faucet with running water is in the kitchen. The washrooms will not be ready for another week.

The hours during which we should be sleeping are spent looking for lice. Judging from the conversations, the results are good. We kill whole colonies of them. In the opinion of the experts, we discover some unusual specimens.

* * *

The Hungarian lying close to the door has very severe pains. A panel of consultants composed of Sawczyc, myself, and a Czech doctor in our barrack, diagnose his ailment as appendicitis. Unfortunately, we cannot help the poor fellow. There is no sick call in this camp.

"*Blockältesters* out!"

It is the usual shout from the *Schreibstube* and the first one in this camp. In spite of our direst expectations, there is good news.

The whole day will be spent in registering. We will receive new numbers for Dachau.

Maks announces happily, "We win one more day. The war is coming to an end!"

This "winning one more day" means being able to rest on the bare boards in our underground hut which is full of irritating smoke because we are using wet wood. What we "win" are a few peaceful hours. We do no work and our bodies are not being deprived of valuable heat.

Early in the morning we receive a visit from the *Kommando* of electricians in the camp. Several of them come from Lodz. They were sent here from Auschwitz sometime during the summer. We bombard them with questions, mainly: What is this place like?

They do not wish to frighten us, so they hesitate before replying. But they finally tell us the truth.

Our camp is number eleven—Dachau XI. There are twelve camps like ours, but only four are occupied. Two months ago they were all filled to capacity. However, even with the constant new arrivals, the high mortality rate has taken its toll so that only four are required. Now these are only half to three-quarters full.

The electricians live in Camp I. The Jews there are chiefly from Lithuania. Camp III houses Hungarian Jews. Camp IV is a hospital in name only; sick people from all the camps are sent there to die. Then there is our Camp XI. The others are empty.

We ask if there are gas chambers here as in Auschwitz where mass murders took place.

They deny it. Here they kill in a variety of ways: with work, beatings, hunger, and extreme climatic conditions. The end result is the same; the only difference is that the suffering lasts longer.

We get no further information from them. In silence, they begin installing the lights.

Maks sighs deeply and whispers that if we do not get employment that will save us from "working for the victory of Great Germany"—in the words of the *Raportführer*—we will die like the thousands of Polish, Hungarian, and Lithuanian Jews before us.

"Medics come forward!"

I jump as though I am jabbed by a needle. I pull Maks and Sawczyc with me, rushing them. Maybe this will be our big chance?!

Unfortunately, we arrive late. The SS doctor, *Obersturmführer* Blank, whom we knew in Auschwitz, stands at the gate to the camp talking with someone. At least a hundred doctors and medics stand around him at a respectful distance.

We have no chance for a position, mainly because of our horrible condition: we have not shaved for a week. We must listen to Blank's loud tirade.

"We don't need sick people. At a time when the State asks for the greatest sacrifice from our Germans, there is no place in the world for sick Jews! Work or death! Understand?!" he shouts.

Then standing arms akimbo, he observes the crowd with an ironic look and asks, "Are all those Mr. Doctors? What?" With a beastly yell he exhorts, "Work! Work, you pigs!"

He announces that, for the entire camp, he will select five medics to apply only the most necessary dressings, to administer first aid, and to transport the critically ill to Sick Camp IV. He concludes with, "There are no medicines now. Dressing material is in short supply and must be used very sparingly."

Two of the doctors talking to Blank are Czechs. No wonder they were chosen, they are friends of the *Lagerältester* who is also a Czech. We cannot judge the degree of suffering nor the depth of their depression. They look relatively good. They are shaved and fairly well dressed. They came from Teresienstadt and Auschwitz and, on that same day, continued their trip with us.

They immediately divide their duties among themselves. Even though there is no sick call, one of them assumes the title of clinic director, and his friend takes the title of assistant. To us they announce that they will try to organize a special barrack for the sick that very day; we must help them find those needing hospitalization.

We return to our barrack in the worst possible mood. We consider ourselves the unhappiest people in the world. The appearance of the sick Hungarian brings us back to our senses. He is vomiting; his abdomen is distended resembling a barrel; he is in terrible pain. His pulse is barely detectable. He is hiccupping, the first symptom of peritonitis.

* * *

"You want to get sick? Go to Camp XI!" Sawczyc just coined this little witticism. He is proud of it and thinks it quite appropriate.

* * *

The *Lagerarzt*'s speech dispels all of our hopes, making it clear that, from now until the end of the war, there will be a brutal struggle for life from which only the strongest will survive. Another thing becomes abundantly clear to us: considering our present physical state, we have virtually no chance to survive.

We take our places in our bunks. Melting snow seeps through the earthen roof. Dirty drops of water fall on our heads.

I recall those times in Lublin and Auschwitz when I was close to death, and how I was always rescued at the last minute. I remember the promise I made to myself then, that I would never break down, but would fight for life with my last breath. Am I a coward who, when faced with his first difficulties, folds his hands and loses his will to continue the struggle?

A mysterious voice whispers in my ear, "It's absurd. You've fought enough. You've nothing more to fight for. You heard the words of the *Lagerarzt*. You saw with your own eyes what was going on today. It's a waste of effort. Just wait quietly for death. Don't struggle and your end will be easier!"

Some strong resolve emerges from within my soul. "Never! Never! I will not surrender! The worse the situation becomes, the harder I will fight—until my last breath."

Immediately after the visit by the political section which gave us new numbers, the newly-organized camp police enter.

"To work!"

I am one of the first to go out. I certainly will gain nothing by sitting in the barrack. Sawczyc and Maks follow my example. In the roll call square, groups have already been assigned to work. Our threesome is added to seven other *Häftlinge*.

The *Kommandant* of our section is the *Raportführer,* himself. He leads us out to the field behind the camp to show us a piece of land covered with tree stumps. We must dig a hole ten meters long, three meters wide and two shovels deep to store potatoes. If we finish by nightfall, we will get two liters of the soldiers' soup with meat from the SS men's kitchen. The tools? Picks, shovels, and two axes are nearby.

The one field worker in our group looks over the area with a professional eye and says, "If we work hard, it is possible to finish this job by nightfall. The stumps will slow us down. We'll leave them for later. Let's start, fellows! It's a matter of soup!"

I spit on my hands and grab a shovel.

Work is hectic in the camp. Groups of *Häftlinge* push carts loaded with stones. Others carry bricks and the masonry mixture. Roofs of unfinished barracks are covered with a layer of earth. Everything is done to the accompaniment of curses interspersed with blows that the O.T. men dispense very generously.

"We're lucky," says Maks. "Nobody is pushing us. Nobody's beating us and we've been promised soup if we complete the work on time."

Somehow the project is progressing. Everyone breathes hard. Our shovels feel as heavy as lead. The soil is frozen; we have to break it up with our picks and tear it with our hands.

But the vision of the SS men's soup releases the last of our energy reserve hidden deep within our muscle fibers.

When we hear the gong, we are almost sorry to cease our work. We receive an unusual dish: a sweet milky soup containing some peculiar kind of kasha. It is very tasty. While it is true that the milk has an odd taste and the sweetness has nothing to do with the use of sugar, it is hot and the milk, even if it is skimmed, contains a small amount of protein which is important for us.

As soon as we have our soup and without waiting for the end of the noontime break, we run back to the field to dig. We find the *Raportführer* there, inspecting our work. He shakes his head in disbelief.

Our hopes are rising. With redoubled energy, we begin digging. No one talks. Not only is it a matter of two liters of soup, but also of precedence. If the *Raportführer* is satisfied, maybe he will ask our group to work inside the camp at some special tasks as promised in his speech. These pleasant reveries make our work more bearable. The picks are striking; the shovels are digging; the pile of soil is growing; the hole gets deeper. Before evening, almost everything is done, and we begin working on the removal of the remaining stumps. The last blows of the axes coincide with the sound of the gong, the end of our working day.

We look at our accomplishment with pride. Sweat pours from our foreheads. We can wring the moisture out our shirts. We breathe heavily, but we succeeded!

The *Raportführer* arrives accompanied by several of the SS guards. "Why are you still standing here?" he demands. "Didn't you hear the gong?"

Sawczyc, who speaks the best German in the group, reminds him of his promise.

"Aha! . . . ." With some difficulty, the *Raportführer* remembers his promise. He is sorry. He received notice that the potatoes will be stored in another camp. We can fill in the hole, and as for the soup. . . . Turning to the guards he says, "Jews are good workers. Promise them some soup and they will complete the most difficult tasks quickly, even surpassing the most qualified workers!" He pauses, turns to us and says, "If you can do a job like that, you don't need soup. Now get going! Move! March!"

We stand like statues. God, that much effort and work! Such great problems overcome with our blood, sweat and tears, and now they are laughing at us! Our legs refuse to respond. We cannot move from our places.

The *Raportführer* grabs a big branch; the SS men remove their belts. They lash out angrily, but not one of us runs. No one cries. Under the rain of blows, we slowly collect our tools. Through our silence we display our deep disdain for the Hitler gang.

The barrack is illuminated now. The stove fills the entire hut with thick smoke. We are happy that our friends cannot see the expressions on our faces as we chew our bread in silence and swallow it together with our tears. Muscles, bones, heart, and lungs rebel against such treatment. In the morning, we cannot get out of bed in spite of the *Blockältester*'s threats and pleas. We are envious of the dying Hungarian.

* * *

There is some commotion in front of the barrack. Two O.T. men enter. Their first victim is the Hungarian. When the unlucky fellow dies not react to their blows, they become angrier and beat him ferociously. We drag ourselves from our bunks and go to the door. Only the last one gets a blow on his back.

We conclude that the activity in the camp is artificial. There is not enough work for everyone. We toil until noon erecting a second barbed wire fence. In the afternoon we push carts containing gravel and stones. After the second run, I go to one side as if to relieve myself. Instead, I hide behind a bush and sit there until evening. My hiding place is not far from where Sawczyc and Maks are working. They do not know where I am. I can see the surprised expressions on their faces when I do not return.

I accidentally meet Josek, the barber. With a little influence, he was assigned to the *Totenkommando,* but he wants to "resign" because there is too much work. He tells me that, in the nearby forest, two helpers and he are burying, on an average, thirty corpses a day.

The fellow from Lodz certainly did not exaggerate when he told us how they finish off people here. When we arrived, we were one thousand one hundred persons.

At the *Lagerführer's* order, the quarantine period is being shortened from fourteen to ten days. In expectation of this new disaster, I spend the days before it ends, walking through all the huts begging anyone I know for help. Unfortunately, in this terrible struggle for a dish of soup and a crumb of bread, no one can afford to be sentimental. The fact that I helped someone in Auschwitz does not give me the right to ask for reciprocity.

The Czechs in the sick bay naturally support their own countrymen. I cannot blame them for that. Not only I, but even old Dr. Szor, who miraculously survived Auschwitz, must leave empty-handed. They can only accept us as patients.

I cannot even get a job as a cleaner in the washroom or toilets, those public institutions in the camp which will be opened to the public any day now.

I knock on the kitchen door and offer my services as a wood chopper. They laugh at me; others have already taken the job. The only friendly face is Zygmunt's. Although he has no influence among the bandits in the kitchen, he signals me to come at a more opportune time, for instance, after the soup is distributed.

During a long roll call on the afternoon of the ninth day, the decision is announced: we will leave the camp for work. With all my possibilities exhausted, I stand in line and wait for a verdict. Nearly five hundred *Häftlinge* have nothing to do. The *Lagerführer,* all the guards, several O.T. men, and the *Lagerältester* walk along our line, pushing us around, dividing, adding, subtracting. . . . Finally all is ready. The entire *Schreibstube* arrives and writes down the numbers of the "cattle" assigned to work.

One hundred will remain to put the final touches to the camp. The rest are divided into two groups: one is the day shift; the other, for the night. Every two weeks they will change. Luckily Sawczyc, Maks and I get the day shift.

For every one hundred workers, the *Lagerältester* assigns *Kapos* and foremen. We are assigned to new barracks. Before we leave, the recently designated *Kapos* announce that tomorrow we will get bread only during the work period and that we should not even think of hiding. Now we must return to our old huts.

I ask Sawczyc to guard my place while I go to the washroom. Crowds of *Häftlinge* stand by the door, waiting to get some water to quench their thirst and to wash. I stand in the cold for over an hour.

When it is my turn, I scrub my neck, face and chest a little. There is no soap and no medicine. The color of my once white shirt makes me giddy. There is no place for me to wash it now. The shoving is so common next to the faucet that I cannot even dress. I put on my jacket and coat, but hold the shirt in the icy air for several minutes. When I decide to wear it, the lice have frozen, and I am comfortable for a few hours.

We waste most of the night talking about what kind of work we might get. We are restless and apprehensive. There is no one to console us, to instill in us some confidence, to offer a ray of hope.

* * *

"Day shift get up! Day shift get up!"

The *Lagerpolizei* are running from barrack to barrack shouting and banging the wooden bunks with their clubs.

"Kaffeeholen!"

It is sheer idiocy. How will we drink it?

"Forward! Get going!"

Several hundred stooped, sleepy figures drag themselves to the roll call square in the dark. We do not even know what time it is.

They count us. Twenty people are missing. The *Lagerältester* is furious because it is almost time to march and our SS escort is waiting at the gate.

It is not very cold, but a strong wind is dispersing the clouds, a sign that there will be a thaw.

The police find the missing twenty. Five of them are very sick. The others have no shoes.

The *Lagerältester* is desperate and notifies the *Raportführer.* His order is short. "The ill should have reported for sick call yesterday. If they failed to do so, it's their own fault. Today, they must go to work!" As for the second problem, that answer is also simple. "They have no shoes? They must go with what they have. If they have nothing, they'll have to go barefoot. March!"

"Caps off!"

The parody of the Auschwitz parade begins. The searchlights are on. Five abreast we pass through the gate. The SS men count us.

"Out! Let's go!"

The escort surrounds us. We march into the darkness.

In the woods, the trees offer some protection from the deadly wind. In a while, we come to a clearing where the wind lashes us with its full fury. Only by holding hands can we remain on our feet.

The guards chase us, but with no results. The sticky snow clings to our wooden shoes so that after a few steps, it forms artificial soles and heels. Moving is almost impossible.

The *Kommandant* threatens us, telling us that tomorrow we will have to rise one hour earlier and we will get no bread. His final words are that he has never seen animals like us and that he is happy that we will all soon die from the work awaiting us.

Fortunately, the severe wind blows away half of his "friendly" talk.

We walk, trying to straddle railroad tracks. Every once in a while, someone falls and is terribly bruised. In the darkness, we recognize that it is the same road on which we traveled to the camp when we arrived.

Our chests ache from the difficult, fast-paced march. Many laggards stretch out the column. The SS men beat them furiously with their rifle butts. The five sick *Häftlinge* dropped in the snow immediately after we left the gate. Three more become ill. The guards' continuous insults give us no encouragement. We walk ever more slowly.

On the horizon we see dense woods. Our fondest dream is to reach it for its protection from the wintry blasts. Sawczyc appears stooped and shrunken. He is no longer the same man we knew. Maks, whose coat is too short, is avoiding the wind by standing behind me or Sawczyc. He prays to God to let him die quickly. When we finally reach the trees, we must wait until the others catch up to us.

Meanwhile, the sick ones have died. This makes it easier in one respect, we do not have to carry them; we just pull them by their legs.

The only path among the trees is a hazardous narrow railroad track. The woods are fenced in by barbed wire. We advance one step at a time. Any fall could result in a fractured skull. When we reach a gate guarded by a watchman in a shack, we guess that the end of our wandering is near.

After a while, we see some lights in the distance, the first ones since we left the camp. A few hundred steps more and we come to a wide road that cuts across the railroad track. Close by is a large wooden structure. A sign illuminated by several lamps announces:

LEONHARD MOLL
BAUUNTERNEHMUNG
MÜNCHEN

We approach our fate.

Sometime in antiquity, slaves built pyramids for their rulers, and, in the course of their construction, thousands died. Today, in the Twentieth Century, there also are slaves working for their despotic rulers, their masters of life and death, and they also build. The only difference between the past and the present is that today's structures are different and the death rate among the slaves is much higher.

* * *

In the middle of the dense forest, life is hectic. We hear machines clanking, hammers banging, and see more lights.

"Work! Work for the good of Great Germany! For victory! For the 'great goal'!"

We stand in front of an unusual building. Its immense cement dome is six to eight stories high. At the very top, men are working by the light of lamps. Under wooden roofs at the bottom, *Häftlinge* operate noisy machines.

At the top of the dome and a bit to one side is a maze of iron bars. We soon realize that we are looking at a modern reinforced concrete building. The siren wails, signaling the end of the shift. At the top and bottom of the dome there is a great deal of activity as O.T. men descend narrow stairs followed by *Häftlinge*.

We learn from those running closest to us that they live in the first camp. The appearance of the others gives them away. They are skeletons, corpses dressed in rags.

With the approach of several imposing guests: SS and O.T. men, and civilians, the *Kapos* feverishly arrange us by hundreds.

"Why aren't they working?" demands an SS man, pointing to us.

"Caps off!" shouts the *Kapo* and, in an apologetic voice, explains that this is our first day. The "gentlemen" shake their heads understandingly and leave.

Our hope that they might send us back to the camp vanishes quickly. One of the O.T. men separates us into sections, then assigns us to some foremen who are emerging from the woods.

"Move!"

The outstretched arm of the hoodlum in the green coat indicates the way to the top of the dome. Carefully we climb up the unusually narrow ladder. Our lack of experience is readily noticeable. The clumsy wooden shoes do not help.

Crash! The first one loses his balance. He tries desperately to regain his equilibrium, but in vain. As he falls, the entire group behind him also drops to the bottom.

The O.T. men think that this is a new form of sabotage and brutally club us. It is our first beating in the new place.

We reach the top. The wind that had given us so much trouble on the ground, now topples us. Several, who do not hold onto the handrail tightly enough, lose their footing, fall, and suffer massive injuries on the iron bars.

The O.T. men are very amused. They laugh so much that they hold their bellies.

An O.T. dignitary comes toward us. All the green uniforms line up respectfully. He mounts an elevation and signals for us to gather around him. He adjusts the Iron Cross on his chest and begins the traditional speech. His shouting can be heard over the howling wind, the grating metal, and roaring machinery.

"Here we work for victory! You stinking shit ought to be proud that you have such a high honor. If you don't understand that and don't value it, you will shortly join your Abraham. There is pity for no one here! You work, and you work until your last breath! Understand?!"

The "holy" work begins. We hand the O.T. men the iron rods.

Every few minutes, a small, but powerful locomotive pushes up many cars loaded with rods. A special *Kommando* from the first camp unloads the contents with lightning speed. The thick, solid, heavy round rods are ten, twelve and sixteen meters long.

Since we have no gloves, our bare hands cling to the ice-cold iron. Given the rods' length, it is no easy task. When they fall, they tear the skin on our fingers and smash our toes. Our job is to carry a rod up the ladder, lower it carefully, and pass it to the O.T. man.

"Zwei Mann, eine Stange!" (Two men, one rod!)

Step by step I carefully descend the ladder with Maks. "Be careful, Tadzek! One missed step means crippling or death!" How well I know that! My nerves are strained to the utmost. I feel like a circus performer under the big tent performing a difficult aerial manoeuvre without a net. Death and injury threaten us from all sides.

After two hours our hands are covered with dried blood. Moisture, rust, and wind dig into our wounds. I grit my teeth trying not to scream from pain.

It is snowing. The wind chases the clouds. As the snowflakes become smaller, they turn to rain. In a few minutes our uniforms are soaking wet. The O.T. men put on rubber ponchos with hoods.

"Move! Quickly!"

There is no pity here. Neither rain nor sleet can stop the tempo of the work.

"Move! Move! Go! Two men, one rod!"

We notice trains below us. Many locomotives are pulling hundreds of cars loaded with stones and pebbles removed from under the dome.

Maks looks at me peculiarly and says, "If I could only lie down on one of those railroad tracks! In a minute, no rain, no wind, no cold . . . nothing and nobody."

"You bastard, shut your mouth!" I retort, angrily. "There's nothing and nobody, only freedom! Freedom is as imminent as vengeance! Don't you know that every beginning is difficult? It will improve! You'll see!" I add, but without much conviction.

We meet Sawczyc and Dr. Szor carrying a sixteen meter rod. Sawczyc is tall; Szor, short. They form an unequal couple, but the foreman ordered it that way. The O.T. men have very little to amuse them on the job.

When the siren sounds, the O.T. men rush to the tables for the noon meal. We remain on top. We are extremely hungry; it is about time we received our bread. A *Kapo* comes up to inform us that everything is badly organized today, but it will be better tomorrow. We will receive our bread tonight.

We have been dealt another blow. Maks looks at me accusingly and murmurs, "So, wasn't I right?" I toss a piece of iron in his direction.

Sawczyc and Szor are surprised at my aggressiveness. I start to explain, but Maks grabs my hand at the last minute saying, "Stop it, Tadzek! I beg you!"

* * *

It is almost dark when the second siren goes off at four o'clock. The O.T. men have completed their shift for the day. Their relief has come and work begins with renewed energy. We are utterly exhausted after a day's work.

"Move! Tempo! Two men, one rod!"

We cannot budge. Once again the SS men use bats on us. Several SS guards climb to the top of the dome to see what the commotion is about.

"Of course! The Jews obviously don't want to work!"

The guards have an idea. A few of the "guilty" are pushed down the dome. When they reach the bottom, the guards yell to them to hurry and come up to work. When the victims do not rise after a few minutes, the SS men grab shovels and run down. We can clearly see how they use the sharp sides of the shovels to batter the men's faces. When the guards climb up again, their coats and boots are splattered with blood. "This is how we punish Jews who don't want to work! Understand?!"

Now I realize that Maks was right. We work by lamplight until seven o'clock. Finally our relief, the night shift, appears at the base of the dome.

We are so pleased to see them that we leave our work and decide to run down, but the wild O.T. men block our way. At the end of the day we still receive a few blows on our exhausted bodies and the order, "Wait here until the relief comes! What's the hurry?!"

"Assemble!"

We form a line; the *Kapos* distribute bread. We load the corpses, eleven of them—one day's "harvest"—on the bread cart that still contains plenty of crumbs.

It takes us two hours to walk back to the barracks. We toiled from four in the morning, when they woke us, until ten o'clock at night on two hundred fifty grams of bread, twenty grams of margarine, three-quarters of a liter of cold watery soup . . . and the work, the bloody work . . . "Honorable! For victory! For the glory of Great Germany!" . . . *Bauunternehmung Leonhard Moll– Munich.* Oh God!

* * *

The barrack is cold. There is no wood for the stove. We have no place to dry our wet shirts, pants, and coats.

"To the washroom! To the barber! Shave! Those who are not shaved will get no bread tomorrow! This is the order of the *Raportführer*!"

We must look good. A corpse is also cleaned before it is sealed in a casket. After a sixteen hour workday, we must drag ourselves to the washroom in a heavy rain until midnight and maybe later.

* * *

When I finally return, the barrack is as dark as a grave. Blindly I push myself toward my bunk, take off my wooden shoes and place them under my head. My wet rags steam on my body. I inhale the sweet moldy vapor and it acts like a narcotic.

As it happened once before in Auschwitz, death is approaching. From the howling wind, from the rain beating against the glass window, a voice enters my consciousness.

Steadily, mysteriously, menacingly it commands, "Enough fighting! Enough suffering! Lie down and wait for your true friend, Death.

"You won't be harmed. You'll rest quietly in the earth. Nobody will hit you. No one will be unjust. The wind won't bother you. Only lie quietly and wait. Maybe someone will try to chase you from your place. He may yell; he may beat you. Don't be afraid! Your body is insensitive to blows. Lie down and wait. It won't be long, not long! An eternal peace will settle over you."

I never felt so good. My head is whirling blissfully.

An icy draft freezes my body. Moonlight appears through the window. The light hurts my eyes, and I want to scream. Oh God! It is my father! It IS my father. I can clearly hear his stern voice, "What are you doing? Remember, you promised!"

The voices are mixed.

"Lie down!"

"No! No!"

"Wait!"

"Death—friend!"

"What are you doing? You promised!"

"Mother! Father! Fredzia!"

"Fight! You must survive! Remember you promised!"

The beloved faces are fading. I rise and run after them. I am sobbing, sobbing loudly in the dark, "I will fight! Yes, I will fight! I swear! Forgive me!"

* * *

I feel someone's hand and hear, "What's happening to you?"

"What a performance you gave us!" Sawczyc and Maks exclaim.

I lie quietly in the bunk determined never to submit. I will fight! This is my final decision.

The wind is singing through the wires. I see my mother's beaming smile and hear her say, "Very good, son!"

"Yes, I will fight!"

* * *

We wade up to our knees in mud. It does not bother me. I am busy concentrating on plans to save myself at any cost.

There must be a way to get some heat in the barrack. We need it desperately, especially during the night when we are sleeping and waiting for our rags to dry.

There are fifty of us in the barrack and plenty of wood at the building site. If each of us brings only a few pieces, it would be enough. During the march, I immediately start a campaign in our group.

"Friends, it's for everyone's benefit. Only a few pieces!"

In my mind I evoke my experiences in Auschwitz. It was bad there, too. The rain drenched me there, but I found help from friend Ivan and the protective coats he made from cement sacks. That same material is here also. Only yesterday I noticed several carloads of cement on a sidetrack.

I can hardly wait for work to start. I decide that, during the noon meal, I will come down from the dome and look around. My nerves are getting the better of me. I grind my teeth in anticipation.

My search does not last long. Not far from the sidetrack is a solidly built structure on a stone foundation. One look convinces me that I have found the right spot. I crawl inside. There are thousands upon thousands of cement sacks. Near the wall is a pile of empty ones reaching to the ceiling. I do not hesitate. I take one for myself, one for Sawczyc, one for Maks, another for replacement and wrap them all around my body. I cannot carry more and still button my coat. I am as round as a barrel. I got too fat in a very short time. I reach for one more; it may be useful.

At the door I meet an O.T. man. I stand transfixed. With a wild look and without a word, he raises his powerful fist and punches me in the nose. Before I can open my mouth, he grabs my neck in his steely grip, drags me to the wall, and beats my head against it. When I think that I am giving up my soul and dying without help, he loosens his grip and pushes me onto a heap of cement.

Blood streams from my nose; I swallow some. There is cement between my teeth; my head is splitting. It takes me a long time before I can utilize my remaining strength to slowly crawl back.

I am late. The others have been working for fifteen minutes. The O.T. man, my master, hits my back with a shovel and demands, "Where have you been, pig?!"

I bend as much as I can to avoid the blows. I even try to smile at Maks and Sawczyc who are passing by.

"Move! Work! March!"

The master accepts no explanations. There is no pity here.

I carry a short iron rod on my shoulder. My spine feels as if it is broken. My knees buckle.

"Move! Two men, one rod! Bring the rods!"

Go down; come up. Go down; come up. We continue without a stop, without a chance to catch our breath. My chest aches. I cough. Every few minutes I spit up some cement mixed with blood, but it is worth it. I have my sacks. Tonight, when there is heat in the barrack, we will make good protective coats for ourselves.

* * *

The sacks are several layers thick. They yield to my nails and teeth only with great difficulty. Unfortunately, I have no other tools. Maks and Sawczyc wonder what I am doing.

After overcoming many problems, one sample raincoat is finally finished. The fellows are delighted. They quickly join me. When the usual cry comes, "Moll workers come forward!" we awaken from a short sleep. Triumphantly, we don our raincoats over our shirts, then put on the dry jackets and coats.

The rainy weather continues. Our outergarments are wet even before we start marching, but the water does not reach our bodies. This is very important for us, giving us a feeling of well-being.

This allows me to think clearly and unfettered. My brain begins to function, and I shed my apathy. I am conceiving a plan to sabotage the work, one that will minimize our loss of strength. Basically, it is very simple and easy to implement. It may be explained in one word: snail, work slowly for the enemy.

Maks, I and Sawczyc with Szor are trying to stay close to each other. We take advantage of every instance of inattention by our supervisors.

We carry a rod for only several meters from where it was unloaded and throw it in the middle of the road, then return and wait in line for the next one. This results in the master O.T. man seeing us often. Our facial expressions exhibit a willingness to work. He gives our foursome his special attention and is quite pleasant to us. During the noon meal, he calls us over and discreetly hands us a small package wrapped in paper in which we find some burned crusts of bread.

If you do not get what you want, you take what you can get. We crumble the crusts into our dishes and then plead with the machinist to give us some boiling water from his steaming cauldron. We pour this liquid into our dishes and we instantly have an improvised bread soup which tastes . . . so help us God. . . . Hundreds of eyes look with envy at our steaming dishes.

After the noon meal, we carry the rods up the ladder and then down the dome to a newly constructed scaffold. Here it is more difficult to deceive, but we do the best we can.

That night Zygmunt waits for me at the camp gate. The dear fellow has been waiting there for more than an hour to tell me that he has a dish of soup for me.

Our threesome has a feast, relishing every spoonful of food. We bless our friend and make further plans to fight.

* * *

Several days later, the situation in the camp becomes more tragic. People have exhausted their last ounce of strength. Hundreds of unbelievably emaciated *Häftlinge* wait in front of the clinic. Their bodies are covered with sores.

One, even two barracks cannot accommodate all of the sick. Normally, there is room for fifty people in the bunks. Nowadays, one hundred and fifty are crowded on bare boards, without covers, and without treatment. They are cold and hungry.

Scores are dying en route to, and during work. Those who fall along the way lie in the mud until the team returns. SS men with flashlights look for them; we drag them back to camp. Those who drop while working, lie in a heap in a small clearing next to the latrine. When the shift ends, there are so many bodies that, try as we might, we cannot put all of the dead, sick, and dying on the carts.

With the exception of the most necessary personnel, all the *Kommandos* inside the camp are being disbanded and sent to fill the gaps in the lines of sufferers who work for Bauunternehmung Leonhard Moll. Even those draconic orders produce little results. The camp is dying very quickly. New victims are needed.

The day finally arrives when they cannot even mobilize a shift of two hundred. There are more supervisors than workers at the building site. We must give up all of our strategic plans. It is impossible to loaf even for a moment. The O.T. men beat us pitilessly for the smallest blunder. Demands keep growing.

"You'll see, Tadzek! One more week and we'll be twenty," Maks consoles me. "Then they'll send us to Garmisch for convalescence. It isn't far from here."

Maks's prediction, that we will be reduced from two hundred to twenty in one week, would have been realized were it not for the arrival of a transport of two thousand Hungarian men and five hundred Hungarian women. The camp is suddenly crowded because part of it is assigned to the women. However, this transport does not help; our situation continues to worsen.

For reasons unknown to us, we move from our barrack to a hut without windows or a stove. We cannot change because other barracks are overcrowded. In the space of two days during which several of our people freeze to death, we organize a stove and a framed window. From where? Those who "organized" them will not tell.

Frost sets in. It has its good and bad effects. We do not wade in mud; our clothes are dry. But the bitter cold affects us tragically. During the sixteen hours that we work, there is no possibility to warm our frozen hands even for a minute. Work on the building becomes more dangerous. One careless step could be crippling which is far worse than death. The body needs more food.

Meanwhile, as if spitefully, Zygmunt loses his position in the kitchen. Now I do not have a single person who is in a position to help me, even a little.

Until now, as we marched to camp, we were content to dream of a warm barrack and a dish of soup that our friend Zygmunt had for us. The return walk created a certain amount of artificially stimulated joy that enabled us to mobilize our reserve strength to withstand further suffering on the following day. Now even this is gone.

Sawczyc breaks down first. My heart bleeds when I see this gentle giant crying like a child. Maks's and my words of sincere consolation do not produce the desired results. The fellow fades from hour to hour. We beg him to go to the clinic. Perhaps, in the sick bay he will be able to rest for a few days. Our pleading is in vain. He is stubborn. He wants to die like a soldier on duty.

Death comes quickly. During the noon pause, the thermometer reaches minus 15° C. The *Kapo* climbs up to tell us to go to the kitchen for some tea. It tastes like a grassy liquid, but it is hot. Sawczyc sits on a tree stump, holds the metallic cup in his hands, and swallows in big gulps. At the same time, he warms the tips of his fingers. Suddenly, he turns to me, opens his mouth as if to say something, but, instead he emits a raspy moan, and falls.

His death does not affect anyone else. Perhaps the only interest they have is in his clothes, but we energetically chase them away.

Maks and I lift the body from the ground and carry it toward the woods. We want to lay our dead friend down at a certain distance from the latrines, but the SS guard watches our every move from behind a bush. With the help of his rifle, he teaches us that a good place for a Jew is on a heap of manure.

Broken-heartedly, silently, we sadly drag ourselves back to camp. A man has left us who was neither a brother nor even a distant relative, but we became very close. Life has its harsh realities, especially in a camp.

A hunger, far worse than any we experienced in Auschwitz, forces us to modify our way of thinking. All the potato peels that the SS men discard are thrown into a ditch. We cannot get to them because the *Kommando* in the camp cleans the area thoroughly before we return from our work. Every few minutes someone collapses. What can we do?! The dreaded spectre of death is very close indeed.

One evening when we can barely stand and when our intestines are twisting from hunger, our ever-searching eyes discover a basket of potatoes in front of the kitchen. In the twinkling of an eye, a crowd of screaming *Häftlinge* forms around the treasure. Afraid that someone will snatch this desirable find, the people grab the raw potatoes and eat them, dirt and all. No one pays any attention to the merciless beatings, or the blows of rifle butts or the warning shots.

"Look, Tadzek! Over there!" Maks shouts.

I notice a rolling potato. Like a wolf, I jump after it just as twenty armed bandits run from the SS guardhouse. I hear Maks's warning shout too late. One SS man sees me picking up the potato and putting it in my pocket. He beats me with his belt; I try to protect my face and head. The hoodlum lashes out repeatedly.

"Come with me!" he yells and takes me to the guardhouse.

Meanwhile, other SS men are shooting, not in the air anymore, but into the crowd around the potatoes.

When the *Raportführer* comes out to see what is happening, the "heroic" SS man points to me and reports with pride, "He was stealing potatoes!" The *Raportführer* is good enough to slap my face several times and then leaves me in the care of the SS man while he sees to the massacre for himself. Slowly the other SS men arrange the *Häftlinge* into lines. Twenty are dead; the twenty-first is missing. Then there is myself. . . .

The night shift is standing in front of the gate. No one is allowed to enter. The *Raportführer* disappears into the SS building. I lick the blood dripping from my nose and rub my aching spots. My only worrisome thought is, "Will the *Raportführer* punish me by taking away my soup?"

Fifteen minutes pass. The *Raportführer*, surrounded by SS men, appears in the doorway of the SS building. The *Lagerältester* runs to him from the gate. The *Raportführer* tells him something; the *Lagerältester* runs back. A short while later, the gong sounds in the camp.

"All barracks come forward!"

Immediately, it occurs to me, "I will probably be shot. Otherwise why would they make such a fuss?"

Holding a large sign, one of the SS guards approaches the *Raportführer*. Meanwhile the entire camp is assembled in the roll call square. The searchlights are on. The gong is booming.

Two SS men lead me into the center of the square. The lights are blinding. I stand quietly. The *Raportführer* hangs a sign around my neck that reads: "I stole potatoes, but they don't taste very good."

One of the guards orders me to open my mouth. When I comply, he stuffs in a dirty potato into it, then leads me to the gate where he positions me so that I face the glaring searchlight on the guard tower. All the *Häftlinge* must parade in front of me. This is cheap entertainment.

When the procession is over, the *Häftlinge* are lined up once again in the square. I hear the *Raportführer* telling the guard on duty, "If this pig moves or removes the potato from his mouth, shoot!" Then the *Raportführer* announces to the *Häftlinge*, "This one will stand here with the potato in his mouth for twenty-four hours. Let this be a warning to all of you!"

The *Totenkommando* drags a cart through the square. On it are twenty bloody bodies. This, too, is a warning.

"Dismissed!"

The camp is quiet. All the searchlights are extinguished except the one on the tower. I hear the guard walking and whistling. It is cold. The bright light shines directly in my face and blinds me as the sun would, but it emits no heat.

I breathe with difficulty. My wide-opened mouth causes my jaws to ache terribly. I try to remove the potato to rest for a minute, but the SS guard in the tower roars, "Hey, you dog!"

The order that he received is clear and unabmiguous. I put the potato into my mouth and assume the prescribed position. The only thing I accomplished in that instant, was that I cleaned the dirt from the potato.

Twenty-four hours . . . what a nice prospect! With envy and despair I think of those who can have some peace and warmth next to the stove for at least a few hours. I am also jealous of those who were shot. Their peace is permanent; they no longer suffer.

I am freezing. The stiffening process starts simultaneously in my legs and arms. In my uncovered hands I feel a slight itching which changes from a needling sensation to excruciating pain. Involuntarily, I start to moan.

The sound escaping from my stuffed mouth must sound

very comical. From time to time the guard utters a horse-like laugh.

I feel as if I can suffer no longer. It occurs to me to plead with the guard to give me the bullet of grace. Then, I suddenly stiffen. The pain disappears. I feel a slight knock under my skull.

Somewhere from afar I hear a cry. The lamps in the roll call square are turned on. Groups of people pass. Also, from a distance, I hear a voice calling, "Tadzek! Courage!"

Something falls near my feet and sticks in the snow. The sounds of steps and voices are receding as the *Häftlinge* enter the woods. The lights are extinguished. I stiffen once again.

I do not care that new groups go to work. It does not bother me that O.T. men, my masters, come into the camp and stand in front of me for a whole minute and hold their bellies from laughter. I do not care when a pinkish light fades in the sky behind the woods and the sun appears. The night shift finally arrives. I hear voices again, only one of which enters my consciousness, "Hold out!"

As time passes, I find it more difficult to distinguish day from night. My eyes are clouded.

"You! Remove your cap!"

Someone pulls my cap from my head. I see nothing; I feel nothing.

"Away! To work!"

Someone pushes me. My legs are stiff, and I fall.

I am grabbed under the arms and pulled. Doors open and a reviving warmth envelops me. Someone massages my legs and face.

I start thawing slowly. The fog in front of my eyes seems to lift a little and finally vanishes. I notice that I am in the sick bay. Someone is putting a dressing on my head. Somebody else places a cup containing a hot liquid into my hand and urges, "Drink!"

I swallow in big gulps. With every drop, I feel my blood circulating faster. A few minutes later, I am strong enough to rise from the stool without help.

From the far end of the barrack I hear the clinic chief's

voice calling, "Give him a few potatoes and let him run! If the *Raportführer* comes, we'll be in trouble."

I must go . . . but where? The only possibility is one of the barracks where the night shift is sleeping now. There is heat there, and I will be able to bake my potatoes. I have had no food for twenty-four hours, and after such a night. . . .

Night is finally here. The *Kapo* enters the barrack and announces, "We're changing to the day shift. Tonight we do not work!"

Shouts of joy greet the *Kapo*'s words. For a moment, I think of Maks and the others who will have to toil for twenty-four hours without a rest. Then I wonder if the whole experience of staying outside the entire night was not the will of heaven to protect me from the tortures of the night shift.

An acquaintance introduces me to the *Kapo*. Although he hesitates, he enters my number on the list of barrack inmates. My new friend, Hilek, disregards the protests of his neighbors and makes a place for me beside him. It is next to the stove. I feel fine.

* * *

Noises remind us that we will start to march in a short while. The thought almost causes me physical pain. A dreadful fear grips me when I realize that I will have to go out into the cold and endure the storm again.

We pass near the spot where, not too long ago, I stood transfixed like a statue. I cannot comprehend how I survived. I share my thoughts with Hilek. "You'll withstand even more if need be," he says optimistically.

We meet the day shift at the building site. I spot Maks who says as he goes by, "Beginning today we get less bread."

It is true. Instead of our quarter of a loaf, we have been cut to a fifth. The quality is also worse. It smells stale and moldy.

I turn my tiny portion of bread in all directions. Looking at his piece, Hilek asks, "How long can one live on this?!"

Work on the building is slowing down because of the frigid weather. Several of our supervisors disappear from the work site to enjoy the warmth of their room. We expend less strength on the job, but suffer more from the cold. As Hilek and I carry the rods, we think of a way to organize a dish of soup.

"If only we could get into the kitchen, ..." muses Hilek.

That gives me an idea. During the noon pause, I run to the cement depot with Hilek. While my friend watches carefully for any imminent danger, I organize several paper sacks. Then we run to the other end of the site where the locomotives arrive, and where there is a mound of coal on the ground. The steam shovel which lifts the coal is nearby. I fill my sack.

Hilek looks at me as if I am crazy and asks, "Why do you want to do that?"

I say nothing. Instead, I throw the sack on my back and, panting from the effort, run upstairs to hide my treasure among the iron rods. Only when the voices downstairs announce the arrival of the night shift and our work is finished for the day, do I tell Hilek of my secret plan.

"Since wood is scarce in the camp and there isn't any other flammable material, even the cooks start to feel the cold. We'll take it to the kitchen and propose that, in exchange for the coal, they give us something to eat. I realize how difficult it will be to transport the fuel to the camp, however, between the two of us, we will manage somehow. Then there's the additional problem of getting into the kitchen which is virtually impossible for a simple *Häftling* because of the ever-watchful camp police."

First Hilek loads the thirty kilo sack on his back. After a few steps he complains that he cannot carry such a heavy load. I take the sack, but after half an hour I, too, feel weak. I clench my teeth. I convince myself that the coal is my only hope and that I must continue at any cost.

When we finally reach the camp and I pass through the gate, I fall to the ground and lie there half-dead for more than a quarter of an hour. I pay no attention to Hilek's pleas for me to get up, or risk getting pneumonia. When my heart quiets down somewhat and does not feel as though it might jump out of my chest, I get to my feet slowly. We drag ourselves to the kitchen.

"Where are you going?" demand two *Lagerpolizei* blocking our way.

"Mr. *Kapo* ordered coal. He told us to come!" I answer as calmly as I can.

The doors to heaven open. I look around. In a small room, ten *Häftlinge* are peeling potatoes. I think, "Oh God, if only I could be among them!"

The *Lagerpolizei* report our arrival. The *Kapo* accepts the coal readily and asks, "What do you want for that?"

Hilek opens his mouth to say something, but I don't let him utter a word. I say, "If it's at all possible, we'd like to peel potatoes."

The *Kapo* is surprised for a moment. He cannot understand why we would want to work day and night, but he does not hesitate for long. He agrees.

We run to the barrack, quickly swallow our soup . . . and hurry back. In a little while we sit over a metallic container with knives in our hands. We begin to work.

The soup we had in the barrack has sharpened our appetites. We wait only long enough for the foreman who is watching us, to turn around for a minute, and the potato, instead of going into the cauldron, ends up in our mouths.

We finish our work around midnight. Each of us receives two liters of good soup. Hilek covers my sweaty face with kisses. He screams elatedly. With a serious face, I say, "Don't be crazy, Hilek! It's late. Let's go to bed."

Four hours of sleep pass all too quickly. In the morning our eyes burn. We yawn noisily, but the important thing is that our stomachs are full. For the first time in ten days I feel a slight contraction in my intestines, a sign that I may have the need to fulfill a normal physiological function.

I decide that the next time we organize another sack of coal, we will divide it evenly between us. Hilek is delighted.

Christmas is approaching. Our hope for two days of rest is vanishing. The rules do not provide holidays for the Jews. Under the supervision of the foremen and the O.T. men, we will work at unloading. The only change in our schedule is that, from Christmas on, we will work in three shifts until the arrival of new transports. This change is necessitated by the alarming rate at which our numbers are diminishing. Also, there are no replacements. Work on the building cannot be stopped because our masters run the risk of being called to the Front which is quickly coming closer.

Roll call lasts several hours. New groups are formed. Fortunately, Hilek and I are assigned to a day shift. We are pleased.

Hilek remarks that, since we started peeling potatoes, I look much better. He adds, patting my hairy cheeks, "Fellow, you're filling out!"

"You idiot, don't give me the evil eye!" I warn him.

The evil comes quickly and unexpectedly.

One night we are more tired than usual. As a result, we work slowly. A small clock on the table indicates that it is midnight. Only half the work is completed.

"Attention!" The voice from the door scares us out of our lethargy.

The *Raportführer* enters the kitchen to conduct one of his surprise checks. He looks into the cauldrons; he inspects the entire kitchen. He pays no attention to the *Kapo* who stands in the middle of the kitchen with his cap in his hand. Finally he comes to our room. Looking at the clock, he asks, "It isn't ready?!"

He kicks the foreman in the stomach and orders all of us to stand in the center of the room. He notices Hilek's muddy coat and my face, unshaven for several days. He does not like the whole *Kommando.* As for Hilek and me, we must be released immediately. He marks down our numbers and announces that if he ever finds us here again during a check, he will shoot the *Kapo,* the foreman, and all the cooks.

We must go. Humbly, we leave. At the last minute, Hilek manages to fill his pockets with potatoes. Our career as peelers is over.

It seems that misfortunes come in pairs. . . .

The next day we go to work over the snow-covered fields as usual. Suddenly the sole of my left foot feels cold. My wooden shoes had been giving me trouble for a long time. As an added precaution, I had wrapped my foot in paper. Now the sole has fallen off the shoe and I am walking with my paper-wrapped foot in the snow.

In the darkness, I begin searching for the missing sole. People are tripping over me. I hear Hilek calling me from the front. He wants to know what happened to me.

My effort is in vain. It is impossible to find what I am looking for. I stand barefoot in the snow and cold for a while and am filled with despair. Ahead of me lies a whole day's work and the walk back. How will I endure it?

In the darkness I cannot find a piece of paper to protect my foot. The snow burns like fire; the pain spreading through my body can only be compared to the torture induced by a dentist drilling on an exposed nerve. I step on stones and barbed wires and scream loudly from the agony. Chased by the SS men and their frantic shouts of "Go faster, man!", the *Häftlinge* run near me. They push; they trip; they yell. I must join them and march forward to work. In this forced trek, nobody pays attention to the suffering of others.

I surpassed the limits of human endurance a long time ago. At the work site, I turn to the *Kapo,* show him my misfortune, and beg him to give me a job where I will step in snow as infrequently as possible.

My prayers are answered. I am assigned to one of several machines that bend the ends of the rods. My work consists of taking the rod off the table and throwing it on a heap. Another man helps me. I decide that, during the noon break, I will organize another cement sack and devise a makeshift boot. Fate seems to smile upon me again.

I think happily that the work lasts only eight hours. Despite the difficulties in the camp, I should be able to organize a new pair of wooden shoes. The most important thing right now is that I am not getting very tired and I do not have to run up and down the scaffolding. My paper boot may conceivably last until the end of the workday.

The machines are operated by *Häftlinge.* One master O.T. man walks around with a bamboo stick. From time to time he looks at the pile of iron rods and expresses his satisfaction or disapproval. The latter he acknowledges by blows with his stick, mostly on the face.

The *Häftlinge* at the machines execute their movements automatically. From the look on their faces, I can clearly detect that their minds are far away. What are they thinking? What are they dreaming?

One of them reveals his secret to me: his future. He dreams of a bright, clean room with a fireplace, but mostly, he dreams of food. In his mind, he plans feasts during which one can be sated with bread and soup. This influences his well-being and instills in him the will to fight for life.

"Try it, friend!" he encourages me. "Then you'll even forget that you're barefoot and hungry!"

I start daydreaming on the way back to camp, and in a few minutes I lose my paper boot. I continue my reverie for the next three days while I go, in vain, to the shoemaker's shop to beg for a pair of wooden shoes. I am still engaged in flights of fancy when, on the orders of the *Raportführer,* I must go to work.

* * *

One evening, my foot aches more than usual. I cannot close my eyes and go to the light. On my sole, I have a big blister full of pus; the slightest touch is extremely painful. I think for a while. With my decision made, I climb down from the bunk and hobble over to the clinic.

"So, dear colleague, we have to cut. . . ."

One scalpel and two clamps are all the instruments available in the clinic. Someone washes the blister with cold water. Another holds my hands in a powerful grip. The dull scalpel cuts into my flesh.

I try to stifle a cry, but it rises in my throat against my will. There are two beautiful, alluring young Hungarian women from Budapest in the clinic. Not having had the opportunity to experience the misery of camp life as yet, they look at me with an expression of fear and distaste. I feel ashamed.

The operation is over; my foot is dressed with a piece of

linen and a paper bandage. I am excused from work for three days and may leave for the hospital.

The hospital barrack is so overcrowded that the nearly two hundred patients sleep in shifts of one hundred each for a few hours at a time. Those who refuse to wake up are thrown to the floor.

The barrack stinks unbearably from pus, dirt, filthy rags, and the excrement-covered patients. The stove smokes. Millions of lice crawl on the boards and the thin pallets of straw. Pneumonia, dysentery, T.B., skin infections, all these cases lie together. They cough and spit at one another, defecate, and smear pus.

I report to the doctor, a young, sympathetic Frenchman. Although he tries, he cannot keep up with the work.

Barrack 4, the main K.B., is overcrowded and cannot accommodate any more patients. Medicine and dressing ma- commodate any more patients. Medicine and dressing ma- terials are lacking. It is a slow and agonizing death.

It is night. The doctor sleeps in the clinic. The sick moan loudly. I want a drink. I cannot get to the water, and snow does not slake my thirst. I sit on the edge of the bunk and place my afflicted foot on the opposite one. Even though I am exhausted and hurting and my eyelids stick together, it is difficult to sleep in such a position. I doze.

By the light of the protected lamp, I see a figure dragging himself to the door. Aha! He probably needs to go out.

A noise near the stove attracts my attention. Some other ghostly individual is tinkering around the stove. He throws in a few boards and blows to start the fire. It begins to smoke. Someone protests weakly, but in vain. The wood catches fire at last and fills the barrack with a welcome crackle. The ghost-like figure places a cup of water on the stove. The other person returns, looks around, and throws something into the cup.

I listen to the moaning of the patients and the bubbling of the boiling water. Someone is begging.

The two figures remove the cup and disappear deep into the barrack. The light goes out. Somewhere, far away, a siren wails, warning that an air raid is imminent. I lie across someone's legs and fall asleep.

I am awakened by loud shouts. Someone hits my injured foot. The hospital barrack is in an uproar. The chief of the section and several doctors are there. The French physician is running around like a madman, cursing and screaming.

What happened?

The mystery is uncovered. Someone cut a piece of flesh from the body of a dead young person. Such acts are occurring in other barracks as well.

I recall the scene I witnessed last night and think of the cup with the boiling water and its contents. No, I will not stay here a minute longer! Let happen what may, I would rather be without a shoe and go to work with a bad foot, otherwise I will become insane.

I share my thoughts with the French doctor. He understands perfectly and wants to help, but unfortunately, he cannot. There is no dressing material. The wound looks terrible. I cannot go on *Kommando* in my condition.

"Do you want to commit suicide? It's your choice, but it's a shame. The Russians are one hundred kilometers from Berlin. The offensive in the West is also advancing at a rapid pace. Think about it."

After some thought, I have an idea. During the day, I will be in the hospital barrack. At night I will hop on one leg to the closest barrack vacated by the night shift.

"It's cold, friend," the Frenchman says.

He gives me two old coats taken from corpses. I wrap myself well in them. It does not help much because the material does not keep me warm. In any event, it is better than nothing. To go out is better than inhaling the stench and far more preferable than being among the dead or the living who, from desperate hunger, cannibalize.

After a week I feel well enough to walk to the shoemaker's shop with the aid of a cane. This time I am lucky. An SS guard is at the door. I promptly report to him to let him know that, despite my illness, I want to go to work and that all I am asking for is a pair of shoes.

Miraculously, one pair of wooden shoes with new tops that

fit me perfectly, is found. I am very happy with them. Triumphantly, I return to the hospital barrack to have my dressing changed.

From the one-eighth of a loaf of bread and half a liter of soup—the portion given to the sick—one can only die. It is far better to carry coal and work hard than to suffer the tortures of hunger every day. In preparation for work, I line the bottom of my shoes with straw and organize a few rags that serve well as improvised socks. Limping slightly, I go to work the next day, but I soon regret my decision.

As the offensive in the Ardennes falters, the SS and O.T. men become furious because they realize that they are losing their last hope for victory. They release their anger for the defeats on us. It is a cruel revenge on helpless victims. Blood is shed on cement and iron.

From a group of *Häftlinge,* walking along the railroad tracks, several are killed by an O.T. man driving a locomotive at full speed. Two SS men, meeting a group of *Häftlinge* carrying bread for everyone, order that it be thrown into the latrine; we suffer for forty-eight hours without our main food supply.

Work on the building stops. The necessary supplies are not arriving. The groups, freed from work, exercise in a small clearing. An SS man, armed with a machine gun, stands behind them watching their routines carefully. Every so often, we hear a volley of shots that resounds tenfold in our ears.

A new cemetery has been prepared in a clearing behind the work site. In a deep ditch dug by a bulldozer, hundreds are resting. On the bread cart, we bring back only those sick ones who had the good fortune to become ill toward the end of the workday. Those who became sick earlier, remain with the corpses and go to the cemetery.

* * *

I begin carrying coal. I am warned about the O.T. man on guard. He has already killed several *Häftlinge.* I consider that those warnings are rumors spread by my dishonest competitors. Nevertheless, as I approach the mound of coal, I look carefully in all directions.

I carry this load to exchange it for a few potatoes; I carry it for a crumb of bread; I carry it for a liter of watery soup. It does not matter that transporting it takes more out of me than the food I receive. It seems to take my mind off the hunger even if only for a short time. At least before I go to sleep, I can give my stomach a little something to digest.

One day I go to the K.B. barrack to sell the coal. When I enter to empty my pack, I suddenly hear someone calling me in a low voice. It is Maks. He has contracted pneumonia and is burning with fever. Next to him Leon Sztajn lies unconscious suffering from typhus.

"Tadzek," whispers Maks, "have pity! Remember I helped you in Auschwitz!"

The water is turned off in the washroom; the water pipe has burst. Despite the risk, I decide to break into the kitchen. This means a beating if I am caught, but for Maks. . . .

I mix with a group of food haulers. I take advantage of the split second when the door opens for the people with the cauldrons. I push the policeman away forcefully, run to the faucet, and fill my canteen with water. By the time the first blows are about to land on me, I jump to the door and run, followed by the shouts and curses of the kitchen personnel.

* * *

In the camp, the plague of lice becomes a horror. It does not matter that the cursed insects poison our every minute making it impossible to rest after work and roll call. The chief danger from the lice is that they can cause a typhus epidemic that threatens the lives of the "valuable" SS men.

On-the-spot procedures produce no helpful results. The baths are not completed yet. There is a lack of basins and shower heads. In the washroom, water is scarce because the pipes keep bursting. Under such circumstances, the administration announces a general disinfection and delousing program.

Toward the end of the workday one afternoon, we wait in vain for our relief shift. We must keep working. The afternoon shift arrives at ten o'clock. They have been deloused. We can expect the same treatment tonight.

When we approach the camp at about eleven o'clock, two SS men direct our group to the first camp. We must walk about six kilometers in terribly cold weather. It is most unpleasant. Nobody seems worried that we have missed our soup and may be terribly hungry after a fourteen hour workday.

Isolated shots behind us make it abundantly clear that the SS men do not play with *Häftlinge*. Our fatigue is so overwhelming that we can barely walk. Our wooden shoes pound the frozen ground in the dark night. How much farther? I breathe with more difficulty. I think with despair that I will not be able to hold out much longer. How far is it? I count the telephone poles: five, twenty, fifty.

At a Y intersection in the road, a motorcycle is parked with its lights off.

"Halt!"

An SS man explains to the guard that there is no room for us in the baths today. We must return.

So back we go. By the time we have walked several kilometers more, we hear the noise of a motor behind us.

"Halt!"

It was a mistake. We must go back. The SS man thought that we came from a different camp.

"Faster! Move!" Boomm! Boomm! Short cries. We keep moving.

"Go on! Move!" The road to the baths is streaked with blood.

How much longer?! I breathe through my wide-open mouth. Thousands of hammers pound in my ears and skull.

"Move! Move! Quicker!"

The road is uphill through woods and fields. Every once in a while some completely exhausted soul lies down with his face in the snow, waiting for the bullet.

Lights are shining through a clump of trees. I close my

eyes, count my steps, open my eyes . . . the lights seem somewhat closer. Maybe I will make it.

Under the glaring searchlight in front of the baths, the SS men count us. Twenty are missing.

"Shot while trying to escape," reports the *Unterscharführer* to the *Kommandant* of the camp.

"Certainly! It's so dark!" says the *Kommandant,* nodding his head understandingly.

The baths are small, accommodating only fifty people at one time. We wait outside until morning. By the time we finally get our half-burned rags back from the delousing chamber, we must begin our march to work.

* * *

"Two men, one rod!"

Someone tries to explain to our master that we worked fourteen hours yesterday and during the night. . . . The *Häftling* receives two slaps in the face and such a forceful kick that he loses his footing, slides and falls down the dome, and is impaled on one of the metal rods projecting five centimeters above the surface of the dome. He shrieks and begs for help. The O.T. men laugh.

"Move! Bring the rods! Tempo!"

It is noontime and we have no bread. We have no strength even to bemoan our fate. Only our eyes speak . . . only they express the limitless torture.

At the end of the workday, I automatically drag myself toward the coal. I do not wonder if I will be able to carry it. I know only one thing: food. Coal is bread. Coal buys a dish of soup. I must carry the black load to camp.

Suddenly, I hear a yell behind me and turn around. From behind a bulldozer, an O.T. man in black overalls runs toward me holding a shovel handle in his fist.

Realizing that my death is imminent, I throw away the sack with its few pieces of coal, to save myself. I try to run, but my legs are buckling. I fall. Above me I hear some loud panting and, "You dog!"

Boom! A black night descends over me.

7 Dachau IV (Kaufering-Krankenlager)

Creak, creak, creak. . . . The sky is blue. I see the tops of trees. Suddenly it gets dark. I have trouble trying to open my eyes.

Creak, creak, again. It is the same: sky, the tops of trees, and the ever present creaking. Where am I? What is happening to me? My head feels as if it weighs a hundred kilograms. My brains are not functioning. They refuse to respond.

I hear someone explaining, "This one wanted to steal coal and was hit over the head by the O.T. man, but he's still alive."

Aha, now I remember . . . slowly, very slowly I remember. It was night, then the bath, work, and then the coal. The O.T. man was running from behind a bulldozer.

Now I am lying in the cart atop a heap of bodies, and the wheels are creaking in the snow. I am lying on my back; that is why I see only the tops of trees and the sky. But I see! So I am alive! What a wonderful thing! I am laughing; I am laughing to myself. I was found just in time! My head is whirling. I faint.

* * *

Putt, putt. Putt, putt. I smell gasoline and almost vomit. Someone holds up my head. It feels as though a rubber tube is choking me. I cough. It hurts to do that.

I regain consciousness. Where am I? Some kind of engine is pulling several carts.

A friend in misfortune says to me, "We're being transported from Camp XI to Camp IV. It will be better there." Then he adds, "You were lucky. They found you when the cart was making the last rounds at the work site."

I've heard enough. I close my eyes and listen to the chugging sound of the engine.

* * *

"Yes, fellow! When you came, they thought that you were dead and wanted to take you straight to the morgue along with the corpses. Fortunately, I recognized you and told them to bring you to this barrack. You were unconscious for several days. You neither ate nor drank; you soiled yourself. Now after all of that, you are still alive."

The Greek doctor is laughing in a very amiable way. I am lying on a big pile of straw, and I am covered with a blanket. The *Stubendienst* explains that my laundry is drying outside.

The Greek is the barrack doctor and *Blockältester,* and is also my old friend from Auschwitz. I helped his brother several times. I was even kind to him once by giving him a portion of bread. He remembered that, and now, after several months, he repays me. When I was lying on the cart, he had difficulty in recognizing me.

I am unable to sort out my feelings for my savior. I do not know whether I should be happy or sad. I am still too weak.

I cannot get oriented. The following day, I ask my Greek friend, "Why is this barrack so empty?"

"It's been that way only for the past two days," he replies. "There's a typhus epidemic ravaging the camp. We have two hundred corpses daily. Only two weeks ago, this place was full. Of the thirty Hungarian doctors, twenty are sick. The head doctor is glad that you're better. As soon as you can get out of your bed, you'll be a medic."

He brings me a loaf of bread and says, "Eat! You'll get cross-eyed!" After a while, he adds seriously, "Don't be afraid. I'm not stealing. These are the portions of those who died. They don't need the bread any longer. The war is ending. The Russians are nearing Berlin. Maybe we'll survive!"

* * *

Two weeks pass before I regain enough strength to enable me to get out of the bunk. In the meantime, the barrack fills up and empties several times.

We divide the portions of bread among the living. Right now, it is our only salvation. The daily ration is eighty grams. Every third day, it is increased to one hundred grams. Three times a week, we are given margarine or sausage. For the noon meal, we receive half a liter of soup made from potato peels. There are no medicines, but a few tablets and capsules are reserved for the high ranking personnel in the camp.

I become a medic. I do not understand my functions too well. In any event, I examine the sick and note the diagnoses on a piece of paper. For the first two days, I argue with the pharmacist to give me the most basic medicines. He laughs at me, and I return to the barrack empty-handed.

A sixteen year old boy, who was lucky enough to survive typhus, is dying from a heart condition. His father expired a week ago; his brother is lying nearby suffering from meningitis.

"Is there nothing for me, Doctor?"

I do not reply. I cannot look into the poor fellow's eyes. Day after day people are dying, and I am unable to help. I cannot take it.

My Greek friend sees my helpless despair and tries to console me. In his barrack, conditions are the same. In all of the other barracks it is no different. How can the doctors and medics help? They are used to it already.

* * *

On the first day of February, we have beautiful winter weather. Not a cloud is visible in the blue sky. The sun is blinding. The sirens in the neighboring villages and towns are continually wailing. We hear an unusual hum.

Anyone with some strength goes outside, defying the SS men's strict orders not to leave the barrack. The guards in the towers are yelling at us.

The sky is full of small shimmering spots: twenty, thirty, fifty. One wave passes. A second follows, bringing hundreds of planes. Suddenly, the earth quakes under our feet. We hear the sound of motors in the distance.

"Drop the bombs! Hit the Germans as often as you can! May God be with you on this journey!" we shout.

Suddenly, it looks as if thousands of snow-white pigeons are falling from the planes. Someone shouts, "Leaflets! Leaflets!" We watch the airplanes with bated breath until the last squadron disappears beyond the woods.

The pieces of paper dance in the air. Unfortunately, the wind blows in the opposite direction. There is no hope that a leaflet will fall into our hands. What a shame!

With intense longing, we wait for news from behind the wires. In the desperate fight for life, one ray of hope is capable of replacing thousands of calories.

Several days after the bombing, the *Kommando* comprised of convalescents finds a crumpled, dirty piece of paper while they are cleaning the latrine. After the sheet is cleaned and dried, we are surprised to find that it is part of a leaflet with a map showing the position at the Front. In the west, the Americans and British are at the Rhine. In the east, the Russians are on the Oder and have entered Slovakia and Hungary. Every day, new Allied successes are reported.

I run into the barrack. It is the first bit of happy news I can bring to the sick in the long time. A weak gleam of joy shimmers in their deeply sunken eyes. On their emaciated faces, faint smiles appear.

* * *

The war is almost over; there can be no doubt about it. Transports of sick, hungry, unbearably tired Jewish *Häftlinge* from every European nation flood into our camp. In the barrack, their number increases daily: eighty, one hundred, one hundred and thirty, one hundred fifty . . . until there are nearly two hundred.

In every European language, "Help!!!" resounds throughout the barrack. They plead desperately for bread.

There is none. Now can I explain to the sick that, for the past two nights, I, the Mr. Medic, have gone to the dump where they throw out the garbage from the kitchen? Can I tell them that I consider myself very fortunate if I find a rotten potato or a few peels sometimes? Whenever I do, a fight usually ensues.

And new transports arrive day and night.

* * *

Hundreds of live skeletons lie dying and suffering in front of the overcrowded barracks and in the streets of the camp. There is no one to take care of them.

The number of corpses is mounting. All those who can stand are forced to dig graves and bury the dead. It does not help. New transports with new victims arrive daily.

In the midst of these hellish events, a rumor circulates through the camp that our suffering will soon end: the SS men decided to bring all the sick to our camp; they will then burn and blow everything into the air, and all the personnel who were in contact with typhus cases must share their fate. The terrible evidence of Hitler's unspeakable crimes must never fall into the hands of the Allies.

"*Blockältesters* and medics come forward!"

The *Lagerältester* delivers a short speech. "In two days an inspection team will arrive. If, by that time, the camp streets are cleared of the corpses, you may be permitted to live until the end of the war. If not. . . ."

Our superior's words make no impression on me nor on the other medics. Let the cooks, *Blockältesters,* supervisors, and all those who have enough to eat do the job.

I return to the barrack and cover myself with my blanket. I rise only to help a *Stubendienst* bring in a cauldron of soup: seventy-five liters for two hundred people.

* * *

The camp's staff appreciates life, judging by the way they work. They take the top off the mobile toilet and put two boards across it. With such an improvised vehicle, they remove forty to fifty corpses on each trip. When the inspection team arrives two days later, there is a semblance of order in the place; we can keep on living. For those who have the will to do so, it is comforting.

As compensation for our labor, we get bread for the first time in a week. For one hundred fifty sick people, the *Blockältester* distributes fifteen loaves. The sick divide it among themselves and fight over the smallest crumb in the wooden crate.

After the loaf is cut into ten parts, lots are drawn. Each participant receives a number from one to ten. One of the group turns his back and another asks him which number is to get this piece. It is a gloomy, tragi-comedy.

* * *

During the first days of March, I get "lucky" when our *Blockältester* contracts typhus. Like all the other staff members of the camp, he cherishes life and is very much afraid of dying. I am exhausted, but, when the *Stubendienst* tells me that the *Blockältester* wants to see me, I crawl down from my bunk.

"Medic, you'll stay with me day and night. I'll reward you. Only help me!"

I am given two blankets and a place near the *Blockältester.* The clinic has ampules of heart medicine and two syringes for my use. I apply cold compresses to his head, check his pulse, and eat. Yes, eat.

I quickly notice several hinged boards near the *Blockäl-*

tester's bed. In a small hidden drawer underneath, the old bandit had amassed many supplies: fat, sausage, bread, cheese, marmalade, and sugar from the time these things were first distributed in addition to the bread.

Right or wrong I take advantage of the situation. Some animal instinct awakens in me, and I tell myself, "He promised to compensate me. These aren't his. He stole them, the hoodlum." I am satisfied to have some justification for my actions.

On the eighth day, the *Blockältester* develops encephalitis. There is no hope. He dies.

No sooner are his remains removed than the *Lagerältester* and several *Blockältesters* run to his quarters. Without a word, they raid his cache, wrap the remaining supplies, and leave quickly taking everything with them. Now my conscience does not bother me any longer. The additional food that I ate for several days, saves my life. That is no exaggeration.

One morning we discover that there are no supplies in the camp, no bread, no potatoes—only clear water. The kitchen doles out hot herb tea twice a day.

The *Totenkommando* has no strength to remove the dead from the barrack. The corpses lie in the bunks among the living. The decomposed bodies smell unbearably.

Cannibalism is an everyday occurrence. With manic expressions on their haggard faces, people tear the bodies of the dead with their teeth. No one has the strength to call this outrage to their attention. Anyway, they will not understand. It is sheer insanity.

Under these circumstances, nobody notices that the American planes are flying lower and lower over the camp every day. No one goes for tea. Who will carry the cauldrons? The *Lagerpolizei* still have some energy and pull a cart through the camp stopping in front of every barrack to distribute the hot liquid to those who want it, but there are fewer and fewer takers.

The entire camp is dying. Hunger is terrible for the first few days, but, after that, one goes on living somehow. The hunger pangs recede slowly. Insidiously, weakness coupled with some numbness sets in as if the whole organism is under the influence of a weak electric current. Slowly I stop distinguishing between day and night. A fog thickens in front of my eyes.

"Hey, medic! How many are alive in your barrack?!"

The question is repeated. Several figures finally approach me and forcibly pull me down from the bunk. I fall on my knees; they help me up. For a long time they harass me, hitting me, pricking me with pins until I come to myself somewhat. Obviously I cannot give them an answer because I do not know how long my semi-consciousness lasted.

"Not long ago there were sixty alive in here," I manage to respond quite logically, while at the same time wondering at the unusual sound of my voice. It seems to be coming from far away and is gruff and dry like that of a man suffering from cholera.

"Wake up, idiot! Packages came from Switzerland. They're saving our lives!"

"Packages? Switzerland? Saving lives?" I mumble uncomprehendingly.

The police take charge of the situation. "You've forty-two alive. You'll get fifty-two packages. Everybody gets one. What's left you'll divide among the men who carry out the corpses. Do you understand?!"

I am quite confused. I do not know where the packages come from. Ten more packages? Corpses?!

The police put the boxes on the floor and count them once more. "Hurry up and distribute these before the rest die!" they order as they leave.

Not a voice is heard in the barrack. I look wide-eyed at the cardboard packages. It is hope! I distinguish the living from the dead only by the shine in their eyes as I walk all over the barrack holding on to things. I place a box in front of every living person: a kilo of sugar, condensed milk, sardines, and much empty space.

I swallow the sugar. Throughout the barrack I hear the noisy smacking of lips, the sound of chewing. Someone moans.

Within minutes there is no trace of a kilo of sugar in my package. I feel a little nauseous. Now for the sardines . . . I break the can open with a sharp stone. Oil! Oh God! The milk! . . . drink the milk!

What am I doing? All together? After such a protracted hunger it may kill me. I am very well aware of that, but some strange hostile force directs my every move. I punch two small holes in the tin can and hold it to my mouth until the loud swish from the can indicates that its contents are in my bottomless stomach. I call myself a pig and do not feel well, but somehow I am able to walk without help.

While I eat, I think of the ten packages that are left. I find four willing workers; I am the fifth. The corpses are light. We put them in a space between the barracks. Now there is some order inside and . . . the packages are ours. Without thinking, the fellows continue to eat. I, on the other hand, once I satisfied my first hunger, regain my self control.

The unexpected help has fatal consequences. At least fifty percent of those who remained alive develop diarrhea. It kills most of the poor fellows who are stricken. Again we carry corpses, this time without pay.

* * *

The world is beautiful; the weather, mild. Spring breezes come from the nearby woods. The sun shines brightly, despite all the horrors occurring here.

My friend, the Greek doctor, is walking toward me. He looks like a ghost and is barely able to stand. He does not seem to notice me until I shout, "Hey, Pepo!"

He stops, looks at me, and opens his mouth as though he wants to say something. After a few minutes, he succeeds. "Oh, it's you! Yes, it's really you! I wanted to see if you're still alive!"

We hear cars on the road. Pepo is pleased as he says, "It must be food for us. Now we'll be saved." Then he adds, "Do you know what those pigs of the SS did? Three transports of packages came for us from Switzerland. Those cursed dogs ate the food in those boxes and then stole half of a fourth shipment. They gave us the rest. May they choke!"

Pepo's hopes are fulfilled to some degree. A line of trucks

enters the camp. It has been a long time since freight trucks came to the kitchen. I notice one with a load of potatoes pulling up there; at least we will have soup. One truck, bringing bread, stops in front of the kitchen. A dozen others are parked, waiting for people to unload several hundred sick people. The few strong ones in the camp are unable to empty the trucks. The impatient SS men climb up and push the people down as if they were garbage.

* * *

The bread and potatoes last for several days. The packages were consumed a long time ago. Hunger menaces us again.

Now nature helps. On the dirt-covered roofs, in front of the wires, and in the small square beyond the last barracks. grass begins to grow. At first, we sort out the juiciest, most "edible" greens. Later we become less choosy. We eat everything except poison ivy and bushes.

Thus time passes as we subsist on a diet of grass, and life goes on among the corpses until the first days of April. We get bread and potatoes only on Sundays. The camp has more dead than living people. I sit outdoors all day because the stench of the cadavers bothers me less there than in the barrack. Nature is blessing us. Grass is growing thickly. The sun warms which is rather rare for this time of year.

What can we expect? I assume, nothing good. We fear that German planes will bomb us someday soon. They will blame the Allies. Meanwhile, they will remove all the shameful traces.

We have received no information about the world situation since the plane dropped the leaflets. For the handful who remain alive, the lack of news is almost as tragic as the hunger we endure. Our tense nerves are strained to the utmost. Freedom is in the air. We feel it instinctively. We sense that the moment of our liberation is at hand. May God grant us strength to survive.

One morning, a trailer truck arrives, bringing one hundred workers from somewhere near the French border. They tell us that the Germans deported them only a few hours before the Allies occupied their town. Americans are only sixty kilometers from us. Another few days and we will be free. "Hold out, brothers!" they urge.

Fearlessly, American planes are flying very low. If the pilots only knew that we are dying of hunger . . . if only. . . .

In the camp meanwhile, strange scenes are taking place. People are trying to conserve their strength. Every move, every unnecessary step is a waste of energy. However, grass must be picked and eaten. Those who are fond of this meatless diet lie on their bellies and eat the grass. SS men in the towers take pictures with their cameras.

A transport of potatoes arrives, three full trucks. Now there is no wood for a fire to heat the cauldrons. Everyone is given fifteen raw potatoes. To those of us who are used to eating grass, the potatoes taste like the finest, tastiest gourmet food in the world.

* * *

A truck arrives pulling several peasant carts linked together; it is a transport from Camp XI. Maks is with them. We greet each other almost tearfully. I thought that Maks had died. He had heard that I had been killed.

"I still have a few potatoes. I'll give you what I have, Maks!"

We improvise a feast. The main course: potatoes, and for dessert: grass.

Maks brings the first definite news. The Americans are still fifty to sixty kilometers away. Two days ago, he still worked for Moll. Construction on the building has been suspended. Camp XI is being prepared for evacuation. The healthy ones are ready to march. The sick ones were sent here.

Maks came on the transport because he thought that he might be able to escape. Unfortunately, there were so many troops on the road that any attempt to run away was sure to fail.

"Yes, Tadzek, these are our last hours. Maybe it's death; maybe, life!"

One afternoon, a contingent of fully armed SS men leave for an undisclosed destination. A few of them and the *Kommandant* will remain in the camp until the very end.

The *Kommandant* issues orders to distribute one-quarter of a loaf of bread and ten potatoes to each *Häftling*. We sense that something important is going to happen. The news from the *Schreibstube* is that the Americans are expected at any hour.

The time spent in waiting is agonizing. One day passes, two, three . . . all with no news, no orders. Sometimes we get a piece of bread; often, not. Many collapse and die.

Maks and I recall our days in Auschwitz with their constant selections, evacuations, and trips into the unknown. Then everything was hopeless. But now? To die at the threshold of freedom?

* * *

We hear loud explosions in the distance. Maks raises his head from the bed and listens, then he shouts joyfully, "Artillery! Artillery! Just like in Auschwitz when the Russians were getting close. But now it's coming from the other direction. Freedom!"

The camp is in turmoil. The police run from barrack to barrack calling everyone who can stand to go to roll call in the square.

We learn that we can choose to be evacuated, or to stay. What should we do? Our lives depend on our choice. I cannot decide.

I am still in a quandry as I accompany Maks to the gate. *Häftlinge* are assembled at the exit. The police take them from the camp and line them up on the road.

The remaining SS men are also preparing to march. They load bread, fat, meat, and sugar from their storehouse onto the carts. There is so much bread that it cannot fit on the carts. The overflow is divided among the *Häftlinge*.

"Tadzek, what will you do?"

"I'm staying, Maks," I reply calmly.

"I'm going. Good luck, Tadzek! Maybe we'll meet!"

"Good luck! Take care of yourself, friend!"

Maks goes through the gate. A moment later the order is issued, "March!"

The first five disappear around the bend. Maks waves his striped cap for good-by. The gate is closed. I remain.

* * *

Several soldiers leave the *Blockführerstube*. Every one of them is about sixty years old. With difficulty, they climb the steps of the guard towers.

I notice some figures sneaking into the open kitchen and leaving loaded with potatoes. I follow their example.

I must descend a ladder to get to the potatoes in the cellar. For a moment I seem to lack strength, but then I await my turn impatiently.

When I get close enough to the potatoes, I feverishly stuff my pockets with them, tighten my belt, and hide more potatoes under my shirt. I resemble a barrel as I climb back up.

Someone in front of me seems to have trouble holding on. At any moment I fear that he will fall on top of me. I extend my hand to steady him. In a little while, the stranger regains his equilibrium and climbs up the last remaining steps. He sits on the ground.

As I am about to pass him, he says, "You, sir, have helped me. I thank you kindly! I am Dr. Reiter from Kielce."

Through the open window I see two SS men running toward the kitchen. Forcibly, I drag my friend out of there. At the last minute, we disappear behind the barrack. We hear the SS guards yelling in the kitchen and then the explosion of a hand grenade. Screams from the cellar shatter the air.

"Those sons-of-bitches! Even now, at the last moment, they're still killing the innocent!"

I pay no attention to Dr. Reiter's remarks. Had we been in the cellar one minute longer, we, too, would have suffered the same fate. All my thoughts are directed toward one objective: how to make a fire to cook or bake our potatoes.

I collect a bundle of straw and find a corpse's eyeglasses. Luckily the sun is still hot, and with the use of lenses, the straw catches fire. I rip some boards from a bunk and break down a door. After slicing the potatoes, I place them on the hot stove. I cook, tend the fire, and worry about nothing else, not even the *Raportführer* yelling at someone nearby.

"You didn't want to go to another camp," he screams, "so you'll go to heaven, perhaps even tonight. A *Kommando* is coming that will blow you and the entire camp to kingdom come!"

Reiter laughs, "I'm curious to know how many potatoes we can bake until tonight."

We can hardly wait until they are ready. The aroma stimulates our saliva and gastric juices.

Every once in a while, someone comes in to ask for permission to use the fire. It may be our last feast before we die. At least we'll have full stomachs before we go straight to heaven.

After three cups of potatoes, our hunger seems to be satisfied. Reiter wants to sleep. I wander over to the wires to see if I can escape. It is impossible.

While we were busy with the potatoes, the camp was surrounded by soldiers. Now our minds can be at peace and we can rest. There is nothing more to do. I regret, to a certain extent, that I did not listen to Maks and join him in the evacuation. I am sorry . . . but not for long. Who knows what will happen to them along the way?

I gather as much straw as I can, remove my shoes and clothes, and cover myself with several blankets. I am comfortable, warm, and feel fine.

"Good night," I hear Reiter say.

* * *

Someone pokes me with a stick.

"Maybe you'll get up, you animal! Do you want to get blown into the air?"

I am very sleepy and rather disoriented.

"So, it hasn't happened yet?" I ask. It is a senseless question.

Reiter, who is stretching leisurely next to me, says, "I dreamt that I was in heaven. It was so pleasant with plenty of potatoes and soup."

We go out in front of the barrack. SS men are placing sticks of dynamite throughout the camp. It is getting dark. Two Hungarian doctors from the *Krankenbau* who remained with us, are running all through the camp begging everyone who has a little strength to help the sick ones who cannot help themselves. They want to move them from the camp.

Just beyond the woods and within several hundred meters of the camp is a railroad track. An evacuation train is expected tonight. Several *Häftlinge* are cutting the wires under the supervision of the SS. Through this improvised gate, we remove the sick and place them on a flat platform near the *Schreibstube*.

I drag Reiter into the camp. Twenty people join us and, together, we help to empty the barracks, systematically working feverishly until late at night. Many in our *Kommando* collapse.

After a while, the SS prevent anyone from returning to the camp. Instead, they order, "Lie down!"

Booooooom! Boom! Booom!

The explosion is deafening. It is followed by another . . . a third . . . a tenth. Fire rises in a smoky column. Our camp is a memory.

I lie on the wet ground next to Reiter. My whole body trembles; I breathe laboriously. Only now do I begin to feel exceptionally tired and utterly exhausted.

The explosions stop; the flames leap heavenward. From the farther side of the wood, we hear the long piecing whistle of a locomotive. We walk to the track, dragging several of the sick ones with us.

When we reach the railroad cars, we lift the feeble ones, and they crawl in. Several hundred helpless souls lie beside the cars. With weak, whining voices, they beg to be thrown into the cars. SS guards and soldiers with rifles wait and watch at the edge of the woods. They can be seen very clearly in the firelight.

In the morning, all is ready. Reiter and I enter a nearby car; someone closes the door. We are moving.

After a few minutes we stop. I look through the only open window and see railroad cars occupied by moaning prisoners from Camps I and III on the next track. Their camps, like ours, were blown up.

The train is maneuvering. When all the cars are coupled, we move again. We can hear the sounds of war in the distance, but as we travel, the explosions and artillery fire sound closer.

"Come, Tadzek! Let's go to sleep. God's will be done. You can do nothing!"

Reiter pulls me away from the window, but I am too nervous to sleep for any length of time. It is daylight. We are stopped at a small station.

"Schwabhausen," I read aloud. The name means nothing to me. However, there is a military train on the next track and, mounted on the open platform, are anti-aircraft and machine guns.

"The bastards are retreating from the Front," remarks an observer.

After a while we hear the locomotive's whistle resembling an air-raid siren. There is much turmoil on the military train. We hear, "Hans! Quick! Get over there!" and then silence. But the stillness lasts only a short while. We hear the sound of motors above us, followed by the roar of diving airplanes. They are firing machine guns.

Trr! Tututu! Trrr! Tutututu!

We hear moaning in our car and notice the sun's rays shining through holes in the walls. The car is being pierced by bullets and looks like a sieve.

More planes are diving. Trrr! Tutututu!

God! They are strafing our train! They do not know that we are here. I run to the door and pull. I want to open it and run. A deadly fear possesses me.

Trrr! Tututu!

Something strikes my head. Fragments of wood injure my face. I wade up to my ankles in blood. I scream to Reiter, "Jump through the window!"

I get to the opening and, without help, struggle to get out

of the car despite the continual shooting. I fall head-first onto sharp stones and bruise myself. I crawl over a high embankment and trip over some wires. After overcoming all these obstacles, I run to the open field as fast as I can.

Meanwhile, the planes turn and shoot at the German military train beside us. Then they return to strafe ours.

In the midst of the whistling bullets and the din of the motors, I hear a voice shouting, "You, come here! It's full of food!"

A few steps from me is a figure in a striped uniform calmly pulling up fresh grass by the handful. He is unaware of anything as he eats with an appetite.

"Thank God!" says the unknown friend when I drop utterly exhausted next to him. "Thank God! I haven't eaten such good grass in a long time!!"

When the planes finally leave, the SS men come out of their holes and surround the train. During the height of the attack, several *Häftlinge* managed to get into the car with the SS guards' supplies and helped themselves. Showing no mercy, the guards and soldiers shoot them. Their victims die with their mouths full of bread and their faces smeared with marmalade.

"We must run," I think to myself as I search for Reiter.

In the meantime, the guards open the cars. The greatest damage was done to those closest to the locomotive of the military train. None of the *Häftlinge* are alive in these cars. Of the fifty in ours, four survived.

The SS men appear quite satisfied with the massacre. I take advantage of their curiosity to pull Reiter, by force, toward the thick bushes at the edge of the woods. We crawl in and take refuge on a patch of moss.

Reiter is afraid. "They'll certainly discover us here!"

I am furious at my friend and scold, "If you wish, you can crawl out. I'm not stopping you. Only don't moan. I'm just as afraid as you are."

We lie on the ground and hold our breaths observing the scene. One hour after the air raid, a locomotive arrives and removes the military train. A while later, the SS men announce through megaphones that anyone, who is able to leave the car unaided, should do so. Several hundred *Häftlinge,* among them some women, are taken to the front of the train where they remove the corpses from the front cars. Then they occupy those places themselves.

The guards round up a group of peasant women from the nearby village. With their help, they pile the dead and severely injured into the rear cars.

The noises of war come still closer. The guards, appearing quite nervous, run like mad to and from the station. Among their shouts and curses we hear, "The locomotive will be here soon."

"Soon" turns out to be night. The engine pulls the front cars carrying the healthy ones. After a little while it returns, and the SS men link the cars with the dead, sick, and wounded.

"Done! Let's go!" shout the SS men.

Through closed doors, we hear the despairing, fearful cries of the people.

"Where are they dragging them?"

Reiter whispers in my ear that there are barrels of gasoline on the station ramp in Schwabhausen and that he saw the SS men doing something near them.

Suddenly, a loud explosion shakes the ground. A sea of fire envelops the area. The successive bursts of the gasoline barrels are synchronized with the rumble of the moving railroad cars. For a short time, we hear the pitiful calls for help, then only the piercing whistle of the locomotive and the clack of its wheels farther down the track. The gasoline burns; the flames hiss.

A shiver passes through my body. I turn to my friend.

"Let's run!"

"Are you crazy? Where to? They'll see us. It's as light as day!"

I do not answer. With Reiter behind me. I try crawling slowly across the clearing to the railroad tracks. We inch up the embankment. Now we are able to see the station building, the nearby camp, and, in the inferno, the contours of the half-burned cars . . . the last crimes of the Germans.

The cannons sound ever closer. The hands of the clock are nearing twelve.

Ending

On the other side of the embankment are dense woods. We grope blindly, hiding among the trees trying to get as far as possible from this cursed place. The flames remain behind us.

In the darkness, we lose our sense of direction and stop. A long time passes before we can adjust to the dark. Reiter stretches out on the ground and begs me to do likewise, ending with, "For God's sake! They'll finish us off in the last minute!"

It gets colder as a wind rises and chases the clouds, letting the moonlight shine into the woods. We sit down behind a thick stump in the stillness and cover ourselves with our coats. I want to look for a better place, but Reiter deters me.

"I beg you, at least wait until morning!" he urges.

I see no sense to it. We must find a safer hideout tonight in case they search. If we are discovered, all will be lost.

"Are you coming?" I ask.

Reiter calls me insane, but he finally agrees.

We reach a clearing where we find traces of a military bivouac. Next to the tent I notice a package. Thinking it is something to eat, I hide it in my pocket.

Looking around, I observe a thick clump of trees beyond the clearing and move toward it. Bushes! . . . just what I was looking for. As we crawl through them, the branches scratch our faces, but we do not mind. Go farther! Go as far as possible! Finally, I decide that we have gone far enough, and we drop exhausted. Some unearthly happiness grips me, and I say, "Friend, maybe we'll survive!!"

The wind blows. The trees are whispering.

* * *

The night passes uneventfully. With daylight piercing the thicket, everything around us appears white. Snow has fallen during the night. The stillness is broken by voices far away.

"Tadzek," whispers Reiter, "maybe they're Americans!"

Some lone German words reach us. Then we hear begging

and crying, followed by a few random shots, then a whole series of them.

The situation is clear. The SS men discovered some escapees. Now, even Reiter realizes the grave danger we faced in the woods.

I remember the package I found last night. In contains a can of German concentrated soup that should be mixed with ten liters of water, however, we eat it right from the can. It is overly spiced, but it saves us from starvation.

"Now what?" asks Reiter.

"What do you mean by 'what'? We'll sit and wait. Don't you like it here?"

The hours drag by more slowly than they ever did before. Every second seems a century. The artillery fire we heard so clearly yesterday is now completely stilled.

"The Germans must have pushed back the Americans," whispers Reiter with utter despair in his voice. "We'll sit here until we die of hunger because, if we get out, they'll kill us as they did the others."

I do not reply. The situation Reiter described is quite possible. Then all of our efforts and suffering will have been in vain. A thought flashes through my mind, "Maybe the Americans are here already, and we are sitting in a thicket."

We hear American planes roaring overhead. A minute later, bullets whizz over our heads, and here we are without any protection. I ask myself, "Would the Americans shoot their own soldiers on their own terrain? No, certainly not!" I am desperate. What if one of the bullets kills me? . . . . This is a horrid, wretched life!

We must gather a little snow to slake our burning thirst. Reiter sucks the water from his drenched coat. I crawl out of the bushes and snap off a snow-covered branch. It makes a loud noise in the woods. This is not being careful on my part, but I am indifferent.

"Let happen what may, Tadzek! Tomorrow morning we'll leave these woods. We can't hold out much longer. Eventually, it's all the same, whether we die from hunger, freezing, or a bullet."

"Yes," I agree, "tomorrow we'll get out. What will happen, will happen!"

We are overly tired after so many sleepless days and nights. Our rags are wet; water runs from them in a stream. The ground is wet. If it freezes tonight, we will certainly die from the cold. Then again, how nonsensical! Who pays attention to such small matters? It is better . . . we will meet our end in our sleep, without suffering . . . around us, a deadly silence.

* * *

It is daylight and time for us to leave. We cannot afford to waste a minute. Our strength is failing fast. We summon up the last of our reserves to keep on going.

We discover a small path. Where does it lead? What awaits us outside of these woods?

With only a few trees separating us from the highway, I observe Reiter. He looks horrible in his rags and a month's growth of beard.

"Maybe you'll scare the Germans, and they'll leave us alone!" I tease.

"Don't worry, Tadzek! You don't look much better."

We hear cars on the highway and can see them through the trees, but, unfortunately, we cannot tell to which side they belong.

"Maybe we should wait a little longer?" asks my friend, losing his courage.

"Maybe you! As for me, I'm going!"

My heart beats as thought it might jump out of my chest. I walk a few more steps . . . and there is the highway. Several cars pass at dizzying speed. God, the American white star! Victory!!!

"Come quickly! We're saved!" I shout, my voice choking with emotion.

I hear loud sobbing behind me. It is Reiter crying like a baby.

"Tadzek, my wife! My little daughter! They weren't fortunate enough to survive."

"Fredzia! . . . ."

Several cadaverous-looking figures emerge from the woods and remain at the edge of the road. The American cars speed by. We would like to give our saviors an ovation, the grandest, loudest one possible. We want to shout our joy and elation, but our nerves and strength are not up to it. Instead of a joyful shout, only a convulsive sob bursts from our throats.

Epilogue

The long American convoy rumbles past us as quickly as the narrow secondary road permits. It is highly questionable if anyone noticed our little ragged group.

After the last truck disappears from sight, we begin despairing once more. Free at last, but. . . . Our last effort to walk some fifty yards from the woods to the clearing and the road, depleted the last of our strength.

Once again we are alone. A few of us start sobbing silently; one prays. Will the Germans return to finish us off at this very last moment of the war after we have already seen our saviors? No one can answer that question. Although we are somewhat numb, our minds still function, however, slowly. Our bodies are broken, and we can do little to alter our fate. We are so spent that we cannot return to the woods to hide. We must remain here.

After waiting quietly for fifteen minutes, we hear vehicles approaching. They are American trucks. The only one in our group capable of expending any effort, is a tall, relatively well-built fellow who waves his cap. The trucks pass by, but the last one stops.

A group of soldiers surround us and start talking. Alas,

none of us can understand or speak English. The soldiers try other languages, even sign language. Eventually one asks, "Anyone here speak Polish?"

With the help of two friends, I move forward with great difficulty and croak, "I do."

The soldier quickly explains that they are the first American troops in the area; that, a few miles back, they saw many like us who had been shot; that many small bands of SS are nearby; that under no circumstances are we to move; that he will radio the medics to take us to the hospital. And indeed, he starts to talk rapidly into a strange contraption he calls a walkie-talkie.

Meanwhile, the other soldiers give us food, water, chocolate, and cigarettes. They bid us good-by, wish us luck, and leave before we can thank them. For a moment we are stunned, then we begin to eat.

My recollection of the events of the next twenty-four hours are quite hazy. Despite the food, our eyes cannot focus, and we see everything as through a thick fog. Our brains cease to function, and we are unable to think.

We wake up in clean beds to find ourselves washed and shaved. We do not know exactly what happened to us. I overhear someone saying that two American ambulances picked us up and that there was some gunfire. I close my eyes and, for the first time in many years, I go to sleep peacefully.

Glossary

Block	Barrack
Blocksperre	Close Barracks
Brotholen	Get bread, fetch bread
Gamel	Completely exhausted prisoner unable to work; used in Maidanek
"Goliath"	Small unmanned tank filled with explosives; attached by cable to underside of a large tank and controlled by the large tank
Häftling(e)	Prisoner(s)
Harasho (Russian)	O.K.
Jawohl	Yes
K.B.	Krankenbau
Kaffeeholen	Get coffee
Kapo	Prisoner in charge of a Kommando
K.L.	Konzentrationlager, concentration camp
Kommandant	Commander
Kommando	Work gang
Krankenbau	Prison hospital, prisoners' sick bay; same as K.B.
Lager	Camp
Lagerpolizei	Camp police (made up of prisoners)
Mittagholen	Get lunch
Muzelman	Completely exhausted prisoner unable to work

Organize	Get whatever one needs
Organization Todt	Nazi para-military labor organization
O.T.	Organization Todt
Reichsdeutsche	True German (i.e. from the Reich, not Volksdeutsch)
"Schmeisser"	Name of machine gun
Schreibstube	Prisoners' record room
Shokhet	Jewish ritual butcher
S.K.	Strafkommando, penal squad
Strassenbau	Road building
Stube(n)	Room(s)
"Sullivans"	Power drill made by the Sullivan Company
Totenkommando	Cadaver squad: bring to morgue, pile corpses for transport, bury corpses
Volksdeutscher	German living in country other than Germany; one professing, or invited to profess, German nationality

SS Personnel

Arbeitseinsatz	In charge of work details, labor assignments
Blockführer	Guard
SS-Hauptscharführer	Master-Sergeant (NCO)
Lagerarzt	SS camp doctor
Lagerführer	SS camp commander
SS-Oberscharführer	Technical Sergeant (NCO)
SS-Obersturmführer	First Lieutenant
Raportführer	Receives reports
SS-Standartenführer	Colonel
SS-Unterscharführer	Second Lieutenant
Waffen-SS	Branch of SS military forces

Prisoners (Häftlinge)

Arbeitsdienst	Nazi "Labor Service"; assigns work details to Kapos
Blockältester	In charge of a barrack
Kapo	See Lagerkapo
Lagerältester	Camp senior
Lagerkapo	Foreman of Kommando
Lagerschreiber	Camp secretary
Oberkapo	Overseer of several Kapos
Stubendienst	Cleans barracks, gets food, assigns prisoners to clean and bring meals
Volksarbeiter	Native worker

DISTRIBUTEURS EXCLUSIFS

Distributeur pour le Canada et les États-Unis
LES MESSAGERIES ADP
MONTRÉAL (Canada)
Téléphone : (514) 523-1182 ou 1 800 361-4806
Télécopieur : (514) 521-4434

Distributeur pour la Suisse
TRANSAT S.A.
GENÈVE
Téléphone : 022/342 77 40
Télécopieur : 022/343 46 46

Distributeur pour la France et les autres pays européens
HISTOIRE ET DOCUMENTS
CHENNEVIÈRES-SUR-MARNE (France)
Téléphone : (01) 45 76 77 41
Télécopieur : (01) 45 93 34 70
histoire.et.document@wanadoo.fr

Dépôts légaux
1er trimestre 2003
Bibliothèque nationale du Canada
Bibliothèque nationale du Québec

Série complète

370 p. 21,95 $

543 p. 24,95 $

432 p. 24,95 $

520 p. 24,95 $

512 p. 24,95 $

392 p. 24,95 $